W9-BQL-479

ST. MARY'S COLLEGE OF MARYLAND
ST. MARY'S CITY, MARYLAND   20686

Malaya, Showing Places Mentioned in the Text

THE BRITISH IN MALAYA 1880–1941

The Social History of a European Community
in Colonial South-East Asia

John G. Butcher

KUALA LUMPUR
OXFORD UNIVERSITY PRESS
OXFORD   NEW YORK   MELBOURNE
1979

Oxford University Press
OXFORD LONDON GLASGOW
NEW YORK TORONTO MELBOURNE WELLINGTON
KUALA LUMPUR SINGAPORE HONG KONG TOKYO
DELHI BOMBAY CALCUTTA MADRAS KARACHI
NAIROBI DAR ES SALAAM CAPE TOWN

● *Oxford University Press 1979*
*All rights reserved. No part of this publication may be reproduced,
stored in a retrieval system, or transmitted, in any form or by any means,
electronic, mechanical, photocopying, recording or otherwise,
without the prior permission of Oxford University Press*

ISBN 0 19 580419 8 (*boards*)
ISBN 0 19 580445 7 (*limp*)

*Printed in Singapore by Dainippon Tien Wah Printing (Pte) Ltd.
Published by Oxford University Press, 3, Jalan 13/3,
Petaling Jaya, Selangor, Malaysia*

To my Parents,
Ruth and Frank Butcher

Preface

S OUTH-EAST ASIA has long attracted the scholar
interested in the history of minority groups. The overseas
Chinese in particular have been the subject of study,
but, as Francis Hsu observed over twenty years ago in an attack
of the obsessive attention then being given to the 'Chinese Problem', the European communities too need to be studied. 'Where',
he asked, 'are the studies of the Belgian minority in the Congo,
the Dutch minority in Indonesia, the English minority in India
and the American minority in Thailand?' Hsu's call for such
studies has gone largely unheeded. In the late 1950s and into the
1960s the more immediate concern of historians, then just
breaking out of the colonial framework which had dominated
South-East Asian historiography, was the study of what in 1961
John Smail called the 'domestic' history of South-East Asia. The
research resulting from this perspective has allowed us to see
South-East Asians making their own history, but it has also made
it possible to take a fresh look at the Europeans, to see them not
only as outsiders bringing change but also as social groups within
a vigorous South-East Asian environment.

My own interest in the Europeans stems from my experience
as a Peace Corps Volunteer in Sabah, for I was fascinated by the
tiny American community of which I was a part, but it was not
until I participated in a seminar on 'Special Social Groups in
Southeast Asia' conducted by Professor Smail that I began to
consider how one might go about writing a social history of a
European community. I was particularly struck by the way in
which G. William Skinner, in his *Chinese Society in Thailand: An
Analytical History*, uncovered the internal dynamics of the Chinese community in Thailand and traced the dramatic changes in
Chinese–Thai relations. The present study has, I believe, gone
some way towards examining one European community in colonial South-East Asia in a similar fashion, but it must be stressed
that much more needs to be done. A full understanding of the
European community in Malaya will only come when scholars
have made much more extensive use of the vast amount of archi-

val material in Malaysia and when, of even more immediate importance, they have also considered in far greater detail than has been attempted here the view from the *kampung*, the estate 'lines', the servants' quarters, the mission school, and the desks of the subordinate officers in the Secretariat by interviewing as many Malaysians as possible of the generation who experienced British rule. In view of the numerous local histories now being undertaken in Malaysian universities by students and staff alike, there is good reason to believe that significant advances in our understanding of Malaya's history and the position of the Europeans in that history will emerge before too long.

This study was originally submitted for the Ph.D. at the University of Hull in November 1975. A short period of research at the National Library of Australia in December 1977 has enabled me to make some revisions, but otherwise very few changes have been made.

Since I began work on this study in 1971 many people and institutions have assisted me in all sorts of ways. During three of my four years in England I was supported by a University of Hull scholarship. I wish to thank the Scholarships Committee for this support and for several travel grants, particularly one which enabled me to do research in Malaysia in the early part of 1973. Among many individuals whom I wish to thank are Paul Kratoska, who made detailed and very constructive criticisms of some of the chapters; Bruce Cruikshank and Jim Jackson, who, among other things, offered useful comments on early outlines of the study; Clive Christie, who read and made suggestions on some of the chapters; John Drabble, who introduced me to the *Planter*, which proved to be a valuable source for this study; Dr. Ivan Polunin, who suggested some readings on medical subjects and who enabled me to xerox relevant materials in the University of Singapore Medical Library; Puan Sri Nik Daud, who sent me photocopies of pages of the original Candidates Book of the Lake Club; Mr. Tan Keat Chye, who helped me with some details on the map of Kuala Lumpur included in this study; Mrs. M. Grace Samuel, who gave me permission to quote from the letters of P. Samuel preserved at the Rhodes House Library, Oxford; and Heather Thompson, Melanie Harris, and Annette Whiting, who typed various drafts of this study. Librarians both in England and in Malaysia gave me a great deal of help. I would particularly like to thank the librarians of the Brynmor Jones Library, University of Hull, who always gave me every possible assistance. Both my wife Lorena and I are grateful to Abu

Hassan bin Haji Omar for all his help during our stay in Malaysia. I have an immense debt to the people I interviewed. Thanks to their help, I was often able to find out information which was not available or only hinted at in the written sources, and always I was able to gain some new insight into colonial society in Malaya. Of the people I interviewed I am especially grateful to Mr. Hugh Allen, Mr. Trevor Walker, and the late Mr. David Gray for their constant willingness to answer my questions. I also wish to thank Mr. Allen, Mrs. Mary C. Hodgkin, the Arkib Negara Malaysia, and particularly Mr. D. H. Simpson of the Royal Commonwealth Society for helping me to collect the photographs included in this study and for permission to publish photographs from their collections. Professor C. D. Cowan and Mr. G. L. Peet, whom I had the good fortune to meet after coming to Perth, made extensive comments on my thesis. They are in no way responsible for the fact that in some cases I have been unable to give their criticisms full justice. And I owe a general debt to my colleague at Murdoch, Jim Warren, whose thoughts on all manner of questions have influenced my own thinking.

I have a very special debt to a number of other people. During the long time he supervised my thesis Dr. D. K. Bassett went over what I wrote with great thoroughness and helped me to clarify my ideas, and was helpful in numerous other ways besides those directly connected with the thesis. On more than one occasion Ivar Oxaal's ideas and encouragement rescued me from the condition which he kindly calls 'creative procrastination'. Finally, it is impossible for me to express how truly grateful my wife and I are to our neighbours in Hull, Betty and Leslie Malam, for all they did for us during our stay in England.

Perth   J. G. B.
December 1978

Contents

Preface   vii
Tables   xiii
Figures and Maps   xiv
Plates   xv
Abbreviations   xvii
Currency   xviii
Note on Spelling   xviii
Glossary   xix

INTRODUCTION   1

1. A POLITICAL AND ECONOMIC SURVEY   4
   The Origins of British Control   4
   The Malay States from Intervention to Federation   7
   The Export Economy after 1900   12
   Political Changes   18

2. A PROFILE OF THE EUROPEANS   23
   Nationality and its Bearing on the Use of Census
      Data   24
   Population Growth   26
   Social Origins and Recruitment   33

3. EUROPEANS IN THE MALAY STATES, 1880–1900   50
   Officials and the Asian Environment   51
   The Growth of European Society in Kuala Lumpur   58
   Health and Hill Stations   68
   After Federation   74

4. THE EUROPEAN COMMUNITY IN TRANSITION, 1900–
   1919   76
   The Changing Position of Civil Servants   78
   Marriage and Salaries   84
   Resolution of the Salaries Question   87
   The Case of the Train Drivers   93

5. TENSION IN EUROPEAN RELATIONS WITH ASIANS, 1904–
   1915   97
      Segregation on the Railways   97
      The Colour Bar in the Civil Service   107
      Europeans and Chinese during the Revolutionary
         Period   112
      European Teams and the Selangor Football League   117
      Some General Observations   120

6. EUROPEAN SOCIETY IN THE INTER-WAR YEARS   126
      Economic Conditions and European Society   126
      Men and Women   134
      Clubs and Social Structure in Kuala Lumpur   147
      The Promise of Hill Stations   157

7. EUROPEAN RELATIONS WITH ASIANS: THE INTER-WAR
   YEARS   167
      General Attitudes   167
      The Europeans in Malayan Society   173
      Asian Participation in European Social Activities   179
      The Rotary Club and Race Relations   188

8. EUROPEAN MEN AND ASIAN WOMEN   193
      Prostitution and Concubinage before the First
         World War   194
      Attitudes toward Sexual Relations between Euro-
         pean Men and Asian Women   201
      The Decline of Concubinage   206
      Mistresses   213
      Prostitution and Venereal Diseases between the
         Wars   217

SOME CONCLUDING REMARKS   223

Appendix 1. Hubert Berkeley: The Last White Rajah
   District Officer   228
Appendix 2. 'The Letter' Case   233
Notes   239
Bibliography   271
Selected List of Persons Interviewed   282
Index   285

Tables

1. The British as a Percentage of Europeans in the F.M.S., 1901–1931 — 24
2. Nationality of Europeans in the F.M.S., 1931 — 25
3. The European Population of Malaya, 1871–1931 — 27
4. Percentage of Employed European Men in the F.M.S. in Agriculture, Mining, and Commerce and Finance, 1901–1931 — 29
5. Educational Background of Civil Servants and Planters Listed in *Twentieth Century Impressions of British Malaya* — 35
6. Monthly Family Budgets of an Official in Perak, 1903 and 1906 — 79
7. Monthly Salaries of Planters and Civil Servants — 91
8. Monthly Family Budgets in 1930: European and Asiatic Standards — 130
9. Marital Status of European Men in the F.M.S., 1911–1931 — 135
10. Occupations and Positions of 77 Men Elected to the Lake Club, July 1925–June 1927 — 155
11. List of Asian Members of the Selangor Club and Selangor Golf Club during the 1920s and 1930s — 182
12. The Japanese Population in the F.M.S., 1891–1931 — 198
13. The European Population of the F.M.S.: Sex Ratios, 1891–1931 — 209
14. Ethnicity of Women from whom European Men Treated at the Sultan Street Clinic Contracted Venereal Disease, 1927–1931 — 218

Figures

1. Growth of the European Population in the F.M.S.,
   1880–1940   30
2. The Maxwell Family   38
3. Distribution by Age, Sex and Marital Status of the
   European Population in the F.M.S. in 1921   140
4. Number of Europeans Treated for Venereal Diseases
   at Government Clinics in the F.M.S., 1925–1938   219

Maps

1. Malaya, Showing Places Mentioned in the Text   *frontispiece*
2. Geographical Distribution of Europeans in the
   F.M.S. in 1921   32
3. Kuala Lumpur in the 1930s   151–2
4. Hill Stations in Malaya   162

Plates

Between pages 108 and 109

1. The leaders of Kuala Lumpur in 1884. (*Arkib Negara Malaysia*)
2. The High Commissioner, Sir John Anderson, and other officials with the Sultan of Selangor at the Sultan's *Istana*, Klang, 1904. (*Royal Commonwealth Society*)
3. Meeting of the Federal Council at Kuala Lumpur, 28 February 1927. (*Royal Commonwealth Society*)
4. Sultan Suleiman of Selangor and Sir George Maxwell at 'Carcosa'. (*Arkib Negara Malaysia*)
5. J. H. M. Robson, founder of the *Malay Mail*. (*Arkib Negara Malaysia*)
6. The Sultan of Perak and the Resident of Perak, 1922. (*Royal Commonwealth Society*)
7. The wedding of Captain Howman at Taiping, 1932. (*Arkib Negara Malaysia*)
8. Panoramic view of Kuala Lumpur in the late 1890s. (*Arkib Negara Malaysia*)
9. A football match in front of the Selangor Club, about 1908. (*Royal Commonwealth Society*)
10. The Chinese section of Kuala Lumpur, 1922. (*Mr. Hugh Allen*)
11. Grandstand at the Ipoh Racecourse, 1890s. (*British Malaya* 6 (*1931*), *180*)
12. A Pierrot Troupe made up of Kuala Lumpur residents, 1901. (*British Malaya*, 8 (*1933*), 92)

Between pages 204 and 205

13. Children and their *amahs* at a party, Kuala Lumpur, 1933. (*Mrs. Mary C. Hodgkin*)
14. A Malay servant. (*Mrs. Mary C. Hodgkin*)
15. Hugh Clifford's Residency at Pekan, about 1894. (*Royal Commonwealth Society*)
16. 'Carcosa', official residence of the Resident-General, late 1890s. (*Arkib Negara Malaysia*)

17. Bungalow of a junior married government officer, Kuala Lumpur, 1930s. (*Mrs. Mary C. Hodgkin*)
18. Interior of the same bungalow. (*Mrs. Mary C. Hodgkin*)
19. Planter's bungalow, 1909. (*Arkib Negara Malaysia*)
20. Estate manager's bungalow, Tanjong Malim, about 1930. (*Royal Commonwealth Society*)
21. Interior view of the same bungalow. (*Royal Commonwealth Society*)
22. Mrs. Treacher, wife of the Resident of Perak, at 'The Hut', Maxwell's Hill, 1890s. (*Arkib Negara Malaysia*)
23. Smoke House Inn, Cameron Highlands (photograph taken in 1952). (*Royal Commonwealth Society*)
24. Hubert Berkeley, District Officer of Upper Perak, about 1922. (*Royal Commonwealth Society*)
25. Hubert Berkeley and his elephants, Upper Perak. (*Arkib Negara Malaysia*)

Abbreviations

Used in the Text

F.M.S.	Federated Malay States
I.S.P.	Incorporated Society of Planters
M.C.S.	Malayan Civil Service

Used in the Notes and Bibliography only

ANM	Arkib Negara Malaysia (National Archives of Malaysia)
BAM	British Association of Malaya Papers, Royal Commonwealth Society, London
CO	Colonial Office Records, Public Record Office, London
FCO	Foreign and Commonwealth Office Library, London
H.C. Deb.	House of Commons Debates
HCO	High Commissioner's Office Files, Arkib Negara Malaysia
JMBRAS	*Journal of the Malayan* [or *Malaysian*] *Branch of the Royal Asiatic Society*
PP	Parliamentary Papers
RH	Rhodes House Library, Oxford

Currency

THE dollar ($) referred to in this study is the Straits Dollar. Before 1906 the value of the Straits Dollar fluctuated; in that year it was fixed at 2s. 4d. sterling.

Note on Spelling

MALAY words, except place names and personal names, have been spelt according to the rules officially adopted in August 1972. Thus 'c' as in *dacing* and *Cina* replaces 'ch'.

Glossary

Amah	A Chinese nurse
Ayah	An Indian or Malay nurse
Dhobi	A washerman
Istana	Palace of a Malay Sultan
Kampung	Malay village
Mem	A European woman
Padang	A parade ground or playing field
Pahit	Literally 'bitter', used for a gin and bitters
Rakyat	The subject class; peasantry
Ronggeng	A Malay dance; a woman who performs such a dance
Stengah	Literally 'half', a half measure of whisky and water or whisky and soda
Syce (or *sais*)	Groom, horse-keeper; chauffeur
Towkay	A wealthy Chinese businessman
Tuan	'Master' or 'lord', the term used by an Asian when addressing a European man
Tuan besar	A European of great importance, such as a high government official, the manager of a large estate, or the head of a firm
Tukang air	Water carrier
Tukang kebun (or simply *kebun*)	Gardener

Introduction

ONE aspect of the British colonial period has been surprisingly neglected by historians of Malaya. Historians have studied the forms of government created by the British and the role of the British in the economic development of Malaya. And as part of their studies of the three main ethnic groups which comprised Malayan society—the Malays, Chinese, and Indians—they have considered the impact of British policies on these groups. They have, in short, looked most closely at the ways in which the British exerted their influence in Malaya's history as policy makers, administrators, and entrepreneurs. Very little attention, however, has been given to the way in which these people lived, how their way of life was influenced by their dominant position in Malayan society, and how as a group or, to use the contemporary term, 'community' within this same society they, like the people they governed, experienced many changes during the colonial period.[1] It is the purpose of this study to look at the British from such a perspective.

The present study can be described as a social history of the Europeans in Malaya rather than of the British, even though most people of European background were in fact British. Whether or not someone was a European had, in most situations, far greater social significance than whether he was British. This study looks both within the European community and at the community in relation to Malayan society. It deals on the one hand with the way in which Europeans adapted to life in Malaya, the occupational and social structure of the European community, and the role of women within the community, and on the other hand with the general position of the Europeans in Malayan society, social relations between Europeans and Asians, the tensions which at times characterized relations between the two groups, and relations between European men and Asian women. At the conclusion of this study it is hoped to show how the concept of a European standard of living (first discussed in Chapter 4) helps us to understand important aspects of both of these broad sets of issues.

During most of the period covered by this study the Malay Peninsula was divided politically into three parts. The three Straits Settlements of Singapore, Penang, and Malacca had become British territory under the East India Company during the last part of the eighteenth century and the first quarter of the nineteenth. In 1867 the Straits Settlements became a crown colony administered by a Governor who was responsible to the Colonial Office in London. The four Malay States of Selangor, Perak, Negri Sembilan, and Pahang became British protectorates between 1874 and 1888 and in 1895 were brought together to form the Federated Malay States. By the First World War Johore, Kedah, Perlis, Kelantan, and Trengganu had also come under British control, but they were not absorbed into the federation; collectively they were known as the Unfederated Malay States. Although reference is frequently made to other parts of Malaya, particularly the Straits Settlements, this study concentrates on the Europeans in the F.M.S. Special attention is given to the state of Selangor and to its principal town, Kuala Lumpur, which became the capital of the federation and which by the 1890s had the largest European population of any town in the four states. The existence of two very valuable local periodicals, the *Selangor Journal* (published between 1892 and 1897) and the *Malay Mail* (1896–1941), and the abundance of other directly relevant sources make Kuala Lumpur especially suitable for a detailed study of the Europeans.

The starting point for this study—1880—has been chosen for a number of reasons. Although British rule in the Malay States began in 1874 it was only by about 1880 that the general outline of British policy toward the states was firmly established. Moreover, the events of these years, when only a very small number of British officials were living in the Malay States, have been the subject of several works.[2] Finally, 1880 was the year in which the Resident of Selangor moved his headquarters to Kuala Lumpur from Klang.

In the present study it is hoped to show the close relationship between the social history of the Europeans and the evolution of British economic and political involvement in the Malay States. Before about 1900 the British in these states were mainly government servants. The British administration grew steadily, but the principal industry, tin, was almost entirely in the hands of the Chinese. Early in the twentieth century Europeans established the plantation rubber industry and began to take a more direct share in the tin mining industry. The sudden increase in the number of Europeans engaged in planting, mining, and commercial activities altered the structure of European society. The improvement in living conditions which resulted from prosperous economic conditions helped to bring about changes in the European way of life. During the inter-war years there were great fluctuations in prosperity, arising from slumps and booms in the export economy, and these too had considerable effect on the social history of the time. Because of their importance in understanding the social history of the Europeans the political and economic changes which occurred between the 1870s and 1930s are outlined in Chapter 1. Some other relevant information about the society in which Europeans lived is presented in the same chapter.

For the sake of clarity it is useful to define at the outset some of the terms as they are used here. Today the term 'Malaysian' refers to anyone, of any race, who is a citizen of Malaysia, but before the Second World War it was used in the censuses to mean 'Malays and other natives of the archipelago'. The term 'Malayan' was used to describe anyone, including Europeans of long residence, who lived in the Malay Peninsula; except in the minds of a very few people it did not imply any sense of a shared national identity. Usually the British referred to the Malays, Chinese, and Indians as 'natives' or 'Asiatics'. By 'natives' they sometimes meant only Malays, but often included all non-Europeans, whether born in Canton, Madras, Kyoto, or in the heart of Pahang. I have used the word 'Asians' for non-Europeans when it has not been necessary to distinguish between ethnic groups.

1

A Political and Economic Survey

The Origins of British Control

UNTIL the 1870s British rule in the Malay Peninsula was confined to the Straits Settlements of Singapore, Penang, and Malacca. The British acquired the island of Penang from the Sultan of Kedah in 1786, and Singapore became British territory soon after Sir Thomas Stamford Raffles established a trading post there in 1819. The British gained possession of Malacca by the Anglo-Dutch treaty of 1824. Except during the Napoleonic war, when Britain occupied the territory, Malacca had been under Dutch rule since 1641, before which it had been ruled by the Portuguese. Because of its location on the main sea route from Europe and India to the Far East, its position in the archipelago, and its status as a free port, Singapore rapidly became the most important of the three British settlements. By 1860 Singapore had a population of nearly 81,000. The largest section of the population were the Chinese, who were engaged in trade or agriculture or worked as labourers. Secret societies played a central role in all aspects of Chinese economic and social life. There were only about 500 European residents in Singapore, but in addition to the officers who administered the Straits government this number included influential merchants, bankers, lawyers, and newspaper editors.[1] By the 1860s both Chinese and British businessmen were taking great interest in the economic potential of the Malay States. The Chinese already had large investments there, while the British hesitated to invest because they feared that the turmoil in the states would prevent them from exploiting this potential. When the Straits Settlements were transferred from the government of India in 1867 it became the Colonial Office's responsibility to decide whether Britain would intervene in the affairs of these states.

Before looking at the events which led to the introduction of British officials it is necessary to describe briefly the society

which existed in the Malay States before British rule. Traditionally the largest political unit in the peninsula was the state. At the
head of each state was a Sultan, who conducted the state's relations with other states and organized its defence in times of war.
The Sultan was the symbol of the state's unity, was its ceremonial
head, and was at the apex of its elaborate social hierarchy.
Despite his ceremonial and social pre-eminence the Sultan had
only limited political control over his realm. The state was
divided into districts, each ruled by a chief. The districts were
usually centred at the mouth of a river or on a section of a river,
for the rivers served as the main means of communication, and it
was along their banks that the small Malay population was concentrated. Although the chiefs had to pay obeisance to the Sultan
periodically, they enjoyed a great deal of independence within
their respective territories. The Sultan's power was to a great
extent confined to his own district. The chiefs' main source of
power was their freedom to raise and spend their own revenues
as they wished. A toll on boats passing through the district was
one of the most important sources of revenue. The chiefs also
administered justice within their own districts and had the right
to demand free labour (kerah) from the peasantry (rakyat). In
order to enhance their prestige and to provide themselves with
needed supporters the chiefs had large numbers of debt-bondsmen and slaves. None of the slaves were Malays since according
to Islamic law only non-Muslims could be enslaved.[2]

Although there were succession disputes and rivalries between
districts the Malay political system was held in a tenuous balance
since no chief was clearly superior to the others in wealth. From
the middle of the nineteenth century, however, this balance was
violently upset by the growing importance of the main mineral
resource of the states—tin. Before the middle of the century a
small amount of tin had been mined by Malays and a few Chinese, but as world demand for the mineral increased Malay chiefs
who controlled areas with rich tin deposits encouraged the
immigration of large numbers of Chinese miners. Other mining
operators were financed directly by Chinese capitalists in the
Straits Settlements. Chinese villages were soon established in the
main mining districts. By 1872 there were between 20,000 and
25,000 Chinese living in Larut in Perak, the most important mining district in the Malay States.[3] Chinese also operated mines
elsewhere in Perak and in Selangor and Sungei Ujong. The village which later became known as Kuala Lumpur had its origins
in about 1858 when a few Chinese traders set up shops near the

junction of the Klang and Gombak Rivers, only a short distance from the tin fields at Pudu and Ampang.[4] The headman of each of these mining centres was recognized by the Malay authorities as the *Kapitan Cina*. Yap Ah Loy, the leading figure in the early history of Kuala Lumpur, was formally installed as *Kapitan Cina* by a Malay raja in 1869.

While some chiefs became rich from tin revenues and so were able to buy arms and hire followers, other Malay leaders borrowed money in the hope of taking control of the main tin producing areas. In Perak the situation was complicated by a succession dispute. In Larut and in the Kuala Lumpur area the two main Chinese secret societies fought for possession of the mines. As civil war between rival coalitions of Malays and Chinese enveloped the states tin production fell greatly, and Chinese capitalists and European commercial interests in the Straits Settlements appealed to the colonial government to take steps to end the strife. A group of British merchants hoped that once peace was restored they might be able to develop tin concessions which they had been granted by the Viceroy of Selangor. For a long time the Colonial Office refused to take any action, but in September 1873 the Secretary of State for the Colonies, Lord Kimberley, instructed the new Governor, Sir Andrew Clarke, to report on conditions in the Malay States and to find out whether Britain might play some role in bringing peace to the states. Whether Kimberley changed British policy towards the Malay States mainly because he feared that another European power, particularly Germany, might intervene first or because he wished to pave the way for British investment in the states is an issue which historians have debated at great length, but it is clear that 'the situation which brought to the fore the problem of British control had largely an economic origin'.[5]

Clarke allowed himself considerable freedom in carrying out the cautious instructions he had received. He first turned his attention to Perak. Without referring to the Colonial Office Clarke arranged for a meeting on Pangkor Island in January 1874 of a number of Perak chiefs and the leaders of the rival Chinese factions. The chiefs agreed to recognize Clarke's choice of one of the Perak claimants, Raja Abdullah, as Sultan and agreed that the Sultan should receive a British officer, called a Resident, 'whose advice must be asked and acted upon in all questions other than those touching Malay Religion and Custom'. The collection and control of all revenue and the general administration of the state was to be regulated by the 'advice' of the Resident. The revenue was to be used to support the Resident and his establishment and finance a Civil List, by which the Sultan and other Malay leaders would receive their incomes. The Chinese headmen who were at Pangkor signed a separate agreement in which they undertook to stop fighting. Within a few months Clarke made similar arrangements to introduce Residents in the states of Selangor and Sungei Ujong.[6]

The Malay States
from Intervention to Federation

During the first few years after the Pangkor Engagement the nature and extent of British 'advice' were far from certain. On the one hand local officials were determined to establish the instruments of effective government and to carry out changes which in some cases clashed with the traditional privileges of the Malay aristocracy. On the other, the Colonial Office wished to keep British involvement in the states as limited and as free from conflict as possible.

The zealous efforts of the first Resident of Perak, J. W. W. Birch, who had spent most of his official career in Ceylon and who was contemptuous of Malay institutions, to take over the collection of revenues and to end debt-bondage and slavery led to his assassination in November 1875. British troops were called in from Hong Kong and India, but by the time they arrived police and soldiers brought in from Penang and Singapore had nearly gained control of the situation. Some members of the Perak royal family and a few aristocrats were implicated in Birch's death; a few, including Sultan Abdullah, were exiled, and two were sentenced to death. The British had thus eliminated those Malays who most actively opposed the British presence and had displayed their willingness to uphold their rule with force. Nevertheless, the Colonial Office refused to consider proposals put forward by the then Governor, Sir William Jervois, that all or part of Perak should be brought under direct British rule. Fearing that annexation would again arouse the anger of the Malays and thus necessitate another costly punitive expedition, the Secretary of State insisted in June 1876 that the Residential system be given a further trial.[7] It soon became clear however that British 'advice' did in fact mean British control. When the new Resident of Perak, Hugh Low, objected to a circular from Jervois's successor, Sir William Robinson, reminding the Residents that they had been placed in the states as advisers, not as rulers, he was assured by the Governor that he could continue to govern as he had been doing but that 'the fiction . . . that the Residents are merely advisers must be kept up'.[8]

Low, who had acquired an intimate knowledge of Malay society during more than thirty years in Sarawak and Labuan, proceeded to accomplish what Birch had set out to do, but unlike Birch he made every effort to gain the co-operation of the Malays. Without in any way relinquishing his own authority Low succeeded at the very least in giving Malays some sense of influencing the way policies which affected them were carried out. Low abolished debt-bondage and slavery only after he had convinced the chiefs that they would no longer need to depend on bondsmen and slaves for labour and had worked out the details of how they would be compensated for their loss. Low also used the State Council, made up of the Ruler, principal chiefs, and Chinese headmen, to discuss legislation. Low's administration was greatly admired by Sir Frederick Weld, who became Governor in 1880, and became the model for the Residential system.

In governing the Malay population the British took over the functions which had previously been performed by the district chiefs. District Magistrates and Collectors (later called District Officers) administered justice and collected land and other revenues, which, unlike in the days before British rule, were now supervised by a central authority, the Resident. The chiefs were given positions as 'Native Magistrates', but in practice they were not expected to do much more than live off their government allowances. Whereas the chiefs were effectively displaced by British officers, the local headmen (*penghulus*) were incorporated into the new administration and paid salaries; they became the direct link between the government and the Malays in the villages (*kampungs*).[9]

Although British officials took over the government from the Sultans and chiefs, the traditional Malay hierarchy was preserved and in some ways even strengthened under British rule. The Sultans achieved a measure of security which they had not enjoyed in the turbulent years before British rule. They were assured of an income with which to maintain a style fitting their position, and now that the chiefs no longer had independent sources of revenue the Sultans were not in danger of being outshone by men of lower rank. As mentioned, the position of the chiefs was somewhat anomalous, but the British did try to make use of their standing in Malay eyes and thereby helped to preserve that standing. Moreover, the British helped to preserve the position of the aristocracy as a class in relation to the *rakyat*. This was done partly by giving a very small number of young Malay aristocrats (most notably two sons of ex-Sultan Abdullah of Perak) posts in the new administration. British educational policy also tended to maintain the distinction between the aristocracy and the *rakyat*. In 1890 the Selangor government opened a school exclusively for young rajas and a few Malays who were not rajas but had a similar status. Although the school did little to prepare its students for anything but subordinate posts in government and was closed in 1894, the idea of a separate school for the Malay élite was revived a decade later.[10] The Malay College, opened at Kuala Kangsar in 1905, drew its students from the aristocracy of the four Malay States and provided them with an education along the lines of an English public school. The British intended that graduates of the college would enter the civil service; a select few did secure such posts, though not until after the First World War. In contrast, educational policy towards the *rakyat* was designed (in later years, it must be stressed, with the approval of some members of the aristocracy) to make them better farmers and fishermen by providing them with a few years of rudimentary education in Malay. English was not taught, even though it was becoming essential for any employment outside the village sphere. It was inadvisable, explained Frank Swettenham, 'to attempt to give the children of an agricultural population an indifferent knowledge of a language that to all but a very few would only unfit them for the duties of life and make them discontented with anything like manual labour'.[11]

The main object of British policy towards the Chinese in the years after the Pangkor Engagement was to encourage tin mining and other commercial activities. It has been estimated that about four-fifths of the government's revenue in Perak and Selangor came from the duty on tin exports and the sale of monopolies to Chinese capitalists (*towkays*).[12] The most important of these revenue farms were for the manufacture and sale of spirits, the running of gaming-houses and pawn shops, the collection of the import duty on opium, and, in some districts, the preparation and sale of cooked opium. The first railway lines, built in the mid-1880s (from Taiping to Port Weld and from Kuala Lumpur to Klang), provided transportation between the main mining areas and the ports and became an additional source of government revenue. It was mainly from Chinese sources that the revenue of Perak rose from $226,000 in 1875 to $4,034,000 in 1895, while that of Selangor increased from \$116,000 to \$3,805,000 during the same period.[13]

Although some British investors had pressed the Colonial Office to intervene in the affairs of the Malay States because they had wanted to open tin mines there, most Europeans who attempted mining during this period were unsuccessful. They lacked the necessary contacts with the labour supplies in China, often used inadequate prospecting techniques, relied on a highly paid staff, and invested too much capital before they were certain of the extent of the deposits. Moreover, unlike the Chinese, European mine operators were not able to depend on an income from various revenue farms when profits from tin were low. For all these reasons nearly all European miners found it impossible to compete against the Chinese. A European firm which bought one of Yap Ah Loy's mines was forced to sell it back to him for a fraction of the original price when the price of tin fell; after Yap re-acquired the property the price of tin began to rise.[14]

At the centre of mining in Selangor was the town of Kuala Lumpur. Until 1879 Yap reigned supreme over the town and surrounding area while the British administration under Captain Bloomfield Douglas carried out its business in the port town of Klang. 'Actually the leading man, not only at Kwala Lumpor . . . , but in Selangor,' observed Isabella Bird during her visit to Klang in 1879, 'is Ah Loi, a Chinaman!'[15] Douglas had stationed some police at Kuala Lumpur, but they lived in Yap's compound and were under his direction. Yap was the principal miner and land-owner and owned the market, gambling booth, and brothels. Under his leadership the town recovered from the devastation of the civil wars. As a result of a rise in tin prices in the late 1870s the town grew rapidly. A British official was posted at Kuala Lumpur at the end of 1879, and the state's administration was moved there the following year. After Frank Swettenham replaced Douglas as Resident in 1882 the face of Kuala Lumpur underwent many changes as officials introduced building rules to make the town (which had been known for its filth and had been destroyed by fire several times) cleaner and safer, moved the market to a better location, and planned the railway.

In his history of early Kuala Lumpur Gullick has described the way in which the town's leadership changed in the years after the arrival of a British administration. Whereas Yap had relied on truly exceptional personal ability and initiative in governing the town's population during and immediately after the civil wars, the British officials who followed him, however much ability and energy they had, tended to apply methods which were standard throughout the British civil service. Moreover, as the functions of administration grew more varied and complex no one man could control all aspects of government in the way Yap had done.[16] One might add that, unlike Yap, the Resident and other officials were part of a larger bureaucracy; they were responsible to the Governor in Singapore and ultimately to the Colonial Office. Room for personal initiative remained, but it was not initiative of the same kind which Yap had exercised under earlier conditions.

After Yap Ah Loy's death in 1885 there were two more *Kapitans Cina*. Yap Ah Shak held the position from 1885 until he died in 1889, and Yap Kwan Seng was *Kapitan Cina* from 1890 until his death in 1902. Though Yap Ah Loy's successors received their appointments from the Resident they were chosen because they already held positions of great prominence and influence within the Chinese community. In the 1880s and 1890s they served as an important link between the British and the Chinese. By the time of Yap Kwan Seng's death the British no longer saw the need for such a link, and the post of *Kapitan Cina* was abolished. The Kuala Lumpur Sanitary Board, formed in 1890, and the State Council were forums where the government could discuss its policies with leading Malays and Indians as well as Chinese. More importantly, by the turn of the century Chinese-speaking officials were taking over the duties which the *Kapitans Cina* had performed.[17] There was, in short, a move to more direct rule over the Chinese.

By the middle of the 1880s officials in the Straits Settlements and at the Colonial Office were satisfied with the success of the Residential system, and in the late 1880s the British confidently extended their control to Pahang and Negri Sembilan (with which Sungei Ujong was later combined). The British had believed that Pahang was extraordinarily rich in mineral resources, but these expectations were not fulfilled. For this reason and because of a rebellion by a major chief in the early 1890s Pahang soon became a financial burden on the Colony. In order to offset this burden, at a time of slump in trade in Singapore, the Governor, Sir Cecil Clementi Smith, proposed drawing upon the surplus revenues of Perak and Selangor. At the same time that they were discussing Pahang's financial problems officials were looking for a way to bring greater unity to the administration of the Malay States in order to make government more efficient and to encourage economic development. After a great deal of debate between officials in the states and in Singapore and at the Colonial Office, it was decided to combine the four states into a federation, to be called the Federated Malay States. The head of the federation was to be known as the Resident-General and would be in a position superior to the Residents but responsible to the Governor. In August 1895 the federation came into being when the Rulers (a term which from 1898 referred to the Sultans of Perak, Selangor, and Pahang and the Yang di-Pertuan Besar of Negri Sembilan) signed an agreement which assured them that the new form of government would not 'curtail any of the power or authority' which they held under the Residential system. By 1895 the Rulers had little power to lose, but federation did mean that they had less personal influence over their respective state administrations. Although the new form of government was known as a 'federation' the powers of the central authority were not subject to formal limitations; nearly all aspects of the government of the states were directed from the headquarters of the F.M.S., Kuala Lumpur. The general administration under the Resident-General and the Railway, Mines, Public Works, Police, and Education Departments all had their offices in Kuala Lumpur. In 1897 and 1903 the Rulers and chiefs met the Governor (who also served as High Commissioner to the Malay States), Resident-General, and Residents at great Durbars, but these meetings were devoted mainly to elaborate ceremony rather than to meaningful discussion of matters with which the Malays were concerned. Furthermore, meetings of the Resident-General, the Residents, and various department heads were held once or twice a year, and it was at these that many important administrative decisions were made.[18]

The Export Economy after 1900

Between 1900 and World War I the hopes for further economic development which officials had had at the time of federation were more than fulfilled. Government revenues, the yardstick by which the British measured progress in these years, increased from $15,600,000 in 1900 to $44,300,000 in 1913.[19] After a slump in the 1890s the tin industry entered a new period of prosperity, and it was during the early years of the twentieth century that the plantation rubber industry was established. By 1909 the railway, which stimulated development and was in turn a source of revenue, extended from the shore opposite Penang

Island to Johore Bahru at the southern tip of the peninsula. From the point of view of this study the most important change was the increasingly active participation of Europeans in the economy. In the years after 1900 Europeans founded the rubber industry and began to take a large share in the tin industry.

Rubber was not the first crop to be grown by Europeans in the Malay States. Coffee planters had opened estates as early as the latter part of the 1870s. Most of the early planters came from Ceylon, where the coffee industry was being destroyed by a fungus. By the early 1890s the main centre of coffee planting was the area between Kuala Lumpur and Klang; in this area planters could take advantage of the railway line both to bring in supplies and to transport their produce. These pioneers were proprietary planters, who opened up and managed their estates with their own resources or with the help of friends and relatives in Britain. Coffee was their principal crop, but parts of their estates were often planted with cacao, tea, cinchona, and pepper as a precaution against a fall in the price of coffee.[20]

By the 1890s rubber (*Hevea brasiliensis*) was another crop which was interplanted with coffee. Rubber had been introduced into Malaya in the late 1870s and planted experimentally at the Botanical Gardens in Singapore and at Kuala Kangsar, Perak, by the Resident, Hugh Low, who had an established reputation as a botanist. Believing that rubber would become an important crop, H. N. Ridley, who was appointed Director of the Botanical Gardens in 1888, experimented with better ways to tap the trees. He also went about encouraging planters to plant more rubber, but he met with little success since the price of coffee was then very high. In the late 1890s, however, the price of coffee fell drastically. Some estates were sold or closed while others were planted with more rubber, which now showed signs of becoming a profitable crop. As the demand for rubber from the expanding automobile industry in the United States became greater and greater the production of rubber became enormously profitable. The London price of a pound of rubber reached 6s. 9d. in 1905, declined slightly in 1907 and 1908, but in 1910 reached the highest level it was ever to attain, 12s. 9d. Because of the high prices the acreage planted with rubber in Malaya (mainly in the F.M.S.) increased dramatically, from about 6,000 acres in 1900 to 541,000 acres in 1910 and 1,074,000 acres in 1913.[21] Since rubber trees take at least five years to mature a relatively small area was in production at the time of the boom prices, but prices remained high enough, except for a time during 1913 and 1914, to ensure producers substantial profits until the early 1920s, when there was a serious slump.

In 1913 Europeans owned three-fifths of the area planted with rubber in Malaya.[22] Nearly all of this area was on estates, while most of the area in Asian hands was made up of smallholdings. This pattern of ownership continued throughout the inter-war years. Of a total of 1,122,068 acres planted with rubber in the F.M.S. in 1924, 55 per cent was on European-owned estates of 100 or more acres; 9 per cent was on Asian-owned estates; 9 per cent was on holdings, owned by planters of various nationalities, of less than 100 but more than 25 acres; and 27 per cent was on smallholdings, principally Malay, of 25 acres or less.[23] A survey conducted in 1932 showed that Europeans owned 296 out of the 308 estates having 1,000 or more acres each while the remaining twelve estates were owned by Chinese.[24]

As the prospects of rubber brightened after 1900 it became clear that the capital required to open a large estate and then maintain it until the trees reached maturity was beyond the means of proprietary planters. The F.M.S. government provided loans to planters opening estates, but most of the capital was attracted from Britain. After 1905 nearly all of the new European estates and most of the old proprietary estates were floated as companies. The long-established merchant houses in Singapore played an important part in the formation of these companies. They had close connexions with the sources of capital in England, and when a company was formed one of these firms acted as agents for the board of directors, checked on the management of the new estates, recruited European managers and assistants, and supplied the estate with the materials it needed for the enterprise. In short, the 'agency houses' attracted capital by assuring investors that their money would be carefully managed and would probably yield a good return—a hope which was more than fulfilled during the boom years, when the dividends of many companies were well over 100 per cent and in some cases were over 300 per cent. As their business as agents flourished these agency houses opened offices in the F.M.S. Two of the best known firms, Harrisons and Crosfield's and Guthrie's, opened offices in Kuala Lumpur in 1907 and 1910 respectively. By 1910 there were also three large British banks in Kuala Lumpur; the Chartered Bank of India, Australia and China had opened an agency there in 1888, while the Hongkong and Shanghai Bank and the Mercantile Bank opened branches at the height of the rubber boom.

In addition to providing loans the government encouraged the plantation rubber industry in two other important ways. First, land was alienated for rubber planting on generous terms, and in Selangor at least officials aided European planters by making it more difficult for smallholders to occupy land located advantageously near government roads. Second, in 1907 the government established the Tamil Immigration Fund in order to stimulate and supervise the recruitment of estate labourers. A massive immigration of labourers was essential not only because of the expanding acreage but also because of the high death rate, mainly from malaria, among those already working on these estates. In 1910 23 per cent of the work force on one Selangor estate died; between 1910 and 1912 one-half of the resident population of the estate died.[25] Although it had been discovered in 1898 that malaria parasites were carried by the anopheles mosquito it was not until shortly before the First World War that British doctors had established which species of the anopheles carried the disease in Malaya and had developed means to control these particular species. One species of malaria-carrying anopheles thrived in the cleared land of newly opened estates, and it was found that it could be effectively controlled by building underground drains and spraying the streams where the insects lived with a mixture of kerosene and oil.[26] The reduction of the incidence of malaria was a great boon to the rubber industry as well as to general public health.

At the same time that Europeans were establishing the plantation rubber industry they were also successfully entering the tin industry. From about 1900 European mine managers were influential in bringing about changes in government policy which were to their advantage. The abolition of various revenue farms after a great deal of pressure from European miners, as well as from other quarters, meant that Chinese capitalists could no longer rely on profits from these farms when the sale of tin was not showing a profit. Partly because of the breaking up of the secret societies, through which they had controlled their labour, and the general demand for labour the Chinese mine owners were also faced with rising labour costs. In addition to labour costs, the fact that much of the richest tin-bearing soil was being exhausted and thus could no longer be as profitably mined by traditional methods meant that mining would now have to be done by highly capital-intensive methods. The Europeans were able to raise this capital by floating limited liability companies. In the late 1890s Europeans succeeded in applying the techniques of hydraulic mining to the extraction of tin, and in 1912 they introduced the first bucket-dredge. The Chinese were unable to raise the immense amount of capital needed to compete with European companies. In 1910 Chinese-owned mines still produced 78 per cent of Malaya's tin, but by 1929 European mines produced 51 per cent of the total. During these years two British firms, the Straits Trading Company, which by the 1890s was already smelting a high proportion of tin mined in the Malay States, and the Eastern Smelting Company, took over nearly all smelting of tin produced in Malaya.[27]

Rubber and tin were the two main supports of the F.M.S. economy and therefore the main sources of government revenue, either directly in the form of duties on exports or indirectly in the form of railway charges or taxes on activities related to rubber and tin. As noted, government revenues soared in the years before the First World War. From these revenues the government was able to create a civil service which was very large in comparison to those of British territories with similar populations; to build railways, roads, and public buildings and finance various social services; and even, in 1912, to give the Imperial government a battleship, H.M.S. *Malaya*. In contrast to the years up to 1919, the period from 1920 onwards was characterized by great fluctuations in government revenues and in the general prosperity of the F.M.S. as the prices of rubber and tin rose and fell in response to changing demand in the United States and Europe. As a result of the post-war slump in America and Europe, F.M.S. government revenues fell from $72 million in 1920 to $52 million in 1922. A return to prosperity in the mid-1920s was followed by a much more severe slump in the early 1930s when the United States was in the midst of the depression. The value of rubber exported from the F.M.S. fell from $202 million in 1929 to $37 million in 1932, while tin exports fell from $117 million to $31 million over the same period. Government revenues, which had reached a peak of $105 million in 1927, dropped from $82 million in 1929 to $47 million in 1933 despite attempts to raise revenue by increasing taxes on imports.[28] It was not until 1937 that the government's revenue recovered to its 1929 level.

Having looked at the role of Europeans in the economic development of the F.M.S. and the economy's dependence on rubber and tin, we need to refer briefly to the population growth which took place as the economy expanded. The population (in round figures) of the four states increased from 419,000 in 1891 to 1,037,000 in 1911 and reached 1,713,000 in 1931. Between 1891 and 1931 the Malaysian population increased from 232,000 to 594,000 as a result of natural increase and immigration from various parts of the archipelago. Their size as a proportion of the total population of the F.M.S., however, declined from 55 per cent in 1891 and 46 per cent in 1901 (when a more reliable census was taken) to 35 per cent in 1931. The reason for the relative decline of the Malaysian population was the massive immigration of Chinese and Indians. The Chinese, who in 1931 were 42 per cent of the population of the F.M.S., came to work in the tin mines, to trade, and, as the rubber industry developed, to work as labourers on estates. Because of their preponderance in commerce and other urban activities the Chinese formed the largest section of the population of towns in the F.M.S. The population of Kuala Lumpur in 1884, after ten years of British rule in Selangor, was about 4,000; it increased to 19,000 in 1891, 47,000 in 1911, and 111,000 in 1931. In 1901 the Chinese comprised 72 per cent of the town's population. By 1931 their share was somewhat smaller, 62 per cent, because of the growing numerical importance of Indians. In 1931 Indians made up 23 per cent of Kuala Lumpur's population, while only 10 per cent were Malaysians. The Indians, comprising 22 per cent of the population of the F.M.S. in 1931, were heavily concentrated in the rubber industry—in 1931 somewhat over half of all Indians were living on estates; the remainder were labourers in other activities such as the railways or were engaged in various forms of trade. In both of the principal immigrant communities men greatly outnumbered women, though the imbalance was gradually reduced as more people were encouraged by improving living conditions to settle in the country and raise families. In 1901 the Chinese community contained 10 females for every hundred males, but in 1931 the figure was 49. For Indians the ratios in 1901 and 1931 were 31 and 55 respectively.[29]

In addition to labourers and traders a small number of non-Europeans were attracted to the Malay States by opportunities for employment in the government. In the early years of British rule a very high proportion of clerks and other subordinates were Jaffna (Ceylon) Tamils, who came from an area where there were many mission schools, and Eurasians, descendants of the Portuguese and Dutch in Malacca, who had received an English education in the Straits Settlements. It was not until local students began to graduate from the Victoria Institution, opened in Kuala Lumpur in 1894, and other English schools that the government and private employers were no longer dependent on immigrants to fill their subordinate staffs.

The population of the F.M.S. was one of great diversity, but this diversity was in fact much greater than has been suggested. The Chinese were divided into numerous dialect groups, of which the largest were the Cantonese, Hakkas, and Hokkiens. One of the smaller groups were the Hailams (Hainanese), who are of interest in this study since they provided the great majority of domestic servants employed by Europeans. Chinese known as Straits or Baba Chinese usually identified themselves with one of the dialect groups, but because of long residence in the Straits Settlements and because they were British subjects and were often educated in English they were a distinct social group. They were more numerous and influential in the Straits Settlements themselves, but some found employment in the Malay States as government subordinates or in business. Among the Indians there was a great diversity of peoples. All Indian estate workers were from southern India, the Tamils being by far the largest group. A small number of Indians came from the Punjab; of these the most notable were the Sikhs, many of whom were originally brought to the states by the British to help form the police forces. Among the immigrant Malaysians were Javanese, many of whom were estate labourers; Banjerese; various Sumatran peoples; and Boyanese, many of whom were employed by Europeans as grooms and later as chauffeurs. In addition to the three main ethnic groups there were small numbers of Siamese, most of whom were in Perak; Japanese, who in the years before the First World War were with few exceptions prostitutes; and, as mentioned, Jaffna Tamils and Eurasians.

Political Changes

As European estates and mines became more numerous and more important to the economy, European unofficials (i.e., those in planting, mining, or commerce as opposed to the various government services) increasingly wanted some say in the formation of government policies. A European mine owner was appointed to the Selangor State Council in 1900, and another unofficial was appointed to the Perak State Council in 1905, but seats on these councils gave unofficials almost no opportunity to affect government policy. Even before 1900 the State Councils had been reduced to bodies which merely ratified decisions already made by the Residents and the Resident-General rather than being places where legislation was initiated. Unofficials therefore wanted some kind of federal council to be created which would give them a meaningful voice in shaping policies which affected their livelihood.

Sir John Anderson, who became Governor in 1904, also wanted some form of federal council. Both Anderson and the Colonial Office believed that a central council would make the passing of legislation much easier and would ensure greater uniformity of legislation within the F.M.S. But it was mainly because he agreed with unofficials that they should take a more active part in government that in December 1907 Anderson requested the Colonial Office's permission to establish a federal council. At the time of federation, declared Anderson in a speech in London,

The one thing that the administration was concerned with was perhaps the opinion of the native rulers and the general work of opening up the country. Now with a very considerable European population, with a large amount of English capital and even foreign capital invested in these states . . . it is desirable that public opinion, the opinion of the influential community, should have more direct outlet and that the Government should be brought more directly face to face with the criticism of those whose affairs they have to manage.[30]

After considerable delay, during which Anderson prodded the Colonial Office by reporting the requests of unofficial groups, such as the Planters' Association of Malaya, for representation on a council, the Secretary of State gave his approval to the Governor's plans. The Federal Council, which met for the first time in December 1909, had four unofficial members as well as the High Commissioner, Resident-General, the four Residents, and the four Rulers. The four unofficials were a prominent Chinese miner and three Europeans: a leading planter, a partner in a large mining firm, and the managing director of the *Malay Mail*, which had long advocated a council. The unofficial members were in the minority and were nominated by the High Commissioner rather than being chosen by particular commercial interests as their representatives. Nevertheless, they vigorously promoted the views of unofficial groups and did influence the government's decisions.

The composition of the Federal Council reflected other aspects of the political situation of the time besides the growing importance of unofficials. Anderson and the Colonial Office made the High Commissioner, rather than the Resident-General, president of the council in order to ensure his position as the overall director of administration throughout British Malaya. The Malay Rulers were in the peculiar position of sitting on a council whose function in theory was to advise the Rulers. They were not expected to take an active part in the proceedings or to attend regularly. They did not have the power of veto, and the council's decisions were binding whether or not they attended. It appears that the Rulers, particularly Sultan Idris of Perak, who often acted as their spokesman, had been led to believe that with the creation of the Federal Council the state governments and State Councils would regain some of the powers they had lost to the Resident-General and federal secretariats after federation. In fact, the new council continued the process of centralization and helped to make the Councils even more insignificant. When in 1910 the Resident-General was given the more modest title of Chief Secretary, Idris believed that this too signified a return of power to the states. Anderson's purpose, however, was to reduce the independence of the Resident-General rather than to loosen the bonds of federation. As it turned out, the first Chief Secretary's powers were much the same as those enjoyed by the last Resident-General.

The issues of decentralization and in particular the post of Chief Secretary were at the heart of the main political controversies of the inter-war years—at least those controversies in which the British were directly involved. In the years after the formation of the Federal Council the Rulers became increasingly dissatisfied with their positions. Their discontent was heightened when they observed the relative independence enjoyed by the Sultans in the Unfederated Malay States. In becoming British Protectorates, Kedah, Perlis, Kelantan, Trengganu, and Johore accepted British Advisers rather than Residents. In 1910, shortly after the northern states had come under British protection, Anderson explained to the Secretary of State that under existing conditions it would be impossible to bring Kedah into the federation. The first British Adviser to Kedah, an official with long experience in the F.M.S. and the Straits Settlements, attempted to administer the state as a Resident would in one of the federated states, but the Malay élite, which was traditionally more unified than those of the west-coast states to the south and which ruled a state which had not been disrupted by mass immigration, successfully retained significant powers.[31] In many ways Johore resembled the west-coast states in the federation, but due to the forcefulness of its Sultans the British had to administer the state with more deference to Malay wishes. The Sultan of Perak had the Sultans of these and the other unfederated states in mind when during a visit to England in 1924 he asked the Secretary of State to restore to the Rulers, Residents, and State Councils the powers which he said were rightfully theirs according to treaties made between the British and the Malay Rulers.[32]

In December 1925 the Governor, Sir Laurence Guillemard, announced his policy of decentralization, the key to which, he said, was the removal of the post of Chief Secretary. Guillemard's proposals met with vehement opposition from European and Chinese unofficials on the Federal Council. They feared either that the High Commissioner, whom they regarded as unsympathetic to the special needs of the F.M.S., would take over the powers held by the Chief Secretary or that if real power were transferred to the states the unity, stability, and hence economic prosperity of the federation would be undermined. Guillemard was forced to lay aside this part of his programme. In order to enhance the dignity of the Rulers he had them replaced in the Federal Council (which by now included several more officials and unofficials than in 1909) by Malay 'unofficials' (most were in fact government servants), who felt more free to participate actively in the debates. Guillemard also gave the states slightly more control over their own finances, but it was the Residents rather than the Rulers who benefited from this change.

In the early 1930s another Governor, Sir Cecil Clementi, embarked on a more ambitious programme of decentralization. It was his aim to forge closer ties between the federated and unfederated states by first giving greater autonomy to the states within the Federation. Clementi's proposals, which included abolition of the Chief Secretaryship, were fought by European and Chinese commercial interests even more strongly than Guillemard's had been. They believed that altering the structure of government in the midst of a severe depression would put the economy in even greater danger. They were also opposed to any trend towards Malay dominance in governing the states. Clementi's successor, Sir Shenton Thomas, did, however, succeed in having the Chief Secretary replaced by a Federal Secretary, who had limited powers and whose official standing was below that of the Residents, enlarging the State Councils and giving them more control over expenditure, and having some departments transferred from federal to state control. Despite these measures the position of the British as the effective rulers of the F.M.S. remained unchanged. The Malay Rulers were still bound to accept the 'advice' of the Residents. Moreover, the state governments and departments were still run in the main by British officers. Finally, the Federal Council, with its official majority, continued to legislate on the most important matters of government. Indeed, it should be pointed out that by enhancing the standing of the Rulers and State Councils, Clementi had hoped to discourage non-Malays from agitating in the future for more democratic representation on the Federal Council.[33] Decentralization, in short, was intended in part as a means of upholding British rule.

From the point of view of this study the most striking feature of the political situation in Malaya during the inter-war years was the absence of any challenge to British rule. There was at times intense political activity among the Chinese, but this was mainly concerned with events which were taking place in China. A large section of the Chinese population took little interest in politics, and some actively supported British rule. Moreover, the British were able effectively to suppress any Chinese organization or individual whose activities they believed might subvert British authority.[34] Indians living in the F.M.S. and the Straits Settlements actively participated in the political questions then affecting their homeland, but they did not challenge British rule in Malaya. Among the local issues which concerned them were government employment, citizenship, and working conditions on estates. As their numbers grew Indians also looked for more effective ways of presenting their views to the government. After receiving many petitions from Indian and Ceylonese groups the High Commissioner appointed a Kuala Lumpur lawyer as the Indian member on the Federal Council in 1928.[35] During the latter part of the 1930s there were signs of a growing political consciousness among Malays. It is notable however that many politically active Malays wished to protect Malay interests in relation to the Chinese rather than to bring an end to British rule and that the most successful political association was dominated by aristocratic Malays, who often professed their loyalty to the British.[36] In European eyes at least, Malaya was therefore a remarkably peaceful place in which to live. 'Altogether,' commented one visitor in the late 1930s, 'Malaya is as happy a land as one could ever hope to find—a Tory Eden in which each man is contented with his station, and does not wish for change.'[37]

2

A Profile of the Europeans

BEFORE going into a detailed description of the European community it is useful to take a very general look at the main occupational divisions within the community. Europeans were divided first of all between officials and unofficials, i.e., all those employed by the government and all those who were in private enterprise of any sort. Officials were in turn divided into the cadet service and the non-cadet service. Beginning in 1920 the cadet service was formally known as the Malayan Civil Service; the term 'civil servant' usually applied only to a member of this sector of the government. Members of the cadet service held general administrative posts from Assistant District Officer all the way up to Resident. As from 1896 they were selected by a competitive examination and spent two or three years as 'cadets' learning an Asian language, usually Malay but sometimes Chinese or an Indian language, and becoming familiar with local laws and regulations. The non-cadet service was in fact not one service but all the professional and technical departments. These included the Police, Railway, Medical, Education, Survey, and Public Works Departments. The distinction between the cadet and non-cadet services was very strictly observed, but the director of the Education Department was invariably a member of the cadet service and sometimes the heads of two or three other departments belonged to the cadet service. Although the non-cadet service consisted of many departments, the service as a whole contained a division which cut across departmental lines. On the one hand there were commissioned police officers and doctors, civil engineers, surveyors, and others with professional or technical qualifications, and on the other there were those who lacked these qualifications and generally held lower positions, such as police inspectors, station masters, train drivers, and prison warders.

The term 'unofficials' covered men in a great variety of occupations. The most important of these were the planters, mine managers, bankers, merchants, and doctors, lawyers, and other pro-
fessionals in private practice.

Nationality and its Bearing on
the Use of Census Data

In Malaya the term 'European' encompassed not only people
from various parts of the British Isles and the continent of
Europe but also Australians, New Zealanders, Canadians,
Americans, and others who traced their ancestry to Europe. As
Table 1 shows, throughout the period covered by this study by
far the great majority of Europeans in the Federated Malay States
were British. Before 1931 superintendents of censuses met with
little success in distinguishing between Britishers of different
national origins. In 1911 Britishers were instructed to identify
themselves with a particular part of the British Isles or the
Empire, but most simply returned themselves as 'British'. Indeed
some were content to identify themselves as 'Europeans'—
'apparently to them a sufficiently marked discrimination for a
resident in a Native State', commented the superintendent of the
census.[1] The 1921 census also failed in its attempt to have
Britishers specify their precise nationality. In the case of both the
1911 and 1921 censuses, however, the fact that over two-fifths of
all Europeans had been born in England indicated that the English were the largest group of Britishers.[2] This was confirmed in
1931 when the British did follow instructions to specify their
nationality. As Table 2 shows, the English accounted for over
half of all Europeans and the Scots for nearly a fifth. The Irish
and Australians were the other large British groups. The largest
non-British groups were the Americans, Dutch, and French.

TABLE 1
The British as a Percentage of Europeans
in the F.M.S., 1901–1931

	1901	1911	1921	1931
Per cent British	85.5	88.9	93.2	91.7

Sources: F.M.S. 1901 Census, Perak Table 3, Selangor Table 3, Negri Sembilan
Table 3, Pahang Table 3; British Malaya 1921 Census, p. 70; British Malaya 1931
Census, Table 35.

TABLE 2
Nationality of Europeans in the F.M.S., 1931

	Number	Per cent
British		
English	3,534	55.7
Scottish	1,191	18.8
Welsh	82	1.3
Irish	378	6.0
Australian	440	6.9
New Zealander	107	1.7
Other British	91	1.4
Others		
Americans	109	1.7
Danish	68	1.1
Dutch	102	1.6
French	104	1.6
Italian	27	0.4
Portuguese	20	0.3
Others	97	1.5
Total	6,350	100.0

Source: British Malaya 1931 Census, Table 35.

The question of nationality is of interest in itself, but it also raises a general problem in the use of census data. This problem arises from the fact that whether an individual was counted as a European depended on whether he told the census enumerator that he was a European or that he belonged to one of the divisions of the European race. A glance at Table 2 reveals that a certain number of people were included under the heading of 'Europeans' even though in all probability they would not have been regarded as such by the great majority of the European community. Probably all of the 'Portuguese' were Eurasians from Malacca. Among the 'French' were some Eurasians and perhaps a few Indians. And many of the Dutch were Eurasians from the Netherlands East Indies.[3] There is evidence that some Malayan Eurasians were included as Europeans because they were ashamed of stating their ethnic identity.[4] The case of the 'Dutch' Eurasians was somewhat different. In the Netherlands Indies the distinction between Europeans and Eurasians was not as clear as it was in British colonial territories. In the twentieth century the social division between Europeans and Eurasians became sharper than it had been, but Eurasians were legally recognized by the Dutch government as being Europeans and were counted as Europeans in the censuses. For this reason Dutch Eurasians who worked in Malaya naturally regarded themselves as Europeans.

It is difficult to know how much the proportion of Eurasians included as Europeans varied from census to census. In 1901 nearly one-fifth of Europeans in Selangor were returned as 'Portuguese', but there were few Portuguese in any of the other states. In 1921 only three persons in the F.M.S. were listed as Portuguese, but there were 107 'Dutch'. It would be safe to estimate that fewer than 5 per cent of those people coming under the heading of 'Europeans' in the 1931 census were people who were not generally accepted by the great bulk of Europeans as belonging to the European community.

To the extent that Eurasians were included as Europeans the census data which are used in this chapter and on many other occasions in this study present a distorted picture of the European community. It is impossible to make adjustments to eliminate this distortion, but it is possible to point to three ways in which the picture might be affected. First, and most obviously, the inclusion of some Eurasians means that the European population was in fact slightly smaller than the census data indicate. Second, since Eurasians generally held clerical and other subordinate positions occupational data may tend to exaggerate the number of Europeans in such positions. Third, since the Eurasian population had a nearly normal age-sex structure the imbalance between the two sexes and between age groups which characterized European society was in reality somewhat greater than the census figures suggest. In view of the relatively small number of Eurasians who were counted as Europeans, however, we can be assured that census data do present a fairly reliable picture of the European community.

Population Growth

For most Europeans Malaya was a place to which they came to work. When the opportunities for employment increased the number of Europeans increased correspondingly, and when existing jobs disappeared the number declined as men returned to Europe or looked for work elsewhere. For reasons to be explained in later chapters, the particular anathema with which the British regarded 'poor whites' ensured that men who had lost their jobs did not linger long in Malaya, and the beliefs Euro-

TABLE 3
The European Population of Malaya, 1871–1931

	1871	1879	1881	1884	1891	1901	1911	1921	1931
Perak					366	661	1,396	2,047	2,359
Selangor		82 (inc. Eurasians)		107 (inc. Eurasians)	190	487	1,348	2,467	2,723
Negri Sembilan					61	140	403	894	878
Pahang					102	134	137	278	390
Total F.M.S.					719	1,422	3,284	5,686	6,350
Straits Settlements	2,429		3,483		4,422	5,058	7,368	8,149	10,003
Unfed. Malay States							413	1,084	1,295
Total British Malaya							11,065	14,919	17,648

Sources: Perak in 1879: Perak 1891 Census; Selangor in 1884: Selangor 1891 Census; Malay States in 1891 and 1901: F.M.S. 1901 Census. Perak Table 1, Selangor Table 1, Negri Sembilan Table 1, Pahang Table 1; Straits Settlements in 1871, 1881, and 1891: H. Marriott, 'Population of the Straits Settlements and Malay Peninsula during the last Century', *Journal Straits Branch Royal Asiatic Society*, no. 62 (December 1912), p. 32 (the 1871 and 1881 figures include the military and transient populations but it is not clear whether the 1891 figure does); Straits Settlements in 1901 and all data for 1911 and 1921: British Malaya 1921 Census, p. 29; all 1931 data from British Malaya 1931 Census, Table 1.

peans had about the harmful effects of long residence in a tropical climate discouraged them from spending their retirements in Malaya. The growth and fluctuations of the European population are therefore to be traced against the background of economic and political developments rather than, as in the case of a settled population, by examining changing birth and death rates.

For the years before 1891, when censuses were conducted in all the states under British protection, it is impossible to know exactly how many Europeans were living in the Malay States. Rough population counts taken in Perak in 1879 and in Selangor in 1884 included Eurasians with Europeans. (See Table 3.) If, as was the case in later censuses, the number of acknowledged Eurasians was approximately the same as the number of Europeans it would be safe to say that there were only about forty Europeans in Perak in 1879 and not many more than fifty Europeans in Selangor in 1884. In 1881 the European population of the west coast states could not have been more than a hundred. In the latter part of the 1880s and early 1890s the number of Europeans increased rapidly. In March 1892 one official remarked that when he arrived in Perak in 1886 there were only about 80 or 90 Europeans in the state but that now there were about 500.[5] The censuses of 1891 gave a total of 719 Europeans in the four Malay States. Over the next ten years the size of the European population nearly doubled.

Until about 1900 the European population increased mainly as a result of the expansion of the government bureaucracy. General administrators and police were joined by engineers, doctors, and others who formed the various professional and technical departments. At the time of the 1891 census of Perak (the only census of that year containing information on occupations) there were 224 European men employed in the state. Of these only 8 were planters, 9 were in commerce, 12 were contractors and builders, and 6 were miners; nearly all of the others were employed in some way by the government. The number of Europeans in planting was undoubtedly somewhat higher in Selangor than in Perak since Selangor contained the principal coffee planting districts. A fairly high proportion of the Europeans living in Pahang in the 1890s were unofficials because of the large number of Australians working at the Raub Gold Mine. At the time of the 1901 census there were 50 European miners in Pahang; 38 of these men were in gold mining.

In the first decade of the twentieth century the character of the European community underwent a great change. Between 1901

TABLE 4
Percentage of Employed European Men in the F.M.S.
in Agriculture, Mining, and Commerce and Finance,
1901–1931
( ) = *number in category*

	1901	1911	1921	1931
Agriculture	12 (107)	42 (881)	47 (1,493)	32 (1,140)
Mining	12 (111)	6 (127)	7 (225)	10 (369)
Commerce and Finance	5 (45)	10 (221)	11 (349)	14 (482)
Total Number of Employed Men	899	2,112	3,200	3,529

Sources: F.M.S. 1901 Census, Perak Table 11, Selangor Table 11, Negri Sembi-lan Table 11, and Pahang Table 11; F.M.S. 1911 Census, Table 42; British Malaya 1921 Census, Table 34 (F.M.S.); British Malaya 1931 Census, Table 130.

and 1911 the population more than doubled. By 1911 the European population of the F.M.S. was nearly half that of the Straits Settlements. During this period the number of civil servants and other government employees increased greatly, but the growth of the various unofficial sections of the community was truly dramatic. The number of men engaged in planting increased eight times, as Europeans flooded in to become managers and assistant managers on newly opened rubber estates. As Table 4 shows, the proportion of European men in the F.M.S. who were planters jumped from 12 per cent to 42 per cent. During the same period the proportion of Europeans engaged in commerce and finance increased from 5 to 10 per cent. There was a slight increase in the number of Europeans in mining, but since the mining methods employed by European companies did not require large numbers of labour supervisors, as in the case of the rubber industry, miners never became a large proportion of the community.

Between 1911 and 1921 the European population increased by 73 per cent, but, as Figure 1 illustrates, the size of the community fluctuated greatly between those dates. The population continued to rise until 1914. On the outbreak of war in Europe

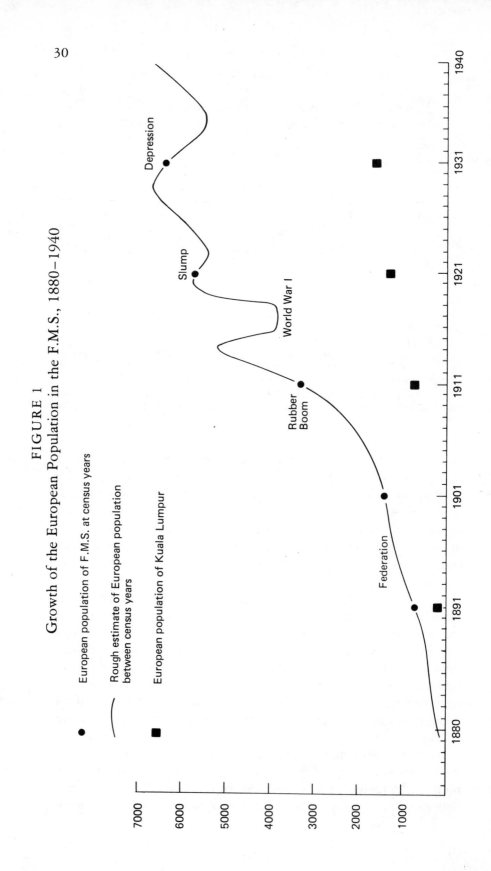

FIGURE 1

Growth of the European Population in the F.M.S., 1880–1940

●   European population of F.M.S. at census years

⌒   Rough estimate of European population between census years

■   European population of Kuala Lumpur

over 700 men left the F.M.S. to serve in the armed forces. There was a further reduction in the population since many of the departing men were accompanied by wives and children.[6] Somewhat more than 200 Europeans who had worked in the F.M.S. were killed during the war.[7] After the Armistice there was a sudden influx of men returning from the war or hoping to begin a career in Malaya. By the time the census was taken in April 1921 many of the newcomers had already left the F.M.S. due to the commercial slump which began in the latter part of 1920.

Having arrived at 1921 we may pause to take a look at some features of the European population in that year. As Table 4 shows, by 1921 nearly half of all employed men were in the rubber industry, while the proportion of men in mining and commerce and finance was nearly the same as it had been at the previous census. The 1921 census tells us little about the sizes of many other occupational groups since some officials in the professional and technical departments are included as 'Civil Service Officials' while others are listed under their respective professions. The relative sizes of the cadet and non-cadet services can however be seen by looking at other sources. In 1918 the cadet service numbered 142 and the non-cadet 894;[8] in 1925 there were 160 members of the M.C.S. serving in the F.M.S. and over a thousand Europeans in the various professional and technical departments. Of the non-cadet services, the Police, Railway, Public Works, and Medical Departments had the largest number of Europeans. Returning to the 1921 census data, a few further points are worth making. As indicated in Table 4, 349 European men were employed in commerce and finance. Of these, the largest number, 173, were proprietors and managers of businesses while 32 were bankers or bank officers. According to the census, 120 European men were employed as commercial assistants and in similar jobs, but it is possible that some of these men were in fact Eurasians. There were also numerous smaller categories of men working outside government such as journalists (8), ministers and mission workers (30), and racehorse trainers and jockeys (4 but no doubt more at certain times of the year). Finally, the census provides information on the few European women who were employed. Seventy-one of them were teachers (both in government and mission schools), 41 were nurses (in government hospitals), 30 were Roman Catholic nuns, and 42 were domestic servants.[9]

In addition to occupations it is useful to refer to the geographical distribution of Europeans at the time of the 1921 cen-

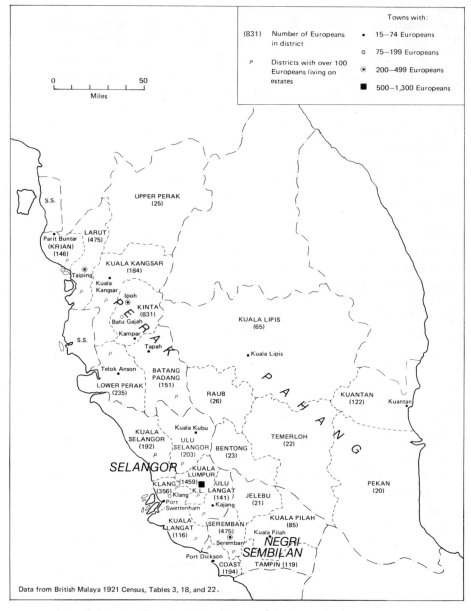

Map 2. Geographical Distribution of Europeans
in the F.M.S. in 1921

sus. Map 2 shows that like the population as a whole Europeans were concentrated along the west coast, the location of the main administrative and commercial centres and planting districts. About 39 per cent of all Europeans were living on estates; the thirteen districts with 100 or more Europeans living on estates formed a belt stretching from Port Dickson and Seremban up to Taiping and Parit Buntar. There were only four towns with 200 or more Europeans, but these towns contained 38 per cent of the European population. Kuala Lumpur had by far the largest number of Europeans—1,267. The other three were Ipoh (427), Taiping (285), and Seremban (202).

After the passing of the slump of the early 1920s the European population again increased, but by 1930 Europeans were faced with a much more severe economic crisis. Perhaps as many as a thousand Europeans left the F.M.S. between 1930 and 1934. A very sizeable percentage of these were planters and their families. As early as April 1931, when the census was taken, only 32 per cent of employed European men were engaged in planting, as compared to 47 per cent in 1921, and only 27 per cent of the European population were living on estates.[10] In contrast to the period after the post-war slump there was no sudden rise in the number of planters when the economy began to recover in 1934. Having been forced to reduce their costs drastically during the depression years, the rubber companies found that they did not need to employ as many planters as they had in the mid-1920s. Where there had once been one European staff member for 500 acres, by 1937 each planter was responsible for about 2,000 acres.[11] It was however necessary to recruit some new planters, and by the mid-1930s commercial firms and the government resumed recruitment. By 1941 the number of Europeans living in the F.M.S. was probably significantly greater than it had been in 1931.

Social Origins and Recruitment

From which social classes in Britain did the British in the F.M.S. come? What motivated them to come to Malaya? By what means were they recruited to work in Malaya? The answers to these questions are complex and the sources limited, but it is possible to make some generalizations and to make broad comparisons between those in various occupations. One of the best sources for studying the backgrounds of the British is an extensive survey of Malaya entitled *Twentieth Century Impressions of British Malaya*, published in 1908.[12] Besides details on the government and commerce of Malaya the book contains biographical data on somewhat over 200 planters, officials, and businessmen. In the first part of this section these data are used to compare the social backgrounds of civil servants, who were the most important group in government service, and planters, who were by far the largest group of unofficials in the F.M.S. The limitations of the data in *Twentieth Century Impressions* are obvious. The biographies of less than half of the civil servants and planters then working in the F.M.S. are included and in many cases very little information is given. The data in the book do however provide a start to answering questions about social background, and these data can be supplemented by information from other sources. Another limitation is that the data were collected in 1907 and therefore any conclusions drawn from these data cannot be said to apply to the whole period covered by this study. But information relating to other times again can be used to supplement *Twentieth Century Impressions*. Moreover, it is worth noting that many of the men listed in the book had been in Malaya since the 1880s and others were to remain there into the 1930s.

A COMPARISON OF CIVIL SERVANTS AND PLANTERS

There are two ways of placing the British who worked in the F.M.S. in the context of British society: by looking at their educational background and by looking at the more limited information on their fathers' occupations. Especially in England the type of secondary education someone received was a strong indication of his family's social class. In Table 5 the educational background of civil servants and planters is shown as far as the information in *Twentieth Century Impressions* permits. A somewhat higher proportion of civil servants than of planters attended one of the seven most famous English public schools—Eton, Winchester, Harrow, Rugby, Shrewsbury, Charterhouse, and Westminster—or one of the other public schools and select grammar schools (such as Manchester and Bedford) which belonged to the Headmasters' Conference, while about equal proportions were listed as having attended other public and grammar schools or having been privately educated. Comparisons are made difficult not only by the lack of data but also by the fact that whereas most civil servants were English perhaps as many as a third of the planters were Scottish. A small number of Scottish schools belonged to the Headmasters' Conference, but in Scotland secondary education

TABLE 5
Educational Background of Civil Servants and Planters Listed in *Twentieth Century Impressions of British Malaya*

	Civil Servants			Planters		
	Secondary Only	*University Degree or Legal Qualif.*	*Total*	*Secondary Only*	*University Degree or Legal Qualif.*	*Total*
The Seven	2	3	5	5	1	6
Other Schools in Headmasters' Conference	5	13	18	19	—	19
Public and Grammar Schools not in H.C., Private Schools	5	2	7	18	1	19
Schools outside British Isles but within Empire	1	—	1	4	—	4
Not Stated	12	8	20	47	—	47
Not British	—	—	—	5	—	5
Totals	25	26	51	98	2	100

Source: Biographical data in Wright and Cartwright, *Twentieth Century Impressions*. Only civil servants employed in the F.M.S. at the time the book was compiled (1907) are included. Planting assistants whose names are listed in *Twentieth Century Impressions* but for whom no biographical information is given have not been included. The eleventh issue of *The Public Schools Year-Book* (London, 1900) has been used to determine whether a school belonged to the Headmasters' Conference.

was in general of a higher quality and available to a greater portion of the population than in England, and thus the type of
school someone attended did not reflect his social class as clearly
as it did in England. Nevertheless, the table suggests that there
was no marked difference in the secondary educational background of civil servants and planters, and therefore that there
was no great difference in the social backgrounds of the two
groups. One point helps us to see both civil servants and planters in relation to British society. Certainly all civil servants and
nearly all planters had some form of education at least to the
age of fourteen, and many of them received this education at
socially exclusive schools. In 1902 only 9 per cent of all
fourteen-year-olds in Great Britain were receiving *any* kind of
full-time education.[13]

Though it was more a sign of differences in academic ability
and interest than of social origins, we may note at this point that
civil servants were far more likely than planters to have been to a
university. Over half of the civil servants listed in *Twentieth Century Impressions* had university degrees, usually from Oxford or
Cambridge but in a few cases from Edinburgh or Trinity College,
Dublin. At the beginning of the twentieth century less than one
per cent of young people of the same age as matriculating students were entering universities in Great Britain,[14] and those
who went on to receive degrees formed an even smaller group.
Several of the civil servants with degrees had also qualified for
the Bar by attending one of the Inns of Court in London. Only
two planters listed appeared to have a university degree. One of
these was a doctor who had abandoned his medical career to take
charge of an estate owned by his brother. Four other planters
had had some university education. Three of them had begun
medical training but had given this up to become planters.

The information in *Twentieth Century Impressions* on the occupations of the fathers of civil servants and planters is, like that on
secondary education, an indication of their social background.
This is given for about a third of the planters and a quarter of the
civil servants, but it is worth considering especially since it is
often given where information on education is lacking. Four
planters were listed as sons of colonels in the British army, while
one was the son of a Major-General. Five were the sons of clergymen and two of doctors. The fathers of three planters had
been in various government services—the Indian Civil Service,
consular service, and Ceylon Civil Service. Five were sons of
Ceylon planters. Among those with commercial backgrounds

were a son of the director of a large insurance firm and a son of
the manager and part-proprietor of a brewery. Others included
the son of a hydraulic engineer and the son of a sheep farmer in
Scotland. C. B. Holman-Hunt's father was the famous religious
artist, William Holman-Hunt. In two cases where the father's
occupation was not mentioned that of a brother was given. One
planter was the brother of a Member of Parliament, while
another was the brother of an actor and theatre owner. One of
the non-British planters was J. de Burlet, whose father had been
Prime Minister of Belgium.

As far as can be ascertained from *Twentieth Century Impressions*
civil servants had broadly similar family backgrounds. Two were
the sons of a sugar planter in Jamaica, and others were the sons
of a stipendary magistrate, a Bradford wool manufacturer, an
army colonel, a London solicitor, and the manager of Lord
Sheffield's properties in Sussex. H. C. Belfield, a Resident, was
perhaps exceptional in being 'the head of an old Devonshire family, a landowner, and J.P.'. Several civil servants were the sons of
prominent Britishers in Malaya. The Resident of Perak, E. W.
Birch, was the son of the first Resident of Perak. The Bishop of
Singapore, G. F. Hose, and a former member of the Straits Settlements Legislative Council, W. Ramsay Scott, had sons serving
in the Malay States. Of all British families associated with Malaya
the best known were the Maxwells. Their ties with Malaya and
other parts of the Empire over four generations are shown in Figure 2.

Various contemporary comments provide further clues to the
social background of civil servants and planters. In 1897 the
editor of the *Malay Mail* observed that cadets 'are mainly
recruited from what is known as the "professional class". The
sons of doctors, clergymen, lawyers, bankers, officers in the army
and merchants form the chief source of supply.'[15] Marwick has
estimated that the upper class constituted 5 per cent of Edwardian society, the middle class 15 per cent, and the working class
80 per cent.[16] For civil servants it would be reasonable to say
that those educated at 'The Seven' and perhaps a few others
came from upper-class families while the great majority had
middle-class backgrounds. From the point of view of its members
the middle class of course contained its own important gradations. In 1914 it was stated that civil servants came from the
'upper middle class',[17] which would certainly include the professions the editor of the *Malay Mail* had referred to earlier. In
1921 a retired civil servant described the M.C.S. as providing an

38

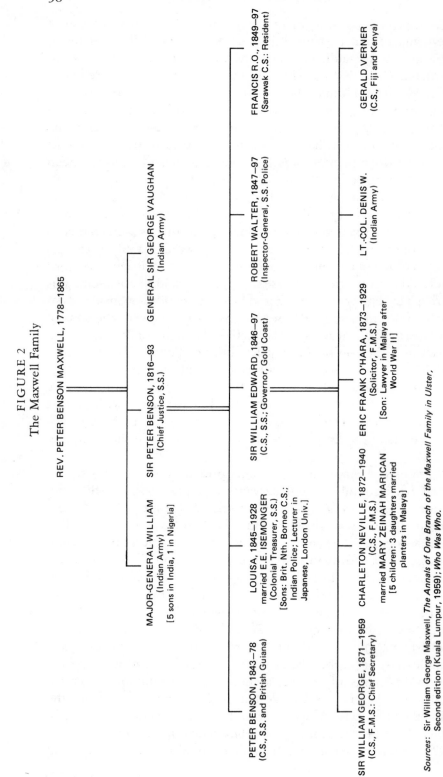

FIGURE 2
The Maxwell Family

REV. PETER BENSON MAXWELL, 1778–1865

MAJOR-GENERAL WILLIAM
(Indian Army)
[5 sons in India, 1 in Nigeria]

SIR PETER BENSON, 1816–93
(Chief Justice, S.S.)

GENERAL SIR GEORGE VAUGHAN
(Indian Army)

PETER BENSON, 1843–78
(C.S., S.S. and British Guiana)

LOUISA, 1845–1928
married E.E. ISEMONGER
(Colonial Treasurer, S.S.)
[Sons: Brit. Nth. Borneo C.S.;
Indian Police; Lecturer in
Japanese, London Univ.]

SIR WILLIAM EDWARD, 1846–97
(C.S., S.S.; Governor, Gold Coast)

ROBERT WALTER, 1847–97
(Inspector-General, S.S. Police)

FRANCIS R.O., 1849–97
(Sarawak C.S.: Resident)

SIR WILLIAM GEORGE, 1871–1959
(C.S., F.M.S.: Chief Secretary)

CHARLETON NEVILLE, 1872–1940
(C.S., F.M.S.)
married MARY ZEINAH MARICAN
[5 children: 3 daughters married
planters in Malaya]

ERIC FRANK O'HARA, 1873–1929
(Solicitor, F.M.S.)
[Son: Lawyer in Malaya after
World War II]

LT.-COL. DENIS W.
(Indian Army)

GERALD VERNER
(C.S., Fiji and Kenya)

Sources: Sir William George Maxwell, *The Annals of One Branch of the Maxwell Family in Ulster,*
Second edition (Kuala Lumpur, 1959); *Who Was Who.*

Note: C.S.–Civil Service.

ideal career for 'the well-educated sons of the upper middle class-es'.[18] In fact, however, the M.C.S. between the wars was not recruited solely from this class. According to Victor Purcell, about a third of the cadets came from the larger public schools ('from Harrow and Winchester down to Uppingham and Repton') and therefore could be said to belong to the upper middle class, while the others came from other public schools in the Headmasters' Conference or from other secondary schools and thus belonged to the lower middle class.[19]

As for planters, the evidence in *Twentieth Century Impressions* indicates that in 1907 the great majority of them belonged to the middle class. At the height of the rubber boom, however, men from a wider range of social backgrounds were attracted to planting. Indeed, one rather superior observer noted in 1912 that the great demand for managers and assistants had finally cleared Penang and other large towns of the loafers and beachcombers who used to hang about bringing discredit to the white race.[20] In 1919 the administrator of a large number of estates was asked by the Bucknill Commission, which was preparing a report on the salaries of government officers, whether nearly all his planters were public school men. 'I rather regret they are not', he replied. 'We have got all kinds. Hitherto there has been no discrimination used in the selection of men.'[21] Jotting in his notebook ten years later, Somerset Maugham claimed that planters could be divided into two classes: 'The greater number of them are rough and common men of something below the middle class, and they speak English with a vile accent, or broad Scotch. . . . There is another class of planter who has been to a public school and perhaps a university.'[22] Maugham's description, however, is not confirmed by planters and others whom I have interviewed. All of them stress the middle-class character of the planting community before the Second World War.

In conclusion, the evidence in *Twentieth Century Impressions* and other sources indicates that a wider range of social backgrounds was represented among planters than among civil servants. This diversity was particularly apparent during the period when the rubber industry was expanding most rapidly. Nevertheless, a large proportion of the planting community came from broadly similar backgrounds as civil servants. It was mainly the fact that most civil servants had an Oxbridge education which distinguished them from planters. This important difference between the two groups can be explained by looking at the various ways they were recruited to work in Malaya.

RECRUITMENT OF CIVIL SERVANTS

During the first decade after the Pangkor Engagement civil servants were recruited to the Malay States from a great variety of sources and in an equally great variety of ways. A few, such as Frank Swettenham and W. E. Maxwell, were seconded from the Straits Settlements Civil Service. Before 1882 members of this service were selected by a competitive examination which they took after being nominated by the Secretary of State; in 1882 the Colonial Office began selecting men for the Straits Settlements, Ceylon, and Hong Kong Civil Services (collectively known as the 'Eastern Cadetships') solely by the results of an open competitive examination. Other officials, such as Hugh Low, who had been stationed at Labuan for twenty-nine years before being appointed Resident of Perak, came to the Malay States after long service in other colonial territories, others had served in Sarawak under Rajah Brooke, and a few were retired naval officers. Many officials were recruited locally. Before being appointed Assistant Resident at Larut, Captain Speedy, who came to Malaya after an adventurous career in Africa and India, had been the commander of a Malay chief's troops during the civil wars. Several of the earliest Collectors and Magistrates were Eurasians from the Straits Settlements. Still others were men of various types who had arrived on the scene and been given jobs. The Italian C. F. Bozzolo, for example, who joined the Perak service in 1880, had mined in Australia and worked as an artisan during the digging of the Suez Canal; his speech was a mixture of Italian, English, French, German, Spanish, and Arabic, and he wrote 'an English of his own invention'.[23] All in all, early Governors found the civil service of the Malay States far from satisfactory. Captain Speedy, who enjoyed wearing Abyssinian costume and playing the bagpipes and conducted an unorthodox administration, was pressured into resigning after only three years at his post. And during his first two years as Governor Sir Frederick Weld dismissed two-thirds of the officials of Selangor for inefficiency.[24] Among those he had removed was the Resident, Captain Bloomfield Douglas.

The next phase in the history of recruitment to the civil service covers the period from about 1883 to 1896. In 1883 the Colonial Office began selecting officers known as 'Junior Officers' especially for service in the Malay States. Most Junior Officers had a public school education, and as a result of their being selected by nomination many of them had personal connexions with important officials in Malaya. Among those selected by nomination at this time were Hugh Clifford, son of Weld's cousin Sir Henry Clifford; C. D. Bowen, son of a friend of the Governor's when Weld was Prime Minister of New Zealand; F. J. Weld, apparently another relative of the Governor's; a son of Sir Frederick Dickson, Colonial Secretary and at various times acting Governor; E. S. Hose, son of the Bishop of Singapore; and two sons of W. E. Maxwell, George and Charleton (see Figure 2). Officials who were selected as Junior Officers usually spent their entire careers in the Malay States, but the Governor had the power to second them to the Straits Settlements Civil Service. George Maxwell, for example, spent some time as a Straits official, as did L. P. Ebden, who had been nominated as a Junior Officer after failing the examination for the Straits civil service.

After 1883 the Residents continued to recruit some officials locally, but they could now be more selective in whom they hired in this way. The Residents showed a definite bias towards public school men who demonstrated some ability at cricket. Cricket was above all others the sport of the late Victorian public schools, and a man who excelled at cricket was regarded as possessing a finer character than the man whose abilities were confined to books and examinations. In the Malay States interest and ability in bookwork was seen not only as unnecessary but also as a possible obstacle to success as an official. 'What we require out here are young public schoolmen—Cheltenham, for preference—who have failed conspicuously at all bookwork and examinations in proportion as they have excelled at sports', one high official was quoted as saying.[25] When J. R. O. Aldworth arrived in Kuala Lumpur in 1889 his record as an athlete at Cheltenham helped to persuade the Resident, Swettenham, to give him a job.[26] As Resident of Perak Swettenham kept an eye out for men who would do credit to both the civil service and the state cricket team, which one sporting official judged as the equal of a good English county team.[27] One of his most successful finds was Oliver Marks, who was invited to work for the Perak government after his brilliant performance for a visiting Ceylon cricket team.[28] There were other men locally recruited who though not renowned for cricket possessed the necessary social attributes. J. P. Rodger was a man of independent means and a barrister; Martin Lister was a son of Lord Ribblesdale; and Arthur Keyser had mixed in high society in England and squandered a large sum of money before heading East in search of employment.[29]

In 1896 both local recruitment and the system of selecting Junior Officers by nomination came to an end. Beginning in that year officials for the Home and Indian Civil Services and the Eastern Services, now including the F.M.S., were all selected by the results of an open competitive examination held in London once a year. All four Residents had been in favour of having a competitive examination, for they regarded several Junior Officers as lacking in education and intelligence, but they wanted the Governor to have the power to nominate the candidates who should be allowed to sit for the examination. The danger of an open examination was, they believed, that the government could no longer be certain of obtaining men who possessed the right physique and character. In expressing his opposition to an open examination, one senior official observed that 'It is a great recommendation to the Malay mind that a man should be a gentleman for the Malay race studies courtesy and is quick to distinguish a gentleman and a man who is either a boor or is under-bred.'[30] Whatever the reasons for which local officials opposed the change, it had two clear results. First, high officials in Malaya could no longer use their influence to secure positions in the civil service for their sons or other relations. Second, the examinations greatly favoured, and were intended to favour, those with both a public school education and a university degree. The great majority of those civil servants listed in Table 5 who had university degrees had been recruited as F.M.S. cadets in or after 1896 or had come from the Straits Settlements Civil Service. As the *Malay Mail* shrewdly noted, what the examination did most was to narrow down 'the field of selection to those who have been educated more or less on the same lines'.[31]

Within a few years after the new system of selection was introduced a clear order of choice developed among those who passed the examination. Those who scored high marks in the examination and had private means usually chose the Home Civil Service. Others who scored high marks but lacked private means tended to choose a career in the Indian Civil Service. Those who scored somewhat lower would have to choose one of the Eastern Cadetships. Even here there was a clear order of choice: Ceylon received first preference, Hong Kong second, and Malaya third. 'It is generally now recognized in Educational and University circles in England', wrote Bucknill in his report on salaries in 1919, 'that Malaya in climate, emoluments and prospects compares for officials unfavourably with the other two colonies.'[32] In 1906, 1907, 1908, 1911, and 1914 all of those who joined the civil service in Malaya performed less well in the examination than any who joined the Ceylon Civil Service. Between 1906 and 1914 only four men who had scored high enough to choose Ceylon if they had wished decided to come to Malaya; a few years later three of them were to express their regret for having made this choice.[33]

The fact that a career in Malaya was regarded relatively unfavourably by candidates did not mean that the civil service in Malaya was getting men of noticeably lower social standing or academic ability than were the other services. This can be shown by looking at the table of marks for the 1909 examination. Of the 214 who sat for the examination there were only seventy-one successful candidates. Because many of those who took the examination and did well had indicated that they were not interested in one of the services, usually the Eastern Cadetships, the seventy-first successful candidate was in fact ranked ninety-eighth out of all who took the examination, but except at the high and low ends of the scale there was not a great range in marks, and, moreover, there was considerable variation in the subjects taken. Most of those who took the examination, whether they were successful or not, had a public school–university education.[34] In any case, in no way were those who chose Malaya the lowest of the examinees, as one writer has stated, nor can it be claimed that they were 'often almost literally the scrapings of the eligibles' barrel'.[35] Those recruited to Malaya were in the upper half of the examinees; the examinees were a remarkably homogeneous group to begin with; and, it may be added, ill health or some other temporary influence sometimes made the difference in whether a man did well enough to choose India and Ceylon or had to settle for Malaya.[36]

During the course of the inter-war years there were some variations in the way civil servants were recruited. For two years after the war cadets were selected partly by examination and partly by their performance during an interview. The 'Reconstruction Scheme', as it was called, was designed to help those men who had been unable to attend university because of war service. In 1921 the Colonial Office returned to the old method of selecting cadets entirely by the results of the examination. In the 1920s a career in Malaya was regarded much more favourably than it had been before the war. Several men who scored high enough in the examination to join the Indian Civil Service instead decided to become civil servants in Malaya. At the same time that the recommendations of the Bucknill Commission made the M.C.S. more attractive, political turmoil in India was making the future of the Indian Civil Service uncertain.[37] In 1932 a new system of recruitment was introduced when the Colonial Office created the Colonial Administrative Service as a step towards combining the civil services of the various dependencies under its control in Africa and Asia. The Colonial Service Appointments Board now selected civil servants according to their personal qualifications as well as their academic record and by the results of an examination which they took after a course of training in England. Though broadening the basis of selection somewhat, the bulk of candidates continued to be drawn from Oxford and Cambridge.

RECRUITMENT OF PLANTERS

After 1896 the civil service of the F.M.S. (and in Britain itself and elsewhere in the Empire) offered a career to a young man of middle-class background who had received a university degree and had passed the competitive examination. Planting in Malaya and elsewhere in the East attracted to its ranks young men who were of similar background but who had not attended a university, had failed to make a success of a career, or had simply become dissatisfied with their career or type of employment. 'The planter', observed a young civil servant named Eric Macfadyen in 1904, 'is usually a younger son whose chief qualification for Colonial life is that there is no room for him at home.'[38] Macfadyen's own case did not conform to this statement since he was soon to give up a promising future in the civil service to become a planter, but it was true that many men had come to planting after making an unsuccessful attempt at some other career. The Kindersley brothers were just two of many planters who had intended to become military officers but had failed the entrance examination.[39] C. R. Harrison had been under great pressure from his father to enter the Army but he failed the physical examination; his mother saw an advertisement for planters and put up the money for him to get started.[40] And in a letter to the *Army and Navy Gazette* in 1892 Major Lake, the father of a Selangor coffee planter, recommended planting as a possible occupation for the many young men who failed one of the competitive examinations.[41]

The variety of experiences of many of the planters listed in *Twentieth Century Impressions* before they began planting would suggest that many had been unsuccessful in a previous career but also that some had turned to planting as a more rewarding occupation. Three had not finished medical training, one had studied the violin at the Royal College of Music, one had given up his medical practice, three had been army officers, several had commercial experience, one had been a solicitor, one had left the Indian Civil Service, and three had been in one of the government services of Malaya. Two had tried ranching in the United States before becoming planters.[42] A perhaps extreme case is that of Cyril Baxendale. As the youngest of four sons of a clergyman less was spent on his education than on that of his brothers, but he seems to have had little interest in further education anyway. After an attack of pneumonia and pleurisy he was sent off to Australia at the age of eighteen. When after five years at various occupations such as farming and serving in the local militia he used up a small inheritance, his brother, then Superintendent of Posts and Telegraphs for Selangor, suggested that he come to Malaya. After brief periods as a journalist and miner Baxendale finally found a job as an assistant on a coffee estate.[43]

Over half of the planters listed in *Twentieth Century Impressions* are mentioned as having had previous planting experience, usually in Ceylon. In the latter part of the nineteenth century and at the beginning of the twentieth planters in Ceylon were recruited as 'creepers'. A creeper was trained by an experienced planter who, if he showed promise, would find him employment as an assistant after his apprenticeship was completed. Many of the planters who came to Malaya from Ceylon had started as creepers. To a lesser extent those who came directly to Malaya began their planting careers in this way. One of these was C. R. Harrison, who claimed to be one of the last of the creepers. The advertisement which his mother answered for him in 1907 stated that a premium of £100 had to be paid for tuition and board during the training period. In itself the premium guaranteed that prospective planters would come from solid middle-class backgrounds, and indeed this was intended. The advertisement which lured Harrison to Selangor concluded by saying: 'Applicants must, of course, find their own passage as well as the premium; good birth and education sine qua non. . . . Public school education preferred and good sportsman.'[44]

As both new estates and the early proprietary estates were floated as companies the system of recruiting creepers came to an end. A man became a planter as a result of being recommended by one of the company's directors, by responding to a newspaper advertisement, or by applying directly to the company's London offices. As mentioned, in the years the industry was expanding most rapidly companies were not very selective in hiring, but by the 1920s they could be more discriminating as to both the social background of candidates and their training. Because of technical developments in rubber planting, companies increasingly looked for candidates with some knowledge of agriculture. Guthrie's, which hired the staffs of all the estates for which it was agent, regularly sent a representative to Aberdeen University, which offered a degree in agriculture, and the Royal Botanical Gardens in Edinburgh, which offered a diploma in the same subject, to interest graduates in a planting career.[45]

THE PROFESSIONAL AND TECHNICAL DEPARTMENTS

We may begin by considering the senior appointments in these departments. Doctors, engineers, surveyors, and most other officers in the professional and technical departments were recruited by the Crown Agents in London, but starting in 1904 commissioned officers in the Police Department were selected by an open competitive examination held by the Civil Service Commission in London each year. As a rule non-cadet officials had been trained in medicine, architecture, agriculture or some other specialized field, but there were two important exceptions. Police officers joined as young men aged between nineteen and twenty-two and received their training during a probationary period in Malaya. The other exception were officers in the Education Department, who were very much like members of the cadet service in that they usually had degrees from Oxford or Cambridge but no professional training.

In 1914 a *Malay Mail* editorial commented that officials in the various professional and technical departments came from 'the same upper middle class at Home' as the cadets.[46] While the information on non-cadet officials in *Twentieth Century Impressions* is even less complete than for cadets and planters, twelve out of the sixty-one named are said to have attended one of the schools in the Headmasters' Conference. At this time the kind of secondary education someone received was (and I have used it as such) a strong indication of his social background. At the same time education, particularly various forms of tertiary education, was not entirely the preserve of upper- and upper middle-class sons. Education was also a means of social mobility. In England and probably to a greater extent in Scotland the son of a lower middle-class or, less frequently, working-class family might by education enter an occupation which was higher than his father's in pay and status. There is some evidence however that social background, as compared to acquired professional qualifications, played some part in selection for service in the F.M.S. In 1911 F. J. B. Dykes, former Chief Warden of Mines and then working in London for the Malay States Development Agency, was asked by the Colonial Office to interview applicants for positions as Inspectors of Mines in the F.M.S. and the Gold Coast. A Mr. Holferd had completed the course at the Camborne School of Mines but had not passed his final examination because he was absent on Yeomanry training. Nevertheless, Dykes recommended him for the vacancy in Malaya because of a testimonial from the head of the school and because of 'his appearance, manner and social position'. A Mr. Thomson had without doubt the necessary professional qualifications. 'He is however somewhat rough, and were there other candidates of better social position' and sufficient experience they, advised Dykes, should be given preference. Thomson was however seen as suitable for the Gold Coast because there 'his dealings would be entirely with Europeans of his own class'. Moreover, in the F.M.S., unlike Africa, the Inspector would have to deal with 'Natives of position' and this required gentlemanly manners. Another candidate was too young but because of his 'nice manner and personal appearance' Dykes said he should be kept in mind for a future vacancy. Finally, another candidate of 'somewhat rough' manner was recommended for the Gold Coast. Not surprisingly it was Holferd who was appointed to the post in the F.M.S.[47] Perhaps Dykes was extreme in his concern for social class, but at least this case would suggest that in selection for the non-cadet services the candidate's social background, as well as his professional qualifications, was carefully considered.

Most of the subordinate appointments held by Europeans were in the Police, Prisons, and Railway Departments. Police inspectors were recruited locally from time-expired sergeants and corporals from military units stationed at Singapore or were recruited from the Metropolitan Police or the Royal Irish Constabulary. The Police Department had a higher proportion of Irishmen than any other government department. European prison warders had the same background as those police inspectors who were locally recruited. Until about 1920 the Railway Department employed a fairly large number of European locomotive drivers and permanent way inspectors. The drivers (who will be considered in Chapter 4) all had previous experience on a British railway. The permanent way inspectors were also recruited from British railways. The Crown Agents wrote to railway companies and, according to a senior engineer who in 1919 said that they would soon be replaced by Asians, advertised 'in the papers read by that class of people'. Before coming to Malaya some permanent way inspectors had been foremen but others had been navvies.[48]

Unofficials other than Planters

The Europeans in this category came from a variety of backgrounds. Of the remaining Europeans listed in *Twentieth Century Impressions* six were mentioned as having attended one of the public schools belonging to the Headmasters' Conference, but it is notable that four of these were lawyers in private practice. Engineering firms and rubber companies employed some European engineers and mechanics of working-class background. Among miners were some men with a public school education, but as a group they were considered by officials and planters to have come from lower social backgrounds and indeed to be somewhat unrespectable. Of higher social origins were the Europeans in the agency houses, large import-export firms, and banks. In that they were more likely to be Scots and unlikely to have a university education they bore a closer resemblance to planters than to civil servants. According to a head of Guthrie's, his firm recruited—by means of private introductions and interviews— public school men 'as a rule'. Officers for the Chartered Bank were recruited by nomination and worked for a period in London on the foreign staff before coming to Malaya.[49] In all cases some personal contact with the company or bank, however indirect, was essential for the young man looking for a job. In no way is this better illustrated than by looking at how D. F. Topham, who later became the managing director of Harper, Gilfillan and Co., first came to Kuala Lumpur.

In 1907 Topham had been working for eight years in a London stock broker's office as an 'unauthorized clerk' at a yearly income of about £130. Because he was very dissatisfied with his work he considered going abroad. He thought first of going to British Columbia but a chance meeting led to his going to Malaya. One of the team members of the Guildford Hockey Club for which he played was a Major Dykes, brother of F. J. B. Dykes, then Senior Warden of Mines in the F.M.S. When he heard of Topham's desire to find a post abroad Major Dykes cabled his brother to ask about a job in Malaya. Very soon Major Dykes received an answer from his brother saying that he had found Topham employment with A. C. Harper and Co. at £250 a

year. The cost of his passage to Malaya was provided by a loan
from the Major. Having joined the company Topham became in
turn the means by which others were recruited. In 1911 he
received a letter from an old friend asking whether he could find
him employment; Topham found him a position in the same
firm. While home on leave the following year Topham received a
cable from his superior asking him to recruit another assistant.
Through a friend of his uncle's Topham got in touch with someone interested in the position; Topham and two sons of the head
of the firm for which the candidate was working had been at the
same public school together. The candidate was given the position and was soon on his way to Kuala Lumpur.[50]

In summary, personal contacts, interviews, examinations,
chance, and the need for certain skills all played a part in
recruitment. Although there were some important differences in
social origins, the methods of recruitment helped to make the
Europeans a remarkably homogeneous group. 'I think my first
feeling', one woman commented shortly after her arrival in
Malaya, 'was that I had never before been a member of a community of which such a large proportion came from one class,
was the product of one form of education and whose outlook on
life therefore was so uniform.'[51]

3

Europeans in the Malay States, 1880–1900

WHEN Isabella Bird visited Sungei Ujong, Selangor, and Perak in 1879 she met the majority of the few Europeans living in those states. At Seremban, which she reached after a tedious journey by steam launch from Malacca, *prahu* up the Linggi River, and then overland by foot and by carriage, she observed how the Resident, Captain Murray, lived alone and performed all the duties of governing 'his little kingdom'. At Klang Bloomfield Douglas ruled as if his Residency expected an imminent siege; Miss Bird was not impressed by the speed with which the Resident's men responded to a pretended alarm. At a church service attended by the entire white population of seven men and two women 'the congregation sat under one punkah and the Resident under another'. After a short stay in Penang Bird reached Taiping by steam launch and gharrie. There the Assistant Resident and the officers in charge of a detachment of Sikhs had a friendly argument every evening at dinner. An uncomfortable elephant ride brought the traveller to Kuala Kangsar, headquarters of the Resident, Hugh Low, whose dealings with the Malays made a very favourable impression on her. 'His manner is as quiet and unpretending as can possibly be, and he speaks to Malays as respectfully as to Europeans, neither lowering thereby his own dignity nor theirs. Apparently they have free access to him during all hours of daylight. . . .' After returning to Taiping Miss Bird was visited by two Ceylon planters who were looking for land on which to cultivate coffee, and she learned of a Scotsman who was already planting in Perak but was intending to give it up. An Englishwoman, 'a product of imperfect civilisation', whom Bird accompanied on the launch back to Penang, was one of the very few other Europeans she met during her five weeks in the Malay States.[1]

In the next few years after Isabella Bird's visit the way of life of Europeans and the nature of the Europeans as a social group underwent many changes. In the decade and a half after the Residency was moved to Kuala Lumpur in 1880 Europeans living there created social institutions which were to endure into the 1930s (and in the case of their main clubs into the 1970s) and emerged as a community characterized by important internal social divisions. Because of their beliefs about the effects of the tropical climate the British, as will be shown, never regarded themselves as settlers, but by the 1890s they were able to lead a way of life more nearly like that in their homeland than they had when Bird visited in 1879. Before examining British social life in detail it is useful to take a general look at how the British viewed the society which they governed and at the changes which took place as the number of Europeans in the Malay States began to increase.

Officials and the Asian Environment

During the early years of British rule officials were brought into constant contact with Malays. In part, this was a result of British policy. From the beginning there was no doubt in the minds of officials in Malaya that whatever the expressed views of the Colonial Office British 'advice' in fact meant direct administration of the states. Nevertheless the Residents did hope to win some acceptance of their policies from the Malays. Birch's assassination in 1875 had led to an expedition into Perak which crushed the main opposition to the British presence there, but it had also demonstrated to the British that they could not rule without any regard for Malay sensibilities. By the 1880s Residents were chosen primarily for their knowledge of the Malays and ability to govern with firmness tempered with tact, the combination of virtues which above all others was valued in these formative years. In the years after Birch's assassination the State Councils served the purpose of allowing Residents to explain their policies, to modify the way they were to be carried out, and to know when a proposed law, regulation, or appointment might be overwhelmingly objectionable to the Malays. At a lower level District Officers were expected by the Residents to keep the government in touch with Asian feelings by being familiar with every aspect of their districts, knowing all the leading people, and being available at all hours of the day to listen to anyone who had complaints about the government or who sought advice on personal or family matters. The District Officers of Sungei Ujong, for example, were advised that since Malays were not accustomed to regular office hours they should be accessible at all times, for otherwise there was the danger of 'discontent brewing . . . without an Officer knowing anything about it'.[2]

Circumstances as well as official policy encouraged close relations between British officers and the people they governed. Since travel about districts on horseback, on foot, or by boat was slow, officers not only spent a considerable amount of time away from their headquarters visiting kampungs but also found it difficult to travel to meet European friends in other stations. One official explained that he had been able to collect a number of Malay folk tales because he was one of those men who 'have for the best portion of their official life been obliged to look for companionship of the native to while away some of their leisure time'.[3]

One of the most striking aspects of this relationship was the admiration officials expressed for Malays. The British abhorred some features of traditional Malay society, such as debt-bondage and slavery, and set about eradicating them. And officials frequently described the Malays as lazy, particularly when they failed to respond as the British hoped they would to some government initiative. The failure of the Malays in one Selangor district, for example, to respond to the District Officer's attempts to have them adopt English ploughs for rice cultivation was explained as a result of their 'natural laziness'.[4] Nevertheless there was much about the Malays and their society which British officials professed to admire. The Malays' love of hunting, fishing, and other sports matched that of English public school men of the late Victorian period. The pageantry of Malay royalty coincided with a love of pomp and circumstance which the British already possessed but which was heightened by their new position as the governing élite of the Malay States. Whether of high or low rank Malays were regarded as perfect gentlemen; the typical Malay was courteous, reserved, and yet intensely proud and always ready to defend his honour.

Although on many occasions British officials expressed their exasperation at the seeming inability of Malays to change their ways, they were greatly attracted to the feudal character of Malay society, which they imagined closely resembled their own society in some era long before the Industrial Revolution. 'Above all things,' wrote Swettenham, the Malay 'is conservative to a degree, is proud and fond of his country and his people, venerates his ancient customs and traditions' and 'fears his Rajas'. Moreover, the Malays had 'a proper respect for constituted authority'.[5] In other words, Malays appeared to show to British officials the same deference which they were accustomed to give their traditional rulers. According to Hugh Clifford, who was for many years acting Resident and then Resident of Pahang, the Malay possessed 'one of the most characteristic qualities of the English gentleman,—he is absolutely and supremely sure of himself'. It was precisely because of this quality that it would never occur to a Malay to 'assume airs of equality or superiority'. It was therefore possible to 'make an intimate friend of a Malay' and to 'share the same hut with him for long periods of time . . . without there being any risk of familiarity breeding contempt, or of the Malay taking advantage of his position to dig you in the ribs or to call you by your Christian name'. It was only those few Malays who had been exposed to too much education, claimed Clifford, who were 'almost as offensive and familiar as a low-caste European'.[6] Statements similar to those by Swettenham and Clifford may be found in the writings of many other officials who worked in the Malay States during this period.[7] The traditional image of the Malays as treacherous pirates lived on in popular literature (such as G. A. Henty's *In the Hands of the Malays*, published in 1905), but it was an image which officials in Malaya made every effort to contradict.

The attitude of British officials towards the Chinese was in many respects the reverse of their views on the Malays. The British had the highest respect for Chinese industriousness. At a time when government revenues depended almost entirely on their enterprise Swettenham described the Chinese as the 'bone and sinew' of the Malay States. He stressed however that it 'is almost hopeless to expect to make friends with a Chinaman, and it is, for a Government officer, an object that is not very desirable to attain. The Chinese . . . do not understand being treated as equals.' By this Swettenham meant that by treating a Chinese as a friend the distance which in fact the British wanted to preserve in their dealings with all Asians was in danger of being breached. A government officer dealing with Chinese, explained Swettenham, had to make sure that they knew who their master was.[8] In the British view the Chinese, with a very few notable exceptions, were not 'gentlemen' in the way Malays of all classes were. Being traders, the *towkays* were engaged in a pursuit which was considered a rather inferior one by English public school men of this period. As for the great mass of Chinese labourers, they were best compared to the urban proletariat of Britain. A young Selangor government officer had this in mind when he explained that the general unpopularity of the Chinese with the British 'could hardly be otherwise, considering that nearly the whole of the Celestial population are coolies pure and simple, who have come from their Father-land with the very smallest assortment of both manners and morals. Would an equal number of English navvies be more law abiding or better behaved?'[9]

As has been suggested, British officials saw certain similarities between Malay society as it existed in the late nineteenth century and the pre-industrial society of their homeland. It is therefore not surprising to find evidence that some officials tended to see themselves as lords of the manor and the Malay *rakyat* as their tenantry. This attitude may have been more prevalent among officials who had close connexions with Irish or English landed society as the two most explicit statements available to me of this attitude come from men of such backgrounds. In letters to his parents, C. D. Bowen, member of an old County Mayo family, was able to relate his experiences in terms which they could readily understand. From Telok Anson he wrote in 1887 that 'when I wake up in the morning there are generally six Malays on the verandah waiting till I have had my bath, etc. It is just the Irish tenantry all over again. . . .' And about his life in a village in Lower Perak he wrote:

> Living in a place like Utan Melintan one just represents the Irish landlord; one goes out in the morning and sees dirty and untidy places and tells the people to get them cleaned up. Their answer is always 'if it pleases your honour we will do it'—which means 'we don't care a pin whether it is done or not'.[10]

And an official familiar with English landed society, Arthur Keyser, District Officer of Jelebu, gave this description of the relationship between officials and Malays:

> English officials . . . are accustomed to pass their lives amongst the Malays, to listen to and help them in their troubles, and to be constantly surrounded by them as followers and companions, and the inmates and affairs of each household are known, much as those of the cottagers on his estate would be to a home-staying country squire in England.[11]

Rather than seeing the Malay *rakyat* in British terms as tenants on an estate, it was also possible for an official to see himself in Malay terms, as a rajah. Robson defined the white rajah District Officer as one who 'expects to receive as his right the usual prostituted homage paid by a ryot to his raja; he on his side acting the part as far as his nationality and position will allow'.[12] One District Officer who certainly fitted this definition was C. F. Bozzolo of Upper Perak. He was said to have punished two Malays who had passed him without giving a respectful salutation; as signs of their less than human behaviour he forced them to obtain dog licences.[13] According to one visitor, Bozzolo ruled his district as a patriarch. He was far enough away from Taiping to be able to 'treat all official communications with contempt'. Bozzolo had a large harem, was 'adored by the natives and has his district in splendid order. . . . He . . . *never* puts on *anything* (even in office) except a hat and a Sarong.'[14]

Even as early as 1890 however the number of white rajah District Officers was very small. By this time conditions had changed sufficiently to make it extremely difficult for an official to rule a district as if it were his personal domain. With the opening of new roads and the improvement of old ones an officer did not need to spend as much time away from his headquarters. More important were the consequences of the fact that, unlike those European adventurers who established themselves as white rajahs in various parts of the archipelago in the nineteenth century,[15] officials in the Malay States belonged to an expanding bureaucratic system and had to conform to its demands. As the amount of paper work increased officials were forced to spend more time in the confines of their offices. The Resident of Negri Sembilan complained in his report for 1896 that treasury work, police court cases, and correspondence were preventing his District Officers from travelling about their districts.[16] Transfers from one government post to another made it still more difficult for an officer to acquire an intimate knowledge of his district. These transfers took place frequently because in order to ensure that the more senior officers filled the more lucrative postings there was a considerable reshuffling of appointments whenever someone went on leave or was promoted.[17]

A further consequence of the growth of the bureaucracy was a decline in the personal authority and independence of District Officers. As the functions of government increased, more and more European officers from the various specialist departments were posted to the districts. The most important of these departments were the Land, Public Works, Police, Survey, and Medical Departments. In Perak, by 1892 the districts of Larut, Kinta, Krian, and Lower Perak each had several officers from these departments. It is notable that the only European officer stationed in Upper Perak was Bozzolo.[18] There was a similar growth in the specialist departments in Selangor. The surveyor, engineer, or doctor was under the supervision of the District Officer, but his main responsibility was to the head of his department in the state capital. Only the land and treasury officers were directly responsible to their respective District Officers.[19]

Several writers commented on the changing position of the District Officer. 'He is a splendid pioneer,' wrote Bowen in 1891 of one of his former superiors, 'but he is not keeping up to the times; he tries to carry on a sort of old Raja rule that does not do now, the country is too much opened up. I used to be a Raja in Selama till the carriage road was finished and with that came civilisation.'[20] In 1897 Robson claimed that there 'is no longer that friendly relationship between many of the District Officers and the people of the country that there used to be'. One well-known District Officer who had been asked a question about the Malays in his district was reported to have replied that he never saw any Malays now. He said that his days were entirely taken up by office work and court cases. Significantly, he added that all his evenings were spent at the local club.[21]

As the number of Europeans increased officials did not need to look to non-Europeans for companionship. As soon as even a few Europeans settled in a district it became possible to form a club. By 1890 there were government-sponsored clubs in every district in Perak except Selama and Upper Perak. In 1892 Taiping had two general sporting-social clubs, a rifle club, turf club, and Masonic Lodge. Kinta district had both a recreation club and a gymkhana club.[22] In 1891 Bowen regularly attended the club at Batu Gajah, ten miles from the town where he was stationed, and served on the club's committee.[23]

How an increase in the number of Europeans in a particular area could change an official's way of life is illustrated by the case of Hugh Clifford. A typical entry from his diary for 1888, when apparently only one other European was living at Pekan, reads:

... To bed at 7.30 am. Up again at 3 pm. Walked—A thief was caught. Slept before dinner—The Bendahara visited me—Went to the Balei & talked to To' Raja, To' Kaya Cheno ... & the Orang Kaya Pahlawan. Talking with Alang till daylight.

Clifford's diary for 1893 contains numerous references to his contacts with Malays both in his official duties and socially, and there are also references to a Malay woman named Meriam who stayed with him (in what capacity is not stated) during part of the year. But that his life had to some extent changed is indicated by such passages as these:

Played L[awn] T[ennis] with Thomas before breakfast & after tea. 5 sets in all. He is not a strong player.

Working at papers nearly all day. Played L.T. with Belfield & beat him 3 sets out of 4—4–6, 6–0, 6–3, & 6–4—dined with Belfield. Won 1197 points at Piquet.[24]

Clifford's diaries confirm his own observation that once a few Englishmen were gathered together in a district they quickly found numerous ways of amusing themselves.[25]

Marriage could also change an official's way of life and hence his relations with the people in his district. The handful of European women who lived in the Malay States were regarded as having made a great sacrifice in giving up the pleasures of life in England to bring 'the comforts and hospitality of home life into the fastnesses of the jungle'.[26] In Victorian England a man was duty bound to do all he could to make his wife as comfortable as possible, but in the Malay States the climate, lack of amenities, and the absence of social life in all but a very few towns placed a special obligation on a husband to look after his wife's welfare. In Clifford's novel *Since the Beginning* the hero, Frank Austin, is plagued by a deep sense of guilt for having brought his wife to the outpost where he is District Officer. Because of his concern for his wife's happiness he no longer enjoys spending hours in leisurely conversation with the Malays. On one occasion he apologizes to his wife for having come home late to join her for tea. 'For some reason or another the Native Chief[s] chose this afternoon as an appropriate day upon which to come and see me in bulk.'[27]

Finally, in looking at the tendency of the European population to become an increasingly self-contained social group it is important to keep in mind one further point. That is that whatever ideas a young man had about Britain's imperial mission, adventures in the jungle, or the fine character of the Malays, he came to the Malay States to make a career. It was therefore more important to cultivate good relations with his superiors in the official hierarchy than to make friends among the Malays and other Asians. This was particularly so because of the great power the Residents exercised over careers. Promotions were in the hands of the Governor, but he generally approved whatever recommendations the Resident made. The Resident also had considerable freedom in dismissing officers whom he claimed were incompetent.

Only civil servants seconded from the Straits Settlements enjoyed security of tenure; they had the right to bring their cases before the Straits Settlements Executive Council and the Secretary of State before they could be dismissed.[28]

Since most Europeans belonged to one of the government services this power of the Resident's gave him enormous influence over the European community. Robson was stretching the truth only slightly when he wrote that if 'the Resident is a sportsman, why we are all death on sport. If the Resident thinks only of work our energy is something frightful to behold.'[29] It has been mentioned that some men received their government jobs partly because of their ability at cricket. Skill in this sport was also one way in which an officer could improve his chances for promotion. In his book *About Perak*, published in 1893, Swettenham claimed that there were not enough Europeans in the state to form cliques and that the popular impression that 'proficiency in cricket is the surest road to Government preferment . . . must be an exaggeration'.[30] An angry reviewer of Swettenham's book, however, insisted that the Resident had no idea of the true extent of his influence over the European community:

The author tells us that cliquism is impossible: he . . . does not know, of course, how a Resident may make or mar a man socially, which goes a long way as to whether he will be a success officially. Needless to say, this power of the Resident's is often misused, and sometimes persons needy and brainless, who have no qualifications of their own to recommend them to the general public, will *kowtow* for the favour of the Resident as the *summum bonum* of all. The rest follows naturally— choice positions, favours of court, life becomes a beautiful dream, and 'no place like the Native States, don't you know'.

Swettenham's critic named one official who had resigned because he believed that his lack of interest in cricket had slowed his advancement.[31]

Clearly, by the 1890s personal relations within the bureaucracy (and hence within the European community), as compared to the relationship between officials and the local population, were increasingly becoming the focus of attention. It is now appropriate to look in detail at the Europeans in the fast-growing town of Kuala Lumpur.

The Growth of European Society in Kuala Lumpur

Until 1879 Kuala Lumpur was completely dominated by the *Kapitan Cina*, Yap Ah Loy. An engineer employed by Yap to run his tapioca factory was probably the only European living in Kuala Lumpur until a government officer and his wife moved there in the latter part of 1879.[32] During Douglas's short period as Resident at Kuala Lumpur the European population consisted of a handful of government officers, a planter, and a mining engineer employed by the *Kapitan Cina*.[33] As the government bureaucracy grew there was a steady increase in the number of Europeans. By the time of the census of 1891 the European population stood at 151. As the population grew there was a corresponding growth in institutions of all kinds. In 1887 Bishop Hose of Singapore consecrated St. Mary's Church on its original site on Bluff Road (the present church was consecrated in 1895); in 1890 the government opened a separate ward near the General Hospital for the care of European patients; and in 1897 the widow of a government officer established the first hotel catering for Europeans. By far the most important institutions for Europeans, however, were their social clubs. Indeed, much of the social history of the Europeans in Kuala Lumpur in the 1880s and 1890s is best understood by looking at the development of these clubs and the roles they played in the community.

In the early 1880s Europeans living in Kuala Lumpur did not have a social club. A Chinese-owned shop, where everything from champagne to boot-laces was sold, instead served as their principal meeting place.[34] In 1884 the Selangor Club was started 'on a very small scale, in a little plank building with atap roof' on the north side of the Parade Ground.[35] Because there was no periodical or newspaper in Kuala Lumpur until the *Selangor Journal* began publication in 1892 there is little record of the sporting and social activities of the club during its first few years. One resident later recalled that 'co-operative dinners at the Club were a feature of those days. Each lady contributed something to the common table: one would send a cold pie, another boiled fowls, another salads, another fruit tarts and so on. All the contributors took their own boys [servants] with them to dine. . . .'[36] One of the club's most important activities in these years was organizing cricket matches with teams from Perak and the Straits Settlements. In 1889 Selangor cricketers travelled to Taiping, where they were defeated by the Perak team. In the following year Selangor enjoyed a close victory in a return match played at Kuala Lumpur.

Although there is little information about the Selangor Club's sporting and social activities at this time, one very fundamental aspect of the club is revealed in the Club Committee's minute book for the years 1885 to 1892, the only volume which has survived. The minutes are not detailed, but they do demonstrate that as *the* European social institution of Kuala Lumpur the Selangor Club played an essential role in keeping harmony within the European community and enforcing a certain standard of behaviour. One man was given three days to resign from the club or be dismissed for having assaulted the club 'boy', a Malay. At one meeting a letter from one member accusing another 'of conduct unbecoming of a gentleman on and outside the Club premises' was read and the committee decided to ask him to resign. Where possible however the committee acted to bring about harmony rather than to punish. At one meeting one member's complaint against another for insulting him in the club reading room was resolved when he received and accepted the other's written apology. And the minutes of another meeting read: 'A complaint is made against a member by the Secretary for misconduct, the said member is called before the Committee and after a lengthy discussion the Committee resolve to drop the question'.[37] Thus the committee decided whether a member's conduct both in the club and outside was 'unbecoming of a gentleman' and brought about expulsion or a peaceful solution. The threat of expulsion must have acted as an extremely powerful force for ensuring that the norms of the European community were upheld. To be expelled from the Selangor Club was in effect to be cast out of European social life. Since the Club Committee consisted of the Resident, who was *ex-officio* president of the club, the Chief Magistrate, and two members nominated by the Resident, as well as five members elected by the club as a whole, misbehaviour could also harm a man's career.

Because of its growing membership the Selangor Club decided in 1889 to build a new and larger clubhouse on the west side of the Parade Ground. Despite substantial loans from the government and from its own members the club soon found itself in deep financial difficulties. In 1890 the club hired its first salaried secretary, Count Bernstorff, to ensure that its finances were properly managed, but during his year in office Bernstorff only added to the club's problems. A short time after his resignation and departure from Kuala Lumpur an unexplained deficit of $1,100 was discovered in his books.[38] With the club in a state of bankruptcy the government suggested liquidation, but the members responded by electing a new committee and asking H. Huttenbach, a leading coffee planter and general merchant, to serve as the club's honorary secretary. Within a short time the club began to flourish. Its revival was attributed partly to Hutten-bach's careful management and partly to the personal use of the club by the acting Resident, E. W. Birch. Birch took great interest in the club's affairs and regularly played football, cricket, and billiards there, as no Resident had done since Swettenham. By October 1892 the club had 140 members.[39] The fact that at the time of the census in April 1891 there were 115 European males (of all ages) in Kuala Lumpur and 145 in the whole state would indicate that many men from outside Kuala Lumpur and perhaps even from outside Selangor, as well as most European men in Kuala Lumpur, belonged to the club.

The Selangor Club's membership also included a small number of non-Europeans. K. Tamboosamy Pillay, a Tamil, was a founding member of the club, and the minutes show that he took an active part in its affairs as a member of the committee. Pillay had come to Selangor from Singapore with the first Resident, J. G. Davidson, in whose law offices he had worked. He eventually became Chief Clerk in the Treasury and for a short time acted as State Treasurer. In 1889 he resigned from government service and both on his own and in partnership with Loke Yew became extremely rich through mining and contracting work.[40] Among Europeans he was famous for the curry tiffins he gave at his home on Batu Road. From the vantage point of Malaya in the 1930s Robson recalled that 'racial distinctions were unknown here in the early days. Tamboosamy was as popular with Europeans as with other races. His position in the community was at the top of the ladder.'[41] In 1889 Raja Muda Suleiman (the future Sultan of Selangor) was asked by the committee to become an honorary member, but there is no record of how much use he made of the club. Probably more Eurasians belonged to the club than did Malays, Chinese, or Indians. In the minutes Thomasz, De Sousa, and other names which almost certainly belonged to Eurasians of Portuguese or Dutch Malaccan descent are mentioned. In 1894 a 'large increase in European and Eurasian members' was noted.[42] Since most of the Eurasian members were fairly low in the government hierarchy it is probable that when the Recreation Club was opened early in 1897 as a gathering place for government subordinates the number of Eurasians in the Selangor Club declined.

One of the most intriguing questions about the early history of the Selangor Club is the origin of its nickname, the 'Spotted Dog'. According to a woman who first went to Kuala Lumpur in 1896 the club was named after Mrs. Syers's dalmatians, which always followed her as she rode in her carriage to the club.[43] Although this has been commonly accepted as a likely explanation, I have found no other evidence to support it. Arthur Keyser, who came to Selangor in 1888, later claimed that he had given the club its nickname after he and a friend had been prevented from taking their turn at the billiards table when two railway employees 'of rough exterior' arrived and appropriated the table. 'I restrained my companion from expressing his resentment, remarking that frequenters of "The Spotted Dog" pub must accept the company as they found it.'[44] Unfortunately Keyser did not say exactly what he meant by men of 'rough exterior'. He may have been referring to Eurasians or, more likely, to the lower-class British. Two men who were in Selangor at about the same time as Keyser later wrote that the nickname referred to the fact that non-Europeans belonged to the club.[45] In any case, the relative openness of the club, rather than being exclusively for men of either a particular social class or race, was responsible for its being called the 'Spotted Dog'.

There was another way in which the Selangor Club was not exclusive. From the beginning or fairly soon after it was founded the wives of members and the few other European women in Kuala Lumpur were allowed to come to the club. Though excluded from the bar the women were allowed to make use of the reading room and to sit on the veranda. Whereas the leading social clubs in the Straits Settlements and apparently in most British outposts in the East (as well as in England itself) were exclusively male preserves, the custom of permitting women to use club facilities was common throughout the Malay States.[46] The presence of even a few women had a definite effect upon the atmosphere of the club. A planter, noting the unusual fact that women were welcome at the Selangor Club, observed that 'not a man is ever heard to murmur at the wholesome restraint which their presence imposes'—even the most 'uncouth' men agreed to wear a collar and tie and to speak more softly than they might if no women were around.[47] This is not to say that men had to be on their best behaviour at *all* times. Indeed Robson commented that for young unmarried men Selangor was a place 'where the trammels of society and the voice of Mrs. Grundy are heard but little of and cared for less'.[48] But in the club, in the presence of European women, men generally conformed to the behaviour which was expected of them.

The activities of the Selangor Club were varied and numerous. In the evening after work men gathered about the bar for a *pahit* or *stengah* or played billiards, while both men and women were able to keep in touch with 'Home' by reading such newspapers and magazines as the *Illustrated London News*, *Punch*, *Ally Sloper*, *Field*, *Lady*, the weekly edition of *The Times*, and *Pall Mall Magazine*. Accounts of the club's sporting activities, mainly cricket and football, take up a great deal of the *Selangor Journal's* pages. Amateur dramatic performances were extremely popular, especially locally written and directed shows which allowed the performers some liberty in commenting on their local society. At one show, for example, the formula for a successful career was outlined in song:

> I soon found the great essential
> Was connections influential
> And my rich relations kindly did the trick,
> And the C.O. got a notion
> That I ought to have a promotion.
> And I naturally got it *rather* quick.
> My mistakes, no doubt were many,
> But that mattered not a penny. . . .[49]

Fancy dress balls at the club were important social events. At one of these a Cantonese Lady, Red Tape, Malay Policeman, Mermaid, and Coloured Gentleman, U.S.A., were some of the characters. Since at the time of the 1891 census 145 out of the 190 Europeans living in Selangor were males it is not surprising that men heavily outnumbered women on these occasions. At the ball just mentioned, which was proclaimed a tremendous success since it lasted until about 4 o'clock in the morning, 62 men and 19 women attended.[50] The importance of this tiny group of women was enormous. The failure of a few women to appear at one ball brought an angry letter from a disappointed man who had travelled a long way to attend. On another occasion just the rumour that several women were planning not to attend prompted the *Selangor Journal* to appeal to the women to let 'no exclusive feelings interfere with their own and other people's enjoyment'.[51] Balls both at the Selangor Club and at the Residency allowed the British to feel closer to their homeland. After complimenting the ladies on their fine dresses, the report of a dance at the Residency commented that it had 'made us inclined to forget that London is not within easy reach'.[52]

Until 1890 the Selangor Club was the only social club for Europeans in Kuala Lumpur. In the 1890s, however, several other clubs and associations were formed. In 1899 the Selangor

Club was described as 'probably the most important institution in Kuala Lumpur' for Europeans,[53] but it no longer occupied the same position it had as the sole European social institution.

The most important of the new clubs was the Lake Club, founded in 1890. The Lake Club was attractively located in the recently completed Lake Gardens, which had been designed by A. R. Venning, the State Treasurer, who had once been a planter in Ceylon. According to the reminiscences of an official who was then serving in Kuala Lumpur, it was also Venning who had originated the idea of forming the new club.[54] Unlike the Selangor Club the Lake Club was exclusively for Europeans. According to the same official, Venning had wished to start a club 'for Europeans only'.

The Lake Club was not only racially exclusive but also from its foundation select in its European membership. In his annual report for 1890 the Resident of Selangor stated that the Lake Club was 'supported by the principal residents'. Among the twenty-eight founding members were the heads of most government departments and other figures prominent in Selangor, but a few leading Europeans at first refused to support the club since they believed that forming a rival club would worsen the position of the Selangor Club, which was then on the verge of collapse as a result of its financial difficulties, and weaken Selangor's ability to challenge Perak and Singapore in cricket and other sports.[55] A look at the names of the founding members indicates that many of them had close personal and business ties with one another. Four colleagues in the firm of Campbell and Co. were founding members; two of these men were brothers of government officers who were also founding members. Two planters who were founding members were in business together. These two had close financial connexions with two other founding members, the two top men in the Straits Trading Company. The head of the Selangor branch of this company was also a founding member.[56]

Despite the close-knit character of its original membership the Lake Club soon established itself as the club for the élite of the European community rather than for one or more cliques within that élite. The facts that the club's entrance fee was four times that of the Selangor Club and that the monthly subscription fee was twice that of the other club helped to restrict membership to men in relatively high positions. Comparing the Lake Club with the Selangor Club, a newcomer to Kuala Lumpur in 1894 observed that the Lake Club 'seemed more select than the other' and that he had been told that it was 'really a most exclusive Club and very difficult to get in'. An official who returned to Selangor after an absence of many years noted that at the Lake Club 'one saw all the rank, beauty and fashion of Kuala Lumpur'. Huttenbach emphasized the changing status of the Selangor Club when he said that whereas it had once been an honour to the Resident to be president of the club it was now much more of an honour to the club that he served as its president.[57]

At about the same time a similar stratification of European society was taking place in Taiping. The Perak Club, the first in the Malay States, was founded in 1880, while the exclusive New Club was opened in 1894.[58] As best as can be established from a brief, discreet report of the founding of the New Club, the increasing number of 'minor persons' in Perak either were not being accepted into the Perak Club or felt uncomfortable in using it because it was dominated by senior civil servants. Because the Perak Club was partially supported by government funds it was supposed to be open to the entire European community, and perhaps a handful of Eurasians and Asians in government service as well, rather than reserved for men in senior positions. It appears that rather than be members of a club with a broad membership the élite of the club's members withdrew to form the New Club. The result was, the reporter noted with regret, 'the formal separation of class and caste'.[59]

In Kuala Lumpur, at least to a regular contributor to the *Selangor Journal*, this clear separation of class, made explicit by what club someone belonged to, was seen as the natural result of the steadily growing number of Europeans. 'It stands to reason that there are people of different education and manners, brought up in a different style and sphere of life, and they by preference naturally associate with their own class. Birds of a feather flock together.' He added that it was natural that people should feel most at home 'amongst their own set', but he criticized those who because of a feeling of superiority ignored 'common rules of politeness' in their dealings with others.[60] Another writer complained that a high official position was all that a man needed to be accorded high social standing; education, literary talent, and other personal qualifications counted for little if they were not accompanied by a large government salary.[61]

In addition to the Lake Club several other clubs and associations were formed in the early 1890s. Interest in horse racing led to the formation of the Selangor Gymkhana Club. The races, which were held once or twice a year, were events to which everyone looked forward with considerable excitement. Horses were regularly imported from Australia by way of Singapore, and then lots were drawn to determine who would get which horse. The *Selangor Journal* followed in great detail the progress of each horse in its training as the race day approached. A race meeting was usually accompanied by a dance and concert at the Selangor Club. In 1895 the Gymkhana Club was reorganized as the Selangor Turf Club, which, unlike its predecessor, allowed professional jockeys to ride at race meetings. A Rifle Association, Hunt Club, and Masonic Lodge were also founded in these years. Next to the Lake Club the most important new club was the Selangor Golf Club, founded in 1893. Scottish coffee planters took the lead in forming the club and in guiding it in its earliest stages. The government allowed the club to use land (which contained a disused Chinese graveyard) in the Petaling Hill area for a course but refused to give the club permanent title to the land.[62] Since golf was practically the club's sole activity during the 1890s, most members belonged to one of the two main social clubs as well, but, as will be related in Chapter 6, the club was in later years to achieve importance as a social club.

Despite the pleasures derived from good fellowship at the clubs some people regarded the predominance of this form of social activity as one of the great drawbacks to life in Selangor. At the club people were reluctant to express their true opinions for fear of offending their ever-present superiors in the official hierarchy. Since people seldom confided in one another they found it difficult to form deep and lasting personal friendships. The public aspect of club life ('a two hours stay amidst a crowd of people') also had the effect of discouraging the formation of friendships. 'A custom has grown up', wrote Robson, 'that entitles a man to consider that he has done his duty to his fellow men if he meets them, chats with them and drinks with them within the precincts of his Club. Hence all his friends lapse to one level.'[63] Nevertheless, in a community where there was little home life and thus little opportunity for alternative forms of social activities the advantages of club life more than outweighed its disadvantages. Referring to the Selangor Club on another occasion Robson exclaimed that 'We could hardly manage to exist without it!'[64]

By the early 1890s Europeans had developed a great variety of social institutions which allowed them to associate with those people with whom they shared similar backgrounds, social standing, and interests. This did not mean, however, that they had entirely cut themselves off from Asians. A small group of Asians participated in some of these social institutions created by Europeans and in turn entertained Europeans in their own homes. Kuala Lumpur in the 1890s was a town with two élites. On one side there were the Britishers who administered the government, and on the other there were the *Kapitan Cina* and a small group of other Asians. Yap Kwan Seng did not have the same authority and independence which his predecessor Yap Ah Loy had exercised, but his influence over the Chinese population was nevertheless very great. British officials in Selangor often acknowledged their dependence on the *Kapitan Cina* and other Chinese leaders for help in controlling the Chinese and in carrying out policies which affected the Chinese.[65] The Dacing Riots of March 1897, in which the Chinese of Kuala Lumpur protested against a government regulation concerning the scales (*dacing*) used by shopkeepers, may have been a sign that the *Kapitan Cina's* influence in this respect was declining, but it is notable that Yap played an important part in restoring peace to the town.[66] The *Kapitan Cina's* position is indicated by the fact that when he went on a trip to China in 1895 Europeans as well as Chinese came to the station to see him off.[67] Social relations between British officials and the Asian élite may be seen both as a reflection of their dependence on one another and as an affirmation of their desire to retain this relationship.

The number of Asian leaders whom the British seem to have regarded as their social equals was probably not much greater than half a dozen. Among them, besides the *Kapitan Cina*, were Loke Yew, whose tin mines made him one of the richest men in Malaya;[68] Yap Hon Chin, elder son of Yap Ah Loy; and Tamboosamy Pillay, regarded by the British as the leader of the Tamil community. Yap Kwan Seng, Yap Hon Chin, and another Chinese belonged to the Golf Club, though they were somewhat conspicuously labelled as 'Chinese Members' and their interest in golf does not seem to have lasted long. Loke Yew, Yap Hon Chin, and Pillay took an early interest in horse racing; during the late 1890s more and more wealthy Asians began to participate in this sport. At a big European wedding Loke Yew, Pillay, and Yap Hon Chin were the only non-Europeans presenting gifts and thus were probably the only non-Europeans who had been invited.[69] Besides Loke Yew and Pillay, the only non-European guests among the 120 or so people who attended a dance at the Residency in December 1897 were two Malays belonging to the Selangor royal family, the Raja Muda and Raja Bot bin Raja

Juma'at, who was one of the leaders of the Malays living in Kuala Lumpur.

These Asians reciprocated by entertaining Europeans. Pillay's famed curry tiffins have already been mentioned, but Yap Kwan Seng, Loke Yew, and Yap Hon Chin entertained Europeans fairly often as well. Neither Loke Yew nor Yap Kwan Seng spoke English, but they were able to converse with their guests in Malay. The *Kapitan Cina* employed an English-speaking secretary who made all the arrangements for the dinners he gave at his garden house in High Street. 'No better dinners have ever been given in Kuala Lumpur', wrote Robson many years later. 'The cooking, the wines and the service were always perfect.'[70] These dinners were usually held when a prominent British official was going on long leave or was being transferred to another state. Judging from reports in the *Selangor Journal* these were enjoyable and relaxing occasions for the European guests. At one dinner given jointly by the *Kapitan Cina*, Loke Yew, and Pillay for the departing Resident, E. W. Birch, it was decided to sing a song which would remind Birch of his school days:

> It happened that a gentleman knew the air of an old Harrow School song, but couldn't remember the words, while another gentleman, who was letter perfect, was no great shakes as a vocalist; it was arranged, however, that the man with a memory should recite while the man with a voice warbled: unfortunately, this unique entertainment did not get beyond the first verse.[71]

After a dinner given by Yap Hon Chin in honour of Captain H. C. Syers, Superintendent of Police, and Dr. E. A. O. Travers, the Residency Surgeon, there were polite speeches but then 'the "strong man" mania seized most of the company and some wonderful feats of strength were attempted'.[72]

Health and Hill Stations

Perceptions of the effects of the climate had a profound influence on the way of life of Europeans in Malaya and throughout the tropics. Europeans believed that physical and mental deterioration were the inevitable results of living for long periods in the tropics. It was therefore, they believed, impossible for them to settle permanently in the tropics and, moreover, essential for them to return to a temperate climate periodically during their careers to recuperate from the effects of their stay and to strengthen themselves for another tour of duty.

Explorations of Africa and other parts of the tropics in the late eighteenth century and early part of the nineteenth led to many attempts by medical men to explain the illnesses which Europeans experienced in these areas. They had before them the undisputed fact that Europeans who went to the tropics were far more likely to fall ill and far more likely to die than those who never ventured out of the temperate latitudes. Since the severity of disease varied so markedly from one climatic region to another it seemed only reasonable to conclude that the climate itself must be in some way the cause of disease. Doctors did not, however, believe that the climate was the sole cause of disease, and so they searched for practical ways to make a sojourn in the tropics safer. As a result of their researches and developments in medicine in general great advances were made in tropical medicine. Improved sanitary practices and the abolition of bleeding and the giving of mercury preparations either as a treatment for 'fevers' or as a means of 'seasoning' men going to the tropics for the first time helped to make a period in the tropics much less hazardous for Europeans. By the middle of the nineteenth century quinine was being regularly and effectively used in the treatment of the most widespread of tropical diseases, malaria, and as a prophylaxis against this disease.[73]

Until the 1880s the term 'malaria' referred not to the disease now known by that name but to the disease-causing poison or 'miasma' which emanated from swamps or was contained in the humid atmosphere of the tropics. Incorrect though the miasma theory of disease was it did play a useful part in limiting the incidence of malaria. In his advice to people travelling to Perak Major McNair recommended the use of a mosquito net partly to keep out annoying insects but especially as a protection against the 'miasma-impregnated moisture' which appeared during the night.[74] In 1880 Laveran discovered that malaria was caused by a living parasite, but it was several years before other medical scientists, now working with more powerful microscopes, confirmed his findings. Scientists then tried to discover the source of these parasites. Some believed that the parasites were to be found in the air when atmospheric conditions, the soil, and vegetation were congenial to their existence. In 1894 Patrick Manson formulated the theory that mosquitoes transmitted the parasites from one individual to another, but it was not until 1898 that Ronald Ross was able to prove this theory.[75]

Despite advances in medical science there were two broad reasons that doctors and laymen alike remained convinced that the tropical climate itself had a deleterious effect on Europeans. First, there seemed to be a great deal of empirical evidence that the climate had such an effect. Despite improvements in sanitation the mortality rate for Europeans living in the tropics was still higher than that for men and women of similar age in England. It was also noted that European children became weak in body and in mind if they were allowed to stay in the tropics past the age of five, six, or seven and that the average age at which European girls born and raised in the tropics first menstruated was lower than that for girls raised in England. Finally, there was the fact, previously mentioned, that the general health of Europeans deteriorated after a long period in the tropics.[76] It is interesting that Europeans living in the Malay States in the 1880s and 1890s considered their 'climate' to be slightly better than that found in other parts of the tropics. In his report for 1896 the Selangor State Surgeon noted that 'malarial fever' was rare except among Europeans living on newly opened estates. (As was discovered in later years, one species of malaria-carrying mosquito thrived in such conditions.) But he went on to say that the 'gradually increasing lassitude and incapacity for active and energetic work or recreation' which Europeans showed was evidence of the climate's effects.[77]

The second reason for the continuing belief in the effects of the climate lay in the nature of the theory which explained these effects. Europeans began by assuming that the temperate latitudes were their natural home, the part of the world where the environment placed the least possible strain on their constitutions. It was known that bodily functions (most notably those associated with sweating) underwent certain changes upon entering the tropics and moreover that these helped the body to adjust to the heat and humidity. Today medical scientists state that temperate-zone men are able to make this adjustment with no ill effects.[78] In the nineteenth century, however, doctors believed that the body never completely adjusted to the new environment and that the physical changes which occurred as a result of residence in the tropics placed an intolerable strain on the body. It was alleged that the liver, spleen, intestines, and skin in particular were burdened to the point that pathological changes eventually took place and that the vitality of the nervous system became depressed. It was assumed not only that degeneration took place regardless of disease but also that when a disease did occur it was partly because the climate had previously weakened the body's resistances. In short, the climate was seen as predisposing the body to disease rather than directly causing disease.[79] Therefore, discoveries of the micro-organisms which we now see as the sole cause of certain diseases did not call into question the belief that the climate had some effect on Europeans.

Many of the fevers Europeans experienced in the tropics were said to be the result of chills. (In 1893, for example, a Selangor District Officer died of an illness resulting from 'a neglected chill'.[80]) Prolonged residence in the heat made the nervous system less responsive and weakened the body's ability to produce heat. The body was thus extremely vulnerable to even a slight drop in temperature. Sojourners in the tropics were advised what clothes they should wear in order to avoid chills. Even though it kept the body rather warm flannel was considered the ideal material for underclothing because its ability to absorb perspiration protected the body against the chilling effects of rapid evaporation.[81] Men were also advised not to take cold baths immediately after exercise or during the heat of the day. It was mainly because of the need to avoid chills that Roland Braddell's father told him never to 'sleep at night with your stomach uncovered'.[82]

The strictest of all rules of tropical hygiene was that a hat had to be worn during the day as a protection against sunstroke. Authorities differed considerably in their views of how sunstroke was caused. Some claimed that the sun's heat on the head caused a form of apoplexy. Others suggested that the sun's glare acting upon the brain through the eyes helped to induce apoplexy. According to another theory the condition resulted from ultraviolet and other rays penetrating the skull. Medical scientists and commercial firms designed sun helmets in different styles according to these various theories, but most authorities were agreed that some type of helmet was absolutely essential. Mrs. Innes attributed the sudden death of Captain Murray, the Resident of Sungei Ujong, in 1881 to his failure to wear his hat for a couple of minutes out in the burning sun.[83] Except as a protection against sunburn and uncomfortable glare it is doubtful whether sun helmets were of any medical use. They certainly were of no use against a sudden and severe attack of malaria, such as may have caused Murray's death. They were also of no value in preventing heat-stroke, the illness against which the helmets might be supposed to give protection, since this condition is caused by an extreme over-heating of the whole body rather than of the head alone.[84] Nevertheless, sun helmets may have served a psychological function. At a time when the nature of disease was very dimly understood those men and women who religiously wore their solar topis and observed the many other rules of tropical hygiene could feel that their fates were not subject to pure chance. 'It was much more satisfying to believe that the dead had broken one or another of a numerous and complex system of taboos.'[85]

Since Europeans believed that their poor health was partly explained by residence in the tropics it was only natural for them to place great faith in a change of climate as a cure for their illnesses and as a tonic against future sickness. In the Malay States officials had a year's leave after every six years of service, but six years was generally considered too long a period to spend in the tropics. In their annual reports the Residents repeatedly appealed to the Colonial Office to give government servants leave every three or at most four years. In 1898 a conference of F.M.S. government doctors passed a resolution declaring that the interests of both the government and its officers would be best served by shortening the period of service between long leaves from six to four years.[86] It was not until shortly before the First World War, however, that the period between leaves was finally reduced.

Since distance and the government's leave policy prevented them from taking frequent trips to their homeland, Europeans looked for other ways to refresh themselves in a cool environment. A trip to the hills also provided relief from the heat of the tropics. The great hill stations of the Himalayas and southern India had their origins in the 1820s. Penang Hill was first used as a hill resort in the days when the East India Company ruled the Straits Settlements. 'Here is a Sanitorium, far-famed over the East, to which many broken down constitutions resort.'[87] The first hill resort in the Malay States was located on the hills to the east of Taiping. The first bungalow was built in 1884 for the use of the Resident of Perak. Two other bungalows—one on Maxwell's Hill and another at the government tea gardens—were built nearby to accommodate Perak government officers, and in 1892 another one was built on Gunung Kledang near Ipoh. Visitors to Maxwell's Hill and the tea gardens were able to arrange with Chinese shopkeepers in Taiping to have regular supplies of food sent to them daily and could relax in a climate which Swettenham said closely resembled that of the Riviera.[88]

In Selangor a single bungalow was built on Bukit Kutu after the Resident, W. H. Treacher, climbed the hill in 1893 to see whether the location was suitable for a resort. To reach Bukit Kutu the visitor took the train from Kuala Lumpur on the recently opened line to Kuala Kubu and then walked, rode, or was carried the seven miles to the top of the hill. Invalids, older women, and babies were transported in chairs which were slung on poles and carried by four coolies each. When a family used the bungalow they brought their servants with them and all the provisions they needed for the period of their stay. When Miss Stratton accompanied a party ascending the hill, two sheep were driven up, and crates of fowls, boxes of tinned food, and the baggage were taken to the top by twenty porters. The only food available on the hill was fresh vegetables, which were grown by the caretaker. The bungalow had four large bedrooms, a dining room, living room, kitchen, and servants' quarters.[89] During the day visitors could play tennis. Shortly after sunset the air cooled rapidly, and by eight o'clock 'the blaze of a wood fire in the grate is fully appreciated; and the visitor feels many miles nearer the old hearth at home'.[90] Bukit Kutu was intended mainly as a place to which to escape from the heat of the lowlands, but it also provided an escape from the pressures of European society. One man who was disenchanted with Kuala Lumpur wrote that when people asked him how he amused himself on Bukit Kutu he wanted to reply that 'if your soul is satisfied with the Lake Club and the Selangor Club; with criticising your neighbour's dress and admiring your own; with tea and scandal; or poker and whisky and soda, by all means stay in Kuala Lumpur, for that is the very place for you'.[91]

Maxwell's Hill and particularly Bukit Kutu were indeed modest resorts when compared to Simla, Ootacamund, and Kodaikanal in India, but the British in Malaya had dreams of building much greater hill stations. As early as 1888 Sir Hugh Low suggested that the highlands on the Perak–Pahang border which had been explored three years earlier by William Cameron might be developed into a health resort and as a place where Europeans could settle.[92] In his report for 1899 the Resident of Negri Sembilan proposed building a hill station which would have a school for European children, and his successor advocated a hill station 'which could be reached after office work, where cool nights could be enjoyed without interruption of office duties in the day, and where the wives and children of officers could stay without long separation from the head of the family'.[93] How far these dreams were to come true will be described in Chapter 6.

After Federation

The political changes which took place following the signing of the federation agreement by the Malay Rulers in the middle of 1895 were accompanied by important changes within European society. Most obviously, the position of the Residents lost some of its former glory. The Residents were now directly responsible to the Resident-General rather than to the Governor, and much of the initiative which the Residents had taken in formulating and carrying out government policies passed into the hands of the man who held this new post. Living in the main town in the Malay States, the Resident-General was now the recognized leader of European society. The changed position of the Residents was accentuated when shortly after federation they were deprived of their entertainment allowances; the Resident of Selangor was also forced to hold a public auction to sell some of his horses and carriages. To an anonymous writer in the *Selangor Journal* all this was a challenge to the idea (which will be discussed in the following chapter) 'that the head of the Government should be surrounded by a certain amount of pomp and state, and that the native mind is beneficially influenced thereby'.[94] In 1897 the Colonial Office restored the entertainment allowances,[95] but the Residents continued to be outshone by the Resident-General. In keeping with the dignity of the new post a house was built for the Resident-General on a small hill overlooking the Lake Gardens. 'Carcosa', as its first occupant, Frank Swettenham, named it, contained dining, drawing, morning, and billiard rooms, five bedrooms, five dressing rooms, office accommodation, servants' quarters, stabling, and quarters for the horse-keepers and gardeners. The new house was neither extravagant 'nor much more than enough for a man with a family', commented Swettenham.[96] Balls at Carcosa were gala occasions at which, were it not for the tropical heat, it would be easy to imagine that 'we were taking part in some big country-house ball at home'.[97]

It is remarkable, however, that the Resident-General did not exercise as great an influence over the European community as the Residents had before federation. The bureaucracy was becoming more elaborate and more specialized and therefore less amenable to the direction of a single individual. Recruitment to the civil service was now entirely in the hands of the Civil Service Commissioners in London, and government officers were now protected against dismissal except according to well-defined procedures. At the same time, the small but steadily growing body of unofficials was beginning to assert itself. In response to petitions from commercial groups, such as the Selangor Planters' Association, who were anxious to protect their investments in the states, in 1896 the government allowed lawyers to practise in the Malay States for the first time. Another important event was the founding of the *Malay Mail* in December 1896. According to its founder, J. H. M. Robson, one of the newspaper's purposes was to give a voice to planters and other Europeans outside the government.[98] In the late 1890s senior officials continued to dominate European social life, but, as the following chapter shows, this too was going to undergo some change in the next decade.

4

The European Community in Transition, 1900–1919

AFTER the turn of the twentieth century the European community underwent many changes. The population grew rapidly, and planters, miners, and men in commerce soon outnumbered government servants. In 1904 a newspaper editor who had last visited Kuala Lumpur at about the time of federation expressed his astonishment at the changes which had taken place there: 'New buildings, new houses, new roads, new industries, new railways, and many new men. The era of work has succeeded the era of play. Planters' and Miners' association meetings take the place of cricket and sports, and the Banker turning out for Rugger, now, is a matter of comment.'[1] It was, moreover, no longer true that a young man could advance his career by displaying his prowess at cricket.[2]

During these years of feverish commercial activity there was much more than a change in the tone of European society. Unofficials were becoming increasingly wealthy as well as numerous, while officials were finding that their salaries did not permit them to emulate the more affluent style of life being set by this emerging section of the European community. The years of prosperity were accompanied by a general improvement in living conditions; Europeans began to see the F.M.S. as more suitable for European women, and as a consequence men wanted incomes which would enable them to marry at a reasonably early age. The first three sections of this chapter describe the changing position of officials during these years, the importance of marriage in their dissatisfaction with their salaries, their appeals for higher salaries, and how in 1919 their complaints were resolved by a special commission. The emphasis in these sections is on the civil servants (cadets). Since they were regarded both in Malaya and at the Colonial Office as the most important of the government services their complaints received the most attention and are therefore the best documented, but whatever salary schemes were decided for them were usually applied in modified form to the senior staff of the professional and technical departments. Those Europeans in subordinate positions in non-cadet services were however treated very differently. To show this difference the final section of this chapter looks at the way in which the grievances of European train drivers, who occupied the lowest end of the European social scale, were handled.

The strains of these years and the way they were resolved bring into sharp focus what was probably the most fundamental idea in European society in Malaya: Europeans believed that they should and indeed must live at a certain standard which was high in comparison to that of the Asian communities or in fact that which they would have enjoyed had they remained in Britain. Though this idea will be elaborated in the following pages the logic behind it needs to be summarized at the outset. Implicit in British thinking about their rule throughout the Empire was the principle that their power was based on prestige rather than military might. 'We govern by prestige, not force', wrote Robson, though he insisted that a readiness to use force when necessary was one element of prestige.[3] One official directing an irrigation scheme in Perak explained how 'my mere presence' inspired the Malays to build stronger dams than they would have constructed alone; in other words, it had been his prestige which had accomplished the task.[4] Since prestige was the basis of power it was absolutely essential to do everything possible to maintain that prestige and to eliminate anything which threatened to undermine it. In the British view, maintaining their prestige was an entirely noble objective for they believed that they would be able to bring Malaya the benefits of their superior skills and methods of efficient and fair government only if they were held in high esteem by the people of Malaya. The maintenance of a high standard of living, particularly by officials, was one way in which British prestige and hence British power was preserved. According to the British, Asians expected their rulers to live in a style befitting their status; if officials (and indeed any European, for reasons to be explained later in this chapter) failed to maintain that standard they would not be respected and would therefore be unable to govern effectively. In brief, the standard of living had to be maintained not merely for the material well-being of officials but for the benefit of the people of Malaya. It had been this logic that the anonymous writer in the *Selangor*

Journal referred to at the end of the previous chapter had used to condemn the cuts in the Residents' allowances shortly after federation.

During the period covered by this chapter the idea that Europeans should live at a certain standard was in no way challenged. What happened was that the standard to which they believed they must adhere was itself rising and that officials found they were less and less able to meet this new standard.

The Changing Position of Civil Servants

When selection by competitive examination was introduced in 1896 for the Home Civil Service, Indian Civil Service, and the four Eastern Cadetships, the F.M.S. Civil Service soon became known in Britain as the least desirable of all the services. In 1898 two men who had resigned after one year as cadets in Perak wrote to *The Times* to warn those taking the examination against considering a career in the Malay States. Foremost among their list of complaints was one that an official's salary was 'quite inadequate for the support of his social and official position'.[5] The Resident of Perak played down the importance of the resignations by implying that the two cadets would not have become successful officers, but he did not deny that salaries were low. In the following year the Secretary of State, Joseph Chamberlain, approved an increase in salaries, but by 1900 civil servants were again expressing dissatisfaction with their emoluments.[6]

Much of the discontent regarding salaries was simply due to fluctuations in the rate of exchange between the Straits dollar and the pound sterling. Officials received their salaries in dollars, so that as the value of the dollar fell—from 4s. 6d. in 1872 to as low as 1s. 6d. in 1902—the amount of money they could remit to Britain for the support of families or relatives or to use while on home leave steadily decreased. To correct this, in 1903 officials were given the opportunity to accept a scheme by which their salaries were expressed in sterling but paid in dollars at the current rate of exchange. Most government servants decided to accept this scheme as a means of protecting their salaries against the falling value of the dollar. Almost immediately after the sterling scheme was introduced, however, the value of the dollar rose markedly and in 1906 was fixed at 2s. 4d. As a result the amount of money which officials received in dollars was greatly diminished.[7]

How the rising value of the dollar affected one civil servant in

TABLE 6

Monthly Family Budgets of an Official in Perak, 1903 and 1906

(All figures in Straits dollars except where otherwise indicated)

	March 1903 Salary—£480 p.a. (Dollar = 1s. 7½d.)	March 1906 Salary—£520 p.a. (Dollar = 2s. 4d.)
Wages		
Cook	14.00	14.00
Boy	14.00	16.00
Ayah	18.00	18.00
Water Carrier	10.00	11.00
Syce	10.00	12.00
Gardener	12.00	12.00
Washerman	10.00	11.00
Total	88.00	94.00
Food, Liquor, Sundries		
Cook's Bazaar Account	44.23	47.60
Milk	14.00	14.00
Bread	4.50	4.50
Coffee	.72	.96
Ice	2.40	.90
Mineral Waters	5.40	5.40
Oil	3.90	3.27
Firewood	6.20	5.00
Horse's Food	12.00	12.00
Shoeing Horse	2.00	2.00
Liquors	24.60	20.88
Groceries	24.00	20.00
Total	143.95	136.51
Total Household Expenses	231.95 (£18 16s. 11d.)	230.51 (£26 17s. 10d.)
Balance	240.67 (£19 11s. 1d.)	126.06 (£14 14s. 2d.)
Net Monthly Salary (after deducting Widows' & Orphans' Fund contribution)	472.62 (£38 8s. 0d.)	356.57 (£41 12s. 0d.)

Source: Memorial of Perak Officials, 1906, Appendix G(I), in Civil Service Committee, *Reprint of Memorials* (Kuala Lumpur, 1917), p. 28.

Note: Expenses are for a married official, apparently with one child. Salaries correspond to those of a civil servant who joined in early 1890s.

Perak is shown in Table 6. Between 1903 and 1906 his salary rose from £480 to £520 per annum but the amount he received in dollars dropped from $473 to $357 per month. Significantly, he did not try to save money by reducing the number of servants he employed; all seven were considered essential for the European home in Malaya. The cook and 'boy', who were usually Hailams, performed most of the household duties. A Malay or Indian *ayah*, or, more commonly, Chinese (usually Cantonese) *amah* was hired to care for the children. The water carrier (*tukang air*), usually a low-caste Indian, had the task of cleaning the toilets, as well as carrying water. Until the 1900s the *syce*, almost always a Boyanese or Malay, cared for the horses and drove the carriage; in the 1900s he quickly adapted to the role of motor mechanic and chauffeur.[8] The gardener (*kebun*) looked after the surroundings of the house. With the exception of the washerman (*dhobi*), who provided his services to many households, all of the servants usually lived in quarters attached to their employer's house. The servants were expected to provide their own food out of their wages. A young European bachelor living in or near a town would usually have his own 'boy' and share the expense of a cook, water carrier, and perhaps a gardener as well with another bachelor.

Since he did not reduce the number of servants he employed, the civil servant whose expenses are given in Table 6 had less money to spend on clothing, furniture, his children's education, leave, recreation, and insurance. As the table suggests, the cost in dollars of running a household at the same standard remained nearly constant between 1903 and 1906, but starting in about 1906 Europeans were also faced with a rise in the cost of living. As a result of memorials presented at the end of 1906 and beginning of 1907 the Colonial Office granted officials a 10 per cent local allowance.[9] The various efforts made by civil servants after 1907 to improve their salaries much more substantially will be described later in this chapter.

The higher cost of maintaining the same standard of living was far from the only reason civil servants were dissatisfied with their salaries. The standard at which they believed they should live was itself rising during the first decade of the twentieth century. This new standard to which they aspired was mainly the result of the prosperity of unofficials, first in the Straits Settlements and then in the F.M.S. In 1901 it was reported that many European merchants and professional men in the Straits had recently retired to Britain with fortunes of between £50,000 and £100,000. The style of living has consequently grown more expensive and everything has increased in price.'[10] Unofficials in the F.M.S. did not enjoy a similar prosperity until the beginning of the rubber boom years in 1906. As A. N. Kenion, a member of the Federal Council, later put it, before 1906 it was 'the exception to find any planter in what one would call affluent circumstances'. The typical pioneer planter had to work hard opening a new estate and, as he waited for the trees to reach maturity, lived in a simple shanty, received little pay, and brightened his life with straight whisky. Beginning with the boom of 1906 his way of life improved markedly. He now had a higher income, a much larger bungalow, and two or three kinds of liquor in his cabinet and could afford to buy a motor-cycle or car.[11] Kenion was perhaps referring mainly to managers and proprietary planters rather than assistants but his comparison does hold true for a large number of planters as the industry prospered. The wealthiest planters were those who had opened estates with their own capital well before the rubber boom, had then had their property floated as companies, and had accepted shares as part of the purchase price. As investors in Europe eagerly put their funds into the rubber industry the value of these shares increased enormously. Alister Macgregor, for example, received shares worth 2s. each when he floated his two estates in 1905; in 1910, when the value of each share had reached 40s., the total value of his shares was £275,000.[12]

Even before the rubber boom officials had been dissatisfied with their salaries, but now their discontent became much more intense. They saw men who were not as highly educated and in many cases, they believed, less capable than themselves suddenly becoming wealthy or at least comfortably well-off. As government revenues soared, their own salaries improved only slightly. At least one cadet—Eric Macfadyen—and several officials in the professional departments left government service for the rewards of planting and commerce. And several retired senior officials, most notably Swettenham, W. H. Treacher, and E. W. Birch, sat on the boards of directors of rubber and tin companies. The 'indecent precipitancy', as *The Times* called it, with which retired administrators became involved in local businesses embarrassed top officials in Malaya and at the Colonial Office.[13] The reputation of the government was further threatened by officials who tried to derive some benefit from the boom by buying and selling shares in local rubber companies. It is not clear how extensive this practice was, but at the height of the rubber boom the

Resident-General wrote that 'it is freely reported that a very large number, if not the majority, of officials', including both senior and junior officers, were participating in such transactions. After a scandal in 1910 in which the names of several public servants were included in the prospectus for a Perak estate the government enforced much more strictly rules prohibiting the involvement of officials in local businesses.[14]

In the rubber districts the prosperity of planters brought about a change within European society. The District Officer had been the undisputed leader, the *tuan besar*, in the district both because of his official position and because he received the highest salary of any European in the area. He was expected to entertain visitors and to set an example by giving more generously to local charities. The District Officer was now, however, somewhat overshadowed by planters who could afford to entertain lavishly. The District Officer, said one official in 1919, 'cannot afford to run a Club bill of half the amount which any senior planter in the District can'.[15] Planters and other unofficials were also more likely than civil servants to own an automobile, which was the surest symbol of whether a man had attained a certain standard of wealth. Without motor-cars, one District Officer insisted, officials were in danger of dropping out of social activities and living at a lower level than other Europeans. 'If only to uphold the prestige of the Government', another official added, every government officer should receive a salary which allowed him to buy a car.[16]

There is no evidence that unofficials received satisfaction from their new ability to lead a more expensive style of life than most officials could. On the contrary, one of the most notable aspects of the civil servants' struggle for higher salaries was the strength with which it was supported by prominent unofficials. In 1910, 1917, and 1918 unofficial members of the Federal Council appealed to the High Commissioner and the Colonial Office to increase the salaries of officials.[17] There were two important reasons for the sympathy and support which unofficials gave officials. In the first place, there were important bonds between the two groups which encouraged them to adopt and maintain a similar style of living. Though the majority of officials had university educations and most unofficials did not, they had often attended the same public schools. These associations were maintained in Malaya both informally and at Old Boys' dinners; a gathering of Old Haileyburians in 1904 was probably the first of these dinners.[18] Whether they were civil servants, planters, or bankers,

Europeans belonged to the same clubs and played sports together.

Unofficials also had practical reasons for supporting civil servants in their plight. They acknowledged that their own prosperity depended upon a contented, efficient civil service. They wanted a civil service to which the best candidates were attracted and which was held in respect by the people of Malaya. Moreover, they were better able to influence—even if in an informal way—the government's decisions if they and officials maintained social contact with one another. Unofficials feared the consequences of officials dropping out of the social life of the European community because of inadequate salaries. An estate manager complained that officials who had to lead secluded lives (i.e., not mixing with other Europeans) got out of touch and, in the case of magistrates, tended to make decisions 'not of such a practical nature as is desirable'.[19] 'Leisure activities', wrote C. Wright Mills in his study of the American 'Power Elite', 'are one way of securing co-ordination between various sections and elements of the upper class.'[20] In Malaya social activities served the same purpose in preserving the unity of the official and unofficial sections of the European community.

Officials were conscious of maintaining their position in the larger Malayan society as well as within the European community. The prosperity of non-Europeans, especially Chinese, during the same period therefore was another reason officials believed they should have higher salaries. The wealth of the Chinese contributed to the rising cost of living and also played some part in setting the higher standard of living to which Europeans believed they must adhere. In the 1890s the wealthiest individuals in the F.M.S. had been Chinese, but the evidence suggests that after 1900 more and more Chinese used their riches to acquire a style of living which was both more opulent and more westernized. Wealthy Chinese hired European architects to build their homes, bought cars, furniture, clothing, and other goods imported from Europe, and trained race horses. In Kuala Lumpur the Resident-General's official residence 'Carcosa' was one of the few European houses which could be compared to Loke Yew's mansion off Batu Road, Loke Chow Kit's home (built in about 1904 and later to become the Empire Hotel) or Loke Chow Thye's home (named 'Birkhall' after a manor in Scotland where he had stayed) on Ampang Road, where many other rich Chinese built their homes.[21] In 1907 the wealthiest Chinese in Kuala Lumpur formed their own social club. Located on a site overlooking the race course, the Weld Hill Club was luxuriously furnished and had the highest subscription fee of any club in the F.M.S.[22]

Marriage and Salaries

Marriage for men pursuing careers in Malaya was extremely expensive. To understand this it is necessary to look first at attitudes common to the middle class of Britain, the class to which the great majority of Europeans in Malaya belonged, and then at the special conditions of marriage in Malaya. In the latter part of the nineteenth century and well into the twentieth the prevailing middle-class attitude was that a man should marry only when he was able to provide his wife all the comforts to which she was accustomed in her parents' home. Moreover, men hesitated to marry until they were sure that marriage would not endanger their ability to meet the expenses needed to maintain their own social position. Marriage therefore was considered out of the question until a man was well-established in his career and could look forward to a steadily increasing income with which to raise and educate his children in the same manner in which he had himself been educated. To enter into an early marriage was considered imprudent or even highly irresponsible. In practice this meant that middle-class men did not marry until their late twenties or early thirties.[23]

The salary which men believed they needed in order to marry in Malaya was much higher than that needed in Britain. This was partly because the standard of living for Europeans in Malaya was higher and much more rigidly defined than the middle-class standard in Britain. 'There is no doubt that as soon as a man arrives in Malaya,' Mrs. Noel Walker wrote in 1912, 'his ideas of what he *cannot* do without become very much enlarged. . . .'[24] And when a man contemplated asking a woman to marry him, noted the *Malay Mail*, he hesitated 'for fear lest he will not be able to give her all the conveniences and accessories which he finds his neighbour has provided for the wife of his bosom'. 'The tendency out here', the paper added, 'is for everyone to live exactly after the style set by the well-to-do; to keep up the same table equipment, to follow the same pursuits, to become in fact dumb treaders of the same social mill.'[25] The cost of marriage in Malaya was made even greater than it was for a man living in Britain because men had to support their wives and children in Britain for long periods; the children had to be educated there and the tropical climate, it was believed, affected women and children more severely than it did men. During the periods when his wife was in Europe a man had to provide her with a home and other comforts appropriate for her social position. At the same time he could not greatly reduce his own expenses in Malaya, for by doing so he would endanger British prestige.

Until the first decade of the twentieth century most men avoided or postponed marriage more because living conditions in the Malay States were not considered sufficiently comfortable for European women than because of low salaries. But after 1900 it became increasingly easy for Europeans living in the larger towns to enjoy the amenities and comforts they left behind in Britain. In Kuala Lumpur medical facilities were improved with the opening of the European Hospital early in 1904. A small school for European girls was opened the following year. In 1910, shortly after the completion of the main railway line, the Singapore Cold Storage Company, which had been providing Singapore residents with beef, mutton, butter, and other products from Australia since 1905, opened a branch in Kuala Lumpur; by 1914 the company had other branches in Klang, Ipoh, Taiping, and Telok Anson.[26] The opening of two fairly large hotels, the Empire Hotel in 1909 and the Station Hotel in 1911, made Kuala Lumpur a much more comfortable place for visitors and newcomers. Finally, the old Singapore firm of John Little's opened a large department store in the centre of Kuala Lumpur in about 1913. It featured electric lifts and fans and a refreshment room which quickly became a popular morning meeting place for European women.

Up until the First World War Europeans who lived far from Kuala Lumpur and other larger towns did not enjoy these comforts. Some men therefore continued to think that it would be irresponsible to marry. 'Could any decent Englishman, when he calls back to memory his home and surroundings in the Old Country,' wrote a planter who lived in a very remote part of Pahang, 'ask any decent girl brought up amid similar conditions to forsake all that that life connotes at Home to share the God-forsaken loneliness, the soul-shattering monotony and the utter dreariness of a rubber estate!'[27] Nevertheless, in the years before the war an ever increasing number of men believed that living conditions were no longer an important deterrent to marriage. More than anything else, salaries determined whether Britishers of middle-class background married and, if so, at what age. It was one of the main complaints of civil servants that their salaries were in fact too low to permit marriage at a reasonably early age.

The attitude of civil servants may be contrasted with that of the few British of working-class origins. Referring to the small European outstation communities in the F.M.S. before the war, Winstedt wrote that 'salaries were so small . . . [that] there was hardly a married official except for the Inspector of Police, *whose class standard was lower*'.[28] Because of their background police inspectors were unlikely to marry women with the same expectations of material comfort as those whom civil servants would hope to marry. Indeed there is evidence that before World War I some men were marrying Eurasian or Asian women knowing that they might never be able to afford a European wife. In 1897 Robson claimed that there were 'numerous' cases of Europeans marrying women 'born and brought up in the East'. Clearly most of these men were relatively low on the European social ladder as Robson indicated that such a marriage was ideal for a 'poor man'.[29] That some police inspectors were marrying local women is suggested by the special clause in their leave regulations which stated that once in seven years free second-class passages to Britain would be given to an inspector and his wife 'provided the wife is not a native of the East'.[30] In 1914 the General Manager of Railways used the same phrase when he revised the leave regulations of European locomotive drivers.[31]

It needs to be stressed that whether officials, planters, and commercial men married concerned not only the men themselves but also the European community as a whole. Many Europeans viewed the lack of women as a blight on the community and hoped that earlier marriages would discourage men from taking Asian mistresses, frequenting brothels, where they were likely to contract venereal disease, and wasting so much time and money around the bar. The Reverend W. E. Horley, chairman of the Methodist-Episcopal Committee on Public Morals, was one of those who believed that these problems would be solved if the government and private employers paid men higher salaries early in their careers to enable them to marry.[32] The *Malay Mail* too hoped to 'render the corporate life of the community the clean and wholesome thing it should be' but claimed that it was the European standard of living rather than the prevailing rate of salaries which was the true villain. A high standard of living might gain the respect of the native population, argued the editor, but adherence to this standard also had the effect of preventing men from marrying and was therefore responsible for the low standard of morals among Europeans. The paper then boldly suggested a lowering of the European standard of living as the first step to encouraging men to marry.[33] The great majority of Europeans, however, considered such a proposal as unthinkable: salaries should be high enough to permit marriage without in any way undermining their standard of living.

The question of marriage affected the salaries issue in still another way. 'There has been an extraordinary amount of intermarriage between the families of civil servants and unofficial residents', wrote a Colonial Office official in 1910.[34] If only because so many men were bachelors and because probably the majority of married men first met their wives in Europe the number of cases could not have been as great as the official suggested. Nevertheless intermarriage must have been very important both in strengthening the bonds between officials and unofficials and in raising officials' expectations for salaries. It is easy to see how even a small amount of intermarriage could cause unofficials to sympathize with officials by making salaries a family concern as well as a matter of prestige. Equally important, it would heighten the desire of officials for a salary similar to that enjoyed by unofficials. A civil servant marrying or even hoping to marry the daughter of a wealthy merchant, banker, or planter would, in accordance with the prevailing British ideas of marriage, want to provide her with a standard of living as near as possible to the one to which she was accustomed.

Having looked at the reasons civil servants were coming to expect a higher standard of living we may now trace their efforts to improve their salaries.

Resolution of the Salaries Question

In 1909 the Secretary of State announced that the allowance which he had granted officials in 1907 would be given for at least another two years. By this time however civil servants were becoming increasingly insistent that their salaries should be improved much more substantially. In 1909 the Civil Service Committee of the Federated Malay States, whom members of the cadet service had elected to act as their representatives, prepared a memorial which was signed by most civil servants and then presented to the High Commissioner, Sir John Anderson, on the question of salaries. The memorial pointed out that the average salary of civil servants was much lower in the F.M.S. than in the Straits Settlements and Ceylon and claimed that this difference was due to the fact that a very high proportion of civil servants in the F.M.S. were stagnating in the lower grades of the service.

(The main body of the civil service was divided into five 'classes', with Class I at the top and Class V at the bottom. The Resident-General and Residents held 'staff' appointments, while the youngest civil servants were known as 'cadets'.) The memorialists therefore hoped that their desire for higher salaries could be met to a great extent by changing the structure of the service.[35]

The High Commissioner and the Colonial Office agreed that there should be an inquiry into the salaries of civil servants in the F.M.S. They also believed that the inquiry should be conducted by someone from the Colonial Office rather than a local committee. In a minute written shortly after the Colonial Office received the cadets' memorial R. E. Stubbs, a permanent official in the Eastern Department, argued that it would be impossible to form a local commission which would not be biased in the favour of civil servants. A commission made up of officials would, he wrote, naturally be liberal in making recommendations regarding their own welfare while a commission of unofficials would be influenced by their close social and personal ties with officials. Stubbs also observed that since the greater part of government revenues came from Chinese sources unofficials would not be restrained by the thought that high salaries for officials would hurt their own prosperity. He therefore strongly supported the view that someone from the Colonial Office should be sent to Malaya to report on salaries.[36] In the event, Stubbs was himself chosen for the task and spent two months in Malaya in the latter part of 1910. By the time he arrived he had been asked by the Secretary of State to report on salaries in the Straits Settlements as well as in the F.M.S.

Despite his cautious reaction to their memorial Stubbs came to have a deep understanding of the reasons civil servants were dissatisfied. Indeed, in his report Stubbs expressed even more forcefully than they had how they viewed their rightful position in Malayan society. According to Stubbs, the expenses of an officer of the cadet service were 'necessarily' much greater than those of an official in England not so much because of higher costs 'as on account of the more luxurious style in which he must live, whether he wishes to do so or not'. A civil servant in Malaya, Stubbs explained:

. . . must conform to a standard which is set for him by other people if he is not to diminish the credit of the Service in the eyes both of unofficial Europeans and of the native communities. He cannot, therefore, live in a cheap house even if he could find one; he cannot dispense with the usual number of servants; he must belong to the usual clubs and generally live as other people do; and if he is a married man or is in charge of a district, he must do a considerable amount of entertaining.

Stubbs went on to explain why the standard to which officials had to conform had risen in recent years. 'It must be remembered that many parts of the Federated Malay States now contain . . . a prosperous and wealthy population of Europeans outside the Government Service, a fact which naturally leads to the setting of a high standard of living.'[37]

Although Stubbs thoroughly understood the officials' point of view his actual recommendations concerning their salaries fell far short of what they had hoped for. He did recommend increasing the salaries of officials in the most junior grades and helping them to achieve higher salaries sooner by reducing the number of years usually spent at the lower end of the hierarchy. Civil servants protested however that these improvements were not great enough to permit men to marry at a reasonably early age. Stubbs stated that a civil servant might be expected to marry at about the age of thirty-two, when, under the proposed scheme, he would be receiving about £600 a year; officials insisted that an income of £700 was necessary for a man to marry 'without incurring pecuniary embarrassment'.[38]

As for the more senior civil servants, Stubbs increased their salaries very slightly but this gain was more than offset by the fact that he took away the privilege they had had of free housing. Moreover, he did not increase the number of posts available in the higher grades. Stubbs's proposals therefore meant that once a man had married his salary would not increase rapidly enough to meet the ever greater expenses of supporting a family and educating his children. 'We submit that an officer should be able to give his sons as good an education as he has had himself', declared civil servants in a further memorial after the Stubbs report was published, 'and that joining the service of this Government should not entail sinking in the social scale.'[39] Finally, a part of officials' salaries under the new scheme was given in the form of a duty allowance, which was not paid when they were away on leave and which was not pensionable. Civil servants were however given no choice by the Colonial Office but to accept the Stubbs scheme. They were warned that the 10 per cent allowance they had been receiving since 1907 would be withdrawn if they did not accept.[40]

The discontent of civil servants reached its peak during the war years. The amount of work officials had to handle increased greatly as many of the younger men left to join the armed forces, prices rose more rapidly than they had before the war, and salaries were increased only slightly by various short-term allowances. During the early part of the war civil servants had refrained from making any efforts to improve their salaries, but after the salaries of their counterparts in the Indian Civil Service were reported on by the Royal Commission on the Public Services in India in 1916 they felt justified in making such efforts. In 1917 civil servants held meetings to decide how best to further their cause.[41] Meanwhile unofficial members of the Federal Council were becoming increasingly outspoken about the salaries of government employees. Their concern was not confined to the cadet service. One speaker, for example, warned that unless police inspectors received much higher salaries they would be tempted to accept bribes or extort money from Asians in order to add to their incomes.[42] It was partly because of the speeches of unofficials in the Federal and Legislative Councils that in May 1918 the Governor, Sir Arthur Young, requested the Secretary of State's permission to form a commission to make recommendations on the emoluments of all government servants receiving their salaries in sterling, i.e., all Europeans employed by the government and a very small number of Asians. In August the Secretary of State agreed to the formation of the Malayan Public Service Salaries Commission.[43]

There was some discussion about the composition of the commission. Civil servants wanted the commission to be made up of local unofficials, since they believed (with good reason) that unofficials would be very sympathetic and most generous in their recommendations.[44] In his original letter to the Colonial Office Young proposed a commission consisting mainly of unofficials and presided over by a judge. In his reply the Secretary of State asked that Sir John Bucknill, Chief Justice of the Straits Settlements, be appointed president of the commission and that an equal number of officials and unofficials serve on it; three officials and three unofficials were eventually selected.[45] The important point is that all of the commission's members resided in Malaya and were therefore thoroughly imbued with the attitudes of the European community. By its terms of reference the commission was limited to investigating and making recommendations on salaries and matters related to salaries, but the commissioners interpreted this very broadly and in some respects went far beyond the terms of reference. The final report and the appendices containing the testimony and written statements of numerous civil servants, members of the professional and technical departments, and unofficials represent the most searching inquiry the British ever undertook into their way of life in Malaya.

In his views on how a civil servant should live Bucknill differed very little from Stubbs. Europeans in the professions and in commerce, declared Bucknill, 'demand from the official who serves them a standard of life which shall be in the main comparable with their own', while wealthy Asians 'even more than his own compatriots expect him to maintain a position of dignity'.[46] Unlike Stubbs, however, Bucknill devised a salary scheme which in fact allowed civil servants to fulfil these expectations. Having found that civil servants were being paid less than bankers, men in commerce, and planters of approximately the same age, the commission recommended increases which placed the salaries of civil servants somewhat ahead of those of most unofficials. It is difficult to be exact in comparing the incomes of planters and civil servants, since the former usually received free housing and sometimes were paid bonuses whereas the latter had various allowances but (except for cadets) had to pay a small rent for their quarters. Nevertheless, Table 7, which compares civil servants' salaries with those of planters employed on one large group of estates, gives some idea of how the Bucknill scheme improved the position of younger officials.

The commission insisted that a civil servant should not be 'condemned to a life of celibacy'.[47] The scheme therefore was designed to allow officers to marry at the age of thirty. Since the

TABLE 7
Monthly Salaries of Planters and Civil Servants
(Dollars per month)

| | Planters | Civil Servants | |
		Stubbs Scheme	Bucknill Scheme
Salary in first year	200	179	275
Salary in eighth year	464	411	525

Source: Bucknill Report, pp. 43–44, 202; planters' salaries given in Appendix V, p. 238. The salaries given for the Stubbs scheme include the duty allowance but not various short-term allowances granted during the war. Salaries under the Bucknill scheme do not include the 10 per cent temporary allowance he also recommended.

scheme not only raised the salaries of the higher grades but also increased the number of senior posts a civil servant could be more certain of a steadily rising income with which to support his family and educate his children. Under the Bucknill scheme salaries were not paid partly in the form of a duty allowance; civil servants thus received their full salaries when on leave and had higher pensionable salaries. The commission therefore met all of the major objections civil servants had had about the Stubbs scheme. The new scheme also provided free passages to Europe every four years for civil servants and their wives and a temporary allowance to meet the sudden rise in the cost of living which occurred after the war. The salary scales which Bucknill recommended for officials in the senior levels of the non-cadet services closely resembled that for the cadet service, though salaries varied from department to department according to the professional qualifications and experience which were required.

Although he did not approve of the way Bucknill had allowed officials giving evidence before the commission to voice their feelings about the overbearing nature of some of their superiors, the Governor was generally pleased with the commission's work and its recommendations. He endorsed the fundamental premise that officials in Malaya could not live as they might in England and that as a consequence their salaries had to be high. 'As an example I would mention that officials who would be quite prepared to travel third class in England must perforce travel first class here.' After making a few small changes in Bucknill's salary scales, Young forwarded the report to the Colonial Office. In a letter to the Governor in December 1919 the Secretary of State described the proposals as 'decidedly generous' but agreed to accept the scheme only because the Malayan economy had been flourishing and showed every sign of continuing to do so. The Colonial Office also accepted Bucknill's proposal that all salaries should be expressed in dollars rather than in pounds. Bucknill's proposal was consistent with his general thesis that salary scales should be designed only with regard to the costs and special obligations which officials in Malaya had to meet—without making comparisons to salaries in other parts of the Empire. But a Colonial Office official hoped that it would also have the advantage of making 'it more difficult for jealous services elsewhere to figure out the sterling equivalent of what we are paying in Malaya'.[48] (The Colonial Office was soon to learn however that the other services were not so easily deceived.) Thus, for the first time since the great expansion in European planting and other economic activities at the turn of the century, officials in Malaya now had salaries which allowed them to maintain what they believed was their proper position both within the European community and·in Malayan society.

The Case of the Train Drivers

One of the premises of the Bucknill report was that the standard of living of *all* Europeans, whether or not they were employed in the government services, should be above a certain level: 'unless a European can earn a wage on which he is able to live decently as a European should he merely brings discredit and contempt upon the British community'.[49] This was by no means a new idea. In the 1860s Cameron had called attention to the danger posed by the presence of unemployed Europeans in Singapore. In 1897 Robson complained that the presence of a few unemployed Europeans in Kuala Lumpur 'does not strengthen our prestige with the natives'.[50] These views were based on the assumption that in Asian eyes distinctions between Europeans of different nationalities and occupations were unimportant, so that any contempt Asians might have for a section of the European community could not fail to damage the prestige of the ruling power. Despite the possible danger to British prestige, the F.M.S. government had however found it necessary to employ a few Europeans in positions for which they received a wage which was not low by Asian standards but which was far below that considered appropriate for Europeans. The largest of these groups was the locomotive drivers, who were recruited in larger numbers as the railway system expanded. In 1912 there were twenty-seven European drivers and by 1919 there were forty-six.[51]

Like other Europeans, train drivers came to Malaya in the hope of earning a better living than they could in Britain. Although their salaries in sterling were slightly higher than they would receive as drivers in Britain they were not high enough to compensate for the greater costs they faced in Malaya. Moreover, their chances for promotion within the Railway Department were extremely slight. In order to increase their earnings most drivers worked between 50 and 100 per cent overtime, or between 12 and 16 hours a day, 6 days a week. A week containing one or more 19-hour days was not unusual. By such extraordinary efforts a driver could earn about as much as a cadet did after only two or three years of service. Evidence given before the Bucknill Commission suggests that these long hours were encouraged by the department so that their basic salary would not have to be raised and in order to keep them so busy they would have no time to get drunk and thus be an embarrassment to other Europeans.[52] Not surprisingly, the long periods of hard work took a heavy toll. During the ten years up to April 1918 two drivers died while in Malaya, seven retired because of ill health, and one died shortly after retirement.[53]

Because of their working-class origins and especially because of their low positions in Malaya the train drivers were totally excluded from European society. The following exchange between Bucknill and a representative of the drivers illustrates their social position very clearly:

> *Bucknill*: Socially, there are not many people here for you, I presume?
>
> *D. Nimmo*: We are on the same level as an Asiatic. We are treated the same by the officials of our department.[54]

In Britain the driver would not have expected to mix socially with public school–Oxbridge men, but in Malaya, where the simple fact of being a European had such importance, their exclusion was humiliating. Whereas most European women regularly went to shop at John Little's or the Cold Storage, the wives of train drivers could seldom afford the goods these stores offered; instead they had to visit various Chinese shops and bargain over the price of everything they bought.[55] The drivers also resented the fact that they were deprived of certain privileges that other Europeans enjoyed:

> When recovering from fevers or sickness,
> Peculiar in tropical climes,
> A change to a cooler temperature
> Works wonders in a very short time,
> So they have bungalows on Taiping Hills,
> Where the cooling breezes blow,
> But they are reserved for the 'high officials',
> And the 'drivers' must stay down below,
> Where the temperature is high and oppressive,
> Work long hours and get little sleep,
> Where they value the broken-down engines,
> And get engine drivers too cheap.[56]

However much they were looked down upon by other Europeans the drivers would not let their superiors forget that they too were Europeans and therefore had, they believed, the same right to a certain standard of living. In a memorial addressed to the Chief Secretary in 1913 twenty-nine drivers complained about their low pay and long hours. They claimed that since other Europeans in the department had been receiving rises they too should do so, 'for there is only one standard of living for Europeans' and the price a European had to pay for imported food was the same regardless of his salary. They also objected to the recent promotion of a few Eurasian drivers from Grade II to Grade I, which had previously been reserved for Europeans. 'We cannot acquire [*sic*] the same standard of living,' the drivers wrote concerning these promotions, 'nor would it be desirable we should if we are to maintain the prestige of Europeans in an Asiatic country.' The drivers urged that a still higher grade should be created which would be reserved for Europeans. A further threat to their standing had occurred when non-Europeans were put in charge of locomotive sheds at several important stations and thus in positions superior to the drivers. Aside from more favourable leave regulations the drivers' memorial brought almost no change in their working conditions.[57] In a letter to the Bucknill Commission in 1919 one driver again reminded the government that it had a responsibility to pay drivers a salary which would 'enable them to live in a manner as befits a European without exposing him to danger of ill-health and an early death'.[58]

Rather than meet the drivers' demands the government had a simpler means of solving the problem of what to do with this 'class of poor whites', as Bucknill described them.[59] It was possible to solve it by giving drivers salaries comparable to those most Europeans received, but a less expensive solution was to replace them with non-Europeans. The Railway Department had been recruiting Eurasians from India since as early as 1908.[60] In 1917 the General Manager of the Railways proposed that all European drivers should be replaced by non-Europeans. After making certain that Asians could be taught how to drive locomotives as well as Europeans, Bucknill endorsed this proposal, but he also recommended some improvements in the European drivers' pay and working conditions in the meantime.[61] Because of the continued expansion of the railway system, because of the steps finally taken by the government to reduce the amount of overtime work, and apparently because few trained Asians were available the government had to request several more drivers from Britain in 1919 and 1920,[62] but these were among the last. By 1930 there were only fourteen European drivers, and in the following year nine men, who had all worked as drivers in Malaya for at least seventeen years, were retrenched and replaced by Asians.[63] In order to improve their position the drivers had tried to use the idea that all Europeans in Malaya should live at a certain standard. In their case, however, the application of this principle simply led to their departure.

The fate of the European train drivers leads us to a point which will be developed later in this study. In theory, the government might have encouraged the hiring of qualified non-Europeans not only as train drivers but at all levels of government. The Royal Commission on the Public Services in India had in fact actively promoted this view in its report prepared three years before the Bucknill Commission began its proceedings.[64] The government of British Malaya claimed to share the goal of employing non-Europeans in high positions, but except in small ways it was never prepared to fulfil this goal in practice. Bucknill argued that in Malaya there was not 'any class of highly educated non-Europeans who are yet qualified to occupy the upper official positions'.[65] There was, however, a more important reason, for, as will be shown in the following chapter, the government applied a colour bar which meant that the higher positions in the government services were almost entirely reserved for Europeans. The principles which guided Bucknill's recommendations ensured that all Europeans in government service would live above a certain level, while the colour bar ensured that at least in the sphere of government employment non-Europeans would not rise above that same level. Together, they formed the basis for the dominant position of the Europeans in Malayan society, not merely as individuals but as a group.

5

Tension in European Relations with Asians, 1904–1915

MORE than any other period covered in this study the time between about 1904 and the First World War was one of tension in relations between Europeans and Asians in the Federated Malay States. The first four sections of this chapter are devoted to specific areas in which there was tension or even conflict between Europeans and Asians during these years. These were the controversy over racial segregation on the railways, the introduction of the colour bar in the civil service, relations with the Chinese during the period of the Chinese Revolution, and the withdrawal of European teams from the Selangor Association Football League. After examining each of these cases in detail it will be possible to make some general observations on tensions in European–Asian relations at this time and then to say a few words on how these tensions were affected by the outbreak of war in Europe.

Segregation on the Railways

Europeans living in the F.M.S. between the world wars prided themselves that the use of public facilities and the enjoyment of public entertainments were not subject to racial segregation. In fact this was not quite true as until 1931 the European Hospital in Kuala Lumpur provided separate medical facilities for Europeans, but this was the only exception. Trains, government rest houses, cinemas, hotels, and churches were not segregated in the same way that similar institutions were in the Southern states of the United States. At the Raffles Hotel in Singapore non-European guests ate in the same dining room as Europeans, but

they were not allowed on to the dance floor;[1] in hotels in the
F.M.S. even this limited form of segregation did not take place.

At the beginning of the twentieth century, however, it was not
at all clear whether the F.M.S. would remain free of racial segregation or would soon have the equivalent of the Jim Crow laws
in the American South. Certainly, it was not then inevitable that
there would be a near total absence of formal segregation in the
F.M.S. Within the European community there were many who
wanted to isolate themselves from Asians. At the same time
there were many Asians who were not sure what pattern of separation might emerge or even what, pattern, if any, already
existed. In 1897 an Asian wrote to the *Malay Mail* to ask
whether government rest houses were intended for the sole use
of Europeans.[2] In 1911 another Asian correspondent asked
whether the recently announced Public Fancy Dress Ball was
really open to the public so that some people who had been considering attending 'would be spared the painful humiliation of
being told again that they are not the public'.[3] In both cases the
writers were assured that non-Europeans were welcome. The
developing controversy over whether to segregate the railways,
which is the subject of this section, shows however that Asians
had every reason to be uncertain of British intentions.

Segregation of railway carriages of course could become an
issue only when the railways had developed to such an extent
that it was a common means of transportation. In the mid-1890s,
when the system was very limited, some railway cars on the
Selangor State Railway were set aside 'For Europeans Only', but
there was so much opposition that this distinction was apparently
removed after a short period.[4] It was not until 1904, by which
time the network had expanded greatly and the various state
lines had been joined, that the question of separate carriages for
Europeans became the subject of often bitter controversy. The
controversy began in the middle of that year when F.M.S. Railway officials decided to have a separate first class carriage marked
'For Chinese'. While all passengers travelling first class paid the
same fare the older, less comfortable carriages were used for
Chinese travellers. When Loke Yew and other prominent Chinese presented a petition to the General Manager of the Railways
they were told that separation of the Chinese had become necessary because European women had been offended by the lack of
manners of many Chinese and had complained to the General
Manager.

In an effort to end the dispute the leaders of the Chinese

community then did two things. First, the Selangor Chinese Chamber of Commerce petitioned the General Manager asking that the 'obnoxious distinction' be removed.[5] Second, Chinese leaders tried to remove the basis of the complaints Europeans had been making about the Chinese on trains. Thousands of copies of a set of rules of etiquette to be observed by Chinese travelling first class were printed at Loke Yew's expense and distributed all over Selangor.[6] A *Malay Mail* reporter provided a translation of these rules. While he may have taken some liberties in his translation, the rules do give a picture of the extent to which the manners of many Chinese contrasted with those considered proper by the British middle class during the Edwardian period. The first rule was that whenever a lady entered a full carriage gentlemen should rise to offer their seats: 'Ladies should always be allowed ample seating room.' Passengers were warned against conversation 'of a coarse nature' in the presence of ladies, not to take off their shoes and squat on the seats, not to smoke or chew betelnut when ladies were near, and not 'to expose parts of one's naked body' or 'to clear one's throat promiscuously'. Passengers were furthermore reminded that a 'first-class carriage is no ordinary, take-it easy concern, but a place reserved for those of the very best circles. No gentleman, therefore, should enter clad in a singlet, or shod with a pair of slippers, but should invariably be dressed in perfect style.' When these rules were written the Chinese believed that the General Manager would soon remove the 'For Chinese' sign. According to the author of the rules, trains would soon have two first class carriages so that 'Oriental and Occidental passengers will naturally separate without any ill-feeling'.[7] Loke Yew and other Chinese leaders distributed the rules because they believed that there would however be occasions when Chinese might have to travel in the same carriage with Europeans.

After a second letter of protest from the Chinese Chamber of Commerce the 'For Chinese' signs were removed, but the new arrangement devised by the General Manager aroused even greater resentment. The first class section of trains were divided into 'A' and 'B' carriages. The 'B' carriage was reserved exclusively for Europeans while the 'A' carriage, which was not as comfortable, was open to anyone else who bought a first class ticket. This aroused the anger not only of the Chinese but also of all other non-Europeans, who as a result of the rule were excluded from the 'B' carriage. This new form of segregation 'shows the ingenuity of the people who are responsible for it', Loke Chow

Kit remarked.[8] When Loke Yew took a seat in the 'B' carriage he was told by a railway subordinate to move to the 'A' carriage, but he was able to stay when a European planter who was travelling in the 'B' carriage told the subordinate to go away. As he boarded a train the next evening at Port Swettenham Loke Yew was again told he could not travel in the 'B' carriage. Instead of moving to the 'A' carriage, however, Loke angrily took a seat in the third class carriage. A few months later Loke Yew's wife and a large number of other Chinese women were reported to have travelled third class to Port Dickson.[9] As a result of the regulation the future of the Malay States Volunteer Rifles, which had only recently been formed, was put in doubt as Eurasian members who were forced to travel in the 'A' carriage when going to or returning from training considered resigning.[10] Apparently there were also occasions when wives were forced to travel separately from their husbands because of the regulation. In some cases the regulation raised the delicate matter of deciding whether a potential first class passenger really was a European; one writer to the *Malay Mail* advised anyone intending to travel in the 'B' carriage to have his genealogy and birth certificate ready in case his European pedigree was questioned by a railway porter.[11]

Among Europeans there appears to have been general agreement that there should be some form of separation in the first class carriages. They pointed to the rules of etiquette as proof that even the Chinese admitted that the manners of many Chinese left much to be desired. There was however disagreement about what kind of separation there should be. Certainly many Europeans had wanted the system of racial segregation, for otherwise the system would not have been introduced, but it is difficult to determine how large a proportion of the European community this was because their views seldom appeared in the *Malay Mail*, which is the main source for studying the controversy. The measure of sympathy which the *Malay Mail* showed for the non-European point of view is hardly surprising as Robson, now the paper's manager, was Loke Yew's local real estate agent. Rather than favouring a system of racial segregation the newspaper's editor and many other Europeans believed that non-Europeans 'of standing' who were familiar with European manners should be allowed to travel with Europeans: 'It is all right to provide separate travelling accommodation for wealthy natives unaccustomed to the ordinary ways of civilized society, but native gentlemen of standing who are accustomed to mix on friendly terms with Europeans feel deeply insulted—and naturally so—if they are treated in this way when travelling on the State railway.'[12] One correspondent who agreed with this view suggested that respectable Asians should be issued with passes to allow them to travel with Europeans if they wished. Providing a separate first class carriage for women was the proposal of Revd. W. E. Horley, who warned that the present policy was causing 'race prejudices and distinctions' in the F.M.S.[13]

The policy had indeed aroused great resentment among Asians, and they proceeded to make their resentment public. There were two organizations, both of which had only very recently been formed, which played a central part in their protest. The first of these was the Chinese Literary and Debating Society, founded at the end of 1903. It appears that the founding of the Society was in part inspired by the visit to Kuala Lumpur in 1903 of Kang Yu-wei, the reform leader, who had had to escape from China after the Empress Dowager came to power in 1898 and who in 1903 was about to return to China. The Society reflected the growth of a small group of Malaya-born, English-educated Asians in Kuala Lumpur. Several of the Society's members had come originally from the Straits Settlements, where opportunities for English education had been long established. The president of the Society was Dr. Ngoh Lean Tuck (later known as Wu Lien-Teh), a Penang-born Chinese who by means of a Queen's Scholarship, which the Straits government had been awarding to one or two non-Europeans each year since 1886, had received his medical training in England and who was currently working for the Institute for Medical Research in Kuala Lumpur. The organization's membership included a few Europeans, among whom was the Protector of Chinese, H. C. Ridges, and its meetings were lively and well attended. One of the early debates was won by those who saw the queue as a badge of Chinese enslavement to the Manchus. The meeting ended dramatically when a Chinese who had supported the motion proclaimed that he wanted to have his queue cut off immediately; amidst loud applause Dr. Ngoh, who had cut off his own queue when he first went to England to study, brought out a pair of surgical scissors and cut it off.[14]

The Debating Society had been active only a year when, in January 1905, they turned their attention to a motion that the introduction of the 'A' and 'B' carriages 'is not in the best interests of the Government nor of the Community'. The proposer, Cheah Boon Teat, observed that respectable traders and merchants from all over Asia were subject to the regulation and asked whether Europeans would not feel offended if they were to visit Japan and were treated in the same way by the Japanese. Cheah appears to have seen the regulation as part of a general trend in government policy. Not long before, a Chinese who had complained that his name appeared in the Government Gazette without the title 'Mr.' in front had been told by an official that 'it is not the practice of Government to gazette any Chinese name with the prefix "Mr.".'[15] More seriously, whereas earlier the government had encouraged Chinese mining with loans and in other ways, Cheah alleged that the government's mining policy was now distinctly unfavourable to the Chinese. The European who opposed the motion did not wholly support the system of racial separation on the trains, but he claimed that some way had to be found to separate Asians who were unacquainted with western manners. He received rather unexpected support from one Chinese who said that since 95 per cent of his fellow countrymen were in fact ill-mannered it was only reasonable that the remaining 5 per cent should suffer a little discomfort for the defects of the great majority, but by a margin of twenty-eight (including at least four Europeans) to four the meeting voted that the system of separate carriages should be abolished.[16]

The second organization to protest against the regulation was the Selangor Chinese Chamber of Commerce, which had been organized early in 1904 with Loke Yew as its chairman. The Chinese Chamber of Commerce played a much greater role in the Chinese community, which was oriented almost entirely to commercial activities, than did similar organizations in western countries, and the government soon recognized this by giving it the privilege of nominating the Chinese representatives on the Kuala Lumpur Sanitary Board.[17] As already mentioned, it was the Chamber of Commerce which had petitioned the General Manager against the 'For Chinese' carriage, only to have it replaced by the 'A' carriage for non-Europeans. As the controversy developed, the Chamber of Commerce became the means by which not only the Chinese but also other non-European elites protested. In February 1905 Loke Chow Kit, a vice-chairman of the Chamber of Commerce, was chairman of a meeting at the Chamber which many prominent Malays, Tamils, and Eurasians as well as Chinese attended to discuss the railway question. At the meeting all agreed that they should arrange a public meeting in the near future. The following month about two hundred people, including Raja Bot, acknowledged as the leader of Kuala Lumpur's Malay community, met and decided to send a telegram of protest to the High Commissioner, Sir John Anderson, in Singapore.[18]

It was only then that the government began to take notice of the resentment that the regulation was arousing, although not with any sense of urgency. Anderson had the telegram returned to Kuala Lumpur to be considered by the Resident-General, Sir William Taylor. According to Taylor there was only a 'sentimental grievance' which had been fostered by a few young Chinese and Eurasians and a few Britishers who simply enjoyed embarrassing the authorities. While 'I personally do not like racial distinctions', he added, the behaviour of Asians travelling first class was 'not always beyond reproach'. Taylor did not think however that cases of bad behaviour were so numerous that segregation was essential, and he suggested that the long open carriages then in use be replaced by carriages which were divided into small compartments so that people would 'in practice segregate themselves'. This solution was in fact similar to the arrangement Chinese leaders had hoped for when they had petitioned against the 'For Chinese' carriage several months earlier. Anderson, who was pictured by some writers in the *Malay Mail* as responsible for the rule but who seems to have had nothing to do with it, asked Taylor to carry out this plan as soon as he could. Meanwhile neither Taylor nor any other official took the trouble to reply to the telegram sent by the public meeting. When more than two months after the public meeting the secretary of the meeting wrote to Anderson to ask whether the government had made a decision, he was told merely that the meeting should have followed the proper procedure and addressed their telegram to the Resident-General, not the High Commissioner, and that 'arrangements' would soon be made to settle the controversy.[19] Besides adding carriages with smaller compartments it appears that some carriages, or compartments, were reserved for women passengers.

Like Taylor, the Secretary for Chinese Affairs, W. D. Barnes, did not take the protest very seriously. In his view, Dr. Ngoh and a few other young men like him 'with more brains than discretion' had been behind the agitation, and he was relieved when Ngoh left Kuala Lumpur to live in Penang. (Ngoh later went to China, where he became an internationally known authority on plague.) Certainly the part Ngoh had played was important— without his guidance the Chinese Literary and Debating Society soon discontinued its meetings—but Loke Yew, who had little or no formal education and was then nearly sixty years old, had at least as much to do with the protest. Barnes was probably correct, however, in saying that the great majority of non-Europeans did not appear to feel any grievance. Those who protested belonged to the tiny minority of non-Europeans who were accustomed to associating with Europeans as equals but now found themselves being treated as inferiors by the railway authorities. Loke Chow Kit may well have been the only Chinese member of the Selangor Club at the time.[20] Dr. Ngoh was the only non-European to attend the Oxford–Cambridge dinner in November 1904, and in the same month he, Loke Yew, and Loke Chow Kit were among the six non-Europeans invited to a great ball at Carcosa.[21] The wealth and position of Loke Yew and Loke Chow Kit is indicated by the fact that they employed a number of Europeans to help them in their business activities.[22] Raja Bot and S. A. S. Chellapa Chetty, two of the non-Chinese who spoke at the public meeting on railway segregation, were members of the Selangor State Council and the Kuala Lumpur Sanitary Board respectively.

Those Asians who had received an English education looked upon the system of separation with particular bitterness. The regulation made many think that despite acquiring the language, culture, and skills of the British rulers they would have to remain in inferior positions simply because they were not of European race. During one of the open meetings at the Chinese Chamber of Commerce, D. A. Aeria, a Penang-born Eurasian who like Dr. Ngoh had been a Queen's Scholar and who had long been a member of the Selangor Club,[23] contrasted the aims of the Education Department with the policy of the Railways:

... the whole trouble arose from the fact that while one Department of Government was doing its best to encourage education, culture and refinement, and, in fact, to raise the moral tone of the community, another Department was compelling those who had some degree of refinement and education to mix, travel and associate with all classes, however repugnant to their feelings it might be. The authorities imparted to us Western ideas and European feelings, and then compelled us to take, and to be contented with, a subordinate position.[24]

Clearly Aeria accepted the superiority of the ideals professed by the British; it was precisely for this reason that he found the denial of his status as an equal particularly embittering. The indignation of those non-Europeans who proudly claimed to be British subjects was heightened still more by the fact that German and other non-British Europeans enjoyed the privilege of travelling in the 'B' carriage while they were excluded.

Although senior British officials had treated it with considerable nonchalance, the Asians' protest at the public meeting had had some effect. In looking at the history of European relations with Asians during the decade before World War I, when the kind of society that would be created was by no means clear, this is a very important point. There was an Asian élite (or rather several élites) which if it wished could effectively resist moves by Europeans to introduce a policy of racial segregation.

For a few years after the regulation enforcing segregation was withdrawn the railways was not a source of racial discontent among either Europeans or Asians. By 1911, however, the controversy re-surfaced as the system of informal separation began to break down. Railway carriages became increasingly crowded as the population grew, Asian incomes rose, and fares were reduced. Moreover, habits which had annoyed Europeans on short trips became doubly irritating now that the trains travelled greater distances. One European complained of sitting in the same carriage with Chinese who 'belched forth garlic fumes', exposed their dirty feet, and carried on conversations with one another across the carriage. Another European directed his ire at English-educated Asians who, he claimed, 'at times make their presence felt in a first class coach, and . . . try to show their equality with Western people by assuming a superiority over their compatriots'.[25] It may have been Asian passengers who had more reason to complain, however. In 1910 two Europeans forced two Tamil women out of the first class section of the railway-owned motor-car which linked Klang and Kuala Selangor to make room for themselves; the following year two or three drunken Europeans entered a compartment which was reserved for women and one 'molested' a Chinese woman.[26] On several occasions planters were accused of rowdiness on the trains.[27]

Despite these incidents it was the behaviour of Asians which received the most attention, and even more than in 1904–5 there was heated controversy about what should be done. Some travellers, both Europeans and Asians, said the issue could be resolved simply by adding more railway carriages, but there were many Europeans who strongly urged a return to the 'A' and 'B' carriages. Racial segregation on the trains, however, was not reintroduced. Even so, either because of mounting pressure from some Europeans or perhaps even before it, railway officials did try to exercise some control over which Asians were permitted to travel first class. At the Kuala Lumpur station no one was supposed to pass through the gate to the platform until he had bought a ticket, but since the window at which first class tickets were sold was located inside the gate the gate-keeper (usually an Indian) had the power to determine who was able to travel first class. Since no platform tickets were sold, the gate-keeper also decided who could go on to the platform to see friends off on the train. Many Asians were infuriated at this system,[28] but for at least three reasons there was no organized protest as there had been in 1905. First of all, there is some evidence that a few Asians were resigned to some form of segregation. 'It is proper to remember', one Chinese wrote, 'that the Europeans are the present governing power in the land and that it is impossible to take off that colour-line.'[29] Second, with the growing use of the automobile wealthy Asians were not so dependent on the trains for travelling about the country. Finally, and most importantly, wealthy, 'respectable' Asians usually were allowed to pass through the gate without tickets. In 1915 one non-European who signed himself 'Greater Britain' asked why at a time when Asian soldiers were fighting shoulder to shoulder with British troops against Germany, Asians in Kuala Lumpur were not even allowed access to the railway platform. To this one Indian replied that distinctions certainly were made but that he himself had never been stopped from entering. 'A man's appearance, the *tout ensemble*,' he wrote with an air of satisfaction, 'always bespeaks his class even to a Sikh watchman.'[30]

In the town of Kuala Lumpur there was another form of informal separation which was if anything more pronounced than that on the railways. A guidebook published by the Railways informed the visitor that Kuala Lumpur was divided by the Klang River into European and Asian quarters, and a government-sponsored handbook noted that one of the advantages of living in Kuala Lumpur was that 'it does not require the European and the Asiatic to live side by side'.[31] Clear though it was this division between European and Asian sections was not supported by a rule which forced people to live in particular areas according to their race. The government reserved the area in the vicinity of the Lake Gardens for senior civil servants, but since senior civil servants were Europeans the area became in effect a European enclave. The residential pattern of Kuala Lumpur was to a great extent the consequence of a policy—the subject to which we now turn—by which nearly all non-Europeans came to be excluded from the civil service.

The Colour Bar in the Civil Service

Starting in 1882 civil servants destined for the Straits Settlements were selected solely by the results of an open competitive examination. The only qualification the candidate had to meet in order to take the examination was that he be a natural-born British subject. No restriction was placed on the race of candidates. The nature of the examination favoured candidates with a public school–Oxbridge education, but there was a very small number of non-Europeans who did have the appropriate education and were able to sit for the examination in London. J. O. Anthonisz, a Ceylonese, entered the civil service in 1883 and P. J. Sproule, a Eurasian from Ceylon, was selected in 1895; both men had degrees from Cambridge. In 1895 the system by which civil servants in the Malay States were selected by nomination was ended, and beginning in 1896 civil servants for the Straits Settlements and F.M.S. civil services were selected by the same examination as for the Home, Indian, Ceylon, and Hong Kong civil services. Among the first civil servants to come to Malaya in this way was E. T. Talma, a Negro from the West Indies who had been educated at Cambridge. The fact that non-Europeans might now serve in the F.M.S. as well as in the Straits Settlements caused some alarm among Europeans in Malaya. In a *Malay Mail* editorial Robson objected to the idea that Eurasians (whom, he declared, seldom possessed 'those robust, rugged, manly attributes which have helped the Anglo-Saxon race to go forth and found the greatest Empire the world has ever seen') and Jaffna Tamils ('sadly wanting in backbone and grit when it comes to analysis of character') might successfully gain admission to the civil service of the F.M.S.[32] More significantly, the Governor, Sir Charles Mitchell, warned the Secretary of State that recruits of Asian or African descent 'would be very unacceptable to the population of the Federated Malay States so that no useful occupation could be found for them'.[33]

The Colonial Office finally took steps to exclude non-Europeans from the civil service when Sir John Anderson became Governor. While still in England Anderson had been told by his predecessor, Swettenham, that the efficiency of the government was being hampered by the number of non-Europeans in the civil service, and he had then unofficially discussed the possibility of a colour bar with the Colonial Office. In a dispatch of 17 August 1904 Anderson reminded the Colonial Office of these discussions and formally requested that non-Europeans be excluded in view of the prejudice ('if it may be properly so called') the great mass of Asians had for non-European officials. A Colonial Office clerk commented that it was the duty of the government 'to educate the natives out of this prejudice' rather than 'to pander to it', but the Colonial Office agreed to Anderson's request and introduced a regulation specifying that future candidates had to be 'of European descent'.[34] An intriguing question is whether the Malay Rulers had any part in influencing Anderson's request. Nearly forty years later W. P. Hume, for many years a civil servant in Perak, claimed that it was because of Sultan Idris's objection to an Indian cadet serving in Perak that the colour bar had been introduced.[35] Whatever the truth of Hume's claim, there is reason to suspect that the colour bar was at the very least not opposed by the Malay elite. In so far as entry into the civil service by examination was concerned the colour bar applied to Malays as to all other non-Europeans, but two or three Malays of aristocratic background had already entered the civil service without taking the examination, and on several occasions the government expressed its goal of increasing 'the number of official appointments for which Malays of high birth are both eligible and qualified'.[36] And the main purpose of the Malay College, established in 1904, was to prepare Malays to take a greater part in government. Nevertheless, there is in the sources available to the writer no clear evidence that Anderson's request for the colour bar was in any way influenced by the wishes of Idris and the other Malay Rulers. In his dispatch of 17 August 1904 the Rulers are not even mentioned.

As a result of Anderson's dispatch candidates for the commissioned grades of the police as well as for the civil service had to be 'of European descent'. Despite the vagueness of this phrase there was no question but that the government intended to exclude Eurasians as well as all other non-Europeans, so that when in 1910 a Eurasian who wished to join the civil service pointed out that he was 'of European descent' Colonial Office officials changed the phrase to 'of pure European descent on both sides'. There now could be no doubt what had been intended.[37] The number of non-Europeans who had actually been able to enter the civil service before 1904 was extremely small. In 1911 there were only about six men in the combined services of the Straits Settlements and F.M.S. who had been

12 A Pierrot Troupe made up of Kuala Lumpur residents which put on a number of charitable performances about 1901. (*British Malaya*, 8(1933), 92)

11 Grandstand at the Ipoh Racecourse sometime in the 1890s. (*British Malaya*, 6(1931), 180)

10 The Chinese section of Kuala Lumpur at the time of the visit of the Prince of Wales in 1922. (Mr. Hugh Allen)

9 A football match in front of the Selangor Club, about 1908. (*Royal Commonwealth Society*)

8 Panoramic view of Kuala Lumpur in the late 1890s. St. Mary's Church at extreme left, the Selangor Club in the foreground, and the Secretariat Building on the other side of the *padang*. (*Arkib Negara Malaysia*)

6 The Sultan of Perak and the Resident of Perak, C. W. Parr, at a
Taiping Gymkhana Club meeting, 1922. (*Royal Commonwealth Society*)

7 The wedding of Captain Howman (standing directly behind the
bride) at Taiping, 1932. Raja Sir Chulan standing at extreme left, his wife
seated second from right; the Sultan of Perak and his wife on either side
of the bride. (*Arkib Negara Malaysia*)

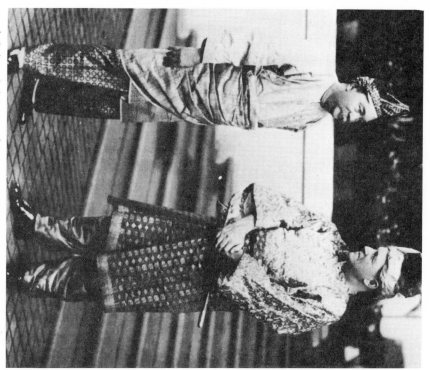

4 Sultan Suleiman of Selangor and Sir George Maxwell at 'Carcosa'. (*Arkib Negara Malaysia*)

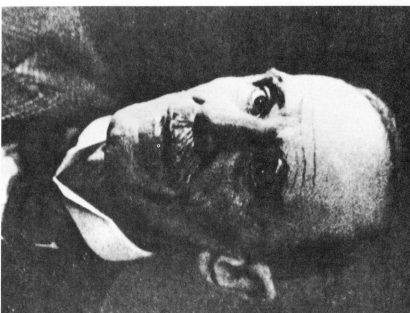

5 J. H. M. Robson, founder of the *Malay Mail*, twice unofficial member of the Federal Council. (*Arkib Negara Malaysia*)

3 Meeting of the Federal Council at Kuala Lumpur, 28 February 1927. At the head of the table is the High Commissioner, Sir Laurence Guillemard. To his right are (in order) the Sultan of Perak, the Resident of Perak, the Sultan of Selangor, the Resident of Selangor, the Yang di-Pertuan Besar of Negri Sembilan, and the Resident of Negri Sembilan. To Guillemard's left are the Chief Secretary of the F.M.S., William Peel, and the Legal Adviser. (*Royal Commonwealth Society*)

2 The High Commissioner, Sir John Anderson, and other officials with the Sultan of Selangor at the Sultan's *Istana*, Klang, 1904. (*Royal Commonwealth Society*)

1 The leaders of Kuala Lumpur in 1884. Seated (left to right): Yap Ah Shak (Yah Ah Loy's successor as *Kapitan Cina*); fourth is Raja Laut; fifth is the Resident of Selangor, J. P. Rodger; sixth is Yap Ah Loy, the *Kapitan Cina*; eighth is Captain Syers of the Police. (*Arkib Negara Malaysia*)

selected by examination before 1904 but who would now be disqualified from taking the examination because of their race.[38] Some of these men had successful careers as civil servants. Anthonisz was for a short time acting Resident of Selangor, Sproule held several top judicial appointments, and Talma was acting Treasurer of the Straits Settlements when he retired in 1924. Nevertheless, they could never hope to reach the very highest positions (Sproule's 'dusky hue' was to disqualify him from becoming Chief Justice of the F.M.S. in 1925),[39] and their social relations with the European community were in some cases very strained.[40]

At least officially, the colour bar applied only to the civil service and the commissioned grades of the police. But the number of non-Europeans who were able to obtain employment in the professional and technical departments was very small. The government tried to maintain the principle that as much as possible a European would never have a non-European as his superior. 'Any European', wrote Anderson, 'would consider it an indignity to be asked to serve under a Eurasian.'[41] This meant that in any particular department a non-European could never hope to be appointed to a position higher than that held by the most junior European in that department. In fact, the government preferred never to appoint a non-European even at the lowest level at which there were Europeans because as a result of seniority he could expect eventually to rise to a position where he would be superior to at least a few Europeans. The government did make exceptions. For example, R. H. McCleland, a Eurasian who in 1901 received a Queen's Scholarship to study engineering in Dublin, rose to the most senior positions in the Public Works Department of the Straits Settlements. But such exceptions were indeed rare and were if anything even rarer in the F.M.S. Dr. E. T. MacIntyre, a Jaffna Tamil who received his initial medical training in Ceylon, was unable to rise above the most junior position a doctor could hold even after he went to England to obtain qualifications which were higher than those held by many of his superiors.[42]

Although the colour bar in the civil service had been in effect since 1904 it did not become a public issue until A. MacCallum Scott, a Liberal M.P. from Glasgow, expressed his opposition to it in the House of Commons in November 1911. Over the next few months Scott persistently questioned the Secretary of State for the Colonies, Lewis Harcourt, and, on one occasion, the Prime Minister, Asquith. While he succeeded in annoying Harcourt, and keeping Colonial Office clerks busy preparing replies for him, the government did not show the slightest sign of wanting to reconsider the colour bar. In Malaya reports of Scott's speeches prompted non-Europeans to protest against the Colonial Office's position, but the number who actively participated in this protest was very small, much smaller than the number who had protested against the system of racial segregation on the F.M.S. Railways. Even before the colour bar was imposed only British subjects had been eligible to take the examination. As only people born on British territory, as compared to British protectorates, were British subjects there were naturally far more British subjects in the Straits Settlements than in the F.M.S. Moreover, although the number was still small, there were more Asians in the Straits Settlements than in the F.M.S. who had received a sufficiently high standard of English education to consider taking the examination or at least to feel strongly about maintaining their right to take it. In the Straits Settlements those non-Europeans who had studied in Britain by means of Queen's Scholarships formed the nucleus of this group. Between 1886 and 1911 only forty-five Straits non-Europeans were awarded scholarships by the government, but these men had an influence far out of proportion to their numbers. In the F.M.S. the government awarded a total of only two scholarships similar to the Queen's Scholarships; neither of the recipients (two Chinese brothers) returned to the F.M.S.—one, a doctor, eventually went to China and the other practised law in Singapore.[43] It is therefore hardly surprising that the protest, limited though it was, was centred in the Straits Settlements rather than in the F.M.S. With the exception of a rather belated letter from a Kuala Lumpur Chinese to a Penang newspaper I have no evidence of protest by Asians in the F.M.S.[44]

The leader of the protest in the Straits Settlements was Dr. Lim Boon Keng, who had received his medical training at Edinburgh by means of a Queen's Scholarship. Lim had earlier resigned from the Singapore Municipal Commission and vowed not to accept any future offer to serve the government. He had made this vow after being told by the head of the Medical Department that a very highly qualified doctor who had applied for a certain position in the department was not being considered simply because he was an Asian. 'I cannot put an Asiatic over European Inspectors', Lim had been told.[45] The unease which Lim and other Straits Asians felt was greatly intensified by the Straits government's decision to discontinue the Queen's Scholarships. One of the two scholarships given annually was abolished in 1908 and the other in 1911. Anderson had argued that the money spent on maintaining two students at a university in Britain would be better spent on improving the general standard of English education in the Straits Settlements. The loss of the principal means by which a handful of them had been able to receive a university education, and thus an opening to successful careers, came as a blow to Straits non-Europeans. Whatever the true reason for which Anderson had abolished the scholarships, many non-Europeans saw this as an attempt by both the government and European unofficials, who had given very strong support for the measure in the Legislative Council, to ensure that they would forever remain in subordinate positions.[46] They therefore tended to regard the introduction of the colour bar as reflecting the government's general attitude toward the aspirations of Straits non-Europeans. When Dr. Lim addressed a meeting of twenty-two prominent non-Europeans (four Chinese, five Malays, six Eurasians, three Indians, three Ceylonese, and one Armenian) protesting against the colour bar in May 1912, he spoke in general terms of the government's policies:

. . . however worthy my posterity may be, they will never be allowed to be more than the most subordinate servants, clerks, and so on, under men who think their white skins are the sole sign of born rulers and administrators, and who have the impudence to declare that we prefer them in authority over us before all others. It is a lie . . . and the House of Commons should be so informed.[47]

At this meeting it was unanimously agreed to present a protest to Parliament through A. MacCallum Scott. Later in the month it was reported that petitions were being 'numerously' signed in Singapore and Penang.[48] Whether Scott ever received the petitions remains a mystery, however, for although he quoted Lim's speech in the House of Commons he never mentioned the petitions. The issue was not raised again until the 1920s.

During the months when they were protesting against the colour bar Lim and other Asian leaders received little support from the main English-language newspapers. The *Straits Echo*, which was edited by an Englishman but owned by a group of Chinese, championed their cause,[49] but the other newspapers supported the colour bar. Indeed, they supported the bar more vigorously than Harcourt had in his replies to Scott's questions. In an editorial which Harcourt quoted as proof that the people of Malaya wanted the colour bar, the *Straits Times* declared that the English, 'as the dominant race in this part of the world', had made alliances with the Malay Rulers, who would be insulted and think that these alliances were not being honoured if men of other races were sent to 'advise' them. Admittedly, there were Asians and Eurasians of great ability and high character, but they could never serve in one of the Malay States and thus, for the sake of efficient and harmonious government, should not be allowed to enter the civil service in the first place.[50] The *Malay Mail* went even further and may well have reflected the view of a large section of the European community. The editor referred not only to the dislike Asians supposedly had for non-European officials but also to the fact that European officials did not want Eurasians or Asians in the civil service. 'No member of the Civil Service who is of mixed Asiatic descent can count upon that measure of cordial assistance and support from his brother officials which is essential for the satisfactory discharge of his public duties.' For this reason alone, the editor wrote, the government had been wise in excluding non-Europeans. The *Malay Mail* also refused to go along with the notion apparently accepted by the *Straits Times* that Asians had the personal qualities required of civil servants. It was true that many Asians had displayed intellectual ability, but despite years of English education they had failed to improve their character because the kind of education they received in Malaya was not modelled on that provided at the public schools and at Oxford and Cambridge. Instead, the editor asserted, Asians were receiving an inferior form of education resembling that given in a Board School in England, so that the government 'now deliberately declares that as a body they are unworthy of positions of trust'.[51] The editor did not, however, suggest that the government bring about changes in the kind of education being offered in Malaya.

Europeans and Chinese during the Revolutionary Period

For the Chinese their New Year was the time of the year's biggest celebrations. Europeans, however, looked forward to the occasion with considerable apprehension. Especially in the Kinta district of Perak European residents feared a rise in crime as the New Year approached and thought that the celebrations would probably turn into destructive rioting. These fears, which the

Chief Secretary once referred to as the 'annual Ipoh scare',[52] were particularly strong as the Chinese New Year of February 1912 approached. During the previous year a number of European mine and estate managers had been held up and robbed by Chinese gangs. The most serious incident took place less than a month before the New Year celebrations when an estate manager was attacked by a Chinese gang, robbed, and left to die. There is no evidence that these robberies and assaults were directed specifically at Europeans (indeed Revd. W. E. Horley appealed to Europeans not to overlook assaults suffered by Asians as well) but a large proportion of the European community saw these events as a particular threat to themselves.[53]

Far more than these incidents it was the general behaviour of much of the Chinese population which aroused apprehension among Europeans or at the very least irritated them. In 1912 there were many complaints that over the previous few years the Chinese had become insolent, independent, and even conceited in their relations with Europeans. Many examples were given to show the existence of this attitude. It was said that European customers were often served abruptly or were ignored in Chinese shops; one European woman felt very insulted because when she went into a goldsmith's in Kuala Lumpur she had been kept waiting while some prostitutes were being served. Another complaint made was that Chinese would not step aside when Europeans were walking through the streets. Noticing that in the Netherlands East Indies the Chinese were restricted to one part of the town, one European argued that the F.M.S. government must also deal firmly with the Chinese: 'Such insolence would never be tolerated in a Dutch Settlement'.[54] It was also alleged that Chinese labourers were displaying 'unreasonable' behaviour. The *dhobis* of Kuala Lumpur doubled their incomes by combining together to charge for each piece of clothing they washed rather than receiving a monthly wage. And in Singapore Chinese who had been brought from China to work in Malaya were refusing to co-operate with the government's quarantine regulations. Finally, though these were by no means new, complaints about Hailam domestic servants employed by the majority of Europeans reached a peak, and Europeans, especially unofficials, renewed efforts to press the government to introduce a system of registration.[55]

Hailam servants were a source of concern in another respect. Chinese showed their support for the revolutionary cause, just then successfully overthrowing the Manchu dynasty, by cutting off their queues. Europeans however found it very appealing that their servants should wear queues, which as a sign of respect the Chinese uncoiled when serving their masters.[56] Europeans therefore objected when the servants either cut their queues off themselves or were forced to do so by those Chinese who supported the revolution more actively. Some Europeans were also wary about what the removal of queues might mean for relations between the Europeans and the Chinese in general. Whereas the queue and a small black cap signified adherence to traditional Chinese manners and customs, wrote one of Kuala Lumpur's leading lawyers, short hair and European-style hats signified 'a desire to be done with old ideas and to claim for the Chinese all the advantages which Europeans have arrogated to themselves in the East'.[57]

It is difficult to determine how widespread and intense the feeling of insecurity was among Europeans as the New Year of 1912 approached. Although it took the view that there would be no trouble the principal planters' journal reported that planters using Chinese labour on isolated estates, 'where the white planting manager is at the mercy of a horde of yellows', were predicting trouble.[58] Apprehension appears to have been greater among unofficials than officials, and more intense in Kinta than in Kuala Lumpur. A writer who claimed to represent the views of a large portion of the European community of Kinta noted that 'race feeling in the F.M.S. has been growing more acute during the last few years' and called upon Europeans to be prepared for a possible confrontation with the Chinese.[59] It was in this atmosphere that the Chief Secretary, E. L. Brockman, had the Malay States Guides put on alert although he personally did not expect they would be needed.[60]

The troops were needed however. In Ipoh and elsewhere in Perak Chinese New Year passed peacefully except for a few minor disturbances,[61] but Kuala Lumpur was the scene of rioting which lasted nearly a week and in which twelve people, all Chinese, lost their lives. The disturbance began as supporters of the revolution who had cut off their queues attacked Chinese who still wore queues and forcibly cut them off, but there was also fighting between Chinese belonging to different speech groups, first between Cantonese, who were also the most enthusiastic revolutionaries, and Hokkiens and then between Hakkas and Hokkiens. The normal business of Kuala Lumpur came to a halt, but otherwise Europeans were affected only indirectly or as a consequence of taking part in returning the town to order. Cricket players visiting Kuala Lumpur for the holidays had to carry their own equipment because there were no rickshaws available, and European domestic life was slightly upset when *dhobis* refused to take any laundry from Europeans for fear that the clothes would be stolen. European volunteers joined the Malay States Guides and the police in finally bringing the riots under control. The most serious moment in the week occurred when a group of rioters attacked the Central Police Station in an attempt to release some prisoners.[62]

From the point of view of this study the most striking feature of the rioting is that it involved only the Chinese. Unlike at the time of the Dacing Riots of 1897 the Chinese were not in any way protesting against the government. All the evidence shows that the European community was in no way a target of any of the rioters. In short, the riot was not a manifestation of the 'racial feeling' which many Europeans had seen mounting in the months before Chinese New Year. But rather than drawing this reassuring conclusion Europeans regarded the riots as a further example of the 'truculence' of the Chinese. The nature and origins of this attitude supposedly displayed by the Chinese was one of the issues considered by a commission which the High Commissioner appointed to examine the causes of the rioting. A number of witnesses and at least two of the three commissioners were convinced that there had been a change in the attitude of the Chinese population toward Europeans.

Two witnesses, however, strongly denied that there had been such a change. One was Dr. Travers, who had long, close ties with Chinese leaders, including Loke Yew.[63] The testimony given by Travers and Loke Chow Thye, one of the most prominent Chinese in Kuala Lumpur, indicates that part of the reason the crowds had got out of hand was that Chinese leaders no longer had the same influence over their fellow countrymen as they had had in the 1890s. The government had steadily taken over those duties of governing the Chinese population which in the nineteenth century it had shared with the *Kapitan Cina* and other leaders. This fact by itself helped to create misunderstanding between the British and Chinese leaders. Indeed, while the commissioners tended to put some of the blame on Chinese leaders for the events at Chinese New Year, these leaders were surprised that the government had been so slow to quell the rioting.[64]

That there had been a change in the attitude of Chinese toward Europeans was also denied by the Chief Secretary.

Brockman suggested that some Europeans tended to see anything short of total submissiveness as a sign of rebelliousness.
'The other day', he quoted a well-known European tin miner as
saying, when giving examples of the Chinese attitude, 'one of my
Assistants found a Chinese walking along a pipe line. He gave
him a cuff on the head and knocked him off the pipe line, and
the Chinese turned round and glared at him!' Brockman agreed
with one of the commissioners that planters employing Chinese
workers might be endangered, but he pointed to the attitude of
the planters themselves as a potential source of trouble.[65] It is
significant that while another witness, H. C. Ridges, a Chinese-
speaking official who had recently retired, believed there had
been a change in the demeanour of the Chinese, he saw this in
part as a reaction to the rude manners of many Europeans with
whom they came in contact.[66] In addition to the examples given
earlier regarding the actions of some Europeans on trains at
about this time, reports of planters and other employers being
prosecuted for rough treatment of their workers would suggest
that if some Asians were becoming less subservient towards
Europeans it was partly due to the behaviour of Europeans themselves.[67]

Most Europeans, however, were not prepared to accept that
their own actions might have played some part in creating the
tensions of the time. Their attitude was hardened when, just as
the commission was concluding its inquiry, further proof of
Chinese 'independence' was provided by a strike of about 150
Chinese employees at four European-owned engineering firms in
Kuala Lumpur. The workers objected to the recent introduction
by the firms of rules that they must give one month's notice
before leaving and that no worker would be employed by
another firm without showing a discharge ticket from his previous employer.[68] According to one of the commissioners, the
workers conceived the idea of going on strike after reading
accounts of recent massive strikes in Britain.[69] Strikes by Chinese workers either in China or in other parts of Malaya were by
no means new—they had not needed to read English newspapers
for such an idea; the strike was probably prompted by the desire
of the workers to maintain as much freedom as possible to move
from one job to another at a time when opportunities for employment were numerous and wages were relatively high. Just as
Europeans saw the Kinta gang robberies as a special threat to the
European community, they also saw the strike as a possible
threat to their position. 'If we are to give in to coolies . . .', an

unofficial member of the Federal Council declared, 'then the position of Europeans in the country will become very difficult.' The Chinese member, Eu Tong Sen, tried to promote a more moderate view by noting that England had strikes too, but this did not win any sympathy for the strikers.[70] Middle-class Englishmen in Malaya had as much antipathy towards the dockers and miners on strike in England as for the Chinese on strike in Kuala Lumpur. None of the engineering employers gave in to the strikers. A few of the workers accepted the new rules and returned to work, but most were replaced by Indians recruited locally or directly from India. The manager of one firm explained that they were 'done with Chinamen'.[71]

European Teams and the Selangor Football League

Of all the aspects of their culture the British introduced to Malaya they were certain that sports, particularly association football, were among the most valuable and important. The British saw sports as a means by which Asians might improve both their physical abilities and their character, by which, in other words, Asians might acquire those qualities such as sportsmanship which were embodied in the image middle-class Englishmen had of themselves. Equally important, sports were seen as a means of promoting good relations between the various ethnic groups. 'It is doubtful', ran a typical passage in praise of sports, 'whether anything in the Federated Malay States has contributed more to the furtherance of the intimate understanding which exists between the various sections of the community than the padangs [playing fields], scattered through the States, upon which all classes meet in friendly emulation.'[72] This section describes how in the years shortly before the First World War relations between Europeans and Asians on the playing field reached a point which was hardly characterized by 'friendly emulation'.

In the 1890s Europeans in Selangor did not play football in an organized league. Occasionally they played against other all-European teams from Perak, Negri Sembilan, Penang, or Singapore. By 1894 there was also an informal competition between teams from Kuala Lumpur, Klang, Kuala Kubu, and Kajang. While the Kuala Lumpur team was entirely European except for one player (the Selangor Club's office boy), the other three teams were about half European and half Asian in membership. These matches do appear to have fulfilled the ideal of bringing

Europeans and other ethnic groups into friendly contact. After an early match between the Klang and Kuala Kubu teams the players enjoyed an excellent dinner at the rest house.[73] In more remote places there were also even less formal games between teams whose players were Asians except for one or two Europeans each. The important point is that in the 1890s Europeans participated in matches which were either between wholly European teams or teams which were racially mixed, rather than in matches between teams which were racially distinct. This meant that a match was not likely to be seen by players or spectators as a contest between two races.

During the 1890s football gained increasing popularity among Asians. The sport was encouraged by the Resident of Selangor, J. P. Rodger, who in 1895 donated a silver cup for which various Asian teams competed.[74] It was not until 1906 that the Selangor Association Football League was founded. To a striking extent the teams in the league were racially defined. In 1912 there were three European teams—the Selangor Club, Casuals, and Klang; three Malay teams—Sultan Suleiman Club, Klang Malays, and Seri Mahkota; a Tamil team, Tamil Union; and a Chinese team, United Chinese. Three teams which had previously competed for the championship had been multi-racial (though entirely non-European or nearly so) in composition—the Recreation Club, Y.M.C.A., and Victoria Institution—but by 1912 all had left the league. The three European teams had earlier considered withdrawing from the league to form a separate European league because, with the exception of the Sultan Suleiman Club, which finished third in 1911, the non-European teams had not provided strong enough opposition, but probably because the European players were unable to form enough new teams for a separate league the three teams remained in the league.[75] At the start of the 1912 season it was clear that the quality of play by Asian teams was improving. As competition for the championship became more intense, spectators, especially Asians, turned up in large numbers to cheer the teams they supported. Since the teams were racially defined games now tended to be seen in the wider context of race relations, which, as we have seen, were very strained at this time. A dispute between two teams therefore could easily take on a larger significance as a dispute between two racial groups.

The 1912 season was marked by several such disputes between European and Asian teams. In one match a member of the Chinese team was admonished by the referee for attempting to strike a European opponent. After another game a Malay player was brought before a magistrate for striking a European player and had to pay a $30 fine. The most serious incident occurred in May during a match between the all-European Casuals and the all-Malay Sultan Suleiman Club, who had not allowed their previous four opponents a single goal. After Casuals had scored a goal, the referee ordered a Malay player off the field for committing a serious foul against a Casuals player. Two of his teammates followed him in sympathy, and the others were encouraged to do so by their Malay supporters, who had been cheering them on with shouts of 'bunuh' ('kill') and 'tendang' ('strike'). Shortly after play was resumed 'blows were struck' between a Casuals player and a Sultan Suleiman player, and a Malay spectator rushed out onto the field to hit the European. While a police officer took the spectator to the police station, the 'referee brought the game to a close and the field was soon the scene of a struggling mass who mostly sympathized with the Malays'.[76]

Among Europeans there was a difference of opinion as to whether the European teams should now withdraw from the league. Claiming that the league simply brought European teams into opposition with 'Asiatics who do not appear to understand what a sporting game is', the editor of the Malay Mail wrote that the European teams should withdraw just as European teams had done from a similar league in Singapore.[77] Indeed this idea received immediate support from the Singapore Free Press, which was more explicit about how deplorable it was for Europeans to play Asians regularly in a league. Whereas foul play between two Europeans produced no lasting ill feeling, the paper stated, foul play between a European and a non-European aroused 'race hatred' and gave the non-European a false opinion of his strength if the European hesitated to strike back.[78] Those who favoured remaining in the league reminded others of the noble purpose for which the British had come to Malaya. 'Great Britain is in this country', one wrote, 'for the education of the races here, not alone in matters of administration, but for the inculcation of the spirit of fair play, pluck, endurance, and sport amongst the people.' He concluded that the standard of sportsmanship among Asians would deteriorate much further if they were deprived of the benefits of playing with Europeans.[79] The fact that there were fewer Europeans in Selangor than in Singapore and that they were spread out over a much wider area, thus making a separate European league more difficult to form, were also arguments in favour of remaining in the league. The Europeans did remain. The league committee suspended two Malay players and one European for the season and one Malay for part of the season, instructed the referees to be stricter, and asked for extra police to control the spectators.[80]

The following season was free of any friction, and when Sultan Suleiman Club won the championship they were even praised for their sportsmanship.[81] The 1914 season, however, saw a return to the tensions of 1912. A Selangor Club player had two ribs broken during a game with Penang Peranakan, a new team apparently made up of non-Malay Muslims. This was soon followed by another dispute involving the Selangor Club team. In addition there were numerous complaints about the 'dirty little tricks' practised by the Asian teams and the constant jeering and foul language of the spectators. The *Malay Mail* again wrote that the European teams (of which only two now remained) should withdraw.[82] One team did so immediately and the Selangor Club players met and voted, with only one man dissenting, to leave the league 'in view of the racial feeling engendered by the attitude of the crowd'.[83] A few days later the Tamil Union team also withdrew; they felt insulted by the withdrawal of the European teams since it implied that they were among those teams which had displayed unsporting behaviour.[84] The ideal that sports should promote harmony and understanding between ethnic groups had not been fulfilled by the Selangor Football League.

Some General Observations

In looking at the tension between Europeans and Asians in the decade before the First World War it is difficult to determine how much was true tension involving both groups or the Europeans and a particular section of the Asian population and how much was simply imagined by Europeans. The controversies over segregation on the railways and the colour bar were by their very nature along racial lines, but in many other cases Europeans found racial overtones where none existed. Gang robberies, an important element of the 'annual Ipoh scare', aroused 'racial feeling', but there is no evidence that these robberies were aimed specifically at Europeans. Punches were not absent in football games between teams of the same race, but because of racial identities and their belief that they must remain aloof and set an example, Europeans withdrew from the Selangor Football League. One may also refer to cases where Sikh police constables or

Chinese spirit farm inspectors (until the farming system was abolished) arrested Europeans on petty charges; other people were annoyed in the same way, but Europeans objected so strongly because *Europeans* were affected. 'During the whole of the time', the outraged editor of the *Malay Mail* recounted of one incident, 'the policemen at the station were giggling and signifying in an irritating manner their amusement at seeing a European in such circumstances.'[85] One visitor to Penang learned how much Europeans feared the slightest appearance of humiliation when an English resident told him why Europeans never carried any money or jewellery when they walked about town: 'You see, we're one white man to three hundred coloured. We have to keep up our personal prestige, and so we try to avoid tempting any one to rob, or steal, from the person by having nothing valuable about us.'[86] Finally, as mentioned, many Europeans believed that the Chinese in particular had become insolent toward them, but there is far more evidence that some Europeans considered anything short of abject servility as insolence. Europeans moreover contributed more than their share to arousing tensions by their own actions. What all these diverse examples illustrate is not only that Europeans saw themselves as superior to other races but that in this period many of them were also filled with a fear of anything which might even appear to threaten their superiority.

The period under review was one of intense jingoism throughout the Empire, but the British in Malaya believed that they had particular cause for an exuberant pride in themselves. 'It is a record of great achievement by courageous and masterful men—such men as are admittedly turned out only by the Anglo-Saxon race', wrote one young official as he surveyed the government's accomplishments and the development of the rubber industry.[87] It was partly because they believed they were as a race responsible for this achievement that some Europeans had wanted the 'A' and 'B' carriages restored shortly before the war. Before 1900 Europeans in Malaya were not slow to extol the qualities of their race, but it had been impossible to pretend that they had been solely responsible for what had been achieved since the economy was almost entirely in Chinese hands. Ironically, at the very time that Europeans were most asserting their superiority the actual cultural differences between them and Asians were diminishing. More Asians had an English education, were aware of western ideas, and were acquiring professional skills which had once been a European monopoly. Even in their

clothing and pastimes Asians now differed much less from Europeans than they had a few years earlier. Far from promoting
harmony, however, the narrowing of the cultural gap aggravated
relations between Europeans and Asians. On the one hand Europeans wished to inculcate Asians with their values and to introduce them to their institutions and pastimes, but on the other as
the gap narrowed they could not feel as certain of their distinc-
tiveness and, by implication, their superiority. It is useful to see
the introduction of the colour bar in 1904 in this light. As the
cultural and educational gap between Europeans and Asians
closed, the colour bar, however it was justified, was the only
remaining means Europeans had of maintaining their superiority
over Asians within the sphere of government activity.

One further aspect of the tension of this period needs to be
mentioned: British attitudes towards events in Malaya were often
coloured by developments in their homeland. This was especially
true in the case of the major confrontations between employers
and workers which took place in Britain between 1910 and the
war. The British in Malaya were because of this turmoil less
tolerant not only, as mentioned, of the strike by Chinese
engineering workers in June 1912 but also of other incidents.
During the rioting in Kuala Lumpur, for example, one writer
suggested that the rioters should be treated with bullets in the
same way white strikers in Manchester had been.[88] Even the
pushing and shoving on the football pitch were seen in the light
of trends in England. The unsportsmanlike tactics supposedly
indulged in by Asian teams resembled those employed by professional footballers in Britain, and the behaviour of the crowds
seemed to resemble that of the undisciplined rabble at matches
in Britain. 'A student of tongues parading the touch-line would
get an amazing revelation of the similarity between the local
crowd and the crowds at the big matches at Home. They come,
in fact, to witness a gladiatorial show.'[89] In short, all those aspects
of their own society which middle-class Britishers most deplored
were in danger of being transplanted to Malaya.

A few months after the outbreak of war Europeans were
embroiled in a conflict with a group of Asians that made the real
and imagined tensions of the previous decade seem inconsequen-
tial when on 15 February 1915 an Indian regiment stationed at
Singapore mutinied. Since the full story of the mutiny has yet to
be told, the reasons the Fifth Light Infantry, a Muslim regiment

consisting of Pathans, who did not participate in the uprising, and Rajputs, mutinied are not clear. Whether it was because of poor morale and lax discipline, resentment over promotions, propaganda emanating from German sources, their fear that they were going to be soon sent to Europe to fight their fellow Muslims the Turks, or for some other reason does not affect this discussion, however, since our main concern is the effect the mutiny had on European attitudes to Asians.[90]

The mutiny began in the afternoon of the second day of Chinese New Year celebrations, when Europeans were enjoying a quiet holiday. After seizing some ammunition and killing two British officers, the mutineers left their quarters at Alexandra Barracks. One large group of soldiers made their way to the Tanglin district and there released the Germans who were being kept as prisoners of war (though in considerable comfort) at the Teutonia Club. During the afternoon other groups from the Fifth roamed about, killing several Europeans attached to the military, European civilians who lived in or happened to be travelling through the area, and a few Asians. Though they had been caught completely by surprise, British officers fairly quickly gathered together a force consisting of Malay States Volunteers, members of the Singapore Volunteer Rifles and the Johore Military Forces, a landing party from H.M.S. *Cadmus*, and the small detachment of the Royal Garrison Artillery stationed at Singapore. Meanwhile, European men hurried about the residential areas collecting their women and children and sending them to hotels in the centre of the city; on the following day most of the women and children were evacuated to ships in the harbour. By the afternoon of 16 February most of the mutineers had been captured or had been killed in skirmishes. In the next few days the forces listed above and landing parties from French and Japanese cruisers which had recently left Singapore but had been called back at the outbreak of the mutiny rounded up most of the remaining men from the Fifth. The mutineers killed a total of forty-four people. Of these five were Asian civilians, three were Malays in the Johore Military Forces, one was a German prisoner of war, and the remaining thirty-five were European civilians, soldiers, and volunteers. As a result of a court martial thirty-seven mutineers were sentenced to death and shot outside the Outram Road Gaol. These were the first public executions since the 1890s.

Not until the Japanese invasion late in 1941 were the lives of Europeans again endangered as they were during the mutiny. But for Europeans the most surprising aspect of the mutiny was not the scale of the killing but that it had been so limited. 'We half feared a rising of all natives, Chinese too,' wrote one woman of the night spent at the Hotel de l'Europe. 'The Chinese boys were to be found that evening and next, many in corners, talking and looking at us, and of course one's imagination gets vivid at such a time and pictures plots and horrors.'[91] On hearing that the mutineers had been rounded up, Europeans living on estates north of Singapore 'breathed a sigh of relief and thankfulness for our escape from dangers untold,—for had the mutiny succeeded, there would have been little chance for us—a few Europeans scattered and far apart, with no means of communication or escape'.[92] The general uprising of all Asians which some Europeans feared did not take place, nor was there even the slightest sign that it would. During the mutiny the Chinese of Singapore continued with their New Year festivities. Even more surprisingly to Europeans, when they returned to their bungalows they found that their Hailam servants not only had not taken advantage of their absence to run off with the silver and other valuables but were ready to serve the next meal. This was a demonstration of 'loyalty' which the British were long to remember.[93] Although one source states that the mutineers were shot in public 'in order to convince the native population that death was the penalty of mutiny',[94] as if all Asians were assumed to have secretly sympathized with the crime, to many Europeans the lesson of the mutiny was that the Asians were not after all one huge mass who were together preparing for the moment when they could eliminate the European community. In keeping with this lesson the Straits Times cautioned its readers against condemning all Indians or even a section of the Indian community because of the deeds of a few Rajput soldiers.[95]

During the war years the British were assured in other ways than by the knowledge that the mutiny could have been worse. In their annual reports the Residents referred to expressions of loyalty from the Malay Rulers, which the British valued all the more since a Muslim nation, the Turks, were allied with the Germans, and to public gatherings, such as one in Kuala Lumpur, attended by all communities, 'each of whom signified after its own fashion its determination to continue the prosecution of the war until victory rested with the British Empire'.[96] Some of the wealthiest Chinese in the F.M.S. donated large sums of money for the war cause; Eu Tong Sen, for example, provided funds for a tank and an airplane. In Singapore there were two especially strong demonstrations of allegiance to the Empire. In March 1915, when rumours were circulating that the mutiny was part of a larger uprising planned by the Muslim community, a gathering of about 3,000 Arabs, Malays, Javanese, and Indian Muslims sent a telegram to the King 'expressing the absolute loyalty of all Mahomedans in the Colony'.[97] And in September of the same year Straits Chinese leaders, including those who had fought the colour bar most strongly, held a great meeting at which they made patriotic speeches and encouraged members of their community to register for local voluntary service and to contribute more money to the war effort.[98] Despite his vow never to serve a repressive British government Dr. Lim Boon Keng accepted a seat on the Legislative Council. But there were signs that Asian leaders had by no means forgotten the issues which separated them and Europeans. Indeed, the support which Asians showed for the British in their time of need made existing inequities seem all the more unjust. Lim had this in mind when in October 1917 he appealed to the government to restore the Queen's Scholarships and to give Asians greater representation on the Legislative Council. If the British were fighting to free the peoples of Europe from German domination, he argued, then 'surely the sons of the Empire, men brought up under the flag and trained in the great ideals and aspirations of Englishmen, have the right to expect that under the flag they will have liberty' and that they will not be denied 'the rights and privileges of free men'.[99] As will be shown in Chapter 7, in the inter-war years the British were again to be faced with pressures arising from Asian aspirations.

6

European Society in the Inter-war Years

T HE first two decades of the twentieth century saw the growing prominence of unofficials both in numbers and in wealth. Their wealth, and indirectly that of all Europeans in the Federated Malay States, of course depended on the prosperity of the export economy. Twice during the inter-war years—in the early 1920s and for a longer period in the 1930s— there were serious slumps. The unstable and generally less prosperous conditions of the inter-war years had effects on European society which were as important, though of a different nature, as those produced by the rubber boom which began in about 1906. It is therefore appropriate to begin this chapter, which deals with several aspects of European society between the wars, with a description of these effects.

Economic Conditions and European Society

The Salaries Commission's report of 1919 was issued after a period of fairly steady economic growth and at a time when prospects for future growth seemed very bright. Both officials and unofficials who presented evidence to the commission confidently predicted that Malaya would continue to enjoy uninterrupted economic prosperity.[1] Because of this prediction it was clear to Bucknill that unless substantial increases were granted the salaries of civil servants would continue to lag behind those of unofficials. Moreover, as was mentioned, it was largely because he believed that the F.M.S. and Straits governments would have the revenue to pay officials higher salaries that in December 1919 the Secretary of State for Colonies accepted Bucknill's recommendations. Within a short time of the Colonial Office's acceptance of the Bucknill scheme, however, the balance which it had achieved between officials and unofficials was upset by the onset of a slump. Since their prosperity was so directly tied to fluctuations in the price of rubber it was the planters, by far the largest group of unofficials, who were most severely affected.

Just after the First World War rubber companies had been very optimistic over the industry's future since there were signs of a boom developing in the United States and Western Europe. As a result companies expanded acreage, re-hired managers and assistants who had returned from war service, and recruited many new planters. In the early part of 1920, however, the western economies entered a period of depression and as a consequence the demand for rubber fell off sharply. Because rubber companies had enlarged their staffs so rapidly immediately after the war the employment of a particularly large number of planters was vulnerable when rubber prices fell in the latter part of 1920.[2] Within a short time companies began dismissing large numbers of European employees. Planters took the initiative in forming their own committee to help unemployed planters and their families, but the editor of the *Planter*, the journal of the Incorporated Society of Planters (I.S.P.), which had been formed by planters in 1919 to promote planting as a profession and to represent the views of planters to the boards of directors in London (but not to act as a trade union), insisted that the government would have to step in to take the bold action required. Not only must the welfare of the planters be considered, wrote the editor, 'but the present state of things tends more than anything else conceivable to destroy European credit and prestige in a native country'.[3]

Early in 1921 the government, which shared the I.S.P.'s view of the harm which would be done to British prestige by the spectacle of unemployed Europeans, formed a European Unemployment Fund and provided a large portion of its funds. By October 1921 the committee had found employment for 163 men, assisted 254 people with grants, and provided 121 men and 56 women and children with passages to England or Australia.[4] 'It was quite impossible', William Peel, the then Controller of Labour who served as chairman of the committee, wrote some years later, 'to retain a number of unemployed white men in the country in the midst of a native population.'[5] In removing unemployed Europeans from Malaya the government had in most cases the co-operation of the men themselves. To be out of work was degrading enough, but, as one planter put it, 'it is a thousand times worse for a white man in a tropical country' to be out of work.[6] Recalling the position of superiority relative to Asians which he had confidently held until the slump and knowing that his fellow Europeans looked upon him as at best an embarrassment, the unemployed European could not help but feel deep personal humiliation in his plight.

A few unemployed planters, however, refused the committee's offer of free passages and instead drifted to Singapore to wait for better times. Since white men were expected not to do work usually done by Asians it was nearly impossible for them to find employment to support themselves while they waited. One visitor wrote that Singapore was 'full of these tragic sights'. He added that they were 'for the most part fine fellows',[7] but in many cases they were not treated as such. A unique glimpse of what it was like to be a 'poor white' in Singapore at this time was provided by Harry Foster, an American who earned his living by writing books on his experiences as a beachcomber in various parts of the world. When Foster approached the Raffles Hotel in his rumpled, dirty clothes a Sikh doorman blocked his way and asked him whom he wanted to see. While Foster waited for the doorman to return, 'a lady on the veranda surveyed me amusedly with her lorgnette. Another lady giggled. A young man stepped to the veranda rail to obtain a better view of me, and said "Ha!" ... as though I were not quite deserving of a complete, "Ha! Ha!".' After working for a short time as a pianist in a wild Chinese-owned saloon Foster was told by a British police officer to leave the city. Two unemployed Englishmen succeeded in earning some money by opening a bootblack stand, but, according to Foster, British officials closed the stand and told the two men 'that shoes were not being shined by white men in the Orient'.[8] When necessary the government used the vagrancy law to deport an indigent European who refused to leave.[9]

By about the middle of 1921 the spirit of unity between officials and unofficials in Malaya which had been so marked at the time of the Bucknill inquiry in 1919 was showing signs of strain. While the salaries of unofficials dropped, civil servants had been granted substantial allowances (20 per cent of an official's basic salary in the case of single men and an additional 20 per cent for married men) to help them keep up with the rising cost of living. In the Straits Legislative Council W. F. Nutt, who as a member of the Federal Council in 1917 had spoken out strongly in favour of higher salaries for civil servants, proposed that these allowances should be reduced; the allowances, he said, had compensated not so much for the high cost of living as for the 'cost of high living'. The government did reduce the temporary allowances by one-fourth, but this was not as much as Nutt had hoped. In replying to Nutt the Governor, Sir Laurence Guillemard, insisted that since government servants did not profit from booms their salaries should not be reduced when there was a depression in trade.[10] It was probably at this time that unofficials began to refer more often to the M.C.S. somewhat pejoratively as the 'Heaven born' (the term long used for the Indian Civil Service), not only because of their superior education and their importance as the governing élite, but also because they now appeared aloof from the financial worries which plagued other Europeans. Despite their salary increases and allowances civil servants were not however entirely satisfied with their conditions of service. With Guillemard's support the Malayan Civil Service Committee (the successor to the F.M.S. and Straits Settlements Civil Service Committees) complained to the Colonial Office in December 1920 about the inadequacy of their pensions. Aware that other branches of the colonial service resented the salary increases the M.C.S. had received as a result of the Bucknill Commission the Secretary of State for Colonies refused to consider the matter.[11]

After reaching a low of 6¾d. per pound in 1922 the price of rubber began to rise until it reached 4s. 8d. in 1925. Conditions for planters improved greatly, but even in the relatively prosperous period in the mid-1920s it would appear that government servants (those in the police and professional departments as well as the M.C.S.) were somewhat better paid than were planters. In the M.C.S. a cadet earned about $325 per month, an officer of Class III (with thirteen to seventeen years of service) earned between $730 and $850, and one of Class I earned between $1,050 and $1,350. On an estate in Perak the six assistants earned between $250 and $475 per month, the senior assistant received $575, and the manager received $1,000.[12] It should be added that whereas the majority of planters in the F.M.S. were assistants and probably had salaries of $500 or less, more than two-thirds of the M.C.S. (those of Class IV and above) received salaries of $570 or more, excluding allowances. Slightly more than a third of civil servants received basic salaries of $800 per month or more and thus enjoyed a standard of living at least as comfortable as that described in detail in Table 8, which compares the officially defined standards for Europeans and Asians in government service. While confirming that planters were in gen-

eral less well paid than government servants, the editor of the
Malay Mail wrote that Europeans in commerce, the banks, and
the law were 'on the average slightly better paid perhaps than
their contemporaries in the public service'.[13] Clearly salaries varied from one section of the European community to another, but
it needs to be kept in mind that very few Europeans earned less
than $250 per month, a salary which permitted a considerably
higher standard of living than the 'Asiatic Standard' outlined in
Table 8. According to an estimate approved by the council of the
I.S.P. in August 1928, the monthly cost of living of a junior
assistant planter in his first year of service was $247, of which
$100 was for food and household necessities, $49 for servants,
$44 for drinks, tobacco, and club expenses, and $20 for clothes,
and of which nothing was spent on rent since housing was provided by the company.[14]

TABLE 8
Monthly Family Budgets in 1930: European
and Asiatic Standards

| Item | European Standard | | Asiatic Standard | |
	Details (only some items)	$ p.m.	Details	$ p.m.
1. Food	Market and cold storage—130	167.00		72.90
2. Drinks and Tobacco	4 bottles whisky, 2 gin, etc.— 36.03; 12 tins cigarettes	47.63		3.60
3. Servants' Wages	Boy—30, cook—30, *tukang air*—20, *kebun*—20, *amah*—35, *syce*—35, *dhobi*—12	182.00	1 servant— 10, *dhobi*, barber, etc.	20.00
4. Light and Water		30.00		6.55
5. Transport	Petrol for 25 miles/day— 25.16	53.47	By bus	11.04
6. Depreciation of car		42.50		—

TABLE 8 (continued)

Item	European Standard Details (only some items)	$ p.m.	Asiatic Standard Details	$ p.m.
7. Education	School for child in Singapore—13; child at prep. school in U.K.: tuition—120; doctor, travel, clothes, etc.—57	190.00		12.70
8. Clothes	(for three in Malaya)	80.00	*Baju, sa-rungs*, etc.	13.00
9. Clubs		61.00		—
10. Rent	(6% of salary)	48.00		30.00
11. Widows' & Orphans' Fund	(4% of salary)	32.00		—
12. Miscellaneous	Dentist, life insurance, holidays, books, etc.	26.40		6.21
Total	Salary of 800 p.m., + 10% temporary allowance, + 10% married allowance	960.00	Salary of 160 p.m., + 10% temporary allowance	176.00

Source: Compiled from data in *Report of the Commission on the Temporary Allowances* (Singapore, 1931).

Note: The European Standard is for an official aged forty with sixteen years' seniority, married with two children, one aged six at school in Singapore, the other aged eight at school in England. The Asiatic Standard is for a member of the General Clerical Service, aged thirty-two with thirteen years' seniority, married with three children, aged eight, six, and three. The *Report* also has data for the 'Eurasian Standard', which differs in small details from the Asiatic Standard but is based on the same monthly salary of $160.

The outstanding feature of a planting career in the inter-war years was its insecurity. By the end of the 1920s the position of planters was again threatened when, as a result of the Wall Street Crash and the depression which followed, the demand for rubber in the United States nearly disappeared. As the price of rubber fell, to less than 2d. per pound in 1932, rubber companies drastically reduced their European staff. It has been reliably estimated that between 1930 and 1933, 30 to 40 per cent of the planting community were retrenched.[15] A large percentage of Europeans in the tin industry were also dismissed, but the total number was much smaller since the tin industry employed far fewer Europeans than the rubber industry did. As in the earlier slump there was an immediate concern about possible damage to white prestige as well as about the welfare of the unemployed. In a letter to the principal employers' association Major Stevens, chairman of the I.S.P., explained that 'this country is expensive to live in, if you are out of work, and when men drift to the cheaper native hotels . . . they lose prestige with the natives'.[16] In October 1930 the government established the European Unemployment Fund, from which the unemployed were given temporary maintenance grants or sea passages from Malaya; about one-third of the Fund's money came from the government while the remainder came from the Ex-Services Association, the I.S.P., and other private sources.[17] In the latter part of 1930 the government formed a special company of the Malay States Volunteer Rifles at Port Dickson to provide temporary employment for Europeans, but when it became clear that economic conditions would not soon improve the company was disbanded.

Most of the planters who remained on the estates willingly had their salaries cut by up to one-third in preference to returning to Britain to face unemployment.[18] As the depression dragged on into 1932 and especially when the rubber industry first showed signs of recovery in 1933, however, planters began to press the employers to restore their salaries to what they had been in 1929. More than anything else planters feared that unless salaries were restored a planting career would no longer attract men 'of the right type', by which they meant men having social backgrounds similar to their own. This would undermine the efficiency of estates, damage the prestige of the planting profession, and deprive the government of the able co-operation it had come to expect from planters in carrying out Britain's mission to the peoples of Malaya.[19] In addition to making these points a statement prepared by the I.S.P. stressed that planters, like all Europeans, had to live in a more expensive style than they would in Britain, whether they wished to do so or not. In words similar to those used by Bucknill in 1919, the I.S.P. appealed to the employers to remember that in Malaya 'a man must, to some degree, conform to a standard . . . which is set for him by other people if he is not to diminish the status of the European in the eyes of the native peoples, and suffer ostracism'.[20] The 'other people' who now set the standard were officials and Europeans in commerce and banking. Finally, in 1936, when planters' salaries had in some but far from all cases improved, one writer expressed his fear of what might happen if a poorly paid planter was unable to meet his social obligations:

The European community in outstations being small, each unit should do his social bit; even if he feels that seeing the same faces, hearing the same voices week in and week out does not compensate him for the expense involved, he should face up to it. It will not do him any good to be thought 'eccentric', or a snob, and if he clings to a hermit existence he may very easily be written off as both.[21]

Although salaries fell to such an extent as to arouse these deep fears among planters it is clear that in general the European standard of living continued to be upheld in the early and mid-1930s. There were two main reasons for this. First, the effect of salary cuts was partially offset by a drop in the cost of living. Official statistics show that between 1930 and 1933 the cost of living for Europeans fell by 18 per cent. The cost of food fell by 29 per cent during this period, and the expense of maintaining a staff of servants fell by nearly as much.[22] The European standard of living was also supported by the selective way in which companies retrenched their staff. Senior managers were retired while large numbers of young assistants were dismissed. A very high proportion of those who remained were experienced men who were too old to hope to find another job but too young to consider retiring.[23] Their salaries were reduced to a level which was far below what was thought proper for men of their position but not necessarily below the generally recognized minimum standard for a European. It is notable that a scholar who resided in Malaya in the worst days of the depression was able to write that the 'distinguishing feature of the situation in Malaya . . . is not that there are some Europeans who are living luxuriously, but that, broadly speaking, there are none who do not live in that fashion'.[24] In the late 1930s there were warnings in the magazine *British Malaya* that a class of 'poor Europeans' might someday develop in Malaya as a result of employers (not only rubber companies) being tempted to ignore European salary standards,[25] but this is not something which took place to any noticeable extent before the outbreak of the Pacific War.

As in the early 1920s, the depression of the 1930s caused unofficials to envy the security enjoyed by government servants. As an economy measure the government took away the temporary allowances which its employees had received since 1919 and retrenched a small number of officials, but government servants were not affected nearly as harshly by the depression as were planters and other unofficials. Nevertheless, on several occasions they appealed to the Governor to restore their allowances. In a memorial presented in December 1931 the Malayan Civil Service Association claimed that in the case of junior government officers who were married and had children the cut in allowances had brought 'their salaries below the level considered necessary for Europeans in the tropics'.[26] In 1937, when economic conditions were clearly improving, the Colonial Office appointed the Chief Justice of Hong Kong to head a commission to recommend whether the temporary allowances should be restored. Although unofficials were pleased that the commission concluded that the allowances should not be restored, they regarded its recommendation, which was approved by the Colonial Office, that married officials be given special allowances to help meet the expense of educating their children in England as further proof of the more favourable position of the government servants.[27] About three years later, however, it was the turn of planters to enjoy a fleeting moment of prosperity. After the outbreak of war in Europe there was a boom of sorts as the American government bought massive quantities of rubber in order to increase stocks in the United States. Those planters who received bonuses based on production did extremely well at this time and so were able to spend more on drinks at the club and on other luxuries than government servants could. 'When the slump was on,' complained one government engineer in 1941, 'the planters were for ever grumbling at the security of the Government officer. Now there's a boom, and we're small fry.'[28]

Men and Women

When in the 1920s Europeans who had lived in Malaya since the turn of the century reflected on the changes that they had observed in European society, they pointed to the influx of European women after the war as the most remarkable change.[29] In Britain there had been a very high marriage rate during the war years, and it appears that an unusually high proportion of men arriving in Malaya for the first time immediately after the war were married. Among government servants the Bucknill salary scheme had the desired effect of making it easier for men to marry. Equally important, living conditions were now considered much more suitable, though still far from ideal, for European women than they had been previously. By about 1920 the threat of malaria had been greatly reduced. In the smaller towns Europeans had clubs, cold storage, and other amenities which earlier had only been found in the main towns. Nearly all districts, observed the superintendent of the 1921 census, now had 'everything that makes life endurable for a white woman in the tropics'.[30] At the same time the automobile greatly reduced the time and difficulty men and women in rural areas had in reaching the social attractions of the large towns. Planters, wrote Richard Curle after his visit to the F.M.S. early in 1921, 'have come to regard motor cars as the one necessity of their social existence. At dusk the roads resound to their hoots as they carry them to the nearest town. . . .'[31]

Table 9 shows both the rising proportion of European men in the F.M.S. who were married and, with the help of British census data, allows us to see how near this proportion came to that in Britain. Between the 1911 and 1921 censuses the percentage of men who were married increased from 33 to 47. Part of this

TABLE 9
Marital Status of European Men in the F.M.S.,
1911–1931
(*Percentage married in each age group*)

Age Group	1911	1921	1931
20–24	4	5	3
25–29	16	25	22
30–34	34	51	54
35–39	54	58	70
40–44	63	67	77
45–49	69	73	78
50–54	60*	76	76
55 and over	77*	61*	71
All men 20 and over	33	47	53

Sources: F.M.S. 1911 Census, Table 14; British Malaya 1921 Census, Table 18 (F.M.S.); British Malaya 1931 Census, Table 112.

Notes: The 1911 census used age categories 20–25, 25–30, and so forth. These have been taken as equivalent to the categories used in the 1921 and 1931 censuses (20–24, 25–29, etc.).

An asterisk (*) is used where the total number of men in the age group is less than one hundred.

increase merely reflects the fact that the proportion of men over the age of thirty (the age by which men of middle-class background might be expected to have married) was somewhat larger in 1921 than in 1911. Thus it is necessary to look within the age groups to find out how much change took place between the two censuses. There was some increase in the percentage among men in the 25–29 age group, but an even greater increase, from 34 to 51 per cent, in the 30–34 age group. It is worth comparing the figures for the seven main towns in the F.M.S. (Kuala Lumpur, Taiping, Ipoh, Seremban, Klang, Kampar, and Telok Anson) and for the remainder of the F.M.S. to confirm the important part improved living conditions in the rural areas played in encouraging marriage. Between the two censuses the percentage of men in the 30–34 age group living in the towns who were married rose from 46 to 59, but the percentage for men living outside these towns rose much more sharply, from 26 to 50.[32]

Between the 1921 and 1931 censuses the increase was less dramatic than it had been during the previous ten-year period. The overall percentage of men who were married rose from 47 to 53. The slight drop in the proportion in the 25–29 age group was probably due to the onset of the slump. There was a small increase among the 30–34 age group and a much greater increase, from 58 to 70 per cent, in the 35–39 age group.

Although the percentage of European men in the F.M.S. who were married rose markedly between 1911 and 1931 it is equally striking that the percentages for 1931 were considerably lower than those for men of the same age in Britain in the same year. In the F.M.S. 22 per cent of European men in the 25–29 age group were married, as compared to 52 per cent of men in the same age group in England and Wales. In the next two age groups the differences were not as large but were nevertheless substantial: in the 30–34 age group 54 per cent of European men in the F.M.S. were married, as compared to 77 per cent in England and Wales; in the 35–39 age group the percentages for the F.M.S. and for England and Wales were 70 and 85 respectively. In the 40–44 age group the difference was somewhat smaller: 77 for men in the F.M.S. as compared to 86 for men in England and Wales.[33]

The fact that in all age groups the proportion of men in the F.M.S. who were married was smaller than that for men in England and Wales but that the difference between these proportions diminished in each successive age group suggests that the pattern of marriage among Europeans in the F.M.S. differed in

two ways from that in Britain. First, the proportion of men in the
F.M.S. who never married was larger than it was for men in Britain. Despite the improvement in living conditions some men
continued to insist that because of its tropical climate Malaya was
no place for European women and children and that it was therefore irresponsible to marry.[34] Some men preferred living permanently with Asian mistresses to marriage to European women,
but as will be shown in Chapter 8 the number of these men was
quite small by the 1920s. It is also possible that a career in an
overseas territory attracted an unusually high proportion of men
who wished to avoid marriage.[35] Second, the statistics show that
those men who did marry tended to do so at a later age than was
usual in Britain, if only because the majority of Europeans in the
F.M.S. came from middle-class families they could be expected
to marry later than was typical for the population of Britain as a
whole. But there were two other reasons, both peculiar to the
European community of Malaya, which were at least as important
in delaying marriage: the attitude of the employers toward marriage and the difficulty men had in finding wives.

Most men were discouraged or actually prevented by their
employers from marrying until they had worked in Malaya for
several years. Marriage was expensive for both the individual and
his employer. A married man had to meet the extra costs of
leaves and holidays, education of children in Britain, and, for
much of his married life, a home in Britain for his wife. Since so
few European women worked, these expenses had to be borne
entirely by the husband. His employer had to provide him with
or subsidize a larger house and (in the case of government servants and some others) pay a great deal more on sea passages.
Moreover, although the government and private employers saw
the advantages of marriage, they were not prepared to pay their
employees salaries which would allow both marriage and adherence to the European standard of living before they were well
established in their careers. In the employers' view a man who
married early in his career would inevitably find himself in deep
financial difficulties, with the result that the quality of his work
would suffer. Because of the need to maintain the European
standard a young married couple was potentially an embarrassment to the community as a whole as well as to the man's employers.

The large British banks had the strictest rules regarding marriage. In addition to their main contract, European employees of
the Chartered Bank were required to sign a separate agreement

stating that they would ask for permission to marry and that they understood that this permission would not be granted until they had been in Malaya for eight years. This was in addition to the period most assistants had already spent at the bank's London headquarters before going to Malaya. When, very occasionally, it was discovered that a bank employee had married without seeking permission he was immediately dismissed. European employees of the large agency houses also signed agreements not to marry without the firm's consent, which would usually be given after the first five-year tour of duty. They too were likely to be dismissed if the agreement was broken, but one informant recalled a case in which the rule was relaxed; this was when an employee who announced that his fiancee was on her way to Malaya and who had not asked permission to marry was able to show that his income from private sources was twice his salary from the agency house.[36]

Planters, except of course the few proprietary planters, also required permission before marrying. One retired planter has written that a planter would be able to marry 'after approval by his manager and also after the manager had the approval of his Agent in the Estate's department of an Agency House, who in turn had written to the Board of the Company'.[37] Although the two were of course closely related, it appears that the age at which a planter could expect to marry depended more on his position and salary than on how many years he had worked for the company. According to testimony given before the Bucknill Commission a planter who proved himself capable in his work would be able to marry after eight years in Malaya, by which time he would have become a senior assistant or manager.[38] In 1933 one planter proposed as ideal a salary scheme which would allow men who had begun work at the age of twenty-three to marry at the age of thirty-one or thirty-two, when they would be receiving a salary twice that at which they had started.[39]

Perhaps no rubber company demanded more of its European employees than did the Belgian-French firm Socfin. In his novel about the company, which he re-names 'Sophia', Pierre Boulle has described how marriage was discouraged by a clause in the contract whereby marriage 'was made to appear in the light of a special reward to those members who had given proof of their loyalty over a number of years'. Marriage added greatly to the company's expenses as it had to provide the couple with a more comfortable bungalow than a bachelor would be given and to cover the cost of the whole family going on leave. According to

Boulle the company was even more concerned that marriage would undermine a planter's total devotion to Socfin. At the same time, it saw an advantage in that upon marriage the employee became much more dependent on the company for financial security, so that the managing director could continue to demand an employee's undivided attention to the needs of the company at any hour of the day, seven days a week, despite objections from his wife.[40]

Unlike most other Europeans, government servants had no formal regulations preventing them from marrying before they reached a certain position or had given a certain number of years of service. The Police Department effectively discouraged marriage however by only recruiting unmarried men as inspectors and by requiring candidates for the commissioned grades to be unmarried.[41] In the M.C.S. early marriage was actively discouraged. Bucknill had designed a salary scheme which allowed civil servants to marry at the age of thirty but not before then. The Governor, Sir Laurence Guillemard, was however alarmed to find that a few civil servants were marrying before that age. In 1923 he proposed to the Colonial Office that cadets should be unmarried when first appointed and that those who married during their first tour of duty (four years) should not receive the extra allowance which was then being given to married officials. According to Guillemard, if officials were allowed to marry at the beginning of their careers they would not be able to spend long periods in rural areas getting to know the people there. If a cadet had to leave his wife to go on tour, worry about her welfare would make 'each night spent on a boat or in a Malay house a penance'. Young married officials would have to be stationed in the larger towns, where they would be burdened with higher expenses, and the government would have few men available for duty in the more remote areas. Although the Colonial Office sympathized with Guillemard's arguments no formal regulation restricting marriage was ever made.[42] An 'unwritten law' however was nearly as effective. Men were discouraged from marrying before completing their first four-year tour of duty, and most men married after their second tour. 'A Head of Department's consent was not obligatory but was always sought.'[43]

Though probably not as important as the formal and informal regulations regarding marriage, a second major reason for the later age at which European men in the F.M.S. married was simply the difficulty they had in finding wives even when they could expect to receive permission. In Malaya the opportunities for

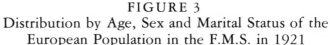

FIGURE 3

Distribution by Age, Sex and Marital Status of the
European Population in the F.M.S. in 1921

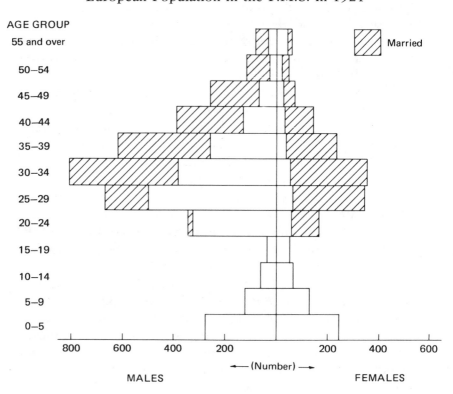

Source: British Malaya 1921 Census, Table 18 (F.M.S.).

meeting eligible women were extremely limited. In marked contrast to Britain, where unmarried women outnumbered bachelors
(especially after the First World War), in the European community of Malaya the number of bachelors was several times greater
than the number of single European women, as Figure 3 illustrates so clearly. It would appear that the alternative some 'poor'
men had chosen in the 1890s and in the early part of the twentieth century of marrying Eurasian or Asian women had become
unacceptable: a representative of the police inspectors had
insisted to the Bucknill Commission that their salaries should be
high enough to enable them to marry European women.[44] The
competition for the small number of unmarried European
women was therefore intense.

These women can be divided into two groups. First, there
were a few single women working in Malaya as teachers, nurses,

and doctors. So many nurses became engaged and then resigned from the Medical Department after a short period in Malaya that one high official complained that the government was running a marriage bureau rather than a medical service.[45] Second, there were the daughters of senior government officials and business-men or sometimes other female relatives of men working in Malaya. Many of them had been born in Malaya and returned there after their education in Britain. They were assured of a constant round of social activities. One man described them as being 'almost blatantly on the marriage market',[46] but it is clear that the number of prospective buyers was indeed great.

Because of the shortage of eligible women in Malaya the majority of men who hoped to marry waited until they were on leave in Britain to look for wives. Sometimes men became engaged to women they had known before going to Malaya, but probably more often to women they had met for the first time while on leave. In either case, marriage was often postponed until the man had returned to Malaya and advanced in his career. In the meantime, of course, his fiancee might decide to marry someone closer home.[47] Even after a woman had boarded the ship to join her husband-to-be in Malaya the danger of losing her was not over. As in Malaya, on board ship women were greatly outnumbered by men and enjoyed a very busy social life. It was therefore not unusual for a man to greet his fiancee after a year or two of separation only to learn that she had been swept off her feet by someone she had met on the ship and had promised to marry him.[48]

As the foregoing discussion has already suggested, the position of women in the European community of Malaya differed mark-edly from that of women in Britain. Some of these differences are described in the remainder of this section.

As in the period before the First World War, married women as well as potential wives were treated with much greater respect and courtesy than they were in Britain. 'In my opinion,' wrote Mrs. Wilson, 'the men of the East are the most charming speci-mens of their sex to be found anywhere.'[49] That the 'plainest woman is a goddess' was the somewhat differing opinion of a journalist who frowned on the way his fellow men showered women with compliments and jumped to their feet when a woman showed the slightest sign of rising.[50] At dances women had no shortage of partners, for if their husbands were not interested in dancing there were many other men who were. The principal reason for the social prominence of women was that they continued to be in the minority. Even at the time of the 1931 census women were outnumbered by men by two to one, as compared to three to one in 1911.[51] There were of course many other women in Malaya besides European women, but European women were the only ones with whom men could associate in public. How European women preserved their social monopoly will be discussed in Chapter 8.

While having greater social prominence women in Malaya had less economic importance than did women in British society. During the war women of all social classes in Britain entered occupations which had previously been filled solely by men. Employment gave women greater opportunities for personal fulfilment and greater economic independence from fathers and husbands.[52] In the inter-war years more European women in Malaya were employed than had been the case before the war but to nowhere near the same extent as women in Britain were. A few women came to Malaya specifically to work as nurses, doctors, or teachers or to serve as missionaries, but the great majority came as wives—of men whose salaries were high enough that they would not need to work. Very few women who had begun or planned careers in Britain were able to pursue these once they came to Malaya. For some of these women the transition to life in Malaya could be extremely difficult. To marry a professional or business woman and bring her to the tropics 'is rather like caging a lioness in the Zoo', warned a writer in the *Times of Malaya*: 'she will live and eat and sleep, and may even reproduce her species, but, given the chance, she will turn round and rend her keeper and destroy him if she can.'[53]

As well as having fewer opportunities for employment European women in Malaya had fewer domestic chores than middle-class women in Britain. Whereas in post-1918 Britain a middle-class family considered themselves fortunate to have one servant, European families in Malaya employed between three and six servants. In 1928 Gibson claimed that five servants—a houseboy, *tukang air* (water carrier), cook, *syce* (chauffeur), and an *ayah* (Indian or Malay nurse) or *amah* (Chinese nurse)—were 'all essential' for a European family.[54] In 1931 the Commission on Temporary Allowances assumed that a married official would have a *kebun* (gardener), as well as those servants listed by Gibson. (See Table 8.) Both Gibson and the Commission added that a *dhobi* had to be contracted to do the family's washing.

Although Europeans believed that they needed more servants than they would in Britain because the heat made household duties irksome and because many homes still lacked plumbing, the number of servants a family employed was dictated as much by custom as by convenience. When the cost of living was rising in the late 1920s the *Malay Mail* observed that all Europeans were required 'by a species of social coercion' to conform to a certain standard of living and therefore could not reduce the number of servants they employed or economize in other ways.[55]

During the slump of the early 1930s many European families did reduce the number of servants they employed,[56] but this appears to have been temporary. In Singapore it was reported that some European women were venturing into the markets for the first time in the hope of saving money.[57] In Kuala Lumpur in the mid-1930s at least it was both unusual and somewhat improper for women to go to the main market, as Mrs. Wilson explained after visiting her daughter: 'A few hardy *Mems*, on economy bent, penetrate these odorous precincts daily. Madge was induced to go once, when she first lived in town—but once only. She fled, before she publicly disgraced herself.'[58] The fact that a servant was able to buy food more cheaply than a European woman could (even after he had given himself a small commission) also encouraged women to stay away from the market. Within the household, husbands often discouraged, though not usually successfully, their wives from taking the management of the servants too seriously in the hope of avoiding friction. Tension was particularly likely if the servants had worked for a man before he married and had enjoyed nearly complete freedom in running the house.[59]

Although they had numerous servants most European women deeply resented any implication that they therefore had little to do but idle away the hours playing bridge, dancing, and gossiping. The organization of a large staff of servants could in fact be a task in itself. During one year, 1920, Mrs. Evans hired three *ayahs*, three cooks, two new 'boys', and a gardener; at any one time there were six or seven servants in the house. In her household account book she kept a careful record of what the cook had spent at the market each day and any advances in wages she had given to servants, as well as what she had herself spent in various stores in Kuala Lumpur.[60] Many women insisted that Asian servants were lazy, inefficient, and sometimes unclean and so required a great deal of supervision. One woman, for example, made this contrast:

The housekeeping at Home is easy; one orders goods and they are sent; it is not necessary to choose and haggle. Here housekeeping is complicated; everything has to be kept locked up and given out in small quantities. . . . People (who do not know!) say the amah does everything. On the contrary; most mothers make all their children's food and this means time. The amahs do the work, but they do not fill the place of an English nurse whom one trusts.[61]

There were cases reported of mothers who preferred to raise their children without any help from an *amah* but these appear to have been extremely rare. Most European children spent a large part of each day in the care of *amahs* and a few were almost completely in their charge. It may be noted that in the case of very young children many *amahs* preferred not to share their duties with the mother since they had their own set ideas on how to raise and control babies. Parents tried to prevent *amahs* from giving their children small doses of opium to placate them during teething and at other times,[62] but otherwise they were able to care for the children in their own way.

While many women felt compelled by criticism from men or visitors to refute the idea that they had little to do in the home, there were others who did admit that their household tasks were slight. Some of these women were clearly trying to find an acceptable way of defining their purpose of being in Malaya. Mrs. Bruce, for example, advised the wives of planters to have more sympathy for the troubles of their husbands in their work and to do all they could to make their lives more pleasant.[63] Similarly, another woman stressed how wives were able to relieve their husbands of the strains which arose from working in a hot climate and among other races and added that far more than in Britain a woman's personality played a large part in her husband's chances for promotion.[64] In addition to their role as wives, an increasing number of women were by the 1930s spending time outside the home in voluntary work such as the Girl Guides. There were also a few women who, though denied opportunities for employment themselves, took an active interest in their husbands' work and in the Asian world about them.[65]

Perhaps the most notable characteristic of married life for Europeans in Malaya was the periods of separation between parents and children and husbands and wives. Although separation was common throughout the period covered by this study, and so has been mentioned earlier, it can be treated more fully in this chapter because in the inter-war years the British were less bound by social convention in writing about some of the personal matters which were involved.

Most Europeans continued to believe that the tropical climate prevented children from developing as they would in Britain. Children were said to thrive up to the age of five or six, but after that age it was claimed that they became 'weedy' and showed signs of mental lethargy. European children were compared to a temperate-climate plant which is at first stimulated by the atmosphere of a hothouse but then begins to wilt. It was also believed that because of the climate girls reached sexual maturity earlier than they would if raised in Britain. In 1928 Dr. G. A. C. Gordon of Singapore boldly argued that European children could remain in the tropics until the age of nine without any damage to their physical health if certain precautions were taken.[66] Although these precautions were seen as useful, most parents did not agree that their children could remain in Malaya until such an advanced age. They had other reasons which were at least as important as the climate for sending their children home to Europe.

Europeans believed that their children's education and moral development would also suffer as a result of prolonged residence in Malaya. Because they were cared for by Asian servants children often grew up learning very little English. Moreover, many Britishers did not want their children to attend local schools where they would have to associate with Asian children and possibly be surpassed by them in schoolwork (thus damaging British prestige) and where, it was believed, they would not receive an education of the same type and quality as the one they would receive in Britain. Equally important, children were believed to be in danger of becoming generally 'precocious' if they remained in Malaya. They were likely to become very demanding, undisciplined, and unable to do anything for themselves since at an early age they learned to take advantage of servants. Though the typical *amah* was 'generally satisfactory with infants', the *Malay Mail* claimed, she 'has no sort of control over an older child and alternates useless threats with equally useless bribes which Master John and Miss Jane view with contemptuous superiority'.[67] At the same time children had few other European playmates who might have been able to put them in their place. There was the further danger that they would learn from the servants more about sex than was felt proper for a young British child. One way to avoid these threats to a child's moral development was to employ a European governess. Very few families did this, however, partly because of the greater expense and partly because her standing relative both to other Europeans and to the Asian servants of a household was very awkward.[68] Most parents therefore believed that their children must be removed from Malaya by the age of five or six and given a regimented education. It was essential, as one woman put it, to have 'the corners . . . rubbed off'.[69] As Figure 3 shows, the number of children who remained in Malaya beyond the age of five or six was indeed very small. Most of those who remained beyond this age were the children of Europeans receiving relatively small salaries.

When a child reached the age at which he had to leave for England his mother had to decide whether to stay with him there or with her husband in Malaya. Some mothers believed that they should be near their children in order to guide them in their formative years, but since most children attended boarding schools their actual influence was often slight. Other women believed that their husbands needed their companionship or feared that unless they remained in Malaya their husbands would degenerate into their bachelor habits, which could consist of anything from wearing dirty clothes to turning to Asian women. Whether or not this happened, long periods of separation were likely to put a severe strain on relations between husband and wife. 'I believe Bruce is very difficult to live with,' wrote one woman of a man whose wife had recently returned to Malaya, 'especially after 7 years "bachelordom". I don't think it pays to leave them out East alone but it is a case of, "children or husbands", & many seem to choose their children.'[70] Probably in most cases the wife tried to compromise by accompanying her husband to Britain on leave but remaining there a few extra months after he had returned to his work in Malaya. When a man who was pursuing a career in Malaya married, both he and his wife foresaw that at least some periods of separation—'the tragedy of the East'—were inevitable. Even if a couple had no children, it was believed that since women were more affected by the climate than men the wife should spend less time in Malaya. Using census data it is possible to estimate that in 1921 about 30 per cent of the married men in the F.M.S. were temporarily separated from their wives. By 1931 the proportion had decreased somewhat to about 23 per cent.[71] The main reason for this decrease was certainly that during the slump fewer Europeans could meet the great costs involved in separation. But a small part of the decrease reflected the steps Europeans were beginning to take to reduce the time husbands and wives had to be separated. These steps will be described in the final section of this chapter.

Clubs and Social Structure
in Kuala Lumpur

In a community where men greatly outnumbered women and family life was made unstable by periods of separation social clubs occupied a position of great importance. 'Practically the only channel of social intercourse', noted a government handbook, 'is through membership of a club.'[72] After a day of work, dealing with people of different languages, cultures, outlook, and (from the British point of view) social standing, the club was the place where people who had something in common could relax with the help of a few drinks and dispense with the stricter conventions. Since club life was nearly synonymous with social life, men and women regularly went to the club even when they were not overly enthusiastic about the companionship; those who did not attend were in danger of being labelled eccentric, aloof, or anti-social.[73] As we have seen, it was partly because of the fear of being unable to meet the expenses of club life that at various times sections of the European community insisted on salaries comparable to those of other sections.

In every small town there was a European club; and often the European employees of the larger estates had their own clubs. These clubs were the centres of social activity for all the Europeans of their particular localities. In contrast, in the towns with large European populations there was usually more than one club and membership was along the lines of position in the community or a common interest. In Kuala Lumpur the three principal clubs were the Selangor Club, the Lake Club, and the Selangor Golf Club. As the most important social institutions for Europeans in the Kuala Lumpur area each deserves some description. After this we can look at the clubs in relation to the structure of European society.

As the largest of the three clubs the Selangor Club enjoyed a reputation as the one to which 'everyone' belonged. It was the one place where all Europeans could meet 'on a level', where the formalities of rank which were so carefully observed at other times could be set aside.[74] While diminishing social distinctions within the European community the club emphasized the division between Europeans and Asians. 'As long as you are white the Club draws few distinctions', Curle observed. 'To be a European is its passport—the title of "Spotted Dog" is growing obsolete—and within those limits it is a democratic institution.'[75]

The Selangor Club's membership was drawn from all over the F.M.S. At the end of 1921 the club had 1,971 members,[76] which was 600 more than the number of European men in Selangor at the time of the census of that year. During the rubber boom years which began in 1906 the rapid increase in membership had put such a strain on the club's facilities that some members had proposed forming separate sports and social clubs, but by 1909 the members had decided instead to greatly expand the existing club's buildings.[77] By the 1920s the clubhouse, which stretched the length of one side of the town *padang*, contained billiards, card, reading, and tiffin rooms, one hair-dressing saloon for men and another for women, and two bars. Of the two bars the more important was the famous long bar, from which women were excluded. It was especially around this bar that all men were believed to be equal. 'The Club bar', claimed the *Malay Mail*, 'plays a prominent part in the process of assessing a man's worth as distinct from his social position.'[78] Next in importance to the long bar was the large reading room at the north end of the club: 'in it you may see how the little world of Malaya wags, since at one time or another anyone and everyone from all over the F.M.S. may be found there'.[79] The reading room served as a ball room as well as a lounge. About 700 people attended the dance given in honour of the Prince of Wales during his visit to Malaya in March 1922. (On this occasion great blocks of ice in which flowers were frozen were placed on stands around the edge of the room to keep the temperature down.) On an important annual social event such as the St. Andrew's Day ball about 500 people would be present. On most Saturdays and sometimes on other days there was a *thé dansant* or a dance at night. Presiding over the club's activities were the General Committee, which consisted of the Resident, who was *ex-officio* president of the club, a vice-president, five members elected at the club's annual general meeting, and two members who were nominated by the Resident. There was also a committee which looked after cricket, rugby, hockey, tennis, and other sports.[80] The day-to-day work of running the club was carried out by the club's secretary and a staff of sixty Hailam servants. Many of the servants lived with their families in quarters conveniently located near the club until the building collapsed in 1936 while repairs were being made on it (one baby was killed and twenty-eight other people were injured).

Although it had tennis courts and a small swimming pool the Lake Club had fewer facilities than the Selangor Club had. As in the 1890s, its most important feature was that it was exclusive. By the 1920s the club may however have become slightly less exclusive than it had been at the beginning of the twentieth century. According to a writer in 1926, 'the days are gone when to belong to it meant that you were at last Someone with a capital S'.[81] In 1908 D. F. Topham had been truly exceptional when, with the influential backing of the Chief Warden of Mines and the European unofficial member of the Selangor State Council, he had joined the Lake Club as an assistant in a commercial firm,[82] but in the 1920s, as will be shown, it was not unusual for assistants in firms and banks to join the club. Nevertheless, the relative exclusiveness of the Lake Club was very often remarked upon in the inter-war years.[83] The fact that the club was known as the 'Tuan Besar' or 'Brass Hat' club would also support the view that it was the preserve of the élite of the European community. The high entrance fee and monthly subscription by themselves limited membership. Although there are no newspaper reports giving its size the Lake Club's membership was clearly much smaller than that of the Selangor Club. The Candidates Book of the Lake Club shows that between August 1921 and August 1931 an average of 35 men joined the club each year whereas the corresponding figure for the Selangor Club was between 150 and 200. By assuming that the ratio of new members to the total membership was very roughly the same for both clubs the membership of the Lake Club may be estimated at between 400 and 600.

In the 1920s the Selangor Golf Club was the smallest but the fastest developing of the three clubs. During the war the government decided to take over the land on Petaling Hill, which had been given to the Golf Club on a temporary lease, to convert part of it into a park, and to sell the remainder. A committee headed by C. F. Green, who was not only chairman of the Kuala Lumpur Sanitary Board but also a past captain of the Golf Club, proposed that the government should give the club land for a new, larger course and money for opening the course and building a clubhouse. The committee also argued that any money which the government received from the sale of the land on the Petaling Hill site should be spent on the European community, since it was only because Europeans had used the site when land prices were low that the government could now sell at a high price. Senior officials rejected this principle ('The demands of the Golf

Club do not err on the side of moderation', the Resident complained), but they did agree to provide the club with land and enough money to open the new course.[84] After considerable discussion between the committee and the government, land to the east of Circular Road was chosen for the new course, which was opened in September 1921 and greatly expanded in the following years.[85] (See Map 3.) The club's membership increased from 294 at the beginning of 1921 to 589 in 1930.[86]

During the 1920s probably the great majority of the Golf Club's members belonged to either the Selangor Club or the Lake Club as well. Unlike the other two clubs the Golf Club was primarily a sports rather than a social club. But this began to change in the 1930s. The club's decision in 1934 to build a swimming pool near the clubhouse directly threatened the other clubs. The controversy which followed filled the pages of the *Malay Mail* more than any other issue of the time except the abdication of King Edward VIII. The Lake Club, which had a small pool, feared that a new pool would draw away some of its membership, while the Selangor Club, which had some vague plans of its own for a pool, saw the plan as a direct attack on its position as the main European social club. The Golf Club asked the Selangor Club whether it wanted to share the expense of building the pool in return for which Selangor Club members could use the pool at certain times. A general meeting of the Selangor Club angrily rejected this offer. 'There is no reason', protested a long-time Selangor Club member, 'why the "Dog" members should have to go to their new rival for their swim.'[87] The Golf Club then decided to build the pool alone, but the Resident of Selangor, T. S. Adams, refused to give the club the needed permission. Only after bitter negotiations between the club and the government were the plans approved.[88] It is clear that with the opening of the pool in 1937 the Golf Club did begin to establish itself more and more as a social club and indeed as a family club. Because of the pool, members were more likely to remain at the club into the evening, and the club's membership of 583 in 1937 jumped to 1,178 four years later.[89]

In somewhat differing ways each of the three clubs exercised strict control over the admission of new members. To join the Golf Club a man had to be proposed by two members and then appear before the club committee for a preliminary scrutiny. If the committee found the candidate suitable his name was posted on a board in the clubhouse, and if no members objected to his becoming a member the committee gave their final approval to

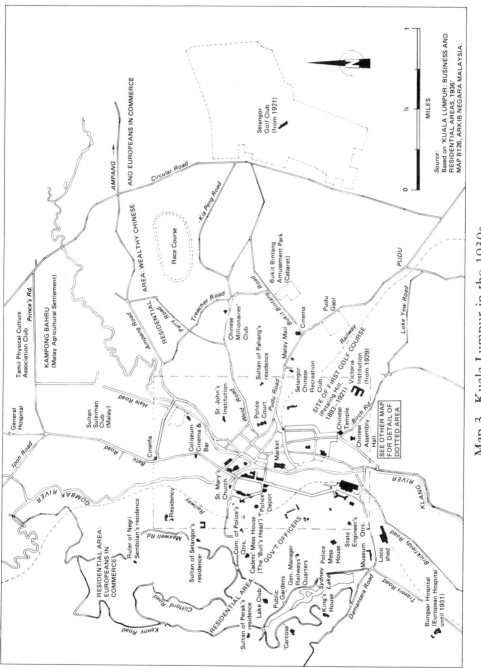

Map 3. Kuala Lumpur in the 1930s

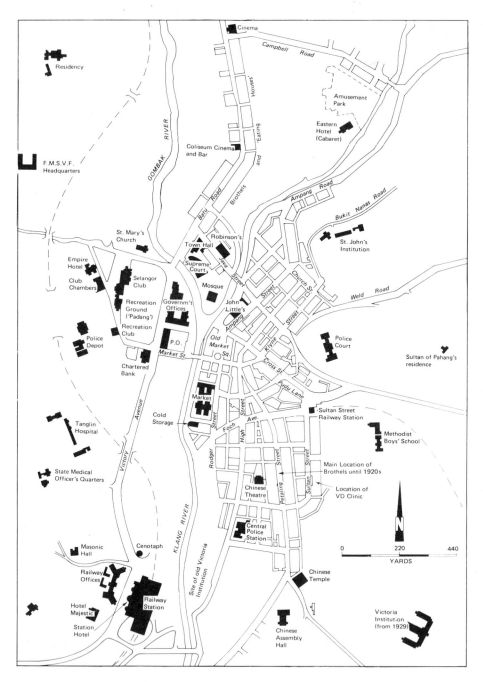

Map 3. Kuala Lumpur in the 1930s (continued)

his membership.[90] To join the Selangor Club a man had to be proposed by a member and seconded by another. His name, address, and occupation were then posted in the club for members to inspect. During the three months he was awaiting election he could use the club's facilities; if he was not elected his sponsors were held responsible for any bad debts he might have incurred during this time. Membership was determined by an election committee which consisted of the club's General Committee, the sports committee, and two members elected specially to serve on the election committee. To be elected a candidate had to receive at least nine votes of a possible sixteen in his favour; if he received three blackballs he was excluded.[91] The large membership of the Selangor Club would suggest that by far the great majority of those proposed for membership were elected.

At the Lake Club potential members were considered by a committee of eight members. A prospective member had to be proposed by two members, who entered his name and occupation in the Candidates Book, which was always open for members to inspect. During the two months before the committee voted on their membership candidates attended social gatherings especially intended to give club members a chance to look them over, which, according to one source, they did 'with a unanimity positively petrifying'.[92] A candidate was also expected to 'call' on the wives of all married committee members by dropping his card into boxes provided at the club. If a woman liked the candidate he was invited to dinner. Otherwise his call was returned by a card from her husband. Whether or not he was invited to dine, the important point was that the candidate had carefully observed the expected etiquette. According to a civil servant who joined the club in about 1923 this procedure was sometimes relaxed. At parties a good dancer found himself quickly accepted by the old members, and at less formal times, such as after watching a game of tennis, 'you could join a table of wives and husbands on whom you had not called and be welcome'.[93] During the period before the election members therefore had the opportunity to decide whether the candidate met their standards, and, equally important, the candidate was able to assess his chances of being elected. It is clear from the Candidates Book that there were two ways by which the few members who were found unacceptable were weeded out. Some were not elected when they received two or more blackballs from the election committee, while about an equal number preferred to withdraw their candidateship when they realized that they were unlikely to be elected.

The fact that the Lake Club was generally recognized as the institution to which the élite of the European community belonged naturally raises a question. What were the occupations and positions of the club's members? In other words, who were the European élite? There are two difficulties in using the club's membership as a means of describing the élite, but it can be argued that neither is serious. First, the Candidates Book, which is the only important club record to have survived the Second World War, only allows us to know who was *joining* the club rather than the total composition of the club at a given time, but because of the care with which new members were selected it can be safely assumed that the new members were of a standing similar to that of the old members or at the very least had attained a certain standing to be considered eligible to join the club. Second, whether a man joined the club was not always a matter of his own position. His election could be aided by the public prominence or standing within the club of his sponsors. D. F. Topham's early admission to the Lake Club has already been given as an example of this, but he was himself to indicate that this was unusual. A candidate might also be rejected because his sponsors were for some reason unpopular at the time rather than because of a low estimation of his personal attributes. But this must have been extremely rare since very few candidates were rejected for *any* reason. Between 1921 and 1931 almost 95 per cent of all candidates were eventually elected.

Between May 1925 and May 1927 eighty-three men were proposed as candidates to the Lake Club. Of these, one was blackballed, two withdrew their candidateship, and there were three who were elected but whose occupations were not given and whose names do not appear in directories or civil service lists. Table 10 shows the occupations and (for all but six individuals) the positions of the remaining seventy-seven, who were elected to the club between July 1925 and June 1927. Using the table it is possible to make some observations about the Lake Club's membership and, with caution, the composition of the European élite.

Obviously, the position which a man had to have reached within his occupation to be considered eligible for membership varied greatly from occupation to occupation. The difference between members of the M.C.S. and government servants in the professional and technical departments is especially striking.

TABLE 10

Occupations and Positions of 77 Men Elected to the Lake Club,
July 1925–June 1927

| | Government | | Non-Government | | | | |
	M.C.S.	Prof. and Tech.[a]	Planters	Mining	Banking	Commerce	Others
Position	Class I and Staff 3 Classes II and III 7 Classes IV and V 3 Cadets 3	Very Senior 7 Senior 16 Junior 2	Managers 4 Assistants 0		Agents 3 Sub-Agents 2 Assistants and Sub-Accountants 4	Partners, Directors, Managers 8 Assistants 5	Editor, *Malay Mail* 2 Lawyers (partners in firms) Dental Surgeon
Able to trace position	16	25	4	0	9	13	4
Unable to trace	0	1	1	3[b]	0	1	0
Total	16	26	5	3	9	14	4

Sources: Candidates Book, Lake Club. The names are taken from the nine pages listing those proposed between 1 May 1925 and 8 May 1927. Further information comes from the *Singapore and Malayan Directory* and the *Malayan Civil List* of various years.

Notes: [a]Government servants in the professional and technical departments have been classified as 'very senior', 'senior', and 'junior' since there was no hierarchy common to all the departments. The seven 'very senior' government servants were: the Chief Justice of the F.M.S. Supreme Court, a judge at the Supreme Court, Ipoh, the acting General Manager of the F.M.S. Railways, the chairman of the Electricity Board, the director of the Rubber Research Institute, and the two top officers attached to the F.M.S. Volunteer Force. 'Senior' government servants were those in charge of a major section of a department (and therefore senior to as many as thirty Europeans in that section) and those of very high professional standing (such as a surgeon). The two 'junior' government servants were a teacher and an inspector of schools.

[b]In the Candidates Book these three were listed as mining engineers.

Although there were about seven times as many Europeans employed in the non-cadet services as in the M.C.S., officials in the professional and technical departments only slightly outnumbered civil servants among new members. Officers of all levels of the M.C.S. were joining; they could expect to join the club soon after being stationed in Kuala Lumpur regardless of their positions within the M.C.S. (This is confirmed by checking names on other pages in the Candidates Book as well as those covering the period being discussed here.) In contrast, most other government servants who joined the Lake Club during this period had well over ten years of service and were heads of departments or important sub-departments. Whatever the fine gradations within the M.C.S., the M.C.S. was as a whole the élite of the government service. During his visit to Malaya in 1928 Major Furse observed that officers of the M.C.S. displayed 'a slightly brahminical attitude towards their colleagues in the professional services'.[94] It is interesting to note that the two junior non-M.C.S. government servants to join the Lake Club during this period were members of the Education Department, who very closely resembled the M.C.S. in educational background.

The table shows that only five planters joined the club during this period and that at least four of them were managers. The view expressed by informants that banking enjoyed a standing almost equal to that of the M.C.S. is supported by the table; four out of the nine bankers who joined were assistants or sub-accountants. During this period the new editor of the *Malay Mail*, two lawyers who were partners in private firms, and a dentist who had his own practice also became members of the club.

Although certain occupations (particularly the M.C.S.) had a higher social standing than others it is important to note that some men from all the major occupational areas were joining the Lake Club. The European élite was therefore made up of men from all the major sections of the community rather than any one section. The government, planting, banking, and various commercial hierarchies were brought together in a wider hierarchy up which Europeans rose as they advanced in their respective careers. The European community was broadly divided into those who belonged to the Selangor Club and a smaller upper group of those who belonged to the Lake Club, but this was a division which most men could, if they wished, bridge during their careers.

The most important division within the European population

was not, as was sometimes implied by contemporary observers, between officials and unofficials,[95] or between those who belonged to the Selangor Club and those who belonged to the Lake Club, but rather between those who belonged to one of the main clubs and those who did not. Despite its claim the Selangor Club was in fact not quite 'everyone's' club. European prison warders, the few remaining train drivers, and jockeys were not acceptable as members (though the last-mentioned were welcome guests at the club after a race) and were unlikely to become more so no matter how long they worked in Malaya.[96] It was only these few Europeans who did not hold high positions and who did not live at the accepted European standard who were not truly part of the European 'community'. According to Wheeler these men served as a reminder to Asians that there were 'grades' among Europeans as among the various Asian groups,[97] but it was partly because they were such a reminder that they were excluded from European society and indeed that their numbers in Malaya were kept as small as possible.

The Promise of Hill Stations

Looking back to the years just after the First World War we must remind ourselves that the British could not imagine the time when they would no longer be the rulers of Malaya. As they assumed their rule was permanent they wanted to do all they could to make life for themselves and future generations of Britishers as comfortable as possible. Hill stations were seen as the most promising of the means by which Europeans might overcome the distressing features of life in Malaya. By the end of the war the government had begun planning Fraser's Hill on the Selangor–Pahang border as a hill station, and in 1925, even before some of the main buildings on Fraser's Hill were completed, the Chief Secretary, Sir George Maxwell, who had played an important part in guiding the development of Fraser's Hill, recommended that the Cameron Highlands should be developed as a much larger hill station. Before describing how these two hill stations were in fact developed it is necessary to explain the reasons there was such a great demand among Europeans for hill stations.

The demand for hill stations arose most of all from continuing beliefs about the effects of the tropical climate on Europeans. In some respects indeed the possible effects of the climate now seemed more mysterious than ever. The discovery of the causes of many major diseases, most notably malaria, in the decade and a half before the war had given Europeans hope that all the diseases and other ailments which they experienced in the tropics might be explained as the result of germs and therefore alleviated by medical science. Even though scientists had not discovered the germs which caused some diseases, wrote Sir Patrick Manson in the 1907 edition of the standard work on tropical medicine, 'their existence . . . may be confidently postulated'.[98] In the inter-war years, however, this spirit of optimism gave way to a feeling that the potential contribution of medical science was not unlimited and that the effects of the climate were greater than they had previously acknowledged.[99] It was precisely because so much progress had been made that it appeared all the more of a mystery that after three or four years in the tropics white men no longer displayed as much energy in their work and that many became nervous and irritable and found it difficult to concentrate and to remember recent events or even important appointments. In addition to this syndrome, known to doctors as 'tropical neurasthenia' and to laymen by such names as 'Malayan head', the rate of suicide among Europeans in the tropics appeared to be extremely high.[100] Although diseases had been controlled the climate remained the same as it had always been and therefore must be in some way considered responsible.

This view of the climate's effects was supported by a great variety of reasoning and evidence. Doctors and laymen alike claimed that in addition to the heat and humidity the monotony of the climate was one of its most harmful aspects, but they did not make it clear whether the nervous system was gradually damaged by a lack of stimulation from changing temperatures or simply that men who were used to marked seasons found the tropical climate boring. In a well-publicized article Kenneth Black, Professor of Surgery at the King Edward VII College of Medicine in Singapore, noted a report that the efficiency of surveyors tended to drop off markedly during the last months of their three-year tours of duty. Although in all probability the men were impatiently looking forward to their leave in Britain, Black took this as evidence of the way in which the climate gradually wore down Europeans.[101] Black also noted that during his visit to Malaya in 1928 W. G. A. Ormsby-Gore, Under-Secretary of State for the Colonies, had remarked that in contrast to officers serving in West Africa civil servants in Malaya showed definite signs of mental lethargy. Black implied that Ormsby-Gore's statement fully supported his own views on the climate's effects. In fact, although Ormsby-Gore had said that the climate had an adverse effect, he had attributed the lethargy mainly to the fact that civil servants in Malaya were out of touch with current thinking in Britain because of their relatively long tours of duty rather than to the fact that they spent longer periods in the tropics.[102] Finally, beliefs about the long-term effects of the climate were often influenced by the attitudes Europeans had towards the peoples who inhabited the tropics. Arising from these attitudes was the fear that over a period of several generations, if not sooner, Europeans might lose their superior vigour and degenerate into the lazy ways of the natives.

A few doctors and a very small number of laymen claimed that the climate had no significant effect on Europeans. Instead they insisted that tropical neurasthenia could be ascribed to the way Europeans lived in the tropics rather than to the tropics themselves. They pointed out that nearly all Europeans thought of themselves as exiles and argued that it was because they longed for home and took no interest in the community about them that many Europeans suffered from boredom and a sense of rootlessness. 'Unless you give up home leave,' G. L. Peet told his readers in his book *Malayan Exile*, 'unless you cease to dream about retirement in a white man's country, and unless you can so attach yourself to Malaya that this country means to you what England used to mean, you can never hope to know beneath the tropic stars the unimaginable peace of an English summer night.'[103] In the view of those who rejected a climatic explanation of neurasthenia the strain of living in the tropics was partly the result of long periods of family separation. In the case of men who had sexual relations with Asian women during their wives' absence this strain was compounded by a sense of guilt for having set aside their marriage vows. According to Dr. G. Waugh-Scott, an estates doctor of long experience, the 'mental disharmony' experienced by Europeans in Malaya was fostered by a more general failure 'to square our manner of living with our ideals of conduct and behaviour' learned in childhood:

We may choose to ignore in our conscious behaviour the fact that intemperance, unkindness, improvidence, impurity, concubinage, etc., are unsocial and wrong, but the unconscious never ignores . . . such matters. Deep down, unsleeping, and always maintaining its conflict with the behaviour which the conscious mind has willed, lies the great herd instinct which regards such conduct as taboo, and until our practice agrees with our deepest principles there can be no real equanimity of spirit.

'Living in sin' is a kind of joke as we mention it round the pahit table, but on through the day and night the never ceasing 'Thou shalt not' of the unconscious is grinding its pathway towards the conscious with serious effects on the peace of mind of those who do not take steps to mend matters.

Much of our indulgence in alcohol and the inordinate rush after pleasures and excitements of all kinds are merely the symptoms of this lack of mental harmony.[104]

While accepting that there were social strains peculiar to life in a tropical dependency, the great majority of doctors and laymen however believed that the climate had *some* effect on Europeans. Separation of husbands and wives, for example, did cause strain, but, they were quick to add, it was certainly in great part the climate's effects on women and children which made separation necessary in the first place. Most Europeans continued to believe that it was essential for men to take six to eight months' leave in a temperate climate every three or four years and for women and children to spend an even shorter time in the tropics.[105]

The great attraction of hill stations was that they provided a change of climate without the necessity of a long, expensive voyage to Europe. Two to four weeks in a hill station each year would, it was believed, help men to maintain their vitality throughout their tours of duty or to remain healthy in the tropics longer if they were unable to take leave. At the same time, because of hill stations families would be able to stay together for longer periods. Children could receive at least the early years of their education at a hill school; as long as they were under European supervision and enrolment was confined to European children they would have most of the advantages of an education in Britain and yet be able to see their parents frequently. Women would be able to spend some of their time with their husbands in the lowlands and some with their children in the highlands. Whole families could be together during holidays and for the few weeks a year when men had local leave. In short, hill stations might some day eliminate 'the tragedy of the East'.

With this as background we can now trace the development as hill stations first of Fraser's Hill and then of the Cameron Highlands.

As the European population grew rapidly after 1900, the demand for more hill stations increased. The existing ones— Maxwell's Hill, Bukit Kutu (Treacher's Hill), Gunung Kledang near Ipoh, and Gunung Angsi near Seremban—had been built on ridges or hill tops and therefore could not be expanded. Unofficials were particularly dissatisfied with the existing hill stations because officials were given first choice on the use of the few bungalows.[106] After about 1905 interest grew in a plateau on the south side of Gunung Tahan in northern Pahang, the highest mountain in Malaya, as a possible site for a truly grand hill station. The idea of a health resort there, to be reached by a railway branching off from the proposed line to Kelantan and then a funicular railway up the mountain, had the enthusiastic support of senior officials. In 1912 the High Commissioner, Sir Arthur Young, and the Chief Secretary, Sir Edward Brockman, climbed Gunung Tahan to investigate its potential as a hill station. (See Map 4.) The view of the mountain from the plateau reminded one member of the party 'of highland scenery in Inverness-shire on the higher rocky grounds where ptarmigan are found'.[107] As a result of the party's very favourable impression the Federal Council supported Brockman's request for funds for further investigations.[108] The project was however never begun both because of the enormous expense of building the railways and because its development would be complicated by the fact that the northern part of the mountain was in Kelantan, which was not part of the F.M.S.[109]

It was the war which provided the impetus for further hill-station development. Because of the shortage of staff and the difficulty of travel to Britain Europeans found it impossible to go on leave. At least three civil servants had physical or mental breakdowns and were forced to retire, three 'died in harness', and two committed suicide. It was believed that although the greatly increased pressure of work was partly responsible prolonged residence in the tropics had tipped the scales to disaster.[110] At a time when a change of climate by taking leave in Europe was impossible a change of climate by altitude became all the more urgent. In 1917 the Bishop of Singapore, C. J. Ferguson-Davie, submitted a report to the government suggesting that Fraser's Hill, where there had been some tin mining since the 1890s, could be quickly developed as a hill station. The location was considerably higher than any of the existing hill resorts and yet was only about five miles from the main road between Selangor and Pahang. By the time the war had come to an end the government had decided to develop Fraser's Hill as a health resort. The road to Fraser's Hill was completed in 1921, and in the next few years the government built a small golf

Map 4. Hill Stations in Malaya

course and over a dozen bungalows. The Red Cross built four bungalows, two of which were primarily for ex-service men and women. The Selangor Club had a clubhouse and other buildings there which could be used by visiting members as well as regular members. Near the golf course there was a public house known as the Maxwell Arms, which was run by Sir George Maxwell's former head 'boy'.

Europeans frequently testified that their visits to Fraser's Hill had given their spirits a great boost. It was warm during the days but so cool at night that they could warm themselves in front of a blazing fire and feel as if they were at home in England.[111] Each bungalow had its own garden where, wrote Mrs. Wilson, 'all the old English flowers, so dear to us, flourished'.[112] Unlike during a typical holiday in Britain, however, parents had to worry little about the care of their children. Every morning at 9 o'clock men and their wives assembled to play golf, one bachelor observed with a touch of exaggeration, 'while in the background were innumerable "Amahs" . . . looking after some thousands of squawking European babies'.[113]

Despite its great charms many people were far from satisfied with Fraser's Hill. As in the case of earlier hill stations built by the government, officials were given priority in accommodation. Unofficials argued very strongly that since Fraser's Hill had been built from public revenues its facilities should be available to all Europeans on equal terms, but the government continued to favour its employees. Companies and other organizations were given the opportunity to lease land, but only Guthrie's, the Straits Trading Company, and the Methodist Mission did so.[114] Individuals were given a similar opportunity to lease land, but, because of the great expense involved, by 1937 only about seven families had built their own bungalows on Fraser's Hill. Even officials had misgivings about Fraser's Hill. Some of them preferred a trip to Brastagi in Sumatra where they could not only enjoy a change of climate but also escape the government atmosphere which prevailed as much at Fraser's Hill as it did in Kuala Lumpur, Taiping, and other towns. It was for this reason that Ormsby-Gore suggested that in the future private enterprise should play a greater part in developing hill stations.[115] Finally, even by the mid-1920s it was clear that the location itself was inadequate. Because of the nature of the terrain the area available at the resort was not large enough to meet the growing needs of the ever-increasing European population. And, as will be mentioned shortly, some Europeans wanted a hill station

which would offer facilities similar to those at Fraser's Hill
(though on a larger scale) but would also have land for agricultural settlement.

Since William Cameron explored the area in 1885 there had
been conflicting estimates of how much land was available in the
mountains of north-west Pahang for use as a hill station. It was
only after further explorations in the early 1920s that its great
potential became known. As the ones who would most benefit
from a new hill station unofficials immediately pressed the government to survey the area and to begin making plans for its
development. In March 1925 the Chief Secretary, Maxwell, led
an expedition which reported on the terrain, soil conditions, and
climate of the highlands.[116] In the following year the government
set up the Cameron Highlands Development Committee to
oversee the planning, but in the view of unofficials progress was
being made at a painfully slow rate. In 1929 an unofficial
member of the Federal Council made an emotional appeal to the
government to hasten the development of the highlands. 'If you
strip the ladies of their lip-stick and their face powder, who do
you get? You see women entirely worn out. You see their health
breaking up. The children are pale and anaemic and undoubtedly
should not be in the country as long as they are.'[117]

Although not as quickly as unofficials wished the government
proceeded with the work of developing the highlands. Despite
the economic crisis the work was encouraged by Sir Cecil
Clementi, who took office as Governor early in 1930. Clementi
foresaw the day when for certain periods of the year the government of Malaya would be carried on at Tanah Rata in the
highlands just as the Indian government moved to Simla during
the hot season.[118] After the main road to the highlands was completed in 1931, smaller roads, a golf course, and a rest house
were built by the government. Most of the remaining work was
undertaken privately. By the mid-1930s there were three hotels.
As in the case of Fraser's Hill the British tried to re-create the
feeling of being in their homeland. One of the hotels was built in
the form of an Elizabethan mansion, and visitors could enjoy
looking at English flowers and eating strawberries with fresh
cream. 'You seem to be in another world up there', wrote one
woman after her return to the lowlands, and 'so much nearer to
England'.[119] By 1935 the long-held dream of hill schools for
European children was becoming a reality. There were two private schools, both run by Europeans and having only European
students, for children up to about the age of thirteen. In 1935

there were only about a hundred European children at schools in the Highlands, but for at least a few families the schools were 'averting much of the tragedy of married life in the East'.[120]

Of all sections of the European community it had been the planters who had most pushed the government to develop the Cameron Highlands. All planters shared the desire for a health resort and hill schools, but some had a special interest in the highlands. At a time when economic conditions gave them little hope of retiring in great wealth to Britain many planters believed that they could spend their retirements in much greater financial comfort in the highlands of Malaya than in their homeland. By opening small estates they hoped to supplement their pensions. Since, unlike in Britain, there was no income tax in Malaya they could expect to save a relatively high proportion of what they earned. It was also believed that the climate in the highlands was ideal for someone who had spent all his working life in the tropical heat: it was cooler than the lowlands and yet not uncomfortably cold as Britain was during much of the year. The climate would of course be ideal for their wives as well. Men who retired at a fairly early age to settle in the highlands could plan to have their children educated at one of the highland schools. Their daughters, one of the first settlers prophesied, would marry men working in the plains and their sons might pursue careers in Malaya and later inherit the property.[121]

In a memorandum apparently prepared late in 1933 L. D. Gammans, Assistant-Director of Co-operation in the F.M.S. and the Straits Settlements, pointed to what he saw as some of the potential disadvantages of European settlement in the highlands. Gammans pointed out that a settler was in danger of cutting himself off from his country of origin and that the highland schools which his children would attend were 'in the very nature of things . . . not likely to compare in education and tradition with the school which the settler himself attended'. Gammans also observed that many prospective settlers were planning to grow crops, such as temperate-climate vegetables, which were already being successfully produced by Chinese gardeners. He warned that since Europeans lacked any clear superiority in market-gardening techniques a settler would be forced to reduce his standard of living to that of his competitors in order to cut his costs. Gammans concluded that prospective European settlers would be better advised to risk their capital in Great Britain or in one of the Dominions, 'where competition, severe as it may be, will be with men of his own race and of an equivalent standard of living'.[122] Gammans's warning, however, was especially directed at Europeans who planned to open medium-sized estates and who would have to rely entirely on the sale of their produce for their income. Perhaps because other officials shared Gammans's views all of the land in the highlands which the government alienated for agricultural purposes was taken up by smallholders and a very small number of large-scale companies.

By 1935 about fifty men, most of whom were retired planters, were living on smallholdings in the Cameron Highlands. Although their numbers were small their importance in the social history of the British in Malaya is indeed great. There were now for the first time a few Europeans who were beginning to look upon Malaya as a home as well as a place to work.

7

European Relations with Asians: the Inter-war Years

IN his book *Malayan Exile*, published in 1934, G. L. Peet recounts how after several years' residence in Kuala Lumpur he accompanied some Chinese friends into town for the first time to watch celebrations for the Moon Cake Festival. 'Have you ever walked down a Chinese street with Chinese friends?' Peet asked his readers. He was sure most had not. 'That is perhaps the most significant feature of our life in this country,' Peet observed, 'that we all live in compartments and only occasionally do we scramble over the dividing walls.'[1] This chapter describes the walls which divided Europeans and Asians in the inter-war years, the degree to which Asians were in fact accepted into European social activities, the special barriers which separated Eurasians from Europeans, and how during this period a small group of Europeans and Asians attempted, by forming a Rotary Club, to change the pattern of European–Asian relations. Before discussing these topics, however, it is useful to describe how Europeans themselves perceived their relations with Asians as these perceptions not only reflected existing relations but also helped to perpetuate them.

General Attitudes

For the most part Europeans living in the Federated Malay States between the world wars looked at their relations with the Asians among whom they lived with great satisfaction and pride. Unlike in South Africa or the American South there appeared to be no racial tension, and the absence of any nationalist movement among the Asian population suggested that they were content with British rule. According to many Europeans in Malaya, there was not only an absence of hostility but also a spirit of goodwill between themselves and the various other ethnic groups. Europeans saw Malaya and relations between the various peoples in it as truly exceptional in the world after the Great War. Robson was warmly applauded by other members of the Federal Council in 1925 when he described the F.M.S. as 'one of the very few territories in the world to-day where there is no real poverty, no unrest, no oppressive taxation, and no racial ill-feeling'. Despite differences in religion and outlook on life, he said, Europeans, Malays, Chinese, and Indians 'all live together in harmony, work together in confidence, and often play together in the best of good fellowship'.[2]

Racial harmony was considered by many Europeans to be Malaya's most precious heritage. The desire on the part of both Europeans and Asian leaders to preserve this heritage was demonstrated most clearly when racial segregation in the use of medical facilities in Kuala Lumpur was removed in 1931. The issue arose in the late 1920s when, because of insufficient funds, the government shelved plans to build a large modern hospital which would have served people of all ethnic groups. The government instead improved facilities at the European Hospital and also at the General Hospital, the main hospital for Asian patients.[3] Prominent Chinese and Indians, however, were far from satisfied with these improvements. They claimed that the General Hospital was still in a deplorable condition and that its new facilities for first class patients were markedly inferior to those provided at the European Hospital. The Indian member of the Federal Council asserted that by its failure to provide equal facilities the government was jeopardizing 'the harmony that has always existed between the rulers and the ruled for so many years in this country—a harmony which has become a tradition and a watch-word of the great Civil Service by which this country is administered'.[4] In April 1931 seven Asians (including two doctors) who had inspected the General Hospital a few months earlier published a report detailing their complaints. Though they found a great deal wrong with the second and third class wards they paid particular attention to the special first class wards, which, they believed, did not provide facilities of the standard which Asian members of the Federal Council and other Asian leaders had the right to expect. 'One can scarcely conceive of refined ladies, whose accommodation in their homes is not in the least inferior to the best European homes in Kuala Lumpur, availing themselves of the special class ward.'[5] The Resident of Selangor and the Principal Medical Officer characterized the report as a collection of inaccuracies and exaggerations, but the High

Commissioner, Sir Cecil Clementi, treated it sympathetically, and it was supported by the leading British newspapers. The report, asserted the *Straits Times*, had 'lanced an abscess which was threatening to poison the corporate life of Kuala Lumpur'.[6] In July, after Clementi had visited the hospital and talked with Asian leaders, the government announced that a new hospital would be built when financial conditions improved and that in the meantime the European Hospital, to be known as the Bungsar Hospital, would be open to European and Asian patients alike. After the announcement both Europeans and Asian leaders expressed relief that a potential threat to racial harmony had at last been removed.[7]

When speaking of the goodwill between themselves and Asians, Europeans included *social* relations only to a limited extent. The great majority of Europeans assumed that social life meant social relations with other Europeans. When, for example, a government handbook stated that the automobile 'has eliminated distance as a bar to social intercourse' it meant that those Europeans living on rubber estates and at mines could now visit Europeans in the towns much more easily than they could before cars were commonly used.[8] Similarly, when the Resident of Selangor opened the new Selangor Golf Club with the words that the club would play a large part in the 'social life' not only of Kuala Lumpur but of all Selangor he had in mind the social life of the *Europeans* living in Selangor.[9] In the view of most Europeans it was only natural that Europeans should want to spend their leisure time in the company of other Europeans; it was not prejudice which separated people but simply that people of similar background, interests, and tastes preferred one another's company. It was for this same reason, a *Malay Mail* editorial argued, that in the larger towns there were social divisions even between Europeans, with the more senior men in one club and the juniors in another.[10]

Thus what seemed remarkable to many Europeans was not how little contact there was between themselves and Asians outside the working hours but rather how much there was under the circumstances. Like Robson in his Federal Council speech, Europeans looked to the sports field as the scene of most amicable relations between the races. Indeed, it can at least be said that the tension which had led the European teams to withdraw from the Selangor Football League in 1914 was nearly absent in the inter-war years. The possibility of racial tension either causing or arising from conflict on the football field was very much less after

World War I. The major competition during this period was
between state teams, which were multi-racial, for the Malaya
Cup, rather than between racially-defined teams. Moreover,
Europeans more often played on departmental or company
teams, which were multi-racial, than on racially-defined club
teams. On those occasions when European teams played Asian
teams tension, and even blows, were not unknown,[11] but on the
whole sport does appear to have been a means of friendly contact
between Europeans and Asians. In cricket the number of non-
Europeans playing on the state and colony teams increased not
only because their interest in the game was growing but also
because the Europeans who organized the teams were more
inclined to select players by ability than by favouring Europeans.[12] In addition to sports, Europeans also pointed to official
and private gatherings where Europeans and Asians mixed as a
sign of goodwill. During one week in 1926, for example, Europeans were guests at a housewarming put on by Alan Loke, Loke
Yew's son, and at the wedding of the daughter of the Chinese
member of the Federal Council, Choo Kia Peng. Gatherings of
this kind were, however, more formal and less frequent than the
dinners given by the Capitan China and other Asian leaders in
the 1890s. At the housewarming just referred to, Alan Loke and
his wife invited the Europeans on a different night from their
other guests.[13]

One reason for the lack of tension, which gave the impression
of harmony, was the code of conduct which most Europeans followed implicitly in their relations with Asians. Europeans were
expected, by other Europeans, not to treat Asians harshly as this
would undermine white prestige. As prestige, rather than military power, was assumed to be the basis of British rule any damage to that prestige was considered a very serious offence. In
1922 two planters who had received small fines for disorderly
conduct and assaulting a Chinese bar-boy in a railway restaurant
car were berated by the *Planter* for behaviour which 'degrades
the European in the sight of the Oriental'. 'It is up to every
decent white man', the editor continued, to 'ostracise them from
the society that they have disgraced. They are pariahs, unfit for
the companionship of honourable men.'[14] In short, it was wrong
that one man should harm another, but infinitely worse that a
European should harm an Asian.

Europeans—at least those most conscious of the special
responsibilities of their race—tried not only to ensure that
Asians were not treated harshly but also to present an example of

good behaviour and moral living to Asians, who they believed looked to them for guidance.

A white man in the tropics is watched as a minor god. He may be hated or liked, despised or respected, but being in the minority he is an object of attention from the moment his native servant has taken in breakfast to the time when he has dismissed the chauffeur or ricksha puller, and moved to bed. From the minute he has entered his office, he is watched by natives and feels, if he has a conscience, that he must give an example, in conduct, wisdom and strength.[15]

One consequence of this need to present a good image was to reinforce the tendency of Europeans to confine their social activities to themselves. Most Europeans found it impossible to act as paragons of virtue throughout the day. They therefore attended clubs and private gatherings that, being confined to Europeans and a very few carefully chosen non-Europeans, allowed them to relax without worrying about what kind of image they were presenting. 'We ate & drank & played games like small children,' wrote a teacher, who in his first months in Malaya took a humorous view of European attitudes, about a party with some friends. 'It was good to put aside our true greatness for a period.'[16]

In the inter-war years Europeans were even more concerned about preserving their prestige than they had been before the war. The Great War itself was seen as a severe blow to white prestige because of the spectacle it provided of Europeans killing one another. In the view of many Europeans the cinema presented the greatest threat to their prestige. On the screen Asians saw white men as criminals, tramps, clowns, and lascivious lovers. They saw them, in other words, as the exact opposite of how the Europeans who governed Malaya wished to portray themselves. In order to protect British prestige the government rigorously censored films,[17] but many Europeans were still far from satisfied that sufficient steps were being taken. During a visit to Malaya in the mid-1930s Bruce Lockhart, who had worked in Negri Sembilan before the war, was pleased to find that a film based on his book *Memoirs of a British Agent* had been banned, but he criticized the government for tolerating too much sex in films.[18] The Asian audience's 'rapture in beholding the bare flesh of a white woman is expressed audibly', moaned another critic of the government's censorship policy. 'Undoubtedly, their respect for the women of the ruling race will be lessened.'[19] It was because they believed that the war, the cinema, and other outside influences were already undermining their prestige that Europeans living in Malaya felt that they should do all they could in their conduct towards Asians not to damage prestige.

Though they feared that their prestige was eroding, most Europeans had, as we have seen, a favourable view of their relations with Asians because of the apparent absence of racial tension and because they had no desire for any more contact than there already was. At the same time there were some Europeans who were dissatisfied, not because they saw any tension in European–Asian relations, but because they wanted more contact with Asians and believed that there were barriers which prevented them from doing so. This dissatisfaction took two forms. A few, such as G. L. Peet, quoted at the start of this chapter, sought to break out of the boredom of their isolation in the European community. A persistent theme of Peet's book *Malayan Exile* was that Europeans were depriving themselves of the interest and stimulation of associating with Asians. In one passage he contrasts the dullness of a European cocktail party with the excitement he observed when some Tamils once gathered in a house near where he lived.[20]

Dissatisfaction with the existing state of European–Asian relations more often took the form of nostalgia for a time at the end of the nineteenth century and the start of the twentieth when, it was believed, associations between Europeans and Asians were closer and friendlier. 'I cannot help feeling that we have lost something,' declared Dr. Travers in 1922 in a speech reflecting on changes he had witnessed in Selangor since the 1890s. 'I feel that there is a loss of that kindness that comes of personal knowledge, of the understanding that comes of that kindly feeling and of the sympathy that is born of understanding each other and each other's point of view.'[21] There was a particular nostalgia for the patriarchal way District Officers had once governed their districts. During the inter-war years only Hubert Berkeley, whose unique career in Upper Perak is described in Appendix 1, was able to rule his domain with little interference from the Resident and the federal secretariat. It was because of this nostalgia, as well as a desire for some decentralization, that the retrenchment commissions which reported in 1923 and 1932 recommended strengthening the role of the District Officer.[22] District Officers continued, however, to be tightly entwined in the government bureaucracy, and particularly when Malays began to replace British officials as Assistant District Officers and District Officers a return to white rajah rule became increasingly unlikely.

The Europeans in Malayan Society

The F.M.S. was a classic example of what Furnivall called a 'plural society'.[23] It was a society containing several ethnic groups, each speaking a different language and following a different culture and religion from the others. It was moreover a society in which ethnic groups tended to concentrate in particular occupations and indeed in which certain occupations were often dominated by one or other of the groups. The majority of rubber tappers were Indians, most mine workers and shopkeepers were Chinese, and nearly all farmers and fishermen were Malays. Almost all government officials were Europeans, as were most managers of large estates. Thus in Malayan society the tendency of people having the same language and culture in common to associate with one another in preference to others was reinforced by the fact that these same people often shared similar roles in the society's economy. The plurality of Malayan society meant that when civil servants or managers of large estates came together on social occasions it was a European gathering. 'Malaya cannot prosper without its Tamil estate coolies, its Chinese mechanics, or its European organisers,' one visitor commented, 'but they have few points of contact.'[24]

Divisions between Europeans of various backgrounds and occupations were important, but in relation to the larger Malayan society the Europeans were a remarkably unified group. This unity derived not only from their strong sense of a common cultural identity and their beliefs regarding the role of Europeans in relation to Asians but also from the fact that the various positions Europeans filled had in common the fact of being at the top. For the unity of the Europeans as a group in Malayan society what mattered was not simply that Europeans held high positions but that such a very small number were to be found in any other position. Because of this fundamental characteristic of the European population the great majority of contacts Europeans had with Asians were with them as subordinates. They were working rather than social relationships. In the government services Europeans held nearly all the high positions; the subordinate positions were filled by Eurasians and Asians. Within each of the many estate communities there was a clear racial hierarchy, with the Europeans at the top as managers and assistant managers, a small number of Eurasian or Indian conductors and office staff in the middle, and then the large Tamil work force. Therefore,

however free of friction or indeed however cordial were relations between Europeans and Asians, in most cases these relations were not between people who were, or considered each
other to be, social equals. In his autobiography Kenneth Blackwell, for example, distinguished between his friendships with
Asians and those with other Europeans. In order to illustrate the
'genuine goodwill' between the British and Asians in Malaya
Blackwell recalled how some Tamil subordinates, for whom he
had refereed football games, came to see him at the railway station as he was about to go on leave, but hesitated to approach
him because 'I was with my *personal* friends', who were Europeans.[25]

   This picture of the position of the Europeans in Malayan society needs to be expanded in three important ways. First, because
of the growing use of English among Asians the cultural bound-
aries of the plural society were becoming less distinct. At the
time of the 1931 census 2.8 per cent of Asians in the F.M.S.
were reported to be able to speak English; in Kuala Lumpur district the figure was 8.7 per cent.[26] The growing use of the English language did not in itself, however, lead to greater social
contact since the relative positions of Europeans and Asians
remained largely unchanged. A high proportion of those Asians
able to speak English were employed as clerks, interpreters, and
overseers and in other relatively subordinate positions; they
belonged to what came to be known in the 1930s as the 'middle
class' of Malayan society. Second, the Europeans were by no
means the only élite in Malayan society. Partly out of tradition
and partly because of British policy, the Malay royalty continued
to maintain, among Malays, a standing and influence over questions of custom and religion which was far greater than many
Europeans were probably aware. Among the Chinese was an
upper class which was distinguished by great wealth. In Selangor
the officers and members of the committee of the Chinese
Chamber of Commerce and the men who were nominated by the
Resident to serve on the Chinese Advisory Board certainly
belonged to this class. The Indian community contained some
prominent businessmen and a small number of successful professional men. Third, and perhaps most importantly, it should not
be forgotten that the position of the Europeans in the government services was based on the political power of the British. It
was within the power of the British as the real rulers of Malaya
to decide how far, if at all, non-Europeans would be allowed into
the higher positions in the government services. In short, British

control over the mobility of non-Europeans in the government services greatly influenced the degree to which non-Europeans would be the official and therefore potentially social equals of Europeans. Before looking at the extent to which Asians did mix socially with Europeans it is therefore necessary to consider how far Asians were being allowed to occupy higher government positions in the inter-war years.

As noted in Chapter 5, the government had in the early years of the twentieth century stated its intention to train young Malays of aristocratic background to take a greater part in the administration of the F.M.S. In keeping with this intention the government created the Malay Administrative Service, but only slowly were Malays allowed to hold positions which were as high as those normally held by the British in the cadet service. Many young British civil servants left Malaya to participate in the First World War, and their places were taken by members of the Malay Administrative Service. By 1917 nearly all Assistant District Officers were Malays. In that year the High Commissioner praised the work being done by these officers, but it was not until 1921 that the British decided to admit a few Malays into the Malayan Civil Service.[27] By 1931 there were only ten Malays in the M.C.S.; six years later this figure had increased to nineteen.[28] The admission of Malays into the M.C.S. did not constitute a significant transfer of political and administrative power away from the British, nor was it intended to do so. In 1929 a government handbook stated that the administration of the F.M.S. 'has benefited greatly by thus satisfying Malay aspirations without sacrificing the country's interest in the efficient conduct of the public service'.[29] Moreover, the British carefully selected only those Malays who had shown after many years in the Malay Administrative Service that they would conform closely to the ideals and standards of the M.C.S. The entrance of a few Malays into the M.C.S. did, however, break down the previously near perfect association between official position and ethnicity. This was itself a change to which some Europeans had to adjust. When G. J. O'Grady, a Public Works Department engineer who had recently arrived in Malaya, had to appear in court in Mentakab, Pahang, to testify on behalf of his Malay chauffeur he was shocked to see that the magistrate was a Malay. 'Was I, a European, to stand up and call a coloured man "Your Worship"?' O'Grady decided to follow the example of another European in the court, who addressed the magistrate respectfully. O'Grady's acceptance of the Malay's position was later made more palatable when he learned that the other European was Theodore Hubback, the Game Warden of Pahang and a true *tuan besar*.[30]

As in the years before the First World War the most active movement on the part of Asians for admission into the civil service took place in the Straits Settlements. The restoration of the Queen's Scholarships in 1924 intensified the desire of the Straits Asians for the right of admission into the M.C.S. since an education at Oxford or Cambridge was regarded as leading naturally to a civil service career. In 1924 the non-European members of the Straits Legislative Council renewed their efforts to have the colour bar removed. What, asked the Eurasian member, was the value of the Queen's Scholarships as long as the colour bar remained? Tan Cheng Lock, the Chinese member from Malacca, protested that while a non-European might, if he were very lucky, become a millionaire or sit on the Legislative Council or Federal Council he was totally excluded from any real participation in governing the country. It was for this reason, Tan said, that Dr. Lim Boon Keng had left Singapore to serve in the Chinese government. After listening to these speeches the Colonial Secretary replied that the government could not admit non-Europeans (other than Malays) into the M.C.S. He stressed that the M.C.S. served the F.M.S. as well as the Straits Settlements and that the British government would therefore have to ascertain the views of the Malay Rulers, to whom it had treaty obligations, before considering any change.[31] Indeed, it was clear that, whatever views the British had, the Malay Rulers and many other Malays were strongly opposed to admitting non-Malay Asians into the M.C.S.[32]

Although their views had little if any influence on the government's policy it is worth noting that the main British newspapers were somewhat less antagonistic to Asian aspirations than they had been before the war. After the Colonial Secretary's announcement in the Legislative Council the *Straits Times* suggested that some scheme might be devised which would admit non-Europeans into the M.C.S. and enable them to fill posts in the Straits Settlements only.[33] A few months later, however, when the Governor rejected a second appeal by Tan Cheng Lock, the newspaper strongly opposed making any concession to non-Europeans: not only were the British bound by treaty to the Malays not to 'impose upon them the control of men of any other race', but also in a country of many races and with some tension between them 'it is the business of the ruling race to rule through men of its own blood and colour'.[34] In contrast to the *Straits Times*, the *Malay Mail* simply commented that the Governor had had the 'unpleasant task' of doing what Britain's obligations to the Malays required him to do.[35] In 1930, when the colour bar was again being discussed, the *Times of Malaya* claimed that there were few local men whose mental capabilities and, even more importantly, moral character would entitle them to become civil servants. The editor did, however, suggest that it was the government's responsibility to develop an educational system which would inculcate such qualities.[36]

After renewed pressure from non-Europeans, particularly Tan Cheng Lock and the Eurasian member of the Legislative Council, Dr. Noel Clarke, the Straits government announced in 1932 the creation of a separate Straits Settlements Civil Service which would be staffed by non-European British subjects. In no way, however, did this upset the dominant position of Europeans in the civil service. Members of the new civil service could not hope for promotion to the M.C.S. Even though in some cases they had exactly the same educational background as members of the M.C.S. their starting salary was less than half that given a newly appointed cadet, and their maximum salary was set at $700 per month, a substantial income, but only what a member of the M.C.S. would earn after about ten years of service. Moreover, members of the new service filled only a few relatively minor posts. By 1935 only two men had been appointed to the Straits Settlements Civil Service, and over the next few years the government made only two more appointments each year. Straits Asians were disappointed with this concession, but in the years before World War II they never organized to challenge the colour bar seriously. Those who wanted the colour bar removed were among the most ardent supporters of British rule. It is remarkable that their appeals for entrance into the civil service were usually accompanied by protestations of loyalty to the King.[37]

In the F.M.S. more and more non-Europeans were employed in the Police Department during the 1920s and 1930s. This represented, however, very little challenge to the racial hierarchy within the department. Non-Europeans were employed as inspectors for the first time, but the Europeans who held that rank either were promoted to a commissioned grade or retired and left Malaya. In Perak, for example, in 1920 all 21 police inspectors were Europeans; in 1924 there were 13 Europeans and 4 Malays;

in 1936 there were 13 Malays, 5 Chinese, 4 Indians, and only 8 Europeans.[38] During this transitional period the department promoted the idea that the remaining European inspectors enjoyed a slightly higher status than their non-European counterparts by paying them much higher salaries and by allowing them to wear a more formal uniform. A very small number of Malays also entered the commissioned ranks of the police, but again the relative position of Europeans and non-Europeans within the department was maintained by not placing Malays in posts where they would have to give orders to the few remaining European inspectors.[39]

In both the F.M.S. and the Straits Settlements more non-Europeans entered the professional branches of government during the inter-war years. The number of non-European doctors increased markedly after the founding in Singapore in 1905 of a medical college, first called the Straits Settlements and Federated Malay States Medical School and then the King Edward VII Medical School, which from 1916 granted degrees which were recognized throughout the British Empire. Non-Europeans in the medical and other professional departments in the government found that their opportunities for further training abroad were severely restricted and that their advancement was extremely slow, even when they had higher qualifications than some Europeans. Gunn Lay Teik, for example, was unable to advance beyond a subordinate grade in the Agriculture Department even though he had a better Cambridge degree than the head of the department.[40] Another example was the case of Dr. A. Viswalingam, whose work as an eye surgeon was very highly regarded by specialists outside Malaya. Viswalingam's application for permission to go to Europe for advanced training in ophthalmology had been rejected by the head of the Medical Department, but Sir George Maxwell had then overruled this decision. Having returned to Malaya, Viswalingam remained in a subordinate position and was not promoted to a grade equal to that of a junior European doctor until after the Second World War.[41] In theory, the standing of Asian doctors within the department was at least higher than that of all nursing sisters and nurses, but in practice this was not quite true. Dr. Mohamed Said, a graduate of the King Edward VII Medical School, recalls how European nursing sisters looked upon Asian doctors as their subordinates and how the doctors' complaints to senior British doctors about the sisters' attitude were ignored.[42]

Despite their grievances Asians in the professional departments made no concerted effort to improve their standing relative to Europeans. Many found compensation in the fact that because of their education and positions they were highly respected by other Asians, even if not by Europeans. Many were also inveterate Anglophiles and remained such even when they found that not being European hindered their careers. Several Asians interviewed for this study expressed admiration for their British teachers and also for British institutions. Charles Bazell, headmaster of the Malay College, was especially admired by his students for having faith in and encouraging their abilities. Finally, whatever they thought about their treatment, most Asians within the professional services, like the Asian population in general, could not imagine the day when British power might be challenged and the British would therefore have to relinquish the privileges associated with their dominance.

Asian Participation in European Social Activities

For Europeans their social clubs were places where people could relax in the company of people who saw each other as having a broadly similar standing and similar interests. Knowing which Asians belonged to the main British clubs therefore enables us to know which Asians were regarded by Europeans as their social equals. There were of course some Europeans who would not accept *any* non-Europeans into their clubs. In 1905 the members of the European club at Raub voted not to admit any non-Europeans,[43] but it should be noted that this decision was taken at a time of rising tension between Europeans and Asians and does not indicate common attitudes between the wars. During the inter-war years the question of admitting Asians to British clubs became an issue on at least three occasions. In about 1922 some members of the New Club at Taiping wanted to offer honorary membership to the European officers of a battalion of Burma Rifles stationed there but to exclude the battalion's Burmese officers, whereupon the younger members of the club threatened to resign unless the Burmese were admitted.[44] A slightly different incident took place in 1927 when the organizers of a Christmas party for children at the Perak Club invited the local Girl Guides, the great majority of whom were non-Europeans, to attend and to provide some of the entertainment. Some parents refused to allow their children to go to the party as they did not want them to mix with the Guides, but most Europeans disapproved of their attitude.[45] Finally, a rather complex case also needs to be mentioned. Up to the early 1930s, the Klang Club had not even made Sultan Suleiman, whose *istana* was near the club, an honorary member, but there were signs the club's attitude to having Asian members was changing. In about 1934 the club wanted Malays of the royal family and Malays in the M.C.S. to become members, but it continued its traditional policy in order to avoid the consequences of having to blackball Tengku Musa-eddin, the Sultan's eldest son and the Raja Muda (heir apparent) of Selangor, who in various ways had made himself very unpopular with the European community. Late in 1934 Musa-eddin became the centre of a great controversy when the Resident of Selangor had him deprived of his title as Raja Muda and then, much against the Sultan's wishes, passed over Suleiman's second son to give the title to his third son, the Tengku Laksamana. Though the government gave in to some of the Sultan's demands and smoothed over the situation in other ways it refused to reconsider the action the Resident had taken. Meanwhile, the Klang Club continued its policy of exclusion, but when Musa-eddin eventually bolstered his standing in European eyes by, among other things, organizing the Tengku Laksamana's coronation as Sultan the club elected all three brothers as honorary members.[46] The general conclusion from all of these cases is that a few Europeans advocated the total exclusion of Asians from their clubs but that during the period between the wars the number who held such a view was steadily declining.

Those Asians who belonged to the British clubs formed an extremely select group. If they were in government service they held higher positions than a European would need to join the club; others were members of the Malay royal families or were very prominent in business. 'The so-called European clubs', recalled a civil servant, 'admitted without distinction the senior Malay officers who were in the Civil Service or Police.'[47] According to a teacher living in Ipoh in the late 1930s, 'a few prominent non-Europeans' belonged to the Ipoh Club and participated in its social activities; the only two he named were Dr. Khong, a doctor with a large private practice and a former Malayan champion tennis player, and the Dato Panglima Kinta.[48] O'Grady noted that the local government doctor, an Indian, was a fully accepted member of the club at Bentong in Pahang.[49] Depending mainly on their interest in European sporting and social activities the Malay Rulers participated in club life. The Yang di-Pertuan Besar of Negri Sembilan played billiards regularly at the Kuala

Pilah Club, and in the late 1930s the Sultan of Pahang was a popular visitor to the European club at Sungei Lembing, where he played tennis.[50]

In Kuala Lumpur both the Selangor Club and the Selangor Golf Club had a small number of Asian members. It should be noted that Asians had several social clubs of their own in Kuala Lumpur and that many of them, including some of very high status, preferred to belong to one of these clubs than to a British club, particularly if they spoke little English and were unfamiliar with western customs. The Chinese belonged to the Selangor Chinese Recreation Club or, if they were extremely wealthy, to the Choon Cheok Kee Loo Club, more generally referred to as the Chinese Millionaires' Club. Tamils belonged to the Tamil Physical Culture Association, and Malays belonged to the Sultan Suleiman Club. (These clubs are shown on Map 3.) The Asians who belonged to the Selangor Club and the Selangor Golf Club were those who most wanted to associate socially with Europeans, either because of interests or friendships established while in England or because of frequent contact in work. Nevertheless, it remains true that an Asian had to be of very high standing in order to become a member of either club.

In the early 1920s probably only two Asians belonged to the Selangor Club and the Selangor Golf Club. Choo Kia Peng and Khoo Keng Hooi were members of both clubs. Choo was a member of the Federal Council and a personal friend of Sir George Maxwell's. Choo's position in the tin industry had helped the Golf Club move to the new site on Circular Road in 1921; it was Choo who negotiated the Club's acquisition of the various mining leases which had been held for this area.[51] Khoo was the managing director of Chow Kit and Co. and had long been active on the Kuala Lumpur Sanitary Board. In about 1924 another Chinese, H. S. Lee, became a member of the two clubs. Lee, a native of Hong Kong, had received his degree from Cambridge (where he was captain of the tennis team) and soon after his arrival in Selangor had quickly established himself as one of the leading miners in the state. During the late 1920s and 1930s three Malays in the M.C.S. became members of the Selangor Club or the Golf Club. Clearly, the increasing participation of Malays in government led to some increase in their participation in European social activities. Table 11, which lists the Asian members of the clubs, suggests that, whereas for Europeans the Selangor Club was 'everyone's' club, for Asians both this club and the Selangor Golf Club were extremely select. A Malay member of

TABLE 11
List of Asian Members of the Selangor Club and Selangor
Golf Club during the 1920s and 1930s

Tunku Abu Bakar (Selangor Club)	Second son of Sultan Ibrahim of Johore; State Veterinary Surgeon, Johore.
Choo Kia Peng (Selangor Club and Selangor Golf Club)	Leading businessman, member of the Federal Council.
Choo Kok Leong (Selangor Golf Club)	Son of Choo Kia Peng, educated at Dulwich College and at Oxford, lecturer at the School of Agriculture at Serdang (Selangor). As the son of a member he automatically became a member, but like any prospective member he was taken around, by his father, to meet members of the club.
Khoo Keng Hooi (Selangor Club and Selangor Golf Club)	Managing director of Chow Kit and Co., chairman of several other businesses, member of the Kuala Lumpur Sanitary Board (died in London in 1928).
H. S. Lee (Selangor Club and Selangor Golf Club)	Educated at Cambridge, leading miner, president of Selangor Miners' Association, member of the Kuala Lumpur Sanitary Board.
Loo Yew Hoi (Selangor Golf Club)	Banker, a trustee of the estate of Loke Yew.
Haji Mohamed Eusoff (Selangor Club)	The Dato Panglima Kinta, member of the M.C.S.
Raja Musa bin Raja Bot (Selangor Club and Selangor Golf Club)	Son of Raja Bot bin Raja Juma'at, member of M.C.S., passed bar examination in England, first Malay lawyer (1929), first Malay judge of the F.M.S. Supreme Court (1938).
Raja Uda bin Raja Muhammad (Selangor Club and Selangor Golf Club)	. . . a close connection of the royal house' of Selangor [Roff, Malay Nationalism, p. 237], member of the M.C.S., Selangor member of Federal Council.

Sources: This list is compiled almost entirely from interviews and personal communications. Some of the information I received is conflicting, but I believe this list is complete and accurate. I am indebted to Mr. Choo Kok Leong (interview, March 1973), Tan Sri Nik A. Kamil (personal communications, 23 April and 15 July 1974), Raja Fuziah Raja Uda (personal communication, 30 July 1973), Mr. T. M. Walker (interview, April 1972), and particularly to Mr. David Gray (interview, June 1972, and personal communications, 13 May 1973 and other dates) and Col. Tun Sir Henry H. S. Lee (interview, February 1973, and personal communication, 5 September 1974). My source for the fact that Khoo Keng Hooi belonged to the two clubs is his obituary in the Malay Mail, 7 May 1928. Biographical data come from directories, interviews, and other sources.

the M.C.S. or an Asian member of the Federal Council could, like Europeans in these positions, become a member of the Selangor Club, but, unlike his European counterpart, a Malay or Chinese police inspector would never be considered as a member nor would he even dream of becoming a member.

Having looked at the extent to which Europeans and Asians mixed in clubs in the F.M.S. it is useful to compare this with the situation in other parts of Malaya. In the Unfederated Malay States, where the traditional Malay élite maintained a much greater control over the governing of their states and where there were therefore more Malays in high governmental positions than in the F.M.S., the number of non-Europeans in the clubs to which Europeans belonged was much greater than in the federated states. This was especially true in Kedah and Johore. Referring to the Kedah Club at Alor Star, one woman wrote that 'all the Tunkus and Malay Heads of Departments were members and joined in all Club activities'.[52] The membership of the Kedah Club remained mainly European, however, because, according to one official who served in Kedah in the 1930s, the junior Malay officials preferred, even if they were on friendly terms with Europeans, the more relaxing atmosphere of their own club to being in the presence of the Regent and the Malay Judge.[53] In Johore Europeans, senior Malay officials, and a few prominent non-Europeans not in government service belonged to the Civil Service Clubs in the principal towns.[54] In Johore Bahru there was also a club known as the International Club, of which Sultan Ibrahim was president. Because of the Sultan's influence the members came from a variety of both racial and social backgrounds and included, one retired civil servant recalls, 'jockeys, riders, polo-players, golfers, Singapore tycoons, penniless princelings and such of his own enormous family ramifications as he was on good terms with'.[55] In the Straits Settlements, where Asians participated in government even less than in the F.M.S., there was much less mixing of Europeans and Asians in clubs than there was in the federation. In Singapore the two main European social clubs, the Tanglin Club and the Swimming Club, were both exclusively European in membership. In 1938 a group of Asians formed their own flying club when the Royal Singapore Flying Club refused to accept Asian members.[56] An exception to the prevailing pattern in Singapore was the Island Club, a 'non-racial' golf club founded in 1932.[57]

Equality of status may be seen as an important pre-condition for social relations between Europeans and Asians, but by no means did it guarantee such relations. Despite the advance in English education among Asians, cultural differences remained which discouraged social relations. The most important of these was the difference between the role of women in the European community and that of women in the various Asian groups. European women freely associated with their husbands and other men on social and public occasions, whereas Asian women remained in the background. Even when Europeans desired social contact with Asians this difference tended to hinder relations.

If a European couple were invited to an Asian gathering the European woman could either mix with the men or sit with the women. Either choice was likely to cause discomfort. If she associated with the men she was not conforming to Asian expectations and might therefore embarrass her husband. If, on the other hand, she associated with the Asian women she was likely to make both herself and the women uncomfortable. The cultural gap between European and Asian women was far greater than that between European and Asian men. Information from the 1931 census reveals that fewer Asian women than men were able to speak English. The percentages of Chinese men and women able to speak English were 3.7 and 2.6 respectively. For Malays the difference was indeed dramatic: 2.3 per cent of men but only 0.1 per cent of women were able to speak English.[58] Unfortunately the census does not tell us how many Europeans spoke Malay, but clearly far fewer European women than men were able to use Malay or any other Asian language at a level above that needed to give orders to their servants. The likelihood of a European woman and an Asian woman having a language in common was therefore extremely small.

It was equally difficult for Asians to conform to the usual style of social life among Europeans. At dinner parties the fact that Malay women knew no English and the European women knew little or no Malay 'imposed something of a strain on the hostess and indeed on all the guests'.[59] During the 1920s and 1930s the number of Asian women who were at home in a European social situation increased but was still very small: the majority of them were the wives of wealthy Chinese. Another bar was that European women were reluctant to invite Asian guests, even when the women came, because the Asian women would be unable to reciprocate by receiving European visitors of both sexes.[60] Europeans were particularly reluctant to invite Malays if, as was often the case, there was going to be dancing as they knew that Malays looked upon western dancing as suggestive of sexual intercourse; Malay men danced with lowly *ronggeng* girls, not their wives, and then without body contact. Swettenham suggested that when there was going to be western dancing it was better not to invite Malays.[61] It appears that European men were more afraid than were the women themselves that the latter might be seen as harlots. A British official serving in Kelantan complained about an Australian woman who had invited the Sultan's sons to parties at her house and had danced with them. When, later, Europeans were guests at the Sultan's palace she and other European women danced with the Sultan and his sons—'a terrible thing for them to do in view of the native's attitude to women'. Since the Malays would have been insulted if the women had refused to dance with them on this occasion, he wrote in his diary, it would have been better if the Australian woman had not asked the Malays to dance in the first place.[62] O'Grady believed that the attitude Asian men had towards women was the main reason it was essential to exclude all but a very few Asians from European social activities.[63]

During the inter-war years a small number of Asian men married European women, whom in most cases they had met while studying in Britain. Such marriages however did not encourage closer social relations between Europeans and Asians. Once an Asian and his European wife had returned to Malaya they found it extremely difficult to fit into either European social life or the social life of the husband's particular community. The European wives were almost always excluded from European society, not only because they had married Asians but also because most of them came from low social backgrounds in England. Only when the woman was married to an Asian of very high position (for example, the wife of Raja Musa of Selangor and, even more notably, the wife of Sultan Ibrahim of Johore) could she be confident of being accepted into European society. The European wife of an Asian also found it difficult to get along with her husband's relatives. This was particularly true if, as often happened, she refused to conform to the role expected of a wife in Asian society and if her husband's relatives had been planning to arrange his marriage to a Malay or Chinese girl upon his return from abroad. In the state of Perak a Malay who had married a European woman had to endure the disapproval not only of his relatives but also of the Sultan. In 1931 a relative of the Sultan's who had married an Englishwoman while he was studying in Oxford (where she worked as an assistant in a local chemist shop) was told by the Sultan to return without his wife, and in 1937 the High Commissioner reported that the Sultan had issued a *titah* (royal command) declaring that no Perak Malay who had married a European woman could hope to hold any office in the state government.[64] In Kedah the government passed a law in 1931 prohibiting members of the Ruling House from marrying Europeans without the consent of the State Council.[65] Inter-racial marriages were also discouraged by a general British policy which made any Asian who married a European woman while living in Europe ineligible for any government assistance to return to Malaya unless he agreed to return without his wife.[66] Under all these pressures marriages between European women and Asian men were not common (though still more common than between European men and Asian women), and those which did take place seldom lasted for more than a few years.[67]

Before concluding these sections which have taken a general look at European–Asian relations it is necessary to say a few words about the special case of relations between Europeans and Eurasians. The cultural differences which impeded relations between Europeans and other non-Europeans were much less pronounced in relations between Europeans and Eurasians. Nearly all Eurasian men and women spoke English, and of all non-European groups they were the ones most familiar with European culture. Nevertheless, the most striking feature of European–Eurasian relations was the lack of social contact between the two groups. Although Eurasians spoke English many did so with an accent, known as 'chee-chee', which was repulsive to English ears.[68] Europeans tended to portray Eurasians in the most unflattering terms. 'Taking the race as a whole,' H. N. Ridley had declared in 1895, 'they are weak in body, short-lived, deficient in energy, and feeble in morals.'[69] It was often said that Eurasians tried to compensate for a deep feeling of inferiority by displaying their importance relative to both Europeans and Asians. Whereas Ridley suggested that Eurasians behaved as they did because of European prejudices, many Europeans believed that their supposed defects were biologically inherent to Eurasians.

An important barrier between Europeans and Eurasians was the position of the latter in Malayan society. By far the great majority of Eurasians were employed in relatively subordinate positions. At the time of the 1931 census 249 out of 541 employed Eurasian males in Selangor were clerks, office assistants, typists, and draughtsmen; others were mechanics, shop assistants, railway workers, and subordinates in the medical services. Only a very small number were in the professions.[70] As a very large proportion of the Eurasians were government employees their means of rising to higher positions were restricted. Eurasians were as a group far more affected by the government's policy regarding the employment of non-Europeans in senior positions than any other section of Malayan society. The generally subordinate character of the Eurasian population was accentuated by the fact that in cases where Eurasians did achieve high status they sometimes ignored their ancestry and successfully identified themselves as members of the European group.[71] Although individuals were occasionally absorbed into the European group, Europeans usually disapproved very strongly when Eurasians tried to consider themselves as Europeans. Eurasians, wrote Peel, should have thought of themselves as a 'definite community and not try to pose as pure whites'.[72]

In the inter-war years some Eurasians did in fact attempt to promote a Eurasian identity. Readers of the *Eurasian Review* were encouraged to take pride in Eurasian accomplishments and to think of themselves as a distinct group in Malayan society. As in the case of the Anglo-Indians in India and the Indo-Europeans in the Netherlands East Indies political developments encouraged a greater sense of unity. Because of the advancement of Malays into the M.C.S. and the moves towards decentralization in the early 1930s, Eurasians feared that their position in Malayan society was in danger of falling rather than improving and that unless they were united they would be unable effectively to protect their interests. 'United we stand; Divided we fall' was the motto which one Eurasian suggested should be adopted by the Eurasian Associations of British Malaya.[73] Though with no success, Eurasians began to claim for themselves some of the privileges which the Malays possessed. In 1938, for example, Eurasians tried unsuccessfully to have the government provide their children with free primary education in English just as it provided Malay children with free education in Malay.[74]

The organization which promoted Eurasian interests in Selangor was the Selangor Eurasian Association. The association was founded in 1919 but showed little sign of activity until a group of young Eurasians revived it in the early part of 1934. A few months later the association had a membership of about 200, which was a substantial proportion of the Eurasian population.[75] In 1936 the association opened its own clubhouse. Though the association had the support of Eurasians in Selangor it was forced to close the clubhouse two years later because of a lack of funds. The association was able, however, to carry on an active sporting programme and helped to bring about the formation of Eurasian units in the F.M.S. Volunteer Force.[76] Clearly, by the latter part of the 1930s the Eurasians of Selangor were beginning to see themselves as a separate group rather than as an appendage of the European community.

The Rotary Club and Race Relations

For the most part neither Europeans nor Asians sought extensive social contacts. It was even more unusual for either Europeans or Asians to attempt to eliminate some of the existing barriers to social relations between them. In the mid-1920s, however, a small group of prominent Asians in Kuala Lumpur took the initiative in proposing that something be done to increase the amount of social contact between Asians and Europeans. How this initiative was received by Europeans is the subject of this section.

According to H. Benjamin Talalla, a leading Indian businessman, early in 1925 he and four other Asians (including Loke Chow Thye, who was at the time president of the Selangor Chinese Chamber of Commerce, and Khoo Keng Hooi) met to discuss 'the need in Kuala Lumpur of a non-communal social club, where men and women of various races could meet on an equal footing'.[77] At about the same time Yap Tai Chi, a son of *Kapitan Cina* Yap Kwan Seng, discussed the possibility of forming such a club with Sir George Maxwell.[78] Asians found support for the idea in a speech given by Sir Cecil Clementi, Governor of Hong Kong, in which he pleaded with Europeans in that colony 'to find ways and means of breaking down these partition walls between various sections of the community' and suggested the formation of a social club open to Europeans and Chinese as just such a means.[79] A Chinese correspondent to the *Malay Mail* said that a 'Concord Club' was needed in Kuala Lumpur as well; in fact, he added, such a club was needed 'whenever the governors and the governed are of different race'.[80]

Among Europeans the idea of a social club drawing its membership from the various ethnic groups was greeted with caution. Some Europeans did believe that they should have more social contact with Asians. The *Malay Mail* insisted, as it often did, that relations between Europeans and Asians were marked by goodwill and mutual respect, but the paper added that although Englishmen and Asians met frequently 'in the course of public duty or business such contacts are except in very rare cases superficial ones, and once the business that has brought them together is accomplished each party goes his own way, withdrawing within the practically watertight compartment of its own community'.[81] In Ipoh, where the idea of a Concord Club was discussed somewhat later than it was in Kuala Lumpur, an official observed that the social contacts Europeans had with Chinese were restricted to farewell dinners given by the latter when the former were going on leave or being transferred to another state.[82] Although many Europeans believed that they should have more social contact with Asians they did not want to go so far as to form a multi-racial social club. Their social needs were already well satisfied by numerous activities within the European community, and they did not want to pay dues for yet another club.[83] Others saw the dietary restrictions which Muslims and Hindus observed as a likely difficulty. Some objected because Asian men would probably not bring their wives and daughters to the club though they would expect to mix freely with European women; the editor of the *Straits Echo* suggested that this objection could be overcome by having the club for men only,[84] but a club for men only was unlikely to receive support either from European men or from their wives. (Unlike nearly all other Europeans, the editor of the *Straits Echo* strongly favoured a Concord Club; it was especially needed, he said, because a growing number of Asians who were educated in Britain and had become used to mixing with the people there were embittered to find on their return to Malaya that social contact with Europeans was now impossible.)[85] In replying to the Chinese correspondent who had suggested a Concord Club, the editor of the *Malay Mail* disagreed with the view that whenever the governors and the governed belonged to different races they should form a social club. Some non-Europeans, the editor declared, would feel embarrassed in more sophisticated company and would make others feel ill at ease as well.[86]

Indeed, although it was never stated so bluntly, the idea of a consciously multi-racial social club violated the basic principle that people usually joined together in a social club because they had a great deal in common rather than because they were aware of their differences. Europeans in Malaya belonged to clubs because, among other reasons, they provided a place where they could be free of the strain of dealing with 'alien outlooks' and where they did not have to worry about what kind of impression they were giving non-Europeans. Maxwell may have been aware of the reluctance of Europeans when he cautioned Chinese who were interested in a Concord Club against expecting it to be well attended during the first few days or even during the first few months.[87] The idea of forming a Concord Club was in fact quietly dropped.

A small group of Europeans, most of them officials, with whom the Asians interested in forming a multi-racial social club had been in touch, suggested that a Rotary Club would be a preferable means of encouraging social contact. Although the Rotary Club differed markedly from a social club in that members only met once a month, and then in a fairly formal setting, the idea was quickly agreed to by the Asians. The first monthly dinner meeting held in July 1928 was attended by nine Europeans, five Chinese, four Indians, and one Malay. The Asians were an extremely select group. Among the Chinese were Choo Kia Peng, Loke Chow Thye, and San Ah Wing, one of the leading businessmen in Selangor. Among the Indians were Talalla and S. Veerasamy, the Indian member of the Federal Council. The Malay at the first meeting was Hamzah bin Abdullah, the first Malay to be promoted from the Malay Administrative Service to the M.C.S.[88] Thus, although there were members of all races, differences in status were kept to a minimum. In keeping with its select nature the club's first meeting was held at the Chinese Millionaires' Club. While maintaining its select character the club's membership grew considerably. In September 1929, when the club was formally inaugurated by an official from Rotary International, there were about fifty members. At this time Europeans and Chinese in Ipoh were considering whether to form a Concord Club, but they abandoned this idea in favour of a Rotary Club. By 1932 there were clubs in Seremban, Klang, Malacca, Singapore, and Penang, as well as in Kuala Lumpur and Ipoh. The membership of the seven clubs in 1932 was made up of 303 Europeans, 94 Chinese, 42 Indians and Ceylonese, 29 Malays, and 30 Eurasians and other non-Europeans.[89]

The Europeans who were active in the formation of the Kuala Lumpur Rotary Club all saw the club as an important link between Europeans and Asians. It is clear that much of their initial enthusiasm for the club was based on nostalgia for a time when, they believed, relations with Asians had been better than in the Malaya of the late 1920s. Andrew Caldecott, the club's first president, said that when he served as an official in Jelebu before the

First World War he had made many friends among the Chinese, Malays, and Indians and had visited them in their homes. According to Caldecott, such informal mixing was no longer possible, but he believed that Rotary, with its emphasis on service to the community, would be a success.[90] L. D. Gammans, the club's first honorary secretary, looked back to a time when towns were small and 'there were frequent opportunities for the various nationalities to meet together socially or on the sports field'. As a result of the growth of towns, the spread of education, the advent of 'doubtful' literature and films, and the existence of subversive political beliefs the old harmony was being endangered. The Rotary Club, said Gammans, was an organization where men of all races could meet as social equals, exchange views, and therefore form bonds of understanding and friendship.[91]

For a few years Europeans in the Rotary movement believed that the clubs were fulfilling this ideal. Only sport was seen as having as great an effect on promoting relations between Europeans and Asians. By about 1934, however, a small number of Europeans and Asians began to question whether in fact the club's goals were being achieved. One hour a week or a month, much of it spent listening to a speaker, was not providing an atmosphere in which men could form lasting friendships. Whether or not Rotary was seen as a success of course depended on one's expectations. The *Malaya Tribune* pointed out that getting men of various races to sit around a table together each week was itself a great accomplishment,[92] but others clearly expected more from the club. The president of the Singapore Rotary Club complained that many club members attended when there promised to be an interesting speaker but not when the only attraction was the companionship of their fellow members.[93] As an intentionally multi-racial club there was also the question of balance of membership. The president of the Ipoh Rotary Club, a Malay civil servant, complained that there were too few Asian members.[94] Also in Ipoh the Asian members were reported to believe that the club was not achieving its goals.[95] Perhaps the strongest criticism came in a speech before the Malacca Rotary Club by Ho Seng Ong, Principal of the Anglo-Chinese School in Malacca. Ho asked his fellow Rotarians not to be content that their weekly luncheon meetings were creating understanding and friendship between men of different races. 'Rotary friendship', he said, 'is often a superficial affair.'[96] Even the editor of the *Malay Mail*, which had for so long carried enthusiastic reports of the Rotary Club, agreed with Ho's appraisal.[97] Because of this dissatisfaction with the Rotary Club a number of Asians and Europeans began to search for a better way of encouraging regular social contact between members of the various races. It was this dissatisfaction which led to the founding of the Suleiman Golf Club in Kuala Lumpur in 1939. The main founder of the club praised the work done by the Rotary Club, but he hoped that the new club would go much further towards fulfilling the ideals contained in the original proposal for a Concord Club.[98]

Neither between members nor between the groups as a whole did the Rotary Club change European–Asian relations as its members hoped. The entrance of a small number of Malays into the M.C.S. had a greater—though still small—effect; they were, if they wished, accepted into the main British social clubs simply because of the positions they held. Clubs reflected and reinforced political realities. It is for this reason that in the states of Kedah and Johore, where the British shared meaningful power with Malays, there was greater social contact between Europeans and Asians. Nevertheless, the Rotary Club was important in the history of European–Asian relations because it marked a growing awareness among both groups of the nature of their relations with one another. It also, as the *Malaya Tribune* pointed out, brought about more contact than there had been, even if this was usually superficial. And if only by such speeches as Ho's the Rotary Club made Europeans more aware than they had been of the views of some Asians.

8

European Men and Asian Women

EVEN in the inter-war years most European men in Malaya did not marry until they were thirty, and some never married. Until the early years of the twentieth century men postponed marriage mainly because living conditions were considered unsuitable for European women. As conditions improved men delayed marriage until they were sure that they could support a wife and continue to adhere to the European standard of living. As was shown in Chapter 6, government and private employers had various formal and informal regulations which were designed to uphold the European standard by preventing early marriage. While social relations with Asians were, as the preceding chapter has shown, very limited, the preponderance of unmarried males within the European group meant that many men turned to Asian women for sexual relations and sometimes for companionship as well. This chapter is concerned with relations between European men and Asian mistresses and prostitutes, the attitudes Europeans held regarding sexual relations with Asian women, and the ways in which concubinage and prostitution changed between the end of the nineteenth century and the inter-war years.

In the case of prostitution much of the discussion which follows relates to the Straits Settlements. European men living in the F.M.S. frequented brothels in the Straits as well as those in the Federation. Indeed, in the pre-World War I period one of a young man's first experiences upon arriving in Malaya for the first time was often a trip to the brothels of Malay Street in Singapore. Some attention is also paid to the broad outline of government policy regarding prostitution both in the Straits Settlements and in the F.M.S., for this is necessary for understanding the way in which Europeans were personally involved in prostitution.

It is unfortunate that because of a lack of information homosexual relations between European men and Asian boys and men cannot also be discussed in this study. One informant estimated that in the 1930s two-thirds of European men at some time had homosexual relations with Asians. Others, however, claimed that such relations were not common. It would seem that the intensity with which homosexuality was condemned must have discouraged such relations from being common. When in the 1930s the diary of a Chinese catamite was discovered by the police the official inquiry which followed brought disgrace to several prominent people and two men committed suicide.[1] It is likely that in his novel *The Soul of Malaya*, published in English in 1931, Fauconnier was suggesting that the intimate relationship between the French planter Rolain and his Malay servant was a homosexual one, but he never makes this explicit.

Prostitution and Concubinage before the First World War

Official British policy towards prostitution in Malaya must be seen against the background of events taking place in Great Britain in the second half of the nineteenth century. Between 1864 and 1869 Parliament passed the Contagious Diseases Acts in an effort to protect soldiers and sailors from venereal disease. The acts required prostitutes in certain garrison and port towns to register with the police and to submit periodically to a medical examination. Women who had venereal disease were detained for treatment and released only when a doctor certified that they were free of disease. Any woman whom the police suspected of being a prostitute also had to undergo a medical examination unless she could prove her character in a police court. The acts represented a victory for those who believed that men had to fulfil their sexual desires from time to time and that therefore it was only reasonable that they should be protected against infection. A growing body of public opinion in Britain, however, vehemently opposed the double standard of sexual morality which was embodied in the acts. Over a period of several years Mrs. Josephine Butler led a campaign to have the acts repealed.[2] During the same period there was a gradual shift among middle-class men away from the view (which was supported by many doctors) that they needed to indulge in sexual intercourse in order to maintain their health. 'Continence even to the point of asceticism', one Englishman observed in 1891, 'has become as universally recognized an obligation of human life as the restraint of other appetites once freely and almost without reproach indulged in even by persons of position and refinement.'[3] As a result of Mrs. Butler's efforts and the changing climate of opinion in Britain Parliament suspended the Contagious Diseases Acts in 1883 and finally repealed them in 1886.

The Contagious Diseases Ordinance which was passed by the Straits Settlements Legislative Council in 1870 closely resembled the Contagious Diseases Acts in Great Britain. Officials and doctors in the Straits Settlements were soon convinced that its provisions were bringing about a sharp decline in venereal disease and also benefiting the prostitutes themselves, the great majority of whom were brought from China by traffickers and sold to brothel-keepers. In 1888, two years after the repeal of the Contagious Diseases Acts in Britain, the Secretary of State for the Colonies instructed the Governor to withdraw the ordinance.[4] At about this time the various State Councils in the Malay States passed (with the Governor's approval) laws requiring the registration of all brothels and prostitutes and requiring prostitutes to submit regularly to a medical examination. In 1894, however, the Secretary of State forced the State Councils to repeal these laws. Officials in Singapore and in the Malay States, and some Asian leaders, deeply resented the Secretary of State's action. In their view compulsory registration had protected prostitutes from the exploitation of brothel-keepers since it ensured that the women were regularly interviewed by government officers. In the late 1890s officials in Malaya succeeded in persuading the Colonial Office that such exploitation was in fact taking place. The Colonial Office therefore allowed laws to be introduced which penalized brothel-keepers who prevented inmates from taking their grievances to the Protector of Chinese or from getting treatment for venereal disease. The Secretary of State prohibited any formal system of registration, but he did permit the Protectors of Chinese in the Straits Settlements and the F.M.S. to keep a list of 'known' brothels and prostitutes. The government was therefore able to conform to the wishes of Parliament and the British public and yet re-introduce some features of the Contagious Diseases Ordinance.[5]

After the introduction of these laws in 1902 the Secretary for Chinese Affairs encouraged both government and private doctors in the F.M.S. to open 'medical clubs' at which prostitutes would be examined and treated for venereal diseases. Several clubs were founded, and probably most prostitutes were regularly examined at them, but they proved to be a great embarrassment to the government. The clubs were supposedly voluntary, but because many of them were run by government doctors brothel-keepers feared that they would be prosecuted for failing to send their inmates to them. The clubs were therefore well attended and, in a few cases, very profitable for the doctors. After the running of the clubs erupted into a scandal in 1907 the Resident-General ordered government doctors to abandon any part they had in them.[6]

As has already been suggested, the views of officials in Malaya on the question of prostitution differed greatly from those which dominated official and public opinion in Britain. Malayan officials insisted that the moral standards which had led to the repeal of the Contagious Diseases Acts in Britain could not be applied to a society made up of many Asian peoples and in which men far outnumbered women in the various immigrant communities. 'Morality', explained Swettenham in 1891, 'is dependent on the influences of climate, religious belief, education, and the feeling of society.'[7]

Most Britishers viewed prostitution as an inevitable feature not only of Asian life in Malaya but also of their own there. They seldom could enjoy the companionship of women of their own race; the average age at which they married was even higher than that for men in Britain; they lived amidst a population which adhered to different standards regarding sexual behaviour; and they lived in a climate which was believed to heighten sexual passions. The British in Malaya therefore felt themselves to be relatively unrestrained by the late-Victorian convention which preached the value of sexual continence. When Robson commented in 1897 that Selangor was 'a country where the trammels of society and the voice of Mrs. Grundy are heard but little of and cared for less' he was referring to the fact the European men in Malaya enjoyed considerable freedom from sexual norms being observed in Britain.[8] In the Straits Settlements and in towns in the F.M.S. it was common for single men to visit brothels, while outside the towns in the F.M.S. it was common for European men to have Asian mistresses.

In Singapore Europeans and also wealthy Asians visited the European and Japanese brothels in the Malay Street area. There were also a much greater number of Chinese brothels in this part of the city, but these were never visited by non-Chinese. Some of the European and Japanese brothels in Malay Street were luxuriously furnished, and each had a large stone veranda where, according to a visitor who was crusading to have the brothels closed, 'the poor, painted creatures, bedecked in their tinsel, sit sipping coffee, smoking cigarettes, and accosting passers-by with the invitation, "Come in here, please".'[9] According to an official count, which may well have been low, in 1905 there were thirty European prostitutes living in eight brothels.[10] All of these women came from southern, central, and eastern Europe. If the police discovered that an Englishwoman was engaged in prostitution she was immediately deported because of the damage which she did to British prestige. In 1912 the *Straits Times* suggested that the presence of European prostitutes of any nationality also undermined British prestige. The paper agreed with the view expressed by the London magazine *Truth* that 'the native who can purchase for his sensual gratification a woman of the same colour as his rulers must . . . feel a lessening of the respect for the authority to which he is accustomed to bow down'.[11] Nevertheless, in the years before the First World War the government made no move to discourage European prostitution, provided that those engaged in it were not of British nationality. Far more common than European brothels were the Japanese brothels which were also in the Malay Street area. The prostitutes in these houses were smuggled out of Japan by traffickers in women, sold to brothel-keepers, and held under indentures.[12] Europeans who frequented European and Japanese brothels in Singapore were to some extent protected from venereal disease since the women regularly submitted to a 'voluntary' medical examination and if necessary received treatment.[13]

There were no European prostitutes in the F.M.S. In 1891 Swettenham observed that 'as a rule . . . the Chinese women are patronized by Chinese men, the Tamils by their own nationals, or, at any rate, by natives of India, while the Japanese and Malay prostitutes draw their clients from Malays, Eurasians and Europeans'.[14] A European seeking a prostitute nearly always went to a Japanese brothel. As Table 12 shows, the number of Japanese women in the F.M.S. increased dramatically during the 1890s and the early years of the twentieth century. In 1911, 900 of the 1,692 Japanese women in the F.M.S. were 'known' prostitutes,[15] and another 129 were, according to the census, brothel-keepers.[16] It was said that any town large enough to have a post office also had a Japanese brothel. In very small towns which lacked a government rest house Japanese brothels not only served their expressed purpose but also were used as hotels by

TABLE 12
The Japanese Population in the F.M.S.,
1891-1931

	1891[a]	1901	1911	1921	1931
Males	14	87	337	757	533
Females	100	448	1,692	1,321	790
Total	120	535	2,029	2,078	1,323
Percentage Females	88	84	83	64	60

Sources: F.M.S. 1901 Census, Perak Table 1, Selangor Table 1, Negri Sembilan
Table 1, Pahang Table 1; F.M.S. 1911 Census, Table 33; British Malaya 1921
Census, Table 16; British Malaya 1931 Census, Table 70.

Note: [a]The census gives no data on the sex of the six Japanese living in Pahang in
1891.

European travellers because of their high standard of cleanli-
ness.[17]

In the main towns Japanese brothels were concentrated along
particular streets. The centre of prostitution in Kuala Lumpur
was Petaling Street, which the government had reserved for
brothels when planning the town in about 1882. In the early
1900s it was a common sight to see European men in rickshaws
going to and from the Japanese brothels on the street.[18] In 1909
the Reverend W. E. Horley of the Methodist Mission, which had
a church and a school a short distance from Petaling Street (see
Map 3), unsuccessfully appealed to the Colonial Office to have
the brothels moved to a different location. The Resident of
Selangor easily persuaded the Colonial Office to drop the matter
by suggesting that Horley's only motive for having the brothels
moved was to increase the value of the mission's property.[19] Up
to 1909 one of the main centres of Japanese prostitution in
Seremban was Locke Road. In 1908 the manager of the Seremban branch of the Straits Trading Company, situated across a
small park from the brothels, complained to the Protector of
Chinese that 'the sights to be seen in the neighbourhood, at
times even in daylight, are of a rather indecent nature'. As a
result of his complaint the government told the women that they
would have to move to two streets where European women were
unlikely to pass.[20] According to one informant who grew up in
Seremban before the First World War, European men seldom
visited brothels in the town. A man would instead send his chauf-

feur to a brothel and have him bring a woman back to his bungalow for the night.[21]

As in Singapore, Europeans who visited Japanese brothels in the F.M.S. were to some extent protected against venereal disease. As mentioned, from 1902 to 1907 government medical officers ran private clinics or 'clubs' at which prostitutes were examined and treated for venereal disease. Each Japanese prostitute had a certificate (with her photograph) which the doctor signed after her weekly examination if she was free of disease. This was done mainly for the benefit of European men, for, as Ohana, the proprietor of two of the 'most fashionable' brothels in Petaling Street, explained, European visitors always demanded to see a prostitute's certificate before having intercourse with her. After 1907, when government doctors were prohibited from running the clubs, private doctors continued to issue similar certificates at the request of the brothel-keepers, who feared that without them they would lose business.[22]

European men looked upon the Japanese women primarily as a means for sexual pleasure, but they sometimes developed strong personal attachments to them. A poem in the *Malay Mail* in 1897 describes the funeral of a Japanese woman and how various Europeans reacted to her death. It begins:

> The funeral bier steals slowly by,
> Fair women turn their heads aside—
> And yet the purest there must die
> As poor love Geisha died.

A young man in town 'who never knew of better love than this', a horseman riding in the jungle far from town, and a man who until he met her had long given up all dreams of love, all mourn her death. The last stanza of the poem again refers to the European women who happened to witness the funeral procession:

> All virtuous the world appears—
> But those who turn aside
> May never win such honest tears
> As fell when Geisha died.[23]

According to Robson, writing in 1894, Japanese women were sometimes engaged by Europeans to work as 'house-keepers', but we can assume that they did more than look after the efficient running of the bungalow. Robson hinted at this himself when he commented that the Japanese housekeeper 'is both pretty and jolly: small wonder then that many a solitary Tuan is only too glad to ask his mirth-provoking little house-keeper to sit down to tea with him'.[24] In order to obtain a Japanese mistress the lonely European had to pay the brothel-keeper a sum of money in order to free her of her indentures. Most of the men who acquired Japanese mistresses in this way were planters. Although some men discarded their mistresses after they had been together a few years, others lived with the same woman for twenty years or more. In a few cases unions formed before World War I were broken only when all Japanese in Malaya were interned at the outbreak of the Pacific War.[25]

Whereas prostitution was mainly an urban phenomenon, concubinage was confined almost entirely to rural areas. In about 1904 a teacher at the Victoria Institution in Kuala Lumpur had a Chinese woman living with him,[26] but this must have been unusual. Referring to the early years of the twentieth century, Sir Malcolm Watson later claimed that some 90 per cent of European men living in outstations had Asian mistresses.[27] To my knowledge there is no way of confirming Watson's estimate, but there is good reason to treat it with respect—Watson's work as a malariologist constantly brought him into contact with planters and officials in Selangor and other parts of the F.M.S. A very high proportion of planters had mistresses in the years before World War I. The rapid growth of the rubber industry after 1900 brought about a great influx of young, unmarried men, and these men lived on estates scattered over a wide area and only loosely connected by the expanding road and rail network. The mistresses of planters, recalled Watson, 'supplied the only companionship which these men had, often from one week to another. They were ... helpmates without whom many more ... men would have succumbed to both alcohol and malaria.'[28] In his memoirs Bruce Lockhart, who was a planter in Negri Sembilan, made several references to the Asian mistresses of planters. Robert Enger, a 'German of good family', had a 'stout, middle-aged Tamil lady' as his mistress; the two of them were often seen riding in and out of Port Dickson in a rickshaw. Lockhart himself had a Malay mistress.[29]

Concubinage was by no means practised only by planters. In his autobiography Winstedt implied that officials in outstations in the early 1900s frequently had Asian mistresses, and he went on to explain the reasons that the practice was common:

No home life, no women friends, no libraries, no theatres or cinemas, not always [a] big enough community for bridge or tennis, no motor-cars, no long walks on account of that labyrinth of trackless jungle: was it any wonder that the white exile took to himself one of the complaisant, amusing, good-tempered and good-mannered daughters of the East?[30]

An Australian railway engineer opening the line through Pahang shortly before the First World War lived openly with a Malay woman. 'My God! I've been in this bloody jungle for fifteen years, and the only things that keep me alive are Siti and the Sydney *Bulletin*!'[31] Hubert Berkeley, Bozzolo's successor as District Officer of Upper Perak, was certainly unusual in that in 1908 he could readily offer a young cadet an attractive Malay schoolmistress both to teach him the language and to keep him company at all hours.[32] Finally, the mistresses of officials are the subjects of several works of fiction, including most notably Clifford's *Since the Beginning*. Among tin miners it is known that William Steward, whose murder in 1911 was the basis of Somerset Maugham's story 'The Letter', discussed in Appendix 2 of this study, had a Chinese woman living with him at the time of his death.

In the years shortly before World War I and particularly after the war concubinage became less and less common. Before tracing this decline it is necessary to look at the attitudes Europeans had concerning sexual relations between European men and Asian women.

Attitudes toward Sexual Relations between European Men and Asian Women

One of the best ways to begin to examine European attitudes regarding sexual relations with Asian women is to look at the flurry of letters which followed an editorial in the *Malay Mail* in November 1922 and a smaller number of letters which appeared in the *Planter* in the early part of 1923. It was the editorial's concluding paragraph which sparked off the correspondence. Whereas women had some choice whether they would live in Malaya, wrote the editor, men had no choice in the matter. 'All men will not lead celibate lives in the tropics. Some may but the majority won't. And this means adding to the mixed population.'[33] Although these words were the immediate cause of the correspondence the time was ripe for a discussion on the question of sexual relations between European men and Asian women. By the 1920s the British were much less reluctant to express their views on sexual matters than they had been before the First World War, though most of the correspondents who replied to the editorial preferred to write under pseudonyms. A more important reason had to do with the economic conditions of the time. Since the early 1900s salaries and living conditions had steadily improved, and as a consequence more and more men had been able to marry. These trends were, however, temporarily halted by the trade slump which began in the latter part of 1920. The *Malay Mail* editorial thus came at a time when men were finding it more difficult to marry and to support a wife in the manner expected by the European community and when therefore it looked as if the average age at which men married would now tend to increase. Because of this prospect some Europeans were asking themselves whether in the long period before marriage men were justified in turning to Asian women for sexual relations. The following pages survey first the correspondence which took place at this time and then other sources which reveal European attitudes.

Among men who wrote letters to the *Malay Mail* and the *Planter* in 1922–3 opinion was divided between those who condoned sexual relations with Asian women and those who condemned it without reservation. The former view was most forcibly expressed by 'Necessitas Non Habet Legem', who wrote that men turned to Asian women 'more from stern necessity than from desire'. He refuted the medical opinion that abstention from sexual intercourse was not harmful to the body. Only when the government and commercial firms encouraged men to marry early in their careers, he argued, would 'laxity of living . . . be a thing of the past'.[34] Two men attacked 'Necessitas's' view with some vehemence. First 'F.M.B.S.-S.' condemned him as a man who was consumed in lust, who showed a dangerous disregard for the prestige of the white race, and who had no pity for the 'outcast children' created by unions between European men and Asian women. Furthermore, he said, 'Necessitas' had 'no thought of bare justice to the pure bride whom he holds it as his right eventually to win'. 'F.M.B.S.-S.' then turned his thoughts to his own daughter who was at school in England: 'Heaven grant that if she marry in this country it may not be to take the place—the room, the furniture, God forgive these men, even the *bed*—of some pitiable dispossessed native prostitute, as I have with bitterness of heart seen happen to many a cherished daughter of parents far away.'[35] In his response to this letter 'Necessitas' asked whether 'F.M.B.S.-S.' could honestly claim to have led a pure life himself before marriage.[36] Similarly, a writer in the *Planter* who had been accused of squandering his salary on a native mistress pointed out that married men in Malaya 'all have pages in their history which are never displayed to the world'.[37] The second writer to attack 'Necessitas' in the pages of the *Malay Mail* wrote that the latter's claim that Europeans could not be continent in the tropics was 'an insult to their manliness and self-control': moral laxity was supposed to be a common trait among Asians, not Europeans. Young men, he stated, should be able to find other channels into which to sublimate their sexual energy.[38] In support of 'Necessitas', however, came a letter from 'Anti-Hypocracy', who accepted sexual relations between European men and Asian women as inevitable under current conditions. In his view the only choice men had was between concubinage and prostitution. Concubinage was preferable because there was less likelihood of getting venereal disease, which men might in turn give to their European brides when they married.[39]

The European women who voiced their opinions in the *Malay Mail* in 1922 all disapproved of sexual relations taking place between European men and Asian women, but they gave somewhat different reasons for their disapproval. 'A Woman' brought up the double standard of sexual morality, that sexual practices which would be condemned for women were tolerated for men. Only if girls insisted, claimed 'A Woman', that their potential husbands had led equally blameless lives before marriage would the problem cease. But the co-operation of those already living in Malaya was essential because brides coming out from England often learned the truth about their husbands only after arriving in Malaya and getting married. Thus it was up to all 'decent minded people' to ostracize all men of 'known laxity of life'.[40] 'Another Woman' also expressed her sympathy for the 'countless disillusioned brides' and agreed that libertines should be drastically dealt with, but she could not help pointing out that the double standard was just as much a feature of society in Britain as it was among the British in Malaya.[41] Of all the correspondents 'All White' was the one most outraged at sexual relations between European men and Asian women, and she went directly to describing what it really was that upset her and probably many other European women. Why, she asked, did men not marry now that living conditions were suitable for white women?

Surely it is not that they prefer black to white. This is truly what hurts us women, the feeling that men prefer a native woman to one of their own. I do not know of K[uala] L[umpur], but out back one hardly dare drive in the town for fear of being confronted by a Tuan along with his native fancy driving about together in a car.

Unlike 'A Woman', 'All White' was not protesting against the double standard. Indeed she seems to have been resigned to it. She was however revolted by the idea of men actually appearing to *like* Asian women. 'I am not a prude, and know few men are pure on their marriage—but I draw the line at color.'[42]

This revulsion by European women at men having close relations with a 'native' woman must have been strongest when a woman found that her own husband had been involved in such a relationship. In Maugham's story 'The Force of Circumstance' Guy, an official in Sarawak (which Maugham visited in 1922), goes home on leave and meets and marries Doris without telling her that he had a Malay mistress and three children by her. Shortly after they return to Sarawak Guy tells Doris that sometimes men turn to Asian women in their loneliness, but she is not disturbed because she assumes that he would never have done this himself. When the continuing appearance of his mistress forces him to reveal the facts of his past, Doris is unable to accept the idea and eventually decides she must leave. 'It is a physical thing,' she tells Guy, 'I can't help it, it's stronger than I am. I think of those thin, black arms of hers round you and it fills me with a physical nausea.'[43]

Guy's failure to persuade Doris to stay derives both from his having had sexual relations with a Malay woman and his inability to convince Doris that this situation had been solely the result of 'The Force of Circumstance'. He had lived with his mistress for ten years, and together they had established quite a family. Bad though it was regarded it appears that much was forgiven if a man gave no hint that the relationship was anything but one based purely on necessity. It was one thing for a man to write, as one did during the 1922 debate, that 'no sane man would ever form an irregular union with a woman, who at best is a sorry makeshift, if he knew that a girl of his own race was willing to share hardships during early years'.[44] It was quite another thing however for men to give the impression, so resented by 'All White', that they actually preferred Asian to European women.

As has been suggested, European men often claimed that they took Asian mistresses out of necessity. It was sometimes also stated that Asian women possessed a physical attractiveness which a European male found very difficult to resist and that the tropical climate made resistance to their charms doubly difficult.

Think of the young assistant standing all day over Asiatic labour, many of them working with breasts and bodies exposed to the sun,

13 Children and their *amahs* at a party, Kuala Lumpur, 1933. (*Mrs. Mary C. Hodgkin*)

14 A Malay servant. (*Mrs. Mary C. Hodgkin*)

15 Hugh Clifford's Residency at Pekan, about 1894. (*Royal Common-wealth Society*)

16 'Carcosa', official residence of the Resident-General, late 1890s. (*Arkib Negara Malaysia*)

17 Bungalow of a junior married government officer, Kuala Lumpur, 1930s. (*Mrs. Mary C. Hodgkin*)

18 Interior of the same bungalow. (*Mrs. Mary C. Hodgkin*)

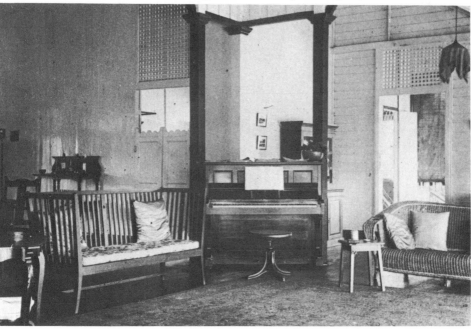

19 Planter's bungalow, 1909. (*Arkib Negara Malaysia*)

20 Estate manager's bungalow, Tanjong Malim, about 1930. (*Royal Commonwealth Society*)

21 Interior view of the same bungalow. (*Royal Commonwealth Society*)

22 Mrs. Treacher, wife of the Resident of Perak, at 'The Hut', Maxwell's Hill, sometime in the latter part of the 1890s. (*Arkib Negara Malaysia*)

23 Smoke House Inn, Cameron Highlands (photograph taken in 1952). (*Royal Commonwealth Society*)

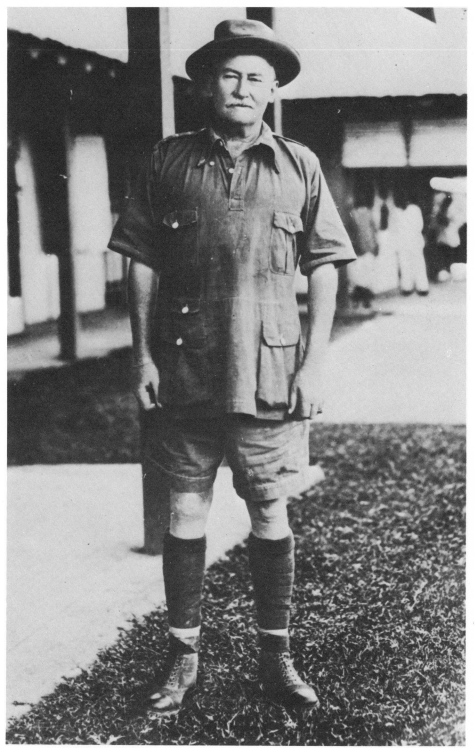

24 Hubert Berkeley, District Officer of Upper Perak, about 1922.
(*Royal Commonwealth Society*)

25 Hubert Berkeley (the middle of the three Europeans in the picture) and his elephants, Upper Perak. (*Arkib Negara Malaysia*)

surrounded by women to whom a few dollars are a fortune for which they would sell the best of themselves, and exposed to all the insidious temptations of the heated tropical zone.[45]

The heat, the climate, had a stirring effect which a man in England cannot fully appreciate. Add to that the sight of a graceful brown form with full breasts scantily covered, a perfect figure, a moon-like face and sensual mouth, framed in a jet-black head of hair, illuminated by dark, soft eyes, and the bachelor would not be human if he did not set his thoughts agoing.[46]

Under these circumstances, it was implied, no man could be entirely blamed for having sexual relations with an Asian woman.[47] By the same token, no man who succumbed to an Asian woman would be thought to have the same lofty feelings towards her that he supposedly would have for a European woman.

Nowhere is the contrast between a man's feelings toward an Asian mistress and then a European wife better drawn than in Clifford's novel *Since the Beginning*, published in 1898, which is to my knowledge the only Malayan novel which has concubinage and marriage as its major theme. Not long after he comes to the Malay state of 'Pelesu' on a visit Frank Austin, a promising young official with a wide knowledge of Malay society, learns through an intermediary that one of the girls living in the Sultan's compound wants to become his mistress. He flatly refuses this suggestion, but when he is told that the girl Maimunah will be bathing in the river the next day and that he can easily see her from the houseboat where he is staying he is tempted to take a look. Seeing her bathing in her green *sarung* Frank is enthralled by her beauty, which derives in great part from her Arabic features, and when she is able to leave the compound secretly late at night to visit his houseboat he manages to tell her she must go away only with the greatest effort. When describing Frank's feelings toward Maimunah the author carefully points out that these 'were not to be dignified with the name of love; but they were born of that overwhelming attraction which the physical beauty of a woman may have for a man, without his heart or his intellect being in any way influenced by her.' Frank succumbs to Maimunah's great beauty and takes her as his mistress. After a while, however, he grows tired of her and decides that he must leave her. After telling Maimunah that he is leaving Malaya for good and giving her the sum of $500, Frank goes to England on leave, meets and marries a girl named Cecily, and brings his bride back to Malaya, where he takes up a post in a different district. The physical attraction Frank had toward Maimunah is contrasted with his pure, deep love for Cecily. There is no hint of base physical passion—when Cecily tells Frank she is going to have a baby it is almost as if it had come about by a miraculous conception.[48]

The Decline of Concubinage

Over a period of about a decade beginning shortly before the First World War the proportion of European men living with Asian women declined markedly. In a letter to *The Times* in 1927 the Bishop of Singapore attempted to refute a statement made in a recently published book that in Malaya 'nearly every' European planter had an Asian mistress. However true it might have been in the past, the Bishop declared, the statement was 'grossly untrue' as far as the present was concerned. His own estimate, made after talking with several men with an intimate knowledge of planters' lives, was that 'less than 10 per cent' of planters had mistresses.[49] According to Sir Malcolm Watson, only 2 per cent of men living in outstation districts had Asian mistresses by the time he left Malaya in 1928.[50] Finally, in 1935 another writer assured the readers of *British Malaya* that although economic conditions were making it difficult for planters to marry they were not being driven into the arms of Asian women: 'the fact is that a custom once prevalent lingers now only to a very limited extent.'[51] Thus, although estimates of how common concubinage was in the inter-war years vary somewhat, it is certain that it was much less common than it had been in the early years of the century. A Colonial Office directive, demographic changes, and opinion within the European community all combined to bring about this sharp decline.

In 1909 the Colonial Office officially declared its disapproval of concubinage. In January of that year Lord Crewe, Secretary of State for the Colonies in Asquith's Liberal government, issued a circular warning officials overseas of the consequences of becoming involved with local women. The incident which provoked Crewe to issue the 'concubine circular', as it was commonly known, took place in Africa rather than Malaya. An acting District Commissioner in Kenya arranged through a local chief to have a young African girl come to live with him and had intercourse both with her and with another girl who was living with, though not married to, an African policeman. It was because the officer's affairs were noticed by the only European woman living in the area and her husband that official action was taken. As a result of the couple's persistent complaints the District Commissioner lost one year of seniority and was told that he would not be allowed to take charge of a district again for at least two years. The lady and her husband, however, saw this as a very mild punishment and therefore appealed to Lord Crewe. They were told that general steps, including the issuance of a circular, were being taken 'with a view of discouraging the practices'. Still unsatisfied, the couple appealed to the British public in a long letter to *The Times*.[52] In response to this letter one Englishman with many years of experience in Africa said that readers should understand that African girls were 'fully developed' at the age of twelve, but another writer and an editorial in *The Times* insisted that the government should take firm action to ensure that 'the practices' did not happen again.[53] Several Members of Parliament raised questions about the case; all said the errant official should have been dealt with more severely, and all asked for an assurance that the government would not allow such acts in the future.[54]

While he did nothing further about this particular case, Crewe issued a confidential circular to officials not only in Africa but also in Ceylon, Fiji, British territories in the Western Pacific, Hong Kong, and Malaya. In addition to a letter to the Governor of each territory there were numerous copies of two enclosures, 'A' which was to be shown to all new officials when they first arrived and 'B' which was for officials already in government service. As Enclosure 'A' was still being shown to government servants in the 1930s it is worth looking at in detail.

Crewe did not dwell on the moral objections to concubinage as he said these were self-evident. Instead he concentrated on the damage such 'ill conduct between Government officials and native women' did to administration. It was impossible for any official to tolerate such practices in others let alone do so himself 'without lowering himself in the eyes of the natives, and diminishing his authority to an extent which will seriously impair his capacity for useful work in the Service in which it is his duty to strive to set an honourable example to all with whom he comes in contact'. Crewe concluded by saying that he did not want to 'cast any reflection' on new officials but only wanted to warn them of 'the disgrace and official ruin which will certainly follow from any dereliction of duty in this respect'.

In only slightly milder language Crewe appealed to those already in the service in Enclosure 'B'. After repeating the same argument against concubinage as in Enclosure 'A' he said that he was sure that concubinage received nothing but 'the gravest condemnation' from civil servants and asked for their co-operation 'in vigorously reprobating and officially condemning all such practices of concubinage between Civil Servants and native women whenever and wherever they are detected'. Crewe, however, wished to have more than the co-operation of civil servants. In his letter to the Governors he made it clear that senior officers were to be told that it would now be part of their duty to take official action 'whenever an instance of conduct to which I have referred comes to their notice'.[55]

Because of a lack of contemporary sources it is hard to know exactly how great an effect the circular had in discouraging concubinage. But it is certain that it had some effect. According to Victor Purcell, who began his career in Malaya soon after the First World War, 'it was the common practice for M.C.S. officers to keep Malay mistresses' until Crewe issued the circular, and several officers decided to marry their mistresses rather than give them up. While claiming to know of several 'successful' Anglo-Malay marriages, Purcell named only that of Charleton Maxwell and a Malay woman, and he did not indicate whether they had married as a result of the circular.[56] A memorandum prepared by the Secretary for Chinese Affairs of the F.M.S. in 1921 or 1922 stated that the circular had not only deterred concubinage but had also discouraged men from visiting 'known' brothels. Many people, he reported, had been led 'to think that occasional lapses from virtue would be considered [as] reprehensible' as living with an Asian woman and as a result now patronized 'sly' (i.e., not 'known' to the Chinese Protectorate) prostitutes.[57] In 1919 Bucknill briefly referred to concubinage and prostitution, but he did not say how these had been affected by the concubine circular. Unless the government enabled men to marry early in their careers, he argued, it 'will reap—even more fully than now—the disadvantages and embarrassments caused by its officers by temporary liaisons with women of non-European race, by all the sordid adjuncts which attach themselves to prostitution and by the unfortunately here only too common concomitant of venereal disease'.[58] This statement would suggest that at the time he was writing Bucknill believed that long-term relationships between officials and Asian women were not common.

The concubine circular discouraged government servants from living with Asian women. At the same time important changes were taking place within the F.M.S. which also helped to bring about a decline in concubinage. The most important of these was the influx of European women which took place after World War

I. As already mentioned in Chapter 6, the proportion of European men who were married increased considerably after the war. The influx of European married women and a smaller number of single women is reflected in the improvement (in the sense of becoming more nearly normal) in the sex ratio in the European population. In 1911 there were, as Table 13(a) shows, 40 females per 100 males, while in 1921 there were 50. The

TABLE 13
The European Population of the F.M.S.:
Sex Ratios, 1891–1931
(*Females per 100 males*)

(a) *By State*					
	1891	*1901*	*1911*	*1921*	*1931*
Perak	41	47	43	50	56
Selangor	31	41	41	54	58
Negri Sembilan	36	30	34	49	53
Pahang	—	24	26	32	54
F.M.S.	37	41	40	50	56
(excluding Pahang)					

(b) *Four Main Towns and F.M.S. excluding Four Main Towns*				
	1891	*1911*	*1921*	*1931*
Kuala Lumpur	31	61	66	65
Ipoh		57	64	64
Taiping		71	75	85
Seremban		47	66	86
Four Main Towns		61	67	68
F.M.S. excl. Four Towns		29	42	48

(c) *On Estates*			
	1911	*1921*	*1931*
	17	38	43

Sources: Selangor 1891 Census; F.M.S. 1901 Census, Perak Table 1, Selangor Table 1, Negri Sembilan Table 1, Pahang Table 1; F.M.S. 1911 Census, Tables 2, 6, and 48; British Malaya 1921 Census, Tables 6, 11, and 43; British Malaya 1931 Census, Tables 3, 18, and 22.

most striking fact revealed by Table 13 is that by 1921 European women were distributed over a much greater geographical area than they had been before the war. In 1921 planters were a slightly older group than they had been at the time of the previous census and thus more likely to be married. For this reason alone more European women were living in rural areas. Moreover, as living conditions and transportation improved European women were less confined to the towns than they had been. Thus, whereas, as Table 13(b) shows, there was a slight improvement in the sex ratio among Europeans living in the four main towns, among Europeans living outside these towns there was a more marked improvement from 29 (females per 100 males) in 1911 to 42 in 1921. Table 13(c) shows that among Europeans living on estates the improvement was even more pronounced, from 17 in 1911 to 38 in 1921. Looking at the sex ratios among Europeans on estates in two of the main planting districts, we find that in Klang there was an improvement from 12.5 to 43 between 1911 and 1921, while in Kuala Selangor there was an improvement from 13 to 49 during the same period. Between the 1921 and 1931 censuses the sex ratios among Europeans living outside the four main towns and among those living on estates improved still further, though not as dramatically as during the previous ten-year period.

These demographic changes contributed to the decline in concubinage in two ways. First, and most obviously, a greater proportion of those men most likely to have mistresses, namely those living in rural areas, were now accompanied by European wives. Second, and perhaps even more importantly, the growing presence of European women in these areas also affected the behaviour of those men who did not have wives. In 1923 one planter commented that there was no need 'to draw pen pictures of the moral conditions prevailing in a district wherein there are white women and wherein there are not' for the difference was obvious.[59] At the very least an outward display of respectability was required whenever a European woman lived in the area. To use the common expression, men never 'flaunted' their mistresses. Referring to the plantations of Malaya in the late 1920s, Alec Waugh wrote that 'there is fairly often a Malay girl who disappears discreetly when visitors arrive'. As long as a man did not appear openly with his mistress, as long as he did not acknowledge her as more than a sexual partner, he had done nothing (to use Waugh's phrase) 'that involves loss of caste'.[60] A European woman could however cause considerable embarrassment if she disapproved even of men who kept their mistresses well in the background. One woman who observed two mattresses being aired outside a bachelor's bungalow broadcast the news that he had an Asian woman living with him.[61] Another woman who was collecting donations on Poppy Day refused to call at the house of a planter who she knew had an Asian mistress.[62] One further demographic change is relevant to this discussion. As pointed out in Chapter 2, during the 1930s rubber companies reduced the size of their estate staff, and they tended to do this by releasing young, unmarried men. Thus, in the 1930s there were even fewer unmarried men living in areas where there were no European women than there had been in the previous decade.

General improvements in transportation and living conditions also contributed to the decline in concubinage. By the 1930s there were very few men who were unable to meet other Europeans regularly for social events. Far fewer men, therefore, felt the need to turn to Asian women for companionship than had been the case before the First World War. 'Whatever loosening of standards may have occurred in the old days of loneliness, imperfect methods of communication and lack of social intercourse,' declared one planter in 1935, 'it is very certain that no such immorality exists today, now that good roads and motor cars have placed neighbours, clubs and relaxation in easy reach of us all.'[63] Some planters nevertheless did have mistresses, but, as has been emphasized, these relationships were conducted with great discretion.

For some planters discretion was needed not only because of the presence of European women but also because the companies for which they worked disapproved of their having mistresses. The management of Socfin, as portrayed in Boulle's novel *Sacrilege in Malaya*, would allow a bachelor to have an Asian woman in his bungalow for a day or two but would take steps to ensure that she stayed no longer than that.[64] Concubinage was also publicly disapproved by the association to which the majority of planters belonged, the Incorporated Society of Planters, which had the aim of promoting planting as a profession. As part of its campaign to improve salaries following the depression the I.S.P. tried to present to employers the view that only the most depraved and incompetent planters were satisfied with present conditions: 'The man who is happy with a native girl [and] who drowns dull care in a plentitude of *stengahs* ... may be satisfied. Steady, thoughtful men are not.'[65] Only the few remaining proprietary planters were relatively free from outside pressures. According to one planter who worked on an estate on the Selangor–Negri Sembilan border in about 1930, the veterans of the Great War who had been given grants of one hundred acres to start their own estates usually had 'a resident "keep"'.[66]

The pressures which discouraged concubinage in rural areas were greatly intensified in the towns. It was acceptable for British officials, planters, bank assistants, and businessmen to visit brothels. To appear in public with a Eurasian or Asian woman, however, could have serious consequences. If a man was seen with a non-European woman his superior would soon find out about it; sometimes the superior's wife was the one who reported the breach. The superior would then call the young man in and warn him never to let it happen again.[67] Such a warning was indeed an effective deterrent. Men wanted to remain on good terms with the local young European women. Moreover, particularly in the 1930s, they could not afford to do anything which would put their jobs in jeopardy. Under these conditions marriages between European men and Asian women were extremely rare; some of the persons interviewed for this study could not recall a single case of intermarriage. 'Our employers, both Government and Commercial,' a Guthrie's employee later explained, 'expected us to remain European in every way and if we had ambitions we did so as much to please our employers as ourselves. Thereby, we ensured advancement in our career.'[68]

In this discussion the decline in concubinage has been explained solely by looking at changes taking place within the European community. But were there any pressures coming from within the various Asian groups which tended to discourage their womenfolk from becoming mistresses to Europeans? Starting about 1910 various nationalist groups in the Netherlands East Indies agitated against concubinage,[69] but to my knowledge there was no similar agitation in Malaya, where there was much less political activity in general than there was in the Dutch colony. In 1941 the leader of Tamil estate workers on strike in Klang district demanded, among other things, 'an end to the molesting of labourers' womenfolk by Europeans',[70] but this demand of course could not have had any effect on the trends which have been described in this section. It is possible that by the 1920s concubinage had become less attractive to Asian women for other than political reasons. They may have resented being kept more in the background than they had been before the war,[71] they may have avoided concubinage because it was now a relatively short-term relationship and therefore one which was less secure than it had been, or they may have found more profitable and attractive opportunities in the towns. All this is however in the realm of speculation, and it is mentioned here only in the hope that evidence might be found to fill in this part of the story.[72] It is however now possible to say something about the background of the women who became mistresses to Europeans and how they came to be mistresses.

Mistresses

According to Winstedt, the Malay mistresses of early officials were women who had been divorced for barrenness by their own menfolk. Although I have no evidence which confirms Winstedt's statement, several informants mentioned that mistresses were women who had been divorced if not for barrenness then for some other reason. Whether or not they had been divorced, it is clear that mistresses were often women who were at least not highly sought after by men in their *kampungs*. Swettenham's description of the Malay mistress of a European in his story 'The Eternal Feminine' as a woman 'born of the people, neither good nor beautiful, nor attractive, nor even young as youth goes in the East'[73] probably applied equally well to the mistresses of other Europeans. When Frank Austin, the hero of Clifford's novel *Since the Beginning*, hears that a Malay girl would like to live with him he supposes that she must be 'the lowest of her kind' to want to become involved in an illicit relationship with a non-Muslim.[74]

A European could not simply take as his mistress a girl whom he found especially attractive. In a story set in Singapore in the 1890s an English official who tries to lure away the beautiful, aristocratic Malay wife of a Malay-Indian businessman not only fails to get the woman but also nearly loses his life.[75] In general, European men accepted the fact that if they took a Malay woman in opposition to her relatives death or serious injury might result. Few bothered to put this to the test. Since Malay women were closely supervised and since they were kept apart on social occasions it was extremely unusual for a man even to know of a woman whom he would like to have as his mistress.

The case of Bruce Lockhart and his Malay mistress Amai was truly exceptional in this respect, but as the best documented example of relations between a European and a Malay woman it is worth considering in detail. And the case illustrates very well the difficulties a man faced if, as was likely, his efforts to have a particular woman as his mistress were opposed by her relatives.

In 1909 Lockhart went to Pantai, a *kampung* a few miles from Seremban, to open a rubber estate. Revelling in his role of being 'the sole representative of the British Raj' in the area he became attracted to the Malays living near the estate and made many friends among them. The leading Malay in the area was apparently the former Dato Klana of Sungei Ujong,[76] who invited Lockhart to watch a *ronggeng* at his home. At this time Lockhart was unable to look about at the women of the royal household because he was seated securely between the Dato Klana and his wife and because the women had their heads covered. To repay the Dato Klana's hospitality Lockhart invited him, his household, and the whole village to his house for another *ronggeng*. It was on this occasion that Lockhart first saw Amai, 'a radiant vision of brown loveliness in a batek skirt and a red silk coat'. Lockhart, who had not spoken to a European woman for over a year and who at the time was steeped in the romance of the East as portrayed in Pierre Loti's novels, was overwhelmed even though he was unable to speak to her. He learned from the village headman that Amai was a relative of the Dato Klana's and that she was married but about to divorce her husband and marry the Dato Klana's cousin. 'The crow does not mate with the bird of Paradise,' the headman warned him, and a British police officer advised him that other women were more easily and safely obtained than one of royal blood.

Lockhart did not however give up his pursuit of Amai. With the headman's help he contacted an old midwife (*bidan*) living in the Dato Klana's household who conveyed to Amai Lockhart's expression of love. Soon after her divorce Lockhart again contacted her with the help of the headman and the midwife to arrange for her to run away from the royal household to come to live with him. Armed with a revolver in case their plans were betrayed, Lockhart went to the meeting place in the jungle, Amai came at the appointed hour, and he led her off to his bungalow. It was then that Lockhart had to face the consequences of his actions. The Dato Klana's wife came to the front of his bungalow to try to persuade him and then to threaten him into giving up Amai, while another relative offered him a beautiful but lowly Malay girl as a substitute for Amai and warned him of trouble if he failed to accept this offer. All Lockhart's Malay friends deserted him, and his Chinese cook left out of fear that the food might be poisoned. Years later Lockhart wrote that he considered converting to Islam to calm the anger of the Malays. After they had been together a few months Lockhart became seriously ill with malaria and eventually was forced to leave Malaya in order to restore his health. When he visited Malaya many years later Lockhart talked with Amai for a few moments and learned that after his departure she had married a local religious leader.[77]

Intermediaries played an essential role in helping a European to find a mistress, just as they did in making marital arrangements in the various Asian communities. An intermediary would locate a girl who wanted to become a mistress and, even more importantly, would find out whether her relatives agreed with the idea. Speaking of 'the more native States', by which he meant the Unfederated Malay States and the predominantly Malay parts of the F.M.S., one civil servant wrote that concern for the welfare of a lonely European sometimes prompted 'an Asiatic to suggest a "companion" to relieve the monotony and loneliness'.[78] A Selangor Malay whom I interviewed claimed that Asian subordinates on estate staffs sometimes helped planters for whom they worked to find mistresses in the hope that by performing this service they would gain some advantage.[79] Servants sometimes acted as intermediaries. 'These relationships . . . begin as a business transaction with the parents of the girl,' wrote Waugh, who was trying to dispel the impression given in some novels about the life of the British in the East that Asian women thrust themselves upon European men, who were powerless to resist their great charms. 'There is no process of selection. It is arranged through the head boy.'[80] According to one informant, a retired planter, a European who wanted a mistress would contact an old Malay woman who specialized in making such arrangements. 'She was generally a divorcee or widow . . . and though it may not have been her only source of income she certainly got a commission from the girl's parents or guardian. . . . She may also have been involved in legitimate bridal arrangements among Malay families.' Furthermore, he recalls, a man living in an area where Islam was strictly observed might have to become, at least temporarily, a Muslim as part of the arrangements in order to satisfy the girl and her relatives. (A Malay informant who lived in Perak in the inter-war years has insisted that Malay girls never lived with Europeans unless the man had become a Muslim and a wedding had been performed.) Another planter interviewed for this study has pointed out that a man might come to have a mistress in one of several ways. A planter who was living alone, he remembers, was sometimes approached by a mother from a nearby *kampung* asking whether he would like to have her daughter as his mistress. She would have obtained some idea from his servants or the labourers on his estate what kind of person he was. Finally, a few planters, as mentioned earlier, had Japanese mistresses, and others had women such as dance hostesses they had met while visiting the large towns.

It would be safe to say that nearly all Malay mistresses came from families very low in the social hierarchy. Becoming a mistress could do little to hurt such a woman's social status and might in fact improve it, while it would very likely enable her (and her relatives) to live a little more comfortably than she would otherwise. When the man with whom she lived married a European woman or retired to Britain a mistress usually received a large sum of money. According to an informant who worked for one of the large British banks in Kuala Lumpur, some men who had retired to Britain made regular payments through the bank to support their former mistresses.

When a planter wanted a mistress he was subject to one severe restriction. It was one of the iron laws of conduct that a planter should not take one of the female labourers on his estate as his mistress. It was feared that such an arrangement would involve him too deeply with his labourers, possibly lead to favouritism, and affect the efficient management of the estate. When a planter was discovered to have broken this rule he could expect to lose his job. Bilainkin quoted one planter as saying that 'only last month a fellow off the next estate went home for the reason that his bungalow had been misused', while another planter said that he had known 'in the years just after the war four or five men sent home in one ship because of this kind of bother'.[81] Bilainkin was trying to correct the impression which he thought was given by Fauconnier in his novel *The Soul of Malaya* that planters freely borrowed the wives of their Tamil workers. It may however have been less a violation of the rule when the woman was not one of the main estate labour force but connected with the planter's household staff. The narrator's mistress in *The Soul of Malaya* is the gardener's wife, while Boulle mentions in his novel that Sophia (as he calls Socfin) 'turned a blind eye on the cook's wife. She did not, properly speaking, form part of the native personnel.'[82] The rule which prohibited a planter from taking a female labourer on his own estate as a mistress contained the implication that 'one's attentions should be confined to the women of the *neighbouring* plantations'.[83] Indeed, according to one informant with a wide knowledge of estates in Malaya, planters sometimes arranged with friends who managed neighbouring estates to have women on their estates come for short visits.

Prostitution and Venereal Diseases
between the Wars

During and immediately after the First World War prostitution underwent many changes in both the Straits Settlements and the F.M.S. The most important of these as far as Europeans were concerned were the demise of the established brothels, the increasing tendency of men to resort to 'sly' prostitutes, and a growing concern about venereal disease.

The European and Japanese brothels located in the Malay Street area of Singapore were closed within a space of five years. The government closed the European brothels after the outbreak of war in Europe, apparently because the great majority of the women in these houses were citizens of countries hostile to Great Britain. The Japanese brothels were closed in 1919 at the request of the Japanese Consul-General in Singapore. As a result of the closure of these brothels European men instead had sexual relations with women who were referred to as 'sly' prostitutes because they worked in hotels, 'eating houses', and private homes rather than in 'known' brothels. Among those with whom Europeans came in contact were Eurasian, Chinese, and 'Muhammadan' (Malay, Javanese, and other Muslim) women. There were also a few Japanese women. After the Japanese brothels were closed Japanese businessmen working in Singapore had brought in some women from their country to serve them as geishas, but as these men imported more women than they needed for their pleasures some of the women became prostitutes. Venereal disease was very common among all of the 'sly' prostitutes with whom Europeans had intercourse, but the rate among Muslim women was particularly high. Among the men themselves venereal disease had become extraordinarily prevalent. In 1921 one authority estimated that about 40 per cent of the European population (presumably adult males) had or had had venereal disease.[84] Two years later the rate was estimated by various experts to be between 25 and 80 per cent.[85]

As noted earlier in this chapter, the concubine circular had encouraged government servants in the F.M.S. to frequent 'sly' prostitutes rather than to visit recognized brothels. In so far as Europeans were concerned, relations with 'known' prostitutes became even less common after most of the Japanese brothels were closed in the latter part of 1920 and the beginning of 1921. Although the majority of the women in these brothels returned to Japan at the urging of the Consul-General, a large number remained. At the end of 1927 there were still 268 'known' Japanese prostitutes in the F.M.S.[86] Many other Japanese women were brothel-keepers and 'sly' prostitutes. Even as the Japanese brothels were being officially closed in Selangor one official observed that 'the Japanese coffee shops and lodging houses which are taking the place of the brothels are undoubtedly cheap brothels for all classes'.[87] At these hotels and eating houses on Petaling Street and along Batu Road, one planter recalls, 'you could get Beer and almost any race of girl';[88] some of the prostitutes were Japanese but the majority were Chinese, Siamese, and women of other races. Europeans sometimes also visited the less ornate Malay brothels which were scattered about the F.M.S. As Table 14 shows, over half of the European men treated for venereal disease at the Sultan Street Clinic in Kuala Lumpur in 1927 claimed that they had contracted the disease from intercourse with Malay women. Although the rate of venereal disease may have been relatively high among Malay prostitutes this fact does indicate that illicit sexual relations between European men and Malay women were fairly common. If we assume that the relative severity of venereal disease among prostitutes of each race remained fairly stable between 1927 and 1931, the table would

TABLE 14

Ethnicity of Women from whom European Men Treated at the Sultan Street Clinic Contracted Venereal Disease, 1927–1931

(Per cent)

	1927	1928	1930	1931
Chinese ('sly')	12.8	19.8	23.6	27.6
Malays	55.2	43.5	28.7	30.3
Siamese	6.1	14.3	31.5	36.0
Tamils	12.3	13.5	5.6	3.1
Japanese	8.4	6.3	4.6	.4
Eurasians	—	2.5	1.4	.4
Europeans	—	—	—	2.2
Others	5.0	—	4.6	—
Total	99.8	99.9	100.0	100.0
No. of cases	179	237	216	228

Source: Annual Reports of the F.M.S. Medical Department.

Note: Spaces marked (—) where ethnic category not used during the year.

FIGURE 4
Number of Europeans Treated for Venereal Diseases
at Government Clinics in the F.M.S., 1925–1938
(Shaded area shows number treated at Sultan Street
Venereal Disease Clinic, Kuala Lumpur, during years for
which separate statistics are available)

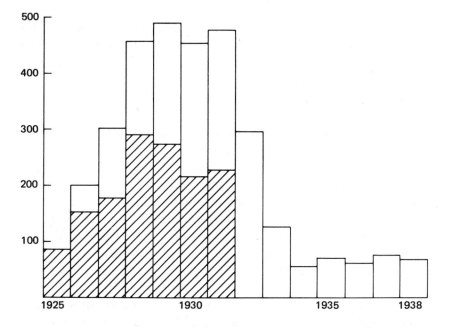

Source: Annual Reports of F.M.S. Medical Department.
Note: For 1925 only the number treated at the Sultan Street Clinic is available.

suggest that over this period European men had less sexual contact with Malay and Japanese prostitutes and greater contact with
Chinese and especially Siamese prostitutes. Sometime during this
period a Siamese brothel was opened on Batu Road.[89]

Venereal disease was probably as common among European
men in the F.M.S. as it was among men in the Straits Settlements. In 1919 a doctor who had a private practice in Kuala
Lumpur said that venereal disease 'is extremely prevalent at the
present time' among European men.[90] As Figure 4 shows, the
Sultan Street Clinic, which was opened in 1924, and other venereal disease treatment centres in the F.M.S. were well attended
by Europeans. The sharp rise between 1925 and 1928 in the
number treated probably does not indicate any significant rise in
the rate of venereal disease among European men. Instead it is

likely that Europeans increasingly tended to obtain treatment from government clinics rather than from doctors in private practice. In each of the years between 1928 and 1931 about one-seventh of all adult European males in the F.M.S. received treatment for venereal disease at a government clinic. There does not appear to have been any stigma attached to visits to the Sultan Street Clinic; one planter who had occasion to use its facilities referred to it as the 'Sultan Street Club'.[91] Nevertheless, an unknown and perhaps significant number of Europeans who had venereal disease did not seek treatment at government clinics.[92] Between 1927 and 1929 about seven European women were treated at government clinics for venereal disease. In all likelihood these women had contracted the disease from their husbands.

During the 1920s the governments of the Straits Settlements and the F.M.S. desperately sought ways of controlling venereal disease. Europeans were by no means the only group in Malayan society to be affected. In 1923 various experts placed the rate of venereal disease for the population of Singapore as a whole at between 25 and 85 per cent; most of these experts believed that the rate was above 50 per cent.[93] In Britain the Venereal Disease Regulations of 1916 empowered local authorities to establish free and confidential treatment centres.[94] A similar policy was pursued in Malaya when the government set up venereal disease clinics in all the major towns. Since the treatment of venereal disease had advanced enormously since the turn of the century men and women who attended these clinics could be fairly certain of being cured. Government officials, doctors, and the general public however believed that more drastic steps had to be taken in order to bring venereal disease under control. In 1923 the Venereal Diseases Committee, appointed by the Governor to report on venereal disease in Singapore, recommended that *all* brothels and prostitutes ('sly', as well as the remaining 'known' Chinese brothels and prostitutes) should be registered, that brothels should be assigned to one part of the city as they had been before the war, and that prostitutes should be required to have regular medical examinations.[95] In short, the committee proposed a system of state regulation of prostitution which was far stricter than that which had existed when the Contagious Diseases Acts were in force in Britain. It was mainly because of their abhorrence of such regulation that an advisory committee set up by the Colonial Office objected very strongly to the Venereal Diseases Committee's recommendations. The advisory commit-

tee also attacked the proposals on medical grounds. It insisted
that the regular examination of prostitutes was not effective in
preventing the spread of venereal disease since a woman might
contract the disease and transmit it to many men before the time
came for her examination. The advisory committee instead
recommended that all brothels should be closed as soon as possible.[96] In 1929 a second committee set up by the Colonial Office
endorsed this recommendation.[97] Despite the opposition of
many Europeans who believed that officials in Britain failed to
appreciate how conditions in Malaya differed from those in
Europe,[98] legislation was passed in the Straits Settlements in
1930 and in the F.M.S. in January of the following year which
made all brothels illegal.

The legislation did not however bring prostitution to an end.
In the early part of 1931 a *Malaya Tribune* reporter discovered
that clandestine prostitution was flourishing in Singapore. During
his tour of the brothels he met many Europeans—'some holding
responsible positions in the Colony!' He also found that many
European prostitutes were working in Singapore. In order to cir-
cumvent the law against brothels these women lived alone or
made calls on their clients.[99] 'We . . . think it is disgraceful', the
Malay Mail declared, 'that European women should be allowed
to practise prostitution among a great Asiatic population, who
are only too apt to judge the character of European nations as a
whole by what is exemplified in individuals here.'[100] Except for
French 'dress makers' who very occasionally visited Kuala Lumpur there were no European prostitutes in the F.M.S.; any white
woman discovered to be engaged in prostitution was quickly
deported. Despite the new legislation the Japanese 'eating
houses' along Batu Road continued to serve as brothels during
the 1930s. One of these houses was particularly well known to
Europeans; the woman who ran it was so trusted that sometimes
young men from outstations would leave their money in her care
during their visits to Kuala Lumpur.[101] Although prostitution
continued, it is clear that the Medical Department's campaign to
reduce the incidence of venereal disease was successful. In the
case of Europeans, as Figure 4 shows, there was a very marked
decrease in the rate of venereal disease during the 1930s.

A new feature of Malayan social life in the 1930s was the
cabarets. Several were opened in Singapore, Penang, and Kuala
Lumpur. In Kuala Lumpur the Bukit Bintang Amusement Park's

cabaret was very popular with the general population of the town, while Europeans usually went to the cabaret at the Eastern Hotel. The main attraction of these cabarets was the dance hostess or 'taxi girl'. The majority of the dance hostesses at the Eastern Hotel were Chinese; the remainder were Eurasians and other Asian girls. When the music started a man would go over to where the girls were sitting and ask one of them to dance; for each dance he would give the girl a ticket (costing 10 cents) from a book of tickets he had paid for earlier in the evening. The taxi girl was paid by the manager by the number of tickets she collected during the night. One visitor to the Eastern Hotel observed that the girls were 'extremely pretty in a fragile, Oriental sense'. When he questioned his host about the propriety of the cabaret he was assured that the girls were not prostitutes. The Europeans present 'simply came to dance without any ulterior motive. They knew perfectly well . . . that any close relationship with an Asiatic woman would be the equivalent of social suicide.'[102] In fact, informants say, some of these girls were prostitutes.[103] Indeed, this was perhaps the most significant aspect of relations between European men and Asian women. A man could pay to dance with an Asian woman at a cabaret. It was also usually condoned if he had sexual relations with an Asian woman. If, however, he wished to appear openly with an Asian woman and to treat her as he would a European woman he was indeed committing 'social suicide'.

Some Concluding Remarks

THIS study began with the purpose of examining, on the one hand, relations within the European community and, on the other, relations between Europeans and Asians. Perhaps what this study has shown more than anything else is the importance of the European standard of living for understanding both of these broad issues. Since the British controlled the administration and since they played a dominant role in the economy it is hardly surprising that many Europeans occupied high positions in Malayan society and that many of them therefore enjoyed a relatively high level of comfort. The important point, however, is, to repeat Emerson's words, 'not that there are some Europeans who are living luxuriously, but that, broadly speaking, there are none who do not live in that fashion'. Whatever was in fact the basis of British rule in Malaya, the British themselves believed that their rule was based on the respect in which they were held by the Asian population and that in order to preserve this respect all Europeans should live above a certain standard. We have seen how at various times during the period covered by this study the British took steps to ensure that this principle was maintained in practice. During the years when planters enjoyed great prosperity the standard of living to which Europeans believed they must adhere rose. As a result government servants appealed to the Colonial Office, ultimately with success, to have their salaries increased to a level which would permit them to observe the new standard. During times of economic crisis the government supported unemployed Europeans or gave them passages out of Malaya because destitute whites were believed to pose a great threat to British prestige. It was for the same reason that the government removed European train drivers from Malaya as soon as it could replace them with Eurasians and Asians.

The fact that the European standard of living was generally maintained affected the whole character of the European community. First of all, it helped to shape the social composition of the community. By offering high salaries employers were able to attract men from the middle class of British society. This was particularly important in the case of private employers, such as rubber companies, since most of the positions which they offered did not require men who possessed definite academic or professional qualifications. Second, the European standard had an enormous effect on social relations. Most Europeans received salaries which allowed them to participate in the same social activities. The general insistence on a European standard prevented the number of 'poor whites' from increasing to the point where they might form a large and distinct European sub-group. There were of course social divisions within the European community. In Kuala Lumpur there was as early as the 1890s a distinction between those Europeans who belonged to the Selangor Club and those who belonged to the more exclusive Lake Club. In Taiping there was a similar distinction between members of the Perak Club and the New Club. The most important division within the European population, however, was between those Europeans who belonged to one of the main social clubs and those who did not. Because so few Europeans lived below the generally accepted standard the latter category was very small indeed. While tending to minimize social differences within the European population, the European standard of living contributed to the social division which existed between Europeans and Asians. Only a very small proportion of the Asian population enjoyed a standard of living as high as that enjoyed by most Europeans. The difference in standards of living was however not the only barrier between Europeans and Asians. Racial prejudice, cultural differences, and the fact that the British only very slowly admitted Asians (and then only Malays) to higher positions in the government services also impeded social relations.

The need to adhere to a certain standard of living had a great impact on personal aspects of the European way of life. As salaries improved and as living conditions became more suitable for European women it became easier for men to marry, but both the government and private employers took steps to ensure that men did not marry before they were able to support their wives in the expected manner. Since most men did not marry until they were about thirty years old, and since there were few unmarried European women in Malaya, men continued to outnumber women even during the inter-war years. It was partly for this reason that European women in Malaya were treated with much greater deference by their menfolk than were women in Britain. Although men outnumbered women, the character of the European community was not changed by the admission of non-European women by intermarriage. A man might have illicit sexual relations with an Asian woman, but if he showed the slightest intention of marrying a non-European he was likely to lose his job. Indeed, the man who married an Asian woman and continued to live in Malaya was usually described as having 'gone native'; he was, in short, no longer accepted as a member of the European community.

This study has also brought out the ambivalent relationship Europeans had with Malaya. We have seen very clearly that Europeans did not regard Malaya as 'home'. Most men began their careers in Malaya when they were in their early twenties, they found wives in Europe, and, largely because of beliefs about the effects of the tropical climate on Europeans, they returned to Europe periodically on leave. They sent their children to Britain to be educated, and they spent their retirements in Britain. During their years in Malaya they enjoyed social activities that were to be found in British society, read British newspapers, and closely followed events in Britain. By building hill stations they even tried to re-create the climate of their homeland. At the same time, the Europeans were changed by their experience in Malaya. Most Europeans were able to enjoy a higher standard of living than would have been the case if they had remained in Britain. For many reasons, not the least of which was this higher standard of living, their social life was if anything more active and varied than that which they would have been able to enjoy in their homeland. Moreover, most Europeans in Malaya were able to exercise far greater authority than was commonly exercised by people of similar social background within British society. Soon after his arrival a European quickly became used to being 'a white man amongst a great many natives'.[1] The attitudes and behaviour of Europeans were profoundly affected by the fact that they were constantly aware of their position in Malayan society and were often very concerned about how they were being perceived by Asians. 'Two Englishmen, one here & one at home,' commented one keen observer of his fellow Europeans, 'might easily be men of different race, language, & religion so different is their outlook & behaviour.'[2] This was perhaps an exaggeration, but it reminds us that Malaya had at least as great an impact on the Europeans as they had on Malaya.

Finally, this study has shown that social relations between Europeans and Asians in the Federated Malay States must be seen against the background of political and economic relationships. Before about 1900 the economy was almost entirely in Chinese hands, and British officials relied on the help of the *Kapitan Cina* and other Asian leaders in governing the Asian population. In Selangor, as we have seen, social relations between the British and Asian leaders were fairly common under these circumstances. As European miners and planters began to gain a much larger share of the export economy and as the government began to rule the Chinese more directly, such relations became less frequent, despite the fact that because of the advance of English education the cultural gap between Europeans and Asians was becoming less pronounced. Nevertheless, Asian leaders retained considerable influence, and Europeans, particularly those who administered the government, did not wish to jeopardize the goodwill which they believed existed between themselves and Asians. We have seen how in 1905 leaders from all the main Asian communities combined to bring about an end to racial segregation on the railways, and how in 1931 Asian leaders (though mainly Chinese and Christian Indians in this case) succeeded in having the European Hospital opened to non-European patients. Although wishing to maintain a public image of cordiality, Europeans did not seek extensive social relations with Asians. Europeans wished to relax in the company of people of similar background and interests. By excluding non-Europeans they did not have to worry whether they were behaving in such a way as to maintain their prestige in Asian eyes. A few Asians did however participate in European social activities. We have seen how during the inter-war years Malay Rulers, Malays in the Malayan Civil Service, and a few other very prominent non-Europeans took part in such activities. In the Unfederated Malay States, where Malays retained a significant role in administering their states, the social division between Europeans and Asians was less pronounced than it was in the F.M.S. In short, this study has shown that although there was a strong tendency among Europeans towards racial exclusiveness the relative importance of Asians in the political and economic spheres influenced the extent to which this exclusiveness was fulfilled in practice.

The European way of life in Malaya as it has been described in these pages came to an abrupt end early in 1942 when British forces surrendered to the Japanese at Singapore. The British could no longer think of themselves as the guardians of Malaya's peoples. 'One man came to me as I was blowing up petrol pumps,' said one government engineer, who was destroying materials which might be used by the advancing Japanese, 'and asked: "Does this mean that our protectors are deserting us?" I couldn't look him in the face.'[3] For the Europeans who lived in Malaya the fall of Singapore was not only a great military defeat, and often the cause of personal suffering, but also a humiliating blow to the prestige which they so cherished. Observing that few Asians helped to resist the Japanese invasion, some Europeans even began to wonder whether their prestige had ever been as high as they had imagined. A few went so far as to explain the British defeat as in part the result of what they regarded as the decadent way of life Europeans had been leading and their failure to mix socially with Asians.[4] Others hoped that once the Japanese were defeated they would be able to redeem themselves in Asian eyes. In 1945 the British did return to govern Malaya, but they found that its people were not prepared to accept their rule for an indefinite period. In 1957 the British relinquished their control over all of Malaya except for the island of Singapore. The transfer of power to a Malayan government did not immediately change all aspects of the life of Europeans (by then including more and more Americans),[5] but it ensured that they would never again occupy the same position in Malayan society that they had before 1942.

Appendix 1

Hubert Berkeley:
The Last White Rajah
District Officer

IN the years just after the First World War there were often complaints by both officials and others about the way in which the position of the District Officers had changed since the formation of the Federated Malay States. Since about 1900, it was asserted, the District Officer had been steadily losing his traditional authority to the Residents and the officials in the federal secretariat in Kuala Lumpur. A mass of government regulations now required the District Officer to refer the most trivial matters to his official superiors. Because the District Officer was so occupied dealing with the mounting piles of correspondence he was no longer free to roam about his district getting to know the people, hearing about their problems and solving them as best he could on the spot, and explaining government policies. In short, it was argued, District Officers—and therefore the government for which they were the local representatives—were losing touch with the people in the districts.

This view of the way in which the role of District Officers had changed overlooked the fact that by the 1890s the growth of the government bureaucracy and, equally important, the growth of European social life had already gone a long way to cutting District Officers off from the people in their districts. Nevertheless, in the 1920s the centralization which had taken place since the turn of the century was seen as the main cause of the loss of contact between District Officers and the population in their districts. In 1922 the District Officer of Kinta, Meadows Frost, made an impassioned plea to the Retrenchment Commission for decentralization. He claimed that an elaborate bureaucracy had been built up which suited Europeans in commerce, mining, and planting and also westernized Chinese, but not the great mass of Asians, especially the Malays. The 'average Asiatic', claimed Frost, 'thinks a great deal of the personality of the officer with whom he has direct dealings and much prefers that the officer shall be able to deal with his particular business at once even though it be in a rough and ready manner rather than be put to the trouble of conforming to a number of regulations which may be very excellent in their way but which he does not understand or care about in the least'.[1] Although the members of the commission agreed with Frost that the role of the District Officer, 'the direct link between Government and the people', should be strengthened, no change was made as they were unable to show that this would help to reduce government spending.[2] In 1932 the Federated Malay States Retrenchment Commission was again to argue the need to give District Officers greater powers so that they would be less burdened with office work and thus free to roam about their districts.[3]

According to Frost, it was essential to restore powers to the District Officers, but it was already impossible to return 'to the patriarchal form of Government' which once existed. In the 1920s there was one District Officer who did rule his district as a patriarch and with a remarkable degree of independence from the Resident and the officials in Kuala Lumpur. This was Hubert Berkeley of Upper Perak, often referred to as the 'Uncrowned King of Upper Perak' or the 'King of Grik'. Unlike most officials, who moved from one part of Malaya to another as they were promoted or temporarily filled posts of other officials who were away on leave, Berkeley spent nearly all of his long period in Malaya in one district. His first position in Malaya was Inspector of Police in the Dindings in 1886. In 1889 he joined the Perak Civil Service, and in 1891 he was stationed in Upper Perak for the first time and served there for short periods until 1902. In 1903 he was promoted to become District Officer of the important Klang district in Selangor, but in the following year he returned to Upper Perak. Except for service as a Captain in the Worcestershire Regiment during the First World War, Berkeley remained in his district until his retirement in 1926 at the age of sixty-two, seven years beyond the age at which most officials retired. During his years in Upper Perak Berkeley came to regard it as *his* district. When J. S. W. Reid, who wrote a short but vivid picture of Berkeley's rule, arrived in the district in 1922 he noticed that the District Office peons each wore 'a large circular silver badge containing the figure of an elephant . . . and the motto "Koh Dhulu"'; Berkeley had adopted this as the district badge, and he used the same design on the rest house dishes and on his personal notepaper.[4]

Most of the many anecdotes about Berkeley relate to the contempt he had for his official superiors and his efforts to maintain his independence from them. He had a comfortable outhouse which, according to one young official who served under him, was decorated with government minute papers and instructions, on which he had written bawdy comments.[5] According to one popularly-told story, he prevented the visit of one high official by having a great tree felled across the road to Grik. When, during the rice shortage which occurred shortly after the

First World War, Berkeley refused to co-operate with a general plan on how rice supplies should be distributed, he was allowed to organize the distribution however he wished within his own district.[6] Even the High Commissioner during Berkeley's last years in Upper Perak, Sir Laurence Guillemard, later acknowledged that Berkeley 'had acquired a position of almost royal authority and independence'.[7]

Berkeley's relative independence was made possible not only by the force of his character but also by the nature of his district. It was one of the districts least affected by the great economic and social changes taking place in Malaya, both because Berkeley discouraged any such changes and because the district offered little attraction to investors. In area Upper Perak was nearly as large as the state of Selangor, but its population was about one-twentieth that of Selangor. Slightly more than three-fifths of this sparse population were Malays; in Selangor just over one-fifth of the population were Malays. In the entire district there were, at the time of the 1921 census, only twenty-five Europeans, of whom all but four were men.[8] In 1922 the only Europeans living in Grik besides Berkeley and Reid were a surveyor and an engineer, both of whom were often away on duty. Berkeley avoided paper work as much as possible; most of the little that needed to be done was left to his Malay assistant and the chief clerk.[9]

Mainly because there were only a few miles of roads, Berkeley almost never travelled by car while in his district. Instead he relied on his horses and elephants. At the rear of his two-storey house were stables and nearby was an elephant loading platform. Elephants occupied an important part of Berkeley's life. One named Awang Padang received considerable attention in Berkeley's diary during a week in 1907:

March 12: Awang Padang throws Che Ngah at 6 P.M. and hurts him badly. Unable to get A. Padang
March 13: Out after Awang Padang all the morning
March 15: out all day after Awang Padang . . .
March 16: out after Padang
March 18: . . . Awang Padang caught[10]

Berkeley took long journeys through his district on elephants, as well as by horse and boat, and on ceremonial occasions at the royal capital of Kuala Kangsar he brought his elephants down from Grik.

In his life at Grik Berkeley followed a leisurely routine. Like Hugh Low, the Resident of Perak when he first came to Malaya, Berkeley enjoyed the company of unusual pets; besides a Siamese cat, he had an otter and two wah-wahs. He got milk from his cows, raised sheep for meat, and had his own padi field. Dressed in a *sarung* and *baju* he proceeded once or twice a week in his two-horse carriage to hot springs a few miles outside Grik where he had built a shallow cement pool and changing hut. 'A Malay syce and groom sat on the dickey and often two or three of his retainers' children shared the back seat with him.'[11] Christmas was the high point of the year. Berkeley invited old friends to stay with him and invited the local population to take part in the festivities. Hundreds of people arrived for the feast provided at Berkeley's (or perhaps the government's) expense. In the afternoon there would be cockfighting on the lawn outside the house, and in the evening large numbers of Malays watched the *wayang kulit*. At other times of the year Berkeley would also hire a *dalang* for *wayang kulit* performances, and he frequently watched *mayong* shows.[12]

It was often said that Berkeley knew the names and life histories of nearly all the inhabitants of his district. Included in his diaries are detailed genealogies of important families and a short history, apparently based on information given to him by local Malays, of Siam's claim to the northern part of the Perak River valley. Berkeley was not only an observer of his district but also personally involved. In 1918 he recorded in his diary: 'Hear of poor Mina's death. Her mother died in 1904—her father a year before at Sumpitan. On Tapong's death July 1906 she came to me aged 10 & and married Nawi Oct 1910. Three little boys.'[13] In a will he wrote in 1907, just before going into the hospital for an operation, he left $1,000 to buy wet-rice land for a boy and a girl, Sari and Kesom, and $200 for a woman named Selama.[14] Berkeley's diaries do not reveal whether Selama was his mistress and Sari and Kesom his children, but this must be considered a strong possibility. Later the same year Berkeley arranged Sari's wedding, for which various local individuals and groups presented several bulls and buffaloes.[15]

The actual governing of Upper Perak was carried out with the least possible formality. Reid recalls accompanying Berkeley on one occasion as he covered his district:

> There would be a land succession case to hear, a civil or land boundary dispute to settle, some small irrigation scheme to inspect, occasionally arrangements to be made for an advance to cover the cost of maintaining and training a newly captured young elephant. Any Malay passed on the way would be spoken to. . . .[16]

In governing his district Berkeley did what he thought was correct and just rather than follow set rules. Early in his career, as a magistrate in Gopeng, Berkeley is said to have decided a civil case in which there was a great deal of conflicting evidence by ruling in favour of the winner of a tug-of-war contest between the two sides.[17] Not surprisingly, Berkeley hated lawyers and discouraged them from entering his district.[18]

It has been suggested that unlike in the case of Bozzolo, Berkeley's equally seigniorial predecessor in Upper Perak, Berkeley's eccentricities aroused great interest and were the subject of numerous stories because, unlike Bozzolo, he came from 'a very important and well-connected English or Irish family'.[19] Indeed, Berkeley belonged to an aristocratic Roman Catholic Worcestershire family; his father was a descendant of the sixth Baron Berkeley, and his mother was a daughter of the third Earl of Kenmare.[20] Such a background may have helped him to get away with being an eccentric, but, equally important, Berkeley combined eccentricity with a complete lack of ambition to be anywhere else but in Upper Perak, a district where his eccentricities did not clash with the demands of economic development. Berkeley was not only tolerated but genuinely admired by many Europeans. He ruled—as best he could since the bureaucracy in Taiping and Kuala Lumpur could not be completely ignored—as a white rajah in a day when such figures appeared only on the pages of Conrad's novels. And at a time when the position of the District Officer was receiving serious consideration Berkeley probably represented to many the ideal District Officer, exercising a close paternal control over the Malays in his district.

In 1926 Hubert Berkeley returned to England to lead the life of a country gentleman. Twice a week he rode to hounds, every year he went to the Derby, and for many years he served on various county committees. In some ways he lived in the same manner as he had at Grik. He raised cows, sheep, and poultry and grew his own vegetables and fruit, and he continued to travel by horse as much as he could. Shortly after the fall of Singapore he died, broken-hearted at Britain's failure to protect the people of Malaya.[21]

Appendix 2

'The Letter' Case

ON the night of 23 April 1911, a Sunday, Mrs. Ethel Proudlock, wife of the acting headmaster of the Victoria Institution in Kuala Lumpur, shot William Steward repeatedly until all six chambers of her revolver were empty. When her husband, friends, and the police arrived on the scene Mrs. Proudlock said that Steward had tried to rape her. News of Steward's violent death caused a sensation among Europeans in Malaya. For months the killing, Mrs. Proudlock's trial, and subsequent events were the main topic of conversation in clubs throughout the peninsula. After a visit to Malaya eleven years later W. Somerset Maugham used the case as the basis for 'The Letter', the best known of his short stories with a Malayan setting.[1] Maugham also wrote a stage version of 'The Letter', and in 1940 the story was made into a film starring Bette Davis. This Appendix recounts, as well as contemporary newspaper reports and official records permit, the events on which Maugham's story is based.[2] The actual case is of interest for two reasons. First, Maugham's story differs from the actual events in many respects. To take just a minor example, the story has the exotic setting of a remote rubber estate rather than Kuala Lumpur.[3] Second, the actual case provides a valuable glimpse into European society at the time. During the trial aspects of people's lives were revealed which under normal circumstances were never mentioned in public, and the passions which the trial aroused reveal some fundamental attitudes Europeans had regarding the position of European women in a colonial society.

As news of Steward's death spread Mrs. Proudlock immediately received the sympathy of most Europeans. Both she and her husband were well known in Kuala Lumpur. She had met William Proudlock, who had taught at the Victoria Institution since 1902, while visiting her father, a Mr. Charter,[4] in Kuala Lumpur. They were married in 1907, when she was nineteen years old. Because of her poor health the couple sailed for England immediately after their marriage. After a child was born the Proudlocks returned to Kuala Lumpur and led what appeared to be a quiet life. They spent most evenings at home at their bungalow near the school, and she helped her husband with his work. He was a member of the Casuals football team and president of the

Selangor State Band, and every Sunday afternoon she sang in the choir of St. Mary's Church. Steward was also well known in Selangor. He had been the manager of a tin mine in Salak South, a few miles south of Kuala Lumpur. In 1911 he was employed as a consulting engineer for a Singapore firm but continued to live at Salak South. Each month Steward, a bachelor, sent part of his salary to his widowed mother in England.[5] He had been an acquaintance of the Proudlocks' since about 1909. William Proudlock was to testify that Steward had come to their bungalow a few times to listen to music and that he and Steward had occasionally met for drinks at the Selangor Club but that he had not seen him since October or November 1910.

After a brief magisterial inquiry early in May 1911 Mrs. Proudlock was committed for trial on the charge of murder. The trial, which took place in June at the Supreme Court, aroused the most intense interest. Except for details which the editor thought were indecent and irrelevant to the case the *Malay Mail* reported the proceedings in full. The reports crowded out news of preparations being made throughout the Empire to celebrate the coronation of King George V. The trial was presided over by Justice T. Sercombe Smith. Helping him to reach a verdict were two assessors, who were both planters. Many Europeans considered it a great injustice that Mrs. Proudlock was not being tried by a jury. The F.M.S. government had abolished trial by jury in 1899 because it believed that juries had often allowed guilty men to escape justice. Swettenham had wanted to retain trial by jury in cases where the accused were Europeans, though he anticipated that there would be some difficulty 'in defining exactly what a white man is'. The Judicial Commissioner at the time argued in the strongest possible terms that if no distinction was to be made between Europeans and Asians the proposed changes should be confined to charges other than capital ones, 'for it will be *impossible* to try Englishmen and Americans for capital offences otherwise than with a jury'. The High Commissioner and the Colonial Office insisted, however, on the complete abolition of trial by jury.[6]

On the opening day of the trial Mrs. Proudlock pleaded 'Not Guilty'. It was accepted by her defence that she had killed Steward. What had to be explained was why she had done it. What had Steward done to provoke her into shooting him? Assuming that she had had good reason to defend herself, had she been justified in responding so ferociously? It was essential to find out how well Mrs. Proudlock had known Steward and whether she had asked him to come to her house on the evening of 23 April. Mrs. Proudlock testified that she had met Steward at the Selangor Club on Saturday, 22 April. At that time she had inquired why she had not seen him recently and had invited him to visit her husband and herself some evening. She was adamant that she had not asked him to come by specifically on Sunday evening, when her husband would be out having dinner with a friend. She denied having been to Salak South to meet Steward during her husband's three-week absence in Hong Kong in December 1909 and January 1910, and she insisted that on the only occasion Steward had come to her house when her husband was away she had invited other people as well.

Like Mrs. Crosbie in Maugham's story, Mrs. Proudlock never varied her account of the killing. Steward arrived shortly after nine o'clock, and, she said, they had discussed religion. When she stood up to get a book she wanted to show him he put his arm around her, kissed her, and told her that he loved her. Then, she said, he put out the light and began to lift her skirt. Her hand 'came in contact with a revolver', she seized it, and when he tried to put her down she shot him. She remembered firing two shots. After that, she insisted under intense questioning, she could remember nothing.

The public prosecutor was unable to prove that any intimate relationship had existed between Mrs. Proudlock and Steward. After his death a police inspector had searched Steward's house at Salak South but had been unable to find letters from any women except his mother and sister. The prosecution was however able to call into question other aspects of Mrs. Proudlock's testimony. Two witnesses testified that Steward had told them that he had an appointment on the night of 23 April, but he had not mentioned where his appointment was. A more important point was the fact that Steward's body had been found some distance outside of the Proudlocks' bungalow. It was obvious that whatever else had happened she had continued to fire at him as he tried to make his way from the bungalow. The rickshaw puller who had taken Steward to Mrs. Proudlock's house and who was waiting to take Steward on his return journey said that he heard two shots, saw Steward stagger down the steps followed by Mrs. Proudlock, and then heard three more shots. Finally, medical examinations both of Steward's body and of Mrs. Proudlock did not show any evidence of attempted rape.

Mrs. Proudlock's defence tried to portray Steward as the type of man who was likely to attempt a rape. Alfred Mace, who had lived with Steward at Salak South, insisted however that he was a moral man, one who always remained calm and never drank to excess. He agreed that Steward had spent a lot on drinks at the Selangor Club but said that this was because he had so many friends. Mace was then asked about the Chinese woman in Salak South who had cried when a police inspector told her that Steward was dead:

Counsel: As far as you know, he had no other relationships with women than with a Chinese woman?

Mace: He might have had.

Counsel: Was she living in the house?

Mace: Yes.

The Chinese woman had lived with Steward for about three months before his death. Mace also said that he believed Steward had once been treated for venereal disease.

According to her defence, Ethel Proudlock had reacted as she had not only because she had been under extreme provocation but also because her mental condition was very unstable. She had been assaulted shortly before the start of her monthly period, when, both her husband and doctor stated, she became unusually sensitive and emotional. Given her mental condition and the shock which she had experienced, her defence argued, it was understandable that she could not recall either firing all six shots or having followed Steward on to the veranda. The defence concluded by saying that it was utterly unthinkable that this girl with a baby face could have planned to commit an atrocious murder.

Despite the defence's plea, on 16 June the judge and·two assessors passed a verdict of guilty. (In 'The Letter' Mrs. Crosbie is acquitted.) Mrs. Proudlock was then sentenced to death by hanging. Upon seeing her husband she burst into tears. In the words of the *Malay Mail*'s reporter, William Proudlock 'leant over the rail of the dock, kissed his wife several times, and spoke consolingly to her, but without avail'. The court was filled with the sound of sobbing, and many remained to 'witness the pathetic scene'. In her distress Mrs. Proudlock apparently failed to hear the judge announce that he and the assessors would make a recommendation for mercy. She was then taken by the police to Pudu Gaol.

At the conclusion of the trial the *Malay Mail* released a mass of letters from outraged Europeans. They objected to the way the public prosecutor had tried to cast doubt on Mrs. Proudlock's moral character. All of the correspondents were convinced of her innocence. 'Are we to consider our wives and daughters so little above the brute creation', asked one man, 'that a defence of their honour is injustified by the laws of the land we live in?'[7]

Meanwhile, William Proudlock sent a telegram to the King asking for a pardon and prepared to have the verdict appealed. Over sixty European women in Kuala Lumpur sent a telegram to the Queen to 'implore pardon at this coronation time'. Within a few days of the verdict two hundred Europeans in Kuala Lumpur had signed a petition on Mrs. Proudlock's behalf. In Penang $2,003 was raised to help finance her appeal, and a meeting of prominent women there sent a telegram to the King and Queen asking them to grant Mrs. Proudlock a free pardon. Mrs. Proudlock also received support from Asians. About 560 Indians signed a petition, and fifty leading Chinese ladies, including Mrs. Loke Yew and the widow of Yap Kwan Seng, presented a petition asking the Sultan of Selangor to pardon Mrs. Proudlock. Europeans were surprised to learn, when the Colonial Office replied to the telegrams sent to the King and Queen, that only the Sultan had the power to grant Mrs. Proudlock a pardon. In England, where newspapers carried reports of the trial, many people were appalled to think that a white woman's fate was in the hands of an 'Oriental potentate', but Europeans living in Selangor knew him as a humane ruler and one who was of course bound to accept the 'advice' of the British Resident. In response to the petitions which he received the Sultan declared that he would await the result of the appeal before he considered whether to grant a pardon.[8]

On 29 June, just two weeks after her sentencing, Mrs. Proudlock unexpectedly withdrew her appeal and placed herself at the mercy of the Sultan. In a letter to her attorney she wrote that although she was innocent of any crime she could no longer stand the suspense and that she would be unable to endure another trial in which she would again be treated as a common criminal.[9] Perhaps she also feared that further investigations would reveal that her relationship with Steward had been more intimate than she had stated during her trial, but unless more sources become available there is no way of knowing whether this was the case. Rumours were circulating that Mrs. Proudlock had visited Steward at Salak South during her husband's absence in Hong Kong,[10] but at the time she withdrew her appeal the public prosecutor had no proof of such a visit. Some time later, however, the government may indeed have learned more about Mrs. Proudlock's relationship with Steward, but we can never be certain of this since the Colonial Office destroyed several sets of correspondence dealing with the case.[11] In short, we may never know whether, as Maugham's story would suggest, Mrs. Proudlock had been in love with Steward and had become incensed when she learned that he had been living with a Chinese woman.

On 8 July 1911 the State Council met at the Sultan's palace at Klang to consider Mrs. Proudlock's plea for mercy. Justice Sercombe Smith, a member of the council, defended the verdict which his court had reached, but he wished to see Mrs. Proudlock's sentence commuted to a term of imprisonment. The Sultan made a strong speech in favour of granting her a free pardon. He took this position, he said, because thousands of people had signed petitions, because Mrs. Proudlock was a mother and in poor health, and because of the recent coronation. The Resident, who had talked about the case with the Sultan before the meeting, had already made up his mind not to oppose the Sultan. He had also told two official members of the council who had doubts about giving Mrs. Proudlock a free pardon that he would not oppose the Sultan. As a result, Mrs. Proudlock was granted a free pardon and immediately released from the gaol. Two days later she left for Penang and sailed on the first ship to England. Sercombe Smith regarded the council's decision as 'a slur upon the assessors and myself, which no independent and self-respecting judge could endure'. He therefore asked to be transferred to a post in the Straits Settlements, but the Colonial Office persuaded him to remain in Kuala Lumpur.[12]

William Proudlock also remained in Kuala Lumpur. He continued to teach and play football, but otherwise his life was far from normal. In a letter to the London gossip paper *M.A.P.* ('Mainly About People')

Proudlock accused the police and the court of having been biased against his wife.[13] A police inspector who Proudlock alleged had 'thrashed' two of his servants when they did not make statements that suited him was given permission by the government to sue for libel. During the trial Proudlock not only failed to prove his allegation but also had to endure some harsh questioning from the inspector's counsel, H. N. Ferrers. Ferrers accused Proudlock of having been afraid that his servants would be able to tell the police that his wife had once visited Steward at Salak South. In an effort to discredit him Ferrers revealed that Proudlock had once had a Chinese woman living with him before his marriage to Ethel Charter. At the conclusion of the trial the judge awarded the inspector the sum of $350 and costs, and criticized the way Ferrers had conducted the case. A few days later Proudlock took a ship to England.[14] Shortly after his letter appeared in *M.A.P.* Proudlock had asked to be transferred to a post in another colony or protectorate, but the Colonial Office informed him that it would be unable to offer him another appointment.[15]

In addition to its deeply personal aspects the events surrounding Steward's death involved the European community as a whole. The trial threatened to give the community a bad reputation in Britain. In a letter to the *Daily Mail* the writer Horace Bleackley declared that Mrs. Proudlock 'appears to have killed in defence of her honour one of the innumerable satyrs with which those Colonies where the male population is largely in excess of the female population are infested'. Europeans in Malaya and those men and women in Britain who had lived in Malaya were infuriated by this statement. European women were in fact treated with the greatest possible reverence, insisted those who replied to Bleackley's letter. 'The white community of Selangor', wrote one resident of that state, 'is undoubtedly as good as, and probably much better than, that of Walton-on-Thames.' One Englishwoman who had lived for four years in Kuala Lumpur explained that 'were it not for the respect with which our men treat us it is certain we could not live safely among natives, perhaps alone all day with Chinese men-servants and a Javanese gardener'.[16] 'We have an idea', added the *Malay Mail*, 'that nowhere at Home are English women more honoured and esteemed than here.'[17] Indeed it was precisely because European women were held in such esteem that Mrs. Proudlock's conviction had been so passionately opposed and that as a result she had been released from prison.

Notes

Notes for Introduction

1. Among the few exceptions to this neglect are J. de Vere Allen, 'The Malayan Civil Service, 1874–1941: Colonial Bureaucracy/Malayan Elite', *Comparative Studies in Society and History*, 12 (April 1970), 149–78, and sections of Emily Sadka, *The Protected Malay States, 1874–1895* (Kuala Lumpur, 1968) and J. M. Gullick, 'Kuala Lumpur, 1880–1895', *JMBRAS*, 28, Part 4 (1955).

2. Among these are C. D. Cowan, *Nineteenth-Century Malaya: The Origins of British Political Control* (London, 1961); C. N. Parkinson, *British Intervention in Malaya, 1867–1877* (Singapore, 1960); J. M. Gullick, 'Captain Speedy of Larut', *JMBRAS*, 26, Part 3 (1953).

Notes for Chapter 1

1. C. M. Turnbull, *The Straits Settlements, 1826–67* (London, 1972), pp. 22–31, 108–27.

2. J. M. Gullick, *Indigenous Political Systems of Western Malaya* (London, 1965).

3. Sadka, *Protected Malay States*, p. 23.

4. According to Pao-Chun Tsou, Pudu Lane was the original site of Kuala Lumpur: *The Urban Landscape of Kuala Lumpur* (Singapore, 1967), pp. 15, 30–1. Pudu Lane is shown on Map 3.

5. Wong Lin Ken, 'Western Enterprise and the Development of the Malayan Tin Industry to 1914', in C. D. Cowan, ed., *The Economic Development of South-East Asia* (London, 1964), p. 150. The background to Kimberley's instructions to Clarke is examined by Cowan, *Nineteenth-Century Malaya*, chapter 4, and Khoo Kay Kim, 'The Origin of British Administration in Malaya', *JMBRAS*, 39, Part 1 (1966), 52–91.

6. Sadka, *Protected Malay States*, pp. 47–9, 181.

7. Ibid., p. 96.

8. Ibid., p. 103.

9. Ibid., pp. 105, 113, 274–89.

10. Rex Stevenson, 'The Selangor Raja School', *JMBRAS*, 41, Part 1 (1968), 183–92.

11. *Annual Report of Perak* (1890), p. 16. Malay education and employment in the government are discussed by William R. Roff, *The Origins of Malay Nationalism* (New Haven, 1967), chapters 4 and 5.

12. Sadka, *Protected Malay States*, p. 332.

13. Ibid., p. 410.

14. Wong, 'Western Enterprise and the Malayan Tin Industry', pp. 137–9; Gullick, 'Kuala Lumpur', pp. 55–6.

15. Isabella L. Bird, *The Golden Chersonese and the Way Thither* (London, 1883), p. 220.

16. Gullick, 'Kuala Lumpur', pp. 125–30.

17. *Annual Report of Selangor* (1902), p. 28.

18. Sadka, *Protected Malay States*, chapter 11; Eunice Thio, *British Policy in the Malay Peninsula, 1880–1910*, Vol. I: *The Southern and Central States* (Singapore, 1969), chapters 5, 6, and 7.

19. Wong Lin Ken, *The Malayan Tin Industry to 1914* (Tucson, 1965), p. 261.

20. James C. Jackson, *Planters and Speculators: Chinese and European Agricultural Enterprise in Malaya, 1786–1921* (Kuala Lumpur, 1968), chapter 9. The following account is based mainly on chapters 10 and 11 of Jackson's study and J. H. Drabble, 'The Plantation Rubber Industry in Malaya up to 1922', *JMBRAS*, 40, Part 1 (1967), 52–77.

21. Figures from Drabble, *Rubber in Malaya, 1876–1922* (Kuala Lumpur, 1973), pp. 213, 216.

22. Ibid., p. 216.

23. *Federal Council Proceedings* (1925), p. B22.

24. Rupert Emerson, *Malaysia: A Study in Direct and Indirect Rule* (New York, 1937), p. 184.

25. C. R. Harrison, 'Ramblings of the Last of "The Creepers"—1', *Planter*, 37 (1961), 345.

26. Sir Malcolm Watson, 'Twenty-Five Years of Malaria Control in the Malay Peninsula', *British Malaya*, 1 (January 1927), 245–6.

27. Wong, *Malayan Tin Industry*, chapter 4; Lim Chong-Yah, *Economic Development of Modern Malaya* (Kuala Lumpur, 1967), p. 54.

28. Figures from Emerson, *Malaysia*, pp. 156, 186–7; P. T. Bauer, *The Rubber Industry: A Study in Competition and Monopoly* (London, 1948), p. 16.

29. Data taken from censuses.

30. Quoted in Thio, *British Policy in the Malay Peninsula*, p. 195. This discussion of political changes up to 1910 is taken from chapter 8 of Thio's book.

31. Sharom Ahmat, 'The Political Structure of the State of Kedah, 1879–1905', *Journal of Southeast Asian Studies*, 1 (September 1970), 115–28; J. de Vere Allen, 'The Elephant and the Mousedeer—A New Version: Anglo-Kedah Relations, 1905–1915', *JMBRAS*, 41, Part 1 (1968), 54–94; Sharom Ahmat, 'Transition and Political Change in a Malay State: A Study of the Economic and Political Development of Kedah, 1879–1923' (unpublished Ph.D. thesis, University of London, 1969), chapter 6.

32. Emerson, *Malaysia*, p. 161; Philip Loh Fook-Seng, 'Malay Precedence and the Federal Formula in the Federated Malay States, 1909 to 1939', *JMBRAS*, 45, Part 2 (1972), 38. The following discussion of decentralization is taken mainly from Emerson, *Malaysia*, pp. 161–75, 325–43.

33. Clementi to Secretary of State, secret dispatch of 3 May 1932, quoted in Loh, 'Malay Precedence', p. 43.

34. See Png Poh Seng, 'The Kuomintang in Malaya, 1912–1941', *Journal of Southeast Asian History*, 2, No. 1 (March 1961), 1–41.

35. Sinnappah Arasaratnam, *Indians in Malaysia and Singapore* (London,

1970), pp. 82–102; Clifford to Amery, 30 December 1927, file 52330, CO 717/59.

36. Roff, *Malay Nationalism*, chapter 7.

37. J. H. MacCallum Scott, *Eastern Journey* (London, 1939), p. 29.

Notes for Chapter 2

1. F.M.S. 1911 Census, p. 39.

2. In 1911, 42 per cent of Europeans had been born in England; in 1921 the figure was 46 per cent. F.M.S. 1911 Census, Table 34; British Malaya 1921 Census, Table 26 (F.M.S.).

3. British Malaya 1931 Census, pp. 74–5.

4. Editorial, 'That Alleged Disrespect', *Straits Echo*, 19 January 1912.

5. C. D. Bowen, letter of 9 March 1892, 'British Malaya As It Was', *Asiatic Review*, 46 (1950), 905.

6. British Malaya 1921 Census, p. 30.

7. By my count there are 215 European names on the cenotaph erected after the First World War and now located at the National Monument, Kuala Lumpur.

8. *Report of the Malayan Public Service Salaries Commission* (Singapore, 1919), p. 33. (This report is hereafter referred to as the 'Bucknill Report'.) The figures include a very small number of non-Europeans.

9. British Malaya 1921 Census, Table 37 (F.M.S.).

10. British Malaya 1931 Census, Table 22.

11. Interview with Mr. T. M. Walker, April 1972.

12. Arnold Wright and H. A. Cartwright, eds., *Twentieth Century Impressions of British Malaya* (London, 1908).

13. David C. Marsh, *The Changing Social Structure of England and Wales, 1871–1961* (London, 1965), p. 218.

14. Ibid.

15. Editorial comment on letter from 'Audi Alteram', *Malay Mail*, 6 October 1897.

16. A. Marwick, *Britain in the Century of Total War* (Penguin Books, 1970), pp. 39–40.

17. 'The Civil Service', *Malay Weekly Mail*, 5 March 1914.

18. J. R. Innes, 'The Malayan Civil Service as a Career', *National Review*, 77 (March 1921), 102.

19. V. Purcell, *The Memoirs of a Malayan Official* (London, 1965), p. 291.

20. F. W. Knocker, 'Penang and the Rubber "Boom"', *Times of Malaya*, 4 January 1912.

21. Testimony of William Duncan, Bucknill Report, Appendix V, p. 239.

22. W. Somerset Maugham, *A Writer's Notebook* (London, 1949), pp. 225–6.

23. *Perak Annual Hand-Book and Civil Service List* (1892), p. 187; R. J. B. Clayton, 'An Account of a Trip from Taiping to Upper Perak in February, 1899', copy of an original letter (RCS); Henry Norman, *The People and Politics of the Far East* (London, 1895), p. 538.

24. Lady Alice Lovat, *The Life of Sir Frederick Weld* (London, 1914), p. 356.

25. G. T. Tickell, 'Early Days in Selangor (1888–89)', *British Malaya*, 2

(January 1928), 231. See also statements by Weld in Lovat, *Life of Sir Frederick Weld*, pp. 390–1, and by Governor Sir Charles Mitchell in Chai Hon-Chan, *The Development of British Malaya, 1896–1909* (Kuala Lumpur, 1964), p. 57.

26. Ibid., pp. 231–2. For another case, see Arthur Keyser, *People and Places* (London, 1922), p. 101.

27. E. W. Birch, 'Malayan Sport in the Earlier Days', *British Malaya*, 1 (May 1926), 24.

28. Obituary of Marks, *British Malaya*, 15 (June 1940), 20; 'The Acting B.R.', *Malay Weekly Mail*, 15 September 1921.

29. Of the officials mentioned in this paragraph, Aldworth, Marks, Rodger, and Lister became Residents and Keyser a District Officer.

30. E. W. Birch, acting Resident of Perak, to Colonial Secretary, 6 January 1896, and letters from the other Residents, enclosed in Mitchell to Chamberlain, confidential of 17 January 1896, CO 273/212.

31. 'The Civil Service', *Malay Weekly Mail*, 5 March 1914.

32. Bucknill Report, p. 35.

33. Ibid., Appendix IVB, pp. 474–6.

34. F.M.S. Despatches from Secretary of State, No. 276, 22 October 1909. ANM.

35. R. O. Tilman, *Bureaucratic Transition in Malaya* (Durham, N.C., 1964), p. 47; Allen, 'Malayan Civil Service', p. 165. Allen's source is Tilman, whose statements come from a misinterpretation of the Bucknill Report.

36. For what it was like to take the examinations, see Sir Richard Winstedt, *Start from Alif: Count from One* (Kuala Lumpur, 1969), pp. 18–19; Leonard Woolf, *Sowing: An Autobiography of the Years 1880–1904* (London, 1960), pp. 192–4, 200–2.

37. Purcell, *Memoirs*, p. 291. Several interviews confirm this.

38. Letter to mother, 20 July 1904, in *Eric Macfadyen, 1879–1934* (privately published, 1968), p. 125.

39. J. H. M. Robson, *Records and Recollections, 1889–1934* (Kuala Lumpur, 1934), p. 25.

40. Harrison, 'Last of the Creepers', p. 341.

41. *Selangor Journal*, 1 (24 February 1893), 179.

42. For another list: 'Who Are the Planters?', *Malay Weekly Mail*, 11 March 1909.

43. C. Baxendale, *Personalities of Old Malaya* (Penang, 1930), p. 52; *Planter*, 2, No. 1 (August 1921), pp. 1, 3, 5.

44. Harrison, 'Last of the Creepers', p. 341.

45. Interview with Mr. T. M. Walker.

46. 'The Civil Service', *Malay Weekly Mail*, 5 March 1914.

47. Dykes to Harding, 22 August and 14 October 1911, enclosed in Brockman to Harcourt, 338 of 18 July 1911, CO 273/374; F.M.S. Civil List (1912). Allen, 'Malayan Civil Service', p. 163, gives an example of the importance of social background in hiring.

48. Testimony of A. Palmer of F.M.S. Railways, Bucknill Report, Appendix V, pp. 64–5.

49. Testimonies of J. A. Robertson, manager of Chartered Bank, Kuala Lumpur, and C. M. Henderson, head of Guthrie's in Penang, Bucknill Report, Appendix V, pp. 129, 215.

50. Topham, 'Autobiography of Douglas Frank Topham...covering the years 1907–1935', written in 1963 (RH), pp. 1–5, 18–19, 21.

51. 'First Impressions', *Malay Weekly Mail*, 30 March 1922.

Notes for Chapter 3

1. Bird, *Golden Chersonese*, quoted passages on pp. 187, 222, 323, 367.

2. *Annual Report of Sungei Ujong* (1888), p. 13. See Sadka, *Protected Malay States*, pp. 213–25.

3. *Selangor Journal*, 2 (6 October 1893), 23.

4. *Selangor Journal*, 4 (20 September 1895), 1.

5. *Malay Sketches* (London, 1895), p. 3.

6. *Studies in Brown Humanity* (London, 1898), pp. 122–3.

7. W. H. Treacher, 'British Malaya, With More Especial Reference to the Federated Malay States', *Journal of the Society of Arts*, 55 (22 March 1907), 503; J. F. A. McNair, *Perak and the Malays* (London, 1878), pp. 201, 297, 415; B. O. Stoney, 'The Malays of British Malaya', in Wright and Cartwright, *Twentieth Century Impressions*, pp. 222–3; Keyser, *People and Places*, pp. 105–6; Hugh Low, *Sarawak* (London, 1848), p. 137. Several aspects of Swettenham's and Clifford's writings are examined by J. de V. Allen, 'Two Imperialists: A Study of Sir Frank Swettenham and Sir Hugh Clifford', *JMBRAS*, 37, Part 1 (1964), 41–73.

8. *The Real Malay* (London, 1900), pp. 38–40.

9. J. H. M. Robson, *People in a Native State* (Singapore, 1894), pp. 17–18. Robson is referred to frequently in this study. Born in 1870, he went to Ceylon in 1889 as a 'creeper' on a tea estate. Later that year he left Ceylon to become a clerk and draftsman in the Selangor Railway Department. By the time *People in a Native State* was written he had become an Assistant District Officer. In 1896 he resigned from government service to found the *Malay Mail*. He edited the paper until 1902. From that year he employed an editor, but he retained control over the paper until the Japanese invasion. He was one of the original members of the Federal Council and served again on the council in the 1920s. He died in internment camp in Singapore early in 1945.

10. Bowen, letters of 21 March and 26 May 1887, 'British Malaya As It Was', pp. 900, 901.

11. Keyser, *From Jungle to Java* (Westminster, 1897), p. 71.

12. Robson, *People in a Native State*, p. 14.

13. Norman, *Peoples and Politics*, p. 539.

14. Clayton, 'Account of a Trip from Taiping to Upper Perak'.

15. See G. J. Resink, *Indonesia's History Between the Myths* (The Hague, 1968), pp. 312–14.

16. *Annual Report of Negri Sembilan* (1896), p. 14.

17. *Selangor Journal*, 5 (18 September 1896), 8–9; editorial, *Malay Mail*, 19 March 1897.

18. *Perak Annual Hand-Book and Civil Service List* (Taiping, 1892), pp. 50–3.

19. Sadka, *Protected Malay States*, pp. 220–1.

20. Bowen, letter of 6 October 1891, 'British Malaya As It Was', p. 905.

21. Editorial, *Malay Mail*, 27 February 1897.

22. *Annual Report of Perak* (1890), p. 22; *Perak Hand-Book* (1892), pp. 60–2.

23. Bowen, letter of 23 October 1891, 'British Malaya As It Was', p. 905.

24. Clifford Diaries (ANM), entries of 13 January 1888, 8 May and 1 October 1893.

25. *Studies in Brown Humanity*, p. 112.

26. The quoted passage is from a report in which the wife of a District Officer is given as an example of such women: *Selangor Journal*, 1 (19 May 1893), 277.

27. Clifford, *Since the Beginning* (London, 1898), p. 161.

28. Sadka, *Protected Malay States*, pp. 124–8, 229–31; Robson, *People in a Native State*, p. 3.

29. Robson, *People in a Native State*, p. 5.

30. Swettenham, *About Perak* (Singapore, 1893), pp. 70, 71.

31. *Pinang Gazette*, 29 September and 2 October 1893. These reviews were reprinted in a pamphlet entitled 'Colonial Criticism' (FCO: Malay States Pamphlet 9).

32. Jackson, *Planters and Speculators*, p. 70; 'Mrs. Dominic Daly', *Malay Weekly Mail*, 26 February 1920. The official and his wife were Mr. and Mrs. D. Daly. Mrs. Daly was Douglas's daughter.

33. 'Memories of Kuala Lumpur', *Malay Mail*, 3 March 1905.

34. Ibid.

35. *Selangor Journal*, 1 (21 October 1892), 37.

36. 'Social Life in Malaya', *Times of Malaya*, 11 September 1929.

37. Selangor Club Minute Book, No. 1, March 1885 to March 1892, minutes of meetings on 20 and 22 December 1889, 21 and 29 October 1890, 22 August 1891. I am indebted to the Committee of the Selangor Club for permission to consult the minute book.

38. *Selangor Journal*, 1 (21 October 1892), 37. 'Bernstorff was some years later heard of in North China where he was A.D.C. to a Chinese Viceroy....' 'Rimba', *Bygone Selangor* (Kuala Lumpur, 1922), p. 49.

39. *Selangor Journal*, 1 (21 October 1892), 37.

40. John Gullick and Gerald Hawkins, *Malayan Pioneers* (Singapore, 1958), pp. 41–5.

41. Robson, *Records and Recollections*, p. 51.

42. *Selangor Journal*, 3 (14 December 1894), 114.

43. Mrs. W. A. H. Stratton-Brown, 'Long Ago in Selangor', life in Selangor 1896–7, written after World War II (RH), p. 5.

44. Keyser, *People and Places*, p. 100. Robson, who incidentally married Mrs. Syers many years after Captain Syers's death in 1897, supported Keyser's claim as the originator of the name. *Records and Recollections*, p. 42.

45. Oliver Marks, 'The Malay States before Federation', *British Malaya*, 8 (January 1934), 192; E. T. McCarthy, *Further Incidents in the Life of a Mining Engineer* (London, 1920), p. 176.

46. Swettenham, *About Perak*, pp. 70–1; H. Conway Belfield, *Handbook of the Federated Malay States* (London, 1902), p. 32.

47. 'Coffee Planting', *Malay Mail*, 17 December 1896.

48. 'Marriage in the East', *Malay Mail*, 17 March 1897.

49. 'The "J.O." ', written and sung by R. G. Watson, *Selangor Journal*, 5 (22 January 1897), 156. Watson himself went on to become a Resident and for short periods was acting Resident-General and Chief Secretary.

50. *Selangor Journal*, 1 (30 December 1892), 114–15.

51. *Selangor Journal*, 4 (4 September 1896), 448; 1 (16 December 1892), 97.

52. *Selangor Journal*, 3 (28 December 1894), 117.

53. *Malay Mail*, 20 January 1899.

54. G. T. Tickell, 'Early Days in Selangor (1888–89)', *British Malaya*, 2 (February 1928), 257.

55. Ibid.

56. Candidates Book 1890–1941, Lake Club, Kuala Lumpur. Information on family and business connexions from *Selangor Journal*, 4 (4 October 1895), 19; *Singapore and Straits Directory* (1891).

57. *Selangor Journal*, 2 (1 June 1894), 306; 3 (21 September 1894), 12; 4 (17 April 1896), 278.

58. Wright and Cartwright, *Twentieth Century Impressions*, p. 875. The New Club was formed in 1892 but within a short time the clubhouse was sold to the Sultan of Perak. In 1893 plans were drawn up for a new clubhouse and in the following year the club was opened.

59. Arnot Reid, 'More About Perak', Article No. 1 (FCO: Malay States Pamphlet 22). The article was almost certainly published in the *Straits Times*, of which Reid was the editor. It is clear from references to Swettenham's book *About Perak* and to the debate on federation, as well as to the building of a new club, that the article was written sometime in the latter part of 1893 or the first part of 1894.

60. 'S. S.', 'About Kuala Lumpur Society', *Selangor Journal*, 2 (9 March 1894), 200.

61. 'Bukit Sembilan', *Selangor Journal*, 1 (11 August 1893), 380. See also Arthur Keyser's novel *An Adopted Wife* (London, 1893), pp. 104–7, where he talks about European society in 'Kuala Taipor'. Regarding the wives of officials, a character comments that 'You can almost place one . . . in the official hierarchy by the tone of her voice'. (p. 107.)

62. Selangor Golf Club, *Twelve Under Fours: An Informal History of the Selangor Golf Club* (privately published, Kuala Lumpur, 1953), pp. 1–23.

63. 'Club Friendships', *Malay Mail*, 17 December 1896. See also 'Coffee Planting' in the same issue of the *Malay Mail*; 'Bukit Sembilan', *Selangor Journal*, 1 (11 August 1893), 381; interview with H. Huttenbach, *Selangor Journal*, 3 (11 January 1895), 147; 'Club Gossip', *Malay Mail*, 4 June 1898; editorial, *Malay Mail*, 14 August 1903.

64. Editorial, 'The Selangor Club', *Malay Mail*, 20 January 1899.

65. On the relationship between the government and Chinese leaders, see Sadka, *Protected Malay States*, pp. 244, 272, 302–10, 318–23.

66. *Selangor Journal*, 5 (19 March 1897), 225–8; Wright and Cartwright, *Twentieth Century Impressions*, p. 898.

67. *Selangor Journal*, 3 (22 March 1895), 217.

68. Loke Yew came to Malaya from China in 1859 at the age of thirteen. After working in a shop in Singapore he opened a shop of his own there. He became involved in tin mining in Larut during the turbulent years before British intervention. After Birch's assassination he secured the contract for supplying food to British troops in Perak. Loke opened tin mines first in Kinta and

then around Kuala Lumpur and in the Bentong district of Pahang. Part of his enormous wealth came from gambling, spirit, pawnbroking, and opium monopolies. In 1915 the British awarded him the C.M.G., and early in 1917 the University of Hong Kong, to which he had given and lent a great deal of money, made him an honorary Doctor of Laws. He died in February 1917. Obituary, *Malay Weekly Mail*, 1 March 1917.

69. *Selangor Journal*, 4 (17 April 1896), 270.

70. Robson, 'Last Century Reminiscences', *Malay Weekly Mail*, 7 January 1931. The secretary was Wee Hap Lang, later a prominent businessman.

71. *Selangor Journal*, 1 (13 January 1893), 130.

72. *Selangor Journal*, 1 (25 August 1893), 389.

73. Philip D. Curtin, *The Image of Africa: British Ideas and Actions, 1780–1850* (Madison, 1964), chapters 3, 7, and 14.

74. McNair, *Perak and the Malays*, p. 417.

75. Andrew Duncan, *The Prevention of Disease in Tropical and Sub-Tropical Campaigns* (London, 1888), 134–7; Charles Singer and E. Ashworth Underwood, *A Short History of Medicine*, second edition (Oxford, 1962), pp. 454–63.

76. E. A. Birch, 'The Influence of Warm Climates on the Constitution', in Andrew Davidson, editor, *Hygiene and Diseases of Warm Climates* (Edinburgh and London, 1893), pp. 1–2, 4–7, 18.

77. *Selangor Journal*, 5 (9 July 1897), 369–70.

78. R. K. Macpherson, 'Acclimitization Status of Temperate-zone Man', *Nature*, 182 (1 November 1958), 1240–1; R. A. Kenney, *Acclimatization to High Temperatures* (Inaugural Lecture as Professor of Physiology at the University of Malaya in Singapore, September 1961).

79. Birch, 'Influence of Warm Climates', pp. 7, 18–23.

80. *Selangor Journal*, 1 (16 June 1893), 310; 1 (30 June 1893), 328.

81. Birch, 'Influence of Warm Climates', p. 20; J. Lane Notter, 'The Hygiene of the Tropics', in Davidson, *Hygiene and Diseases*, pp. 26–30; Duncan, *Prevention of Disease in Tropical Campaigns*, pp. 37–9.

82. Braddell, *The Lights of Singapore* (London, 1934), p. 21. See also McNair, *Perak and the Malays*, p. 418, and Dr. S. C. G. Fox, *The Principles of Health in Malaya: Some Suggestions to New Comers* (Taiping, 1901), p. 2.

83. Emily Innes, *The Chersonese With the Gilding Off*, 2 vols. (London, 1885), I, 189.

84. E. T. Renbourn, 'Life and Death of the Solar Topi', *Journal of Tropical Medicine and Hygiene*, 65 (August 1962), 203–18.

85. Curtin, *Image of Africa*, p. 80.

86. *Annual Report of Sungei Ujong and Jelebu* (1889), p. 8; *Annual Report of Sungei Ujong* (1890), p. 11; *Annual Report of Negri Sembilan* (1896), p. 15, and 1899, p. 15; *Annual Report of Selangor* (1898), p. 12; *Annual Report of Perak* (1897), p. 15; 'Proceedings of the F.M.S. Medical Congress', enclosed in Mitchell to Chamberlain, 140 of 18 May 1899, CO 273/251.

87. J. T. Thomson, *Some Glimpses into Life in the Far East* (London, 1864), p. 70.

88. A. Hale, 'Hill-Stations and Sanitaria', in Wright and Cartwright, *Twentieth Century Impressions*, pp. 251–2; *Perak Hand-Book* (1892), p. 163; Swettenham, *About Perak*, p. 72. The location of early hill stations is shown on Map 4.

89. Mrs. Stratton-Brown, 'Long Ago in Selangor', p. 11.

90. 'Bukit Kutu', *Selangor Journal*, 4 (15 May 1896), 305.

91. 'Treacher's Hill', *Selangor Journal*, 4 (10 July 1896), 378–9.

92. Minute dated 29 September 1888, quoted in 'A Report by the Chief Secretary on a Visit to Cameron's Highlands in March 1925', Council Paper No. 13, *Federal Council Proceedings* (1925), p. C129.

93. *Annual Report of Negri Sembilan* (1899), p. 16, and 1902, p. 19.

94. *Selangor Journal*, 5 (23 July 1897), 375. For other references to the changing position of the Resident: editorials, *Malay Mail*, 6 January, 3 and 24 April 1897.

95. Mitchell to Chamberlain, 8 of 7 January 1897, with enclosures, CO 273/228.

96. Minute by Swettenham, enclosed in Mitchell to Chamberlain, 53 of 6 April 1897, CO 273/228.

97. Clifford, *Malayan Monochromes* (London, 1913), p. 275.

98. 'Agin the Government?', *Malay Mail*, 24 April 1897.

Notes for Chapter 4

1. W. Makepeace, 'Through the States: A Ten Days Trip', *Singapore Free Press*, 29 October 1904. Wright and Cartwright, *Twentieth Century Impressions* (1908), pp. 580–1, noted the declining general enthusiasm for cricket.

2. 'Commercial Travellers', *Malay Weekly Mail*, 29 January 1914.

3. *Malay Mail*, 26 April 1897. For a very interesting discussion on prestige, from which some of my ideas are taken, see Harold Nicolson, *The Meaning of Prestige* (Cambridge, 1937).

4. C. W. Harrison, Land Officer in Larut, quoted in *Annual Report of Perak* (1908), p. 11.

5. Letter from 'Oxonian and Cantab', *The Times*, 25 October 1898.

6. *Annual Report of Perak* (1898), p. 4; *Annual Report of Negri Sembilan* (1899), p. 17; Civil Service Committee, Federated Malay States, *Reprint of Memorials, Minutes, Correspondence, Despatches, and Schemes, 1900 to 1917* (Kuala Lumpur, 1917), p. 1.

7. Bucknill Report, pp. 3–4, 133.

8. 'We will teach your Syce to drive it', said advertisements for the Albion Motor Car in the *Malay Mail* in 1901.

9. Bucknill Report, p. 134.

10. Swettenham to Colonial Office, 17 May 1901, in Civil Service Committee, *Reprint of Memorials*, p. 7.

11. Bucknill Report, Appendix III, p. 4.

12. R. H. Bruce Lockhart, *Return to Malaya* (New York, 1936), pp. 177–8.

13. *Annual Report of the F.M.S.* (1911), p. 30. The article in *The Times* the Chief Secretary was referring to was on 'Northern Nigeria and its Problems' (25 September 1911), but he regarded its observations as applying to retired Malayan officials as well. In 1907 the Secretary of State had issued a confidential circular to all senior colonial officials trying to discourage them from later, during their retirements, becoming directors of companies operating in territories where they were then serving. Elgin to all Governments, 15 February 1907, CO 854/168. For the Colonial Office's reaction to Swettenham's busi-

ness dealings in Johore, see J. de V. Allen, 'Johore, 1901–1914', *JMBRAS*, 45, Part 2 (1972), 1–28.

14. Resident-General to Anderson, 24 January 1910, enclosed in Anderson to Crewe, confidential of 19 April 1910, and Anderson to Crewe, 215 of 9 June 1910, both in CO 273/361.

15. Testimony of R. J. B. Clayton, Bucknill Report, Appendix V, p. 236.

16. A. S. Haynes and H. R. G. Leonard, Bucknill Report, Appendix III, p. 61.

17. *Federal Council Proceedings* (1910), pp. B74–77; 1917, pp. B29–31; 1918, pp. B32–35.

18. *Malay Mail*, 7 September 1904. At least three of the ten who attended were planters.

19. J. McCulloch, Bucknill Report, Appendix III, p. 73.

20. C. Wright Mills, *The Power Elite* (New York, 1956), p. 88.

21. Born and educated in Penang, Loke Chow Kit and his brother Loke Chow Thye were two of the leading mine owners in Malaya and both were involved in numerous other business activities. Loke Chow Kit was part-owner of Chow Kit and Co., the largest general store in Kuala Lumpur. In the early 1900s Loke Chow Kit was one of the principal opium farmers, while his brother was vice-president of the Selangor Anti-Opium Society. Both sent their children to Britain to be educated. Wright and Cartwright, *Twentieth Century Impressions*, pp. 160, 533, 923–4.

22. Ibid., pp. 856–7; *Malay Mail*, 22 July 1907.

23. See J. A. and Olive Banks, *Feminism and Family Planning in Victorian England* (Liverpool, 1964), chapters 5 and 6.

24. *Times of Malaya*, 7 March 1912. The passage comes from a cook book and housekeeping guide prepared by Mrs. Walker, the wife of a civil servant.

25. 'F.M.S. Salaries and Marriage', *Malay Mail*, 3 March 1913.

26. K. G. Tregonning, *The Singapore Cold Storage, 1903–1966* (Singapore, n.d.), pp. 3, 10–13.

27. Letter from 'Ulu Pahang', *Malay Mail*, 8 March 1913.

28. Winstedt, *Start from Alif*, pp. 17–18. Emphasis added. Winstedt adds that an inspector's income 'was not always confined to his salary'.

29. 'Marriage in the East', *Malay Mail*, 17 March 1897.

30. F.M.S. Civil Service List (1904), p. xxvi.

31. HCO 795/1914.

32. Editorials, *Malay Mail*, 20 February and 3 March 1913; letter from 'Trentside', ibid., 6 March 1913. Concubinage and prostitution will be discussed in chapter 8.

33. 'The Lack of Women', *Malay Mail*, 8 September 1913.

34. Minute by R. E. Stubbs, 7 February 1910, on Anderson to Crewe, 18 of 13 January 1910, CO 273/360.

35. Memorial of F.M.S. Cadets, in Anderson to Crewe, 18 of 13 January 1910, CO 273/360.

36. Stubbs minute of 7 February 1910, on ibid. Stubbs had been at the Colonial Office since 1900. In 1913 he became Colonial Secretary of Ceylon. In 1919 he was appointed Governor of Hong Kong. He later served as Governor of Jamaica, Cyprus, and Ceylon. He was knighted in 1919.

37. 'Report of Mr. R. E. Stubbs on the Salaries and Classification of the Cadet Service in the Malay Peninsula', Council Paper No. 10, *Federal Council*

Proceedings (1911), pp. C56–57.

38. 'Further Memorial from the Cadet Service Regarding the Report of Mr. Stubbs', Council Paper No. 1, *Federal Council Proceedings* (1912), paras. 15 and 16 of memorial.

39. Ibid.

40. Bucknill Report, pp. 141–50.

41. Civil Service Committee, *Reprint of Memorials*, pp. 128–31.

42. A. N. Kenion, *Federal Council Proceedings* (1917), p. B30.

43. Young to Long, 13 May 1918, and reply by Long, 12 August 1918, Council Paper No. 21, *Federal Council Proceedings* (1918), pp. C118–122.

44. Civil Service Committee, *Reprint of Memorials*, p. 131.

45. Before becoming Chief Justice of the Straits Settlements in 1914, Bucknill had held legal appointments in the Transvaal, Cyprus, and Hong Kong, where he had been Attorney-General. In 1920 he left Malaya to become Puisne Judge of the Patna High Court. He was knighted in 1916 and died in 1926. The three officials on the salaries commission were H. Marriott, Auditor-General of the Straits Settlements; Oliver Marks, a District Officer in Perak; and C. J. Saunders, Registrar of Companies and Official Assignee, Bankruptcy Office. The three unofficials were R. J. Addie, a partner in Boustead and Co.; A. K. E. Hampshire, manager of Boustead, Hampshire and Co., Kuala Lumpur; and F. M. Elliot, partner in the old Singapore law firm of Rodyk and Davidson.

46. Bucknill Report, p. 169. Despite the stress laid on the views of Asians, only one Asian, Choo Kia Peng, a leading miner in Kuala Lumpur, presented evidence to the commission. According to Bucknill, some prominent Chinese had spoken at public meetings 'with pity and contempt of the salaries paid to their Judges'. (p. 160.)

47. Bucknill Report, p. 201.

48. Young to Milner, 352 of 11 August 1919, with reply by L. S. Amery, 17 December 1919, and minute by A. E. Collins, 31 October 1919, CO 273/484.

49. Bucknill Report, p. 201.

50. John Cameron, *Our Tropical Possessions in Malayan India* (London, 1865), p. 281; *Malay Mail*, 15 March 1897. For similar statements: letter from 'L.', *Singapore Free Press*, 22 November 1888; Wright and Cartwright, *Twentieth Century Impressions*, p. 195.

51. *Singapore and Straits Directory* (1912); Bucknill Report, Appendix IV, p. 364.

52. Testimony of Deputy Locomotive Superintendent, Bucknill Report, Appendix V, p. 80.

53. Ibid., Appendix IV, p. 407.

54. Ibid., Appendix V, p. 206.

55. Letters to the commission from D. Nimmo and B. Nelson, ibid., Appendix IV, pp. 397–8, 403–6.

56. 'The White Slaves of Malaya', by 'Veritas', *The Railway Review* (London), 5 July 1912.

57. Memorial from Drivers, letters by the General Manager and the High Commissioner (Young), HCO 795/1914.

58. Letter from B. Nelson, Bucknill Report, Appendix IV, p. 404. Because of their lack of formal education the drivers were at a disadvantage in presenting their case. The first part of the sentence from which the quotation is

taken reads: 'The Government having incurred the liability of bringing European drivers out to this country have the moral right to pay them a sufficient salary to . . . ' (continuing as quoted).

59. Ibid., Appendix V, p. 78.

60. HCO 1760/1908; 290/1913.

61. Bucknill Report, pp. 105–6, 207, 226–7, and Appendix IV, pp. 407–9 (General Manager's memorandum).

62. HCO 6/1920; Guillemard to Milner, 628 of 31 December 1920, CO 717/5.

63. *Singapore and Malayan Directory* (1930); Clementi to Passfield, 382 of 19 June 1931, file 82439, CO 717/84.

64. Bucknill Report, p. 162.

65. *Report of the Royal Commission on the Public Services in India*, PP, 1916, VII (Cd. 8382), pp. 60–3. Unlike the Bucknill commission, the Royal Commission had a few prominent outsiders, including H. A. L. Fisher and J. Ramsay MacDonald, as members.

Notes for Chapter 5

1. Raymond Kennedy, *The Ageless Indies* (New York, 1942), p. 162. For a description of an incident which almost certainly took place at the Raffles Hotel in which a Eurasian woman was refused admission to the ball room: 'European', letter to *Straits Times*, reprinted in *Malay Weekly Mail*, 29 April 1926.

2. 'Asiatic', letter to editor, and editorial comments, *Malay Mail*, 25 August 1897; also, editorial, 'Rest Houses', *Malay Mail*, 14 October 1897.

3. 'Public' to editor and reply by 'K. I. V.', *Malay Mail*, 22, 24 May 1911.

4. This brief period of segregation on the railways is referred to in a letter from 'Speaking Tail', *Malay Mail*, 9 October 1897, and in an editorial, *Malay Mail*, 2 December 1904.

5. *Malay Mail*, 29 August 1904, and the account of the dispute given by Loke Chow Kit, *Malay Mail*, 10 February 1905.

6. *Malay Mail*, 22 August 1904.

7. *Malay Mail*, 29 August 1904.

8. *Malay Mail*, 10 February 1905.

9. Editorial, *Malay Mail*, 28 November 1904; *Malay Mail*, 14 March 1905.

10. Editorial, *Malay Mail*, 20 December 1904.

11. Letter from 'Substratum', *Malay Mail*, 30 November 1904.

12. Editorial, *Malay Mail*, 28 November 1904.

13. Letters from 'Fanny' and W. E. Horley, *Malay Mail*, 30 November and 8 December 1904.

14. S. M. Middlebrook, 'Pioneers of Chinese Reform in Malaya', *Straits Times Annual 1941*, p. 85; Wu Lien-Teh, *Plague Fighter* (Cambridge, 1959), pp. 227–31; A. Talaivasingham, *Malayan Notes and Sketches* (Singapore, 1924), pp. 27–8.

15. *Malay Mail*, 19 January 1905.

16. *Malay Mail*, 31 January 1905. Several of the fifty or so people who

attended the meeting must have abstained from voting.

17. Wright and Cartwright, *Twentieth Century Impressions*, p. 855. The first Chinese Chamber of Commerce in Malaya was the one at Penang, founded in 1903. The Singapore Chinese Chamber of Commerce was founded in 1906. Ibid., pp. 617, 714.

18. *Malay Mail*, 10 February, 15 March 1905.

19. Telegram, letters, and minutes contained in HCO 377/1905. W. D. Barnes's comments, referred to in the next paragraph, are in a minute in the same file.

20. Wright and Cartwright, *Twentieth Century Impressions*, p. 160.

21. *Malay Mail*, 10, 11 November 1904.

22. There was a special irony about the fact that Loke Yew and Loke Chow Kit had been excluded from the 'B' carriage since for a short time they had operated the Selangor State Railway. The government had leased the railway to Loke Yew and another Chinese to help speed the completion of the first lines. Loke Chow Kit had been the traffic manager at that time. Editorial, *Malay Mail*, 28 November 1904; Wright and Cartwright, *Twentieth Century Impressions*, p. 160.

23. He became a member in 1894: *Selangor Journal*, 2 (13 July 1894), 348.

24. *Malay Mail*, 10 February 1905. It is not clear whether this is a direct quote or a paraphrase of Aeria's speech.

25. Letters from 'Fair-Play' and 'A Little Learning is a Dangerous Thing', *Malay Weekly Mail*, 3 April 1913.

26. S. Sivagurunather to High Commissioner, 30 September 1910, HCO 1456/1910; letter from 'Onlooker', *Malay Mail*, 30 August 1911.

27. Letters in *Malay Mail*, 3, 6 November 1911.

28. For example, letters from 'Gander', *Malay Mail*, 24 June 1912, and 'A Straits-born Chinese', *Malay Weekly Mail*, 26 March 1914.

29. 'Another Passenger', *Malay Weekly Mail*, 11 June 1914.

30. Letter from 'Greater Britain' and reply by Kumar Singhan, *Malay Weekly Mail*, 22 July 1915.

31. F.M.S. Railways, *Pamphlet of Information for Travellers* (1914), pp. 27–8; C. W. Harrison, *Illustrated Guide to the Federated Malay States* (London, 1910), p. 91. It was a sign of growing sensitivity by Europeans after the war regarding their relations with Asians that the quoted passage appeared in the 1920 edition (p. 89) of the *Illustrated Guide* but was deleted from the 1923 edition.

32. *Malay Mail*, 1 October 1897, and editorial comments on letter from 'Audi Alteram' in issue of 6 October 1897.

33. Mitchell to Chamberlain, quoted in Chai Hon-Chan, *The Development of British Malaya, 1896–1909* (Kuala Lumpur, 1964), p. 56.

34. Anderson to Lyttelton, confidential of 17 August 1904, and minute by R. E. Stubbs, 12 September 1904, CO 273/300.

35. Letter from Hume, *British Malaya*, 17 (March 1943), 127. Hume and Sir Richard Winstedt (pp. 126–7) were refuting Sir George Maxwell's statement in the previous issue of *British Malaya* that the Rulers were not opposed to admitting Chinese and Indians.

36. *Annual Report of Perak* (1901), p. 16. See also *Annual Report of the F.M.S.* (1902), p. 24; *Minutes of the Conference of Chiefs of the Federated Malay States*, supplement to *Perak Government Gazette*, 9 October 1903, pp. 8–11; Anderson to Colonial Office, 1 September 1910, quoted in Allen, 'Anglo-Kedah Relations', p. 76.

37. 32 H.C. Deb. 5s., 1385–86 (6 December 1911); 38 H.C. Deb. 5s., 1907–8 (22 May 1912).

38. 32 H.C. Deb. 5s., 390 (29 November 1911).

39. Minute by Collins, 18 September 1925, on Hose to Secretary of State, telegram of 14 September 1925, CO 273/529.

40. Discrimination against non-European civil servants is mentioned by Lim Boon Keng, 'Race and Empire with Special Reference to British Malaya', *The Great War from the Confucian Point of View, and Kindred Topics* (Singapore, 1917), pp. 110–11; editorial, *Straits Echo*, 2 August 1912.

41. Anderson to Lyttelton, confidential of 17 August 1904, CO 273/300.

42. S. Chelvasingam-MacIntyre, *Through Memory Lane* (Singapore, 1973), pp. 20, 22, 24, 40–1, 43.

43. C. Bazell, 'Education in Singapore', in Makepeace, *One Hundred Years of Singapore*, I, 471–2; Song Ong Siang, *One Hundred Years' History of the Chinese in Singapore* (London, 1923), pp. 329–30.

44. Letter from 'S. H.', *Straits Echo*, 9 August 1912.

45. *Straits Echo*, 17 May 1912.

46. Letter from A. W. Gooneratne, *Singapore Free Press* (weekly), 20 March 1912; Lim, 'Race and Empire', p. 110; letter from Lim read by Scott, 40 H.C. Deb. 5s., 560 (27 June 1912); A. H. Carlos, 'The Eurasians of Singapore', in Makepeace, *One Hundred Years of Singapore*, I, 369.

47. *Straits Echo*, 10, 17 May 1912. Lim's speech was read out in the House of Commons by Scott: 40 H.C. Deb. 5s., 562–63 (27 June 1912).

48. *Straits Echo*, 31 May 1912. The petition is quoted in Song, *Chinese in Singapore*, p. 480.

49. Much of the information which Scott used to question Harcourt was supplied by the paper's editor, Tom Wright. 'That Colour Bar', *Straits Echo*, 16 August 1912.

50. 'A Question of Race', *Straits Times*, 4 March 1912; letters and editorial comments in issues of 6 and 7 March. For editorials expressing a similar view: *Singapore Free Press* (weekly), 28 March 1912, and the *Times of Malaya*, 15 August 1912.

51. *Malay Mail*, 20 July 1912.

52. Testimony of E. L. Brockman, *Proceedings of the Commission Appointed to Enquire into the Disturbances in Kuala Lumpur and District at the Chinese New Year, 1912* (Kuala Lumpur, 1912), p. ccxciv. Hereafter cited as 'Riot Commission Proceedings'.

53. Editorial, reports, and letter from Horley, *Times of Malaya*, 8 February 1912.

54. Riot Commission Proceedings, pp. xlvii, ccxviii; quotation in letter from 'Vox', *Malay Mail*, 21 February 1912.

55. *Grenier's Rubber News*, 17 February 1912; *Singapore Free Press* (weekly), 25 January 1912; Riot Commission Proceedings, p. clxxxviii; discussion on registration of servants in *Times of Malaya*, 4 January 1912, and numerous other sources.

56. Europeans had insisted that their servants adhere to this custom. 'I was always careful . . .', explained Mrs. Innes, 'to see that my Chinese servants did not behave to me with what I knew were outward marks of disrespect. If my cook came to me with his pigtail curled round his head, and no jacket on, I used to send him back to dress himself properly before I would condescend to order the dinner.' *Chersonese With the Gilding Off*, I, 214–15.

57. Riot Commission Proceedings, pp. xiv, cclxv–cclxvi; letter from H. N. Ferrers, *Malay Mail*, 23 February 1912.

58. *Grenier's Rubber News*, 17 February 1912.

59. Letter from 'Volunteer', *Times of Malaya*, 8 February 1912.

60. Brockman to Commandant, Malay States Guides, 9 February 1912, Riot Commission Proceedings, Appendix I, p. ccci.

61. HCO 293/1912.

62. *Malay Mail* reports, reprinted in Robson, *Records and Recollections*, chapter 7; *Annual Report of Selangor* (1912), p. 10; *Report of the Secretary for Chinese Affairs* (1912), p. 3.

63. As State Surgeon Dr. Travers had cared for Yap Kwan Seng during his last illness. Travers left government service in 1908 to go into business with Loke Yew and to set up a private practice. Shortly before the rioting he had operated on Loke Chow Kit for appendicitis.

64. Riot Commission Proceedings, pp. cxxii–cxxviii, ccxviii–ccxix.

65. Riot Commission Proceedings, p. ccxcviii.

66. Riot Commission Proceedings, p. xlviii.

67. In 1908 nine Selangor planters were charged with assaulting a Tamil *kangany* (labour foreman) who had refused to make the labourers under him work since they had not been paid for several months; the workers then attacked the Europeans, who in turn fired back: Anderson to Crewe, 251 of 30 July 1908, CO 273/341. Some Perak planters received light fines for beating their labourers: Resident of Perak to Resident-General, 9 February 1910 (para. 6), HCO 512/1910. Reports of two other planters receiving light fines: *Malay Mail*, 10 May, 25 July 1912. One case which caused a sensation among Europeans was the murder of Dr. Barrack in Pahang in 1908. He and the man with whom he was travelling, a Mr. McLean, were attacked by a group of Chinese. The group's target was McLean, who with another European had employed some of the group on contract and, according to evidence which was not presented at the trial or reported in the newspapers, had cheated them of large sums of money on numerous occasions. HCO 1350 and 1542/1908.

68 *Malay Mail*, 12–15, 17, 20 June 1912.

69. W. F. Nutt, Riot Commission Proceedings, p. ccxcviii (24 June 1912).

70. *Federal Council Proceedings* (1912), pp. B26–27; editorial, *Malay Mail*, 29 July 1912. During a visit to London Eu had been unable to get a taxi-cab because of a strike by cab drivers.

71. *Malay Mail*, 2 and 25 July 1912.

72. Wright and Cartwright, *Twentieth Century Impressions*, pp. 848, 850.

73. *Selangor Journal*, 3 (30 November 1894), 87–8; 2 (24 August 1894), 410–12.

74. Rodger's belief in the value of sports for Asians was particularly strong: *Annual Report of Selangor* (1894), p. 21; report on the opening of the Recreation Club, *Malay Mail*, 16 February 1897.

75. Editorial and report, *Malay Mail*, 6 November 1911.

76. Editorial and report (from which the quotations are taken), *Malay Mail*, 2 May 1912; letter from 'Spectator' in issue of 3 May 1912.

77. *Malay Mail*, 2 May 1912.

78. 'Sporting Notes', *Singapore Free Press*, 8 May 1912.

79. Letter from 'Break the "Rotters"', *Malay Mail*, 3 May 1912.

80. *Malay Mail*, 6 May 1912.

81. *Malay Mail*, 11 November 1913.

82. Editorial, letter from 'F. D. S.', *Malay Weekly Mail*, 26 March 1914; editorial in issue of 2 April 1914.

83. *Malay Mail*, 25 March 1914.

84. *Malay Weekly Mail*, 2 April 1914.

85. Editorial and report, *Malay Mail*, 27 May 1907. Also editorials of 7 November 1904 and 26 June 1907.

86. J. Johnston Abraham, *The Surgeon's Log* (London, 1911), p. 88. Abraham visited Penang in 1907.

87. Frederic Knocker, 'Rubber-Planting in the Federated Malay States' (first published in 1907), *A Malayan Miscellany* (Kuala Lumpur, 1924), pp. 149–52.

88. 'S.', 'The Turbulent Town', *Malay Mail*, 27 February 1912.

89. 'League Football', *Malay Weekly Mail*, 26 March 1914.

90. I have used a few contemporary sources but have relied mainly on the account by R. W. Mosbergen, 'The Sepoy Rebellion (A History of the Singapore Mutiny, 1915)' (B.A. Honours thesis, University of Malaya, Singapore, 1954).

91. 'A Lady's Experiences in the Singapore Mutiny', *Blackwood's Magazine*, 198 (December 1915), 785.

92. 'E. M. M.', 'Experiences of a Planter's Wife in Earlier Days', *Malay Weekly Mail*, 30 July 1931.

93. L. Guillemard, *Trivial Fond Records* (London, 1937), p. 115; 'Experiences in the Mutiny', p. 783; Horace Bleackley, *Tour in Southern Asia* (London, 1928), p. 150; Governor Young quoted in Song, *Chinese in Singapore*, p. 482; Sir George Maxwell, *Federal Council Proceedings* (1921), p. B109.

94. Bleackley, *Tour in Southern Asia*, p. 148. See also 'Experiences in the Mutiny', p. 793, and Clive Dalton, *A Child in the Sun* (London, 1937), p. 272.

95. Quoted in Donald and Joanna Moore, *The First 150 Years of Singapore* (Singapore, 1969), pp. 555–6.

96. *Annual Report of Selangor* (1916), p. 23. For similar statements on Asian support for the British: *Annual Report of Perak* (1914), p. 37; *Annual Report of Negri Sembilan* (1914), p. 33; *Annual Report of Pahang* (1918), p. 27.

97. Young to Secretary of State, 89 of 11 March 1915, and enclosures, CO 273/421.

98. *Straits Chinese and the Great War* (Singapore, 1915).

99. *Proceedings of the Straits Settlements Legislative Council* (1917), p. B122.

Notes for Chapter 6

1. Bucknill Report, Appendix III, replies to Question 3.

2. For a full discussion of the slump in the rubber industry, see Drabble, *Rubber in Malaya*, chapter 6.

3. *Planter*, 1, No. 6 (January 1921), 26.

4. *Planter*, 2, No. 3 (October 1921), 29.

5. Sir William Peel, Colonial Service Notes, 1897–1935, written in early 1940s (RH), p. 75. Peel was later Chief Secretary of the F.M.S. and then Governor of Hong Kong.

6. 'Planter' to *The Financier* (London), reprinted in *Planter*, 1, No. 9 (April 1921), 35.

7. H. Norden, *From Golden Gate to Golden Sun* (London, 1923), p. 14.

8. Harry L. Foster, *A Beachcomber in the Orient* (New York, 1923), pp. 188–239, quoted passages on pp. 194, 217.

9. Peel, Colonial Service Notes, p. 76.

10. *Proceedings of the Straits Settlements Legislative Council* (1921), pp. B101–104 (4 July).

11. Guillemard to Milner, 72 of 10 February 1921, forwarding memorial dated 10 December 1920, and reply by Amery, 9 April 1921, CO 273/509. Amery also snubbed Guillemard's request for more favourable leave conditions for government officers. Guillemard to Milner, 710 of 28 December 1920, and reply by Amery, 9 March 1921, CO 273/503.

12. Manager's Annual Report on the Chersonese Estate for 1927 (typescript, preserved by the estate's agents, Thomas Barlow and Bro., Plantation House, Mincing Lane, London). Data on the salaries of civil servants come from *Malayan Civil Service List* for April 1927.

13. Ashley Gibson, *The Malay Peninsula and Archipelago* (London, 1928), p. 112.

14. *Planter*, 9 (September 1928), 39.

15. G. A. Hodgson, 'The Incorporated Society of Planters, 1919–1969', *Planter*, 45 (December 1969), 647–8.

16. *Planter*, 11 (August 1930), 47.

17. *British Malaya*, 6 (August 1931), 116; *Malay Weekly Mail*, 6 December 1934.

18. The salary of one senior assistant, for example, was cut from $375 to $285 per month. A. S. Taylor, 'Harking Back: 1929–1933', *Planter*, 50 (May 1974), 158, 160. Mr. T. M. Walker, to whom I am indebted for several points concerning planters' salaries in the 1930s, doubts that salaries were cut by more than one-third. Personal communication, 20 February 1975.

19. Editorial, *Planter*, 12 (May 1932), 289–90; I.S.P. memorandum on 'Unfair Treatment of Planters', ibid., 13 (August 1932), 14–17; letter from 'One of Them', ibid., 16 (September 1935), 422.

20. Incorporated Society of Planters, *A Statement Upon Questions Relating to the Salaries Emoluments and the General Conditions and Terms of Service of Planters on Rubber Estates and Other Plantations in British Malaya* (Kuala Lumpur, 1934), p. 9.

21. 'Rubber Planting in Malaya', *Planter*, 17 (January 1936), 16.

22. 'Malaya: Average Prices ... and Cost of Living 1934', in *Annual Reports of the Straits Settlements for the Year 1934*, p. 373.

23. S. Cunyngham-Brown, *The Traders* (London, 1971), p. 255; personal communication from Mr. T. M. Walker.

24. Emerson, *Malaysia*, p. 488. He was also referring to the Netherlands East Indies.

25. *British Malaya*, 12 (July 1937), 61; 13 (October 1938), 141; 13 (February 1939), 245.

26. Memorial of 17 December 1931, enclosed in Clementi to Cunliffe-Lister, confidential of 23 January 1932, file 92301, CO 717/88.

27. *British Malaya*, 12 (July 1937), 61; 12 (December 1937), 198.

28. Quoted in Douglas Bailey, *We Built and Destroyed* (London, 1944), p. 29.

29. Knocker, *Malayan Miscellany*, pp. 36–7; J. S. M. Rennie, *Musings of J.S.M.R.* (Singapore, 1933), p. 101. Eric Macfadyen, 'Other Times, Other Ways', *British Malaya*, 1 (June 1926), 45–6.

30. British Malaya 1921 Census, p. 53. See also p. 101.

31. Curle, *Into the East* (London, 1923), p. 168.

32. F.M.S. 1911 Census, Table 14; British Malaya 1921 Census, Table 18 (F.M.S.). The 1931 census does not give separate data on age, sex, and marital status for people living in towns.

33. Data for England and Wales calculated from *Census of England and Wales 1931: General Tables* (London, 1935), Table 10.

34. See, for example, letter from 'Ceylon Planter'. *Planter*, 3 (March 1923), 498.

35. This was suggested by Dr. David Forsyth during discussion on a paper read by Millais Culpin, 'An Examination of Tropical Neurasthenia', *Proceedings of the Royal Society of Medicine*, 26 (1933), 921.

36. Interviews with Mr. J. F. Fenwick, Mr. J. L. Kennedy, and Mr. T. M. Walker, April 1972.

37. Personal communication from Mr. Hugh Allen, 19 July 1972.

38. William Duncan, Bucknill Report, Appendix V, p. 239.

39. A. J. Reid, *Planter*, 14 (August 1933), 5–6.

40. Boulle, *Sacrilege in Malaya*, translated by Xan Fielding (London, 1959), pp. 74–5. Boulle worked for Socfin before the Second World War.

41. Bucknill Report, Appendix V, p. 61; R. L. German, *Handbook to British Malaya* (London, 1926), p. 59.

42. Guillemard to Duke of Devonshire, 379 of 16 July 1923, CO 717/28.

43. Personal communication from Mr. David Gray, 5 December 1973.

44. Bucknill Report, Appendix IV, p. 282.

45. *British Malaya*, 6 (August 1931), 116.

46. K. R. Blackwell, 'Malay Curry', unpublished autobiography written in 1945 (RH), p. 194.

47. For a short story about a District Officer who commits suicide after his sweetheart writes to say that she cannot wait for him any longer and that she has accepted another man's proposal of marriage: *Times of Malaya*, 9 November 1922.

48. If the man she had originally intended to marry had paid for her voyage to Malaya the intruder was expected to pay back to him the cost of her passage. Interview with Mr. J. S. H. Cunyngham-Brown, February 1973.

49. Margaret Wilson, *Malaya the Land of Enchantment* (Amersham, 1937), p. 97, and a similar statement on p. 140. See also a novel by Jessie A. Davidson, *Dawn: A Romance of Malaya* (London, 1926), p. 28.

50. George Bilainkin, *Hail Penang!* (London, 1932), pp. 38–9, and similar views on pp. 127–8.

51. These ratios are for men and women aged twenty or more. F.M.S. 1911 Census, Table 14; British Malaya 1931 Census, Table 112.

52. Marwick, *Britain in the Century of Total War*, pp. 107, 170.

53. 'Advice to the Assistant', reprinted in *Planter*, 10 (June 1930), 302.

54. Gibson, *Malay Peninsula*, p. 120. The same list is given in a Malayan Information Agency pamphlet, *British Malaya: General Description of the Country and Life Therein* (London, 1929), pp. 28–9.

55. 'The Cost of Living', *Malay Mail*, 14 May 1928. See also letter from

'Exile', *Malay Weekly Mail*, 21 May 1931, on the inflexible nature of the European standard of living.

56. G. I. Gun Munro, 'Malaya Through a Woman's Eyes', *Crown Colonist*, 1 (April 1932), 226.

57. R. N. Walling, *Singapura Sorrows* (Singapore, 1931), pp. 9–10.

58. Wilson, *Malaya the Land of Enchantment*, p. 64.

59. 'The Planter's Wife', *Planter*, 14 (November 1933), 180; C. W. Harrison, *The Magic of Malaya* (London, 1916), pp. 125–6; Carveth Wells, *Six Years in the Malay Jungle* (Garden City, New York, 1926), pp. 33–4; *Straits Times Annual 1940*, p. 139.

60. Mrs. D. B. Evans, Household Accounts Ledger for 1920 (RH).

61. Letter from 'Married Woman', *Malay Weekly Mail*, 5 October 1922.

62. J. N. Dugdale, *How to Keep Healthy in the Tropics* (Singapore, 1930), p. 140; Blackwell, 'Malay Curry', pp. 197–8.

63. Mrs. E. Bruce, 'Planters' Wives', *Planter*, 1, No. 1 (August 1920), 27, 29.

64. 'F. G.', 'Random Impressions of a Woman in Malaya', *Malay Weekly Mail*, 2 July 1931.

65. As for example Katherine Sim, who wrote *Malayan Landscape* (London, 1946).

66. Gordon, 'The Health of the European Child in Singapore and Malaya', *Malayan Medical Journal*, 3 (1928), 32–40.

67. 'The Amahs' Ring', *Malay Weekly Mail*, 23 March 1922.

68. H. W. Toms to editor, *British Medical Journal*, 1931, vol. 1, p. 1091; Gordon, 'Health of the European Child', p. 34; F. B., 'European Nursery Governesses', *Malay Weekly Mail*, 11 February 1926. In 1921 there were forty-two European women employed as domestic servants in the F.M.S.; in 1931 there were only three. British Malaya 1921 Census, Table 34 (F.M.S.); British Malaya 1931 Census, Table 130.

69. Letter from 'A Member's Wife', *Planter*, 2 (May 1922), 145. Other sources used for this and the previous paragraph include: an article criticizing Dr. Gordon's views, *Malay Mail*, 5 April 1928; Dugdale, *How to Keep Healthy in the Tropics*, pp. 134–8; A. R. Neligan and others, 'Discussion on the Adaptation of European Women and Children to Tropical Climates', *Proceedings of the Royal Society of Medicine*, 24 (1931), 1315–33, especially 1322 and 1328; *Straits Times* editorial, reprinted in *British Malaya*, 4 (July 1929), 100; R. J. H. Sidney, *Malay Land* (London, 1926), pp. 88–9.

70. Letters of Mrs. Nancy Bateson (Centre for South-East Asian Studies, University of Hull), 3 March 1941.

71. These figures have been calculated from this formula:
100(1−[number of married women/number of married men])
I have made the assumption, which is in fact largely correct, that no Europeans were married to Asians. British Malaya 1921 Census, Table 18 (F.M.S.); British Malaya 1931 Census, Table 112.

72. German, *Handbook to British Malaya* (1926), p. 47.

73. R. J. H. Sidney, *In British Malaya Today* (London, 1926), pp. 244–5; Boulle, *Sacrilege in Malaya*, p. 73; 'Rubber Planting in Malaya', *Planter*, 17 (January 1936), 16.

74. Sidney, *In British Malaya*, p. 245; editorial, *Malay Weekly Mail*, 25 May 1922.

75. Curle, *Into the East*, p. 144. As will be shown in chapter 7, more non-

Europeans did join the club in the years after Curle's visit in 1921.

76. *Malay Weekly Mail*, 30 March 1922.

77. *Malay Mail*, 28 February, 2 September 1907; *Malay Weekly Mail*, 2 September 1909.

78. Editorial, *Malay Weekly Mail*, 25 May 1922. The editor adds: 'Sir Laurence Guillemard once remarked on the good fortune of the European community of Selangor in having a place like the Selangor Club where all could meet on a level.'

79. 'F. B.', 'Our Clubs', *Malay Weekly Mail*, 21 January 1926.

80. 'Selangor Club Rules and Bye-Laws, 1935' (with amendments to September 1946), preserved at the Selangor Club. I was unable to locate an earlier set of rules.

81. 'F. B.', 'Our Clubs'.

82. Topham, 'Autobiography', p. 11.

83. Gibson, *Malay Peninsula*, p. 115; Curle, *Into the East*, p. 140; Sidney, *Malay Land*, pp. 84–5; Purcell, *Memoirs*, p. 101; H. P. Bryson, 'Twenty-Nine-and-a-Half Years in the Malayan Civil Service', written in 1963 (BAM), para. 28; Scott, *Eastern Journey*, p. 35; interviews.

84. Green to Chief Secretary, 17 and 20 May 1917; Resident, E. G. Broadrick, to Chief Secretary, 6 June 1917; minutes by Sir Arthur Young, all in HCO 1198/1917; Selangor Golf Club, *Twelve Under Fours*, pp. 36, 39–40.

85. Selangor Golf Club, *Twelve Under Fours*, pp. 40–7.

86. *Malay Weekly Mail*, 25 May 1922; Selangor Golf Club, *Twelve Under Fours*, p. 56.

87. Letter from 'Life Member', *Malay Weekly Mail*, 29 March 1934.

88. Selangor Golf Club, *Twelve Under Fours*, pp. 64–6; *Malay Weekly Mail*, 22 and 29 March, 31 May 1935, and many other issues.

89. Selangor Golf Club, *Twelve Under Fours*, p. 67.

90. Personal communications from Mr. David Gray, 5 December 1973, 18 February 1975.

91. 'Selangor Club Rules and Bye-Laws, 1935'.

92. 'F. B.', 'Our Clubs'.

93. Bryson, 'Twenty-Nine-and-a-Half Years in the Malayan Civil Service', para. 29.

94. Ralph Furse, *Aucuparius: Recollections of a Recruiting Officer* (London, 1962), p. 207.

95. Ambrose Pratt, *Magical Malaya* (Melbourne, 1931), p. 34; Emerson, *Malaysia*, pp. 30, 474. It may be noted that both Pratt and Emerson visited Malaya in the depression, when the two sections disagreed strongly over several matters of government policy.

96. In Taiping, where the main long-term prison was located, European warders had their own social club.

97. L. Richmond Wheeler, *The Modern Malay* (London, 1928), p. 169.

98. Manson, *Tropical Diseases*, fourth edition (London, 1907), p. xiv.

99. For examples of this shift of attitude, which took place at different times for different writers: Dr. A. Balfour, 'Problems of Acclimatisation', *The Lancet*, 205 (4 August 1923), 245; Sir Aldo Castellani, in Neligan and others, 'Discussions on the Adaptation of European Women and Children to Tropical Climates', p. 1319; 'Health in the Tropics', *Malayan Medical Journal*, 7 (1932), 132–3. A useful survey of various points of view in the mid-1920s is: Glenn

T. Trewartha, 'Recent Thought on the Problems of White Acclimatization in the Wet Tropics', *Geographical Review*, 16 (1926), 467–78.

100. For references to the high suicide rate among Europeans in Malaya: Bishop of Singapore to editor, *British Medical Journal*, 1926, vol. 1, p. 503; Kenneth Black, 'Health and Climate with Special Reference to Malaya', *Malayan Medical Journal*, 7 (1932), 103–4; Robson, *Records and Recollections*, p. 69; Winstedt, *Start from Alif*, pp. 100–4; source cited in note 104. I came across many reports of suicides in newspapers and in official correspondence. The annual reports of the F.M.S. Medical Department give no statistics on suicides by Europeans, but it seems certain that the rate was in fact high.

101. Black, 'Health and Climate', p. 101.

102. Black, 'Health and Climate', pp. 102–3; *Report by W. G. A. Ormsby-Gore on His Visit to Malaya, Ceylon, and Java in 1928*, 1928–9, V (Cmd. 3235), p. 24.

103. Peet, *Malayan Exile* (Singapore, 1934), pp. 59–60. Peet was the *Straits Times* reporter in Kuala Lumpur. Other writings stressing the effects of exile include: 'A Planter's Lot', *Planter*, 17 (May 1936), 216; editorial, 'The White Man in the Tropics', *British Medical Journal*, 1926, vol. 1, p. 909; M. Carthew, 'The Aetiology and Prophylaxis of Mental Irritability in Europeans in the Tropics', *Journal of Tropical Medicine and Hygiene*, 30 (1927), 113–17; Culpin, 'An Examination of Tropical Neurasthenia', pp. 911–17.

104. Waugh-Scott, 'On Mental Hygiene in the Tropics', presidential address to the Malayan Branch of the British Medical Association, *Malay Weekly Mail*, 8 April 1931.

105. Memoranda by Dr. A. L. Hoops and 'Singapore Medico', *Planter*, 13 (December 1932), 162–3; I.S.P., *Statement Upon Questions Relating to Salaries*, pp. 10–11; Dr. S. C. Howard, 'The Malayan Climate Versus the White Races', *Malay Mail*, 7 December 1932; Dugdale, *How to Keep Healthy in the Tropics*, p. 129; German, *Handbook to British Malaya* (1926), p. 14; Sir Malcolm Watson, during discussion on Culpin, 'An Examination of Tropical Neurasthenia', p. 921.

106. Editorial, *Malay Mail*, 2 March 1905.

107. *Annual Report of Pahang* (1912), p. 23.

108. *Federal Council Proceedings* (1912), p. B11.

109. This and the following three paragraphs are partly based on articles by Sir George Maxwell in *Malaya*, 1952: 'Has Gunong Tahan Been Jilted?', August, pp. 27–9; 'The Early Days of Fraser's Hill', September, pp. 35–7, and October, pp. 23–7.

110. Bucknill Report, p. 162, Appendix V, pp. 28–9. Young doubted whether either overwork or the climate was mainly responsible for the early retirement of the three civil servants mentioned by name in the report. One had a family history of mental disorders and was suffering from syphilis; the second had cerebral syphilis; and the third had a family history of mental illness though his condition was 'no doubt aggravated by residence in the tropics'. Young to Milner, confidential of 11 August 1919, CO 273/484.

111. In January 1925 the mean maximum and mean minimum temperatures in degrees Fahrenheit were 70 and 61 respectively. The corresponding figures for Kuala Lumpur were 89 and 71. German, *Handbook to British Malaya* (1926), p. 19.

112. Wilson, *Malaya the Land of Enchantment*, p. 92. For other ecstatic comments: Walling, *Singapura Sorrows*, pp. 61–7; Scott, *Eastern Journey*, pp. 47–8; Rennie, *Musings of J.S.M.R.*, pp. 111–17.

113. Letters of P. Samuel (RH), 6 May 1931.

114. Since Europeans in Malaya were so convinced of the curative powers of a visit to a hill station it is surprising that so few companies built bungalows for their employees. Maxwell suggested that the London boards of directors were responsible for this parsimony. *British Malaya*, 4 (July 1929), 82.

115. *Report by Ormsby-Gore*, p. 25.

116. Council Papers No. 13, 14, and 15, *Federal Council Proceedings* (1925).

117. E. N. T. Cummins, *Federal Council Proceedings* (1929), p. B77.

118. 'Chronicle of the Development of the Cameron Highlands . . . 1926–1931 . . .', Council Paper No. 13, *Federal Council Proceedings* (1932), p. C156.

119. Letters of Mrs. Nancy Bateson, 18 May 1941.

120. *Development of the Cameron Highlands up to the End of 1934 and Information Concerning the Highlands* (Kuala Lumpur, 1935); A. B. Milne, 'Planting in the Cameron Highlands', *British Malaya*, 11 (August 1936), 103.

121. *Singapore Free Press* editorial, reprinted in *British Malaya*, 2 (November 1927), 188; 'Hill Stations', *Planter*, 2 (July 1922), 220–5; paper read by C. C. Footner, *Planter*, 16 (October 1935), 465.

122. Gammans, 'The Development of Cameron Highlands: Some Marketing Problems', apparently written in 1933 (RH), pp. 2–6.

Notes for Chapter 7

1. Peet, *Malayan Exile*, pp. 55–6.

2. *Federal Council Proceedings* (1925), p. B77.

3. *Federal Council Proceedings* (1929), p. B28; 1930, pp. B75–76.

4. *Federal Council Proceedings* (1930), p. B99.

5. 'Report of the Sub-Committee Appointed to Visit the General Hospital, Kuala Lumpur', enclosed in Scott to Passfield, 359 of 10 June 1931, Clementi to Passfield, 523 of 10 August 1931, file 82436, CO 717/84.

6. 'An Asiatic Hospital', *Straits Times*, 22 April 1931. See also editorial in issue of 18 April 1931.

7. Reports and editorial, *Malay Weekly Mail*, 30 July 1931. It must be pointed out that the opening of the European Hospital to non-Europeans benefited only a small section of the Asian community. By 1933 the Bungsar Hospital did not have facilities to provide food to Muslim, Sikh, and Hindu patients. According to a *Malay Mail* editorial, those Chinese and Christian Indians who could afford treatment at the Bungsar Hospital had given up their efforts to improve medical facilities for the community as a whole. 'Kuala Lumpur Hospitals', *Malay Mail*, 30 January 1933.

8. Malayan Information Agency, *British Malaya*, p. 27.

9. Selangor Golf Club, *Twelve Under Fours*, p. 50.

10. 'East and West', *Malay Weekly Mail*, 29 April 1931.

11. Blackwell, 'Malay Curry', pp. 178, 210; Bryson, 'Twenty-Nine-and-a-Half Years in the Malayan Civil Service', para. 32.

12. Editorial, 'The King of Games', *Malay Mail*, 23 June 1928.

13. *Malay Weekly Mail*, 14 January 1926 (reports) and 21 January 1926 (editorial).

14. 'Pariahs', *Planter*, 2, No. 7 (March 1922), 44. See also a *Pinang Gazette* editorial about the harm done to British prestige by some rowdy European spectators at a vaudeville performance in Penang: *British Malaya*, 2 (February 1928), 269.

15. Bilainkin, *Hail Penang!*, p. 69. See also Blackwell, 'Malay Curry', pp. 20, 78, and 178.

16. Letters of P. Samuel, 6 November 1930. See also G. J. O'Grady, 'If You Sling Enough Mud', unpublished autobiography written in 1945 (RH), p. 258; Raymond Kennedy, 'The Colonial Crisis and the Future', in R. Linton, ed., *The Science of Man in the World Crisis* (New York, 1945), p. 318.

17. Rex Stevenson, 'Cinemas and Censorship in Colonial Malaya', *Journal of Southeast Asian Studies*, 5 (September 1974), 209–24.

18. Lockhart, *Return to Malaya*, pp. 103, 126.

19. Bleackley, *Tour in Southern Asia*, p. 195.

20. Peet, *Malayan Exile*, pp. 22–6.

21. *Malay Mail*, 11 December 1922. Dr. Travers was speaking at a large Chinese banquet to which many Europeans had been invited. This was the first such gathering to be held in many years.

22. See Appendix 1.

23. J. S. Furnivall, *Colonial Policy and Practice* (New York, 1956; first published Cambridge, 1948), pp. 303–12.

24. 'First Impressions', *Malay Weekly Mail*, 30 March 1922.

25. Blackwell, 'Malay Curry', pp. 223–4. Emphasis added.

26. Calculated from British Malaya 1931 Census, Tables 210, 211, 212. These figures are for all Asians except those few listed under 'others' in the census. According to the superintendent of the census, 'the test of ability to speak English, which was defined as "ability to carry on a conversation" therein, was somewhat strictly applied in practice' (p. 91).

27. Roff, *Malay Nationalism*, pp. 104–9; *Federal Council Proceedings* (1917), p. B45.

28. *Malayan Civil List* (1932); *Malayan Establishment Staff List* (July 1937).

29. C. W. Harrison, *Some Notes on the Government Services in British Malaya* (London, 1929), p. 65.

30. O'Grady, 'If You Sling Enough Mud', p. 32. It was also true that Europeans charged with minor offences increasingly had their own cases dealt with by Malay magistrates. A controversial case is reported in the *Times of Malaya*, 28 August 1929.

31. *Proceedings of the Straits Settlements Legislative Council* (1924), pp. B33–35.

32. For Malay views see C. M. Turnbull, 'British Planning for Post-war Malaya', *Journal of Southeast Asian Studies*, 5 (September 1974), 240–1, and letter from 'A Malay', *Malay Mail*, 26 November 1924.

33. 'Council Matters', *Straits Times*, 15 April 1924.

34. *Straits Times*, 5 November 1924.

35. 'Legislative Council', *Malay Mail*, 5 November 1924.

36. 'Asiatics and the Service', *Times of Malaya*, 15 January 1930.

37. *British Malaya*, 7 (October 1932), 131–2, and 7 (April 1933), 270; *Proceedings of the Straits Settlements Legislative Council* (1933), pp. B29–31, 102–104; 1939, pp. B78–80.

38. *Singapore and Straits Directory* (1920), *Singapore and Malayan Directory* (1924 and 1936).

39. Interview with Encik Mohamed Din bin Mohamed Shariff, April 1973. Encik Din became a police inspector in Perak in 1925.

40. Sir George Maxwell, 'The Mixed Communities of Malaya', *British Malaya*, 17 (February 1943), 118.

41. Ibid.; interview with Mr. G. L. Peet, January 1978.

42. Interview with Tan Sri Dato' Dr. Mohamed Said, March 1973.

43. *Malay Mail*, 23 February 1905.

44. Bryson, 'Twenty-Nine-and-a-Half Years in the Malayan Civil Service', para. 31. Bryson implies, but does not state, that because of the threat the Burmese officers were in fact admitted.

45. *British Malaya*, 2 (February 1928), 254.

46. Yeo Kim Wah, 'The Selangor Succession Dispute, 1933–1938', *Journal of Southeast Asian Studies*, 2 (September 1971), 169–84; T. S. Adams, Report on the Raja Muda of Selangor, 15 May 1934, enclosed in Caldecott to Maffey, confidential of 17 May 1935, file 33376, CO 717/105; S. W. Jones to Federal Secretary, 11 March 1939, enclosed in Thomas to MacDonald, confidential of 6 April 1939, file 51973, CO 717/140.

47. Bryson, 'Twenty-Nine-and-a-Half Years in the Malayan Civil Service', para. 31.

48. Anthony Hill, *Diversion in Malaya* (London, 1948), pp. 62–3.

49. O'Grady, 'If You Sling Enough Mud', p. 31.

50. *British Malaya*, 8 (September 1933), 100; interview with Miss Nona Baker, March 1972.

51. Selangor Golf Club, *Twelve Under Fours*, p. 42.

52. Agnes Davison, 'Some Autobiographical Notes and General Reminiscences', written after World War II (RH). See also Peel, Colonial Service Notes, p. 87.

53. Interview with Mr. E. C. G. Barrett, April 1972.

54. W. C. S. Corry, Typescript of Tape-recorded Interview Covering Career in the Malayan Civil Service, 1923–1953, conducted in 1969 (RH), p. 3.

55. Personal communication from Mr. J. S. H. Cunyngham-Brown, 10 March 1973.

56. *British Malaya*, 12 (March 1938), 266.

57. *Straits Times*, 29 August 1932.

58. British Malaya 1931 Census, Tables 210 and 211. See note 26 of this chapter.

59. Bryson, 'Twenty-Nine-and-a-Half Years in the Malayan Civil Service', para. 31.

60. 'Good Fellowship', *Malay Weekly Mail*, 21 December 1922.

61. Swettenham, *British Malaya* (London, 1908), p. 147; and also Rene Onraet, *Singapore—A Police Background* (London, 1947), p. 32.

62. A. G. Morkill, Diary Kept While in Kelantan, 1915–1917 (RH), 10 April 1917.

63. O'Grady, 'If You Sling Enough Mud', pp. 255–6.

64. Clementi to Grindle, 14 July 1931, and enclosures, file 82424, CO 717/83; Thomas to Ormsby-Gore, confidential of 1 July 1937, file 51736/1, CO 717/126. Thomas and the Secretary of State approved of the Sultan's attitude since they feared that marriages between Malay men of high rank and European women would lead to succession disputes. In the same letter

Thomas mentioned that 'we have been very near a scandal in Perak where a European woman allowed herself to become the mistress of a Malay'.

65. Morkill to Ezechiel, 19 September 1932, and other correspondence, file 92398, CO 717/92.

66. Scott to Passfield, 2 April 1931, Kelantan 283/1931 (ANM). I am indebted to Thomas Willer for this reference.

67. Sources for this paragraph include Bilainkin, *Hail Penang!*, pp. 101–6; Purcell, *Memoirs*, p. 298; interviews with Encik Mohamed Din bin Mohamed Shariff, April 1973; Dato Abdullah bin Mohamed, April 1973; Tan Sri Dato' Dr. Mohamed Said, March 1973; Raja Tan Sri Zainal bin Raja Sulaiman, March 1973; Mr. David Gray, June 1972; Mr. E. C. G. Barrett, April 1972.

68. According to Blackwell, European parents almost never employed Eurasian nurses because they feared it would be impossible to eradicate this accent after their children had returned to Britain. 'Malay Curry', p. 198.

69. Ridley, 'The Eurasian Problem', in *Noctes Orientales: Being a Selection of Essays Before the Straits Philosophical Society Between the Years 1893 and 1910* (Singapore, 1913), p. 54.

70. British Malaya 1931 Census, Table 131.

71. 'Quarterly Letter', *Eurasian Review*, 1, No. 6 (December 1935), 19; Gibson, *Malay Peninsula*, p. 42.

72. Peel, Colonial Service Notes, p. 137.

73. J. M. Jansen, in the *Eurasian Review*, 1, No. 2 (October 1934), 15; other articles and letters in the *Eurasian Review* and a letter from R. V. Chapman, *Malay Weekly Mail*, 15 March 1934.

74. 'Memorandum on the Report of the Committee Appointed to Enquire into Unemployment in Selangor', Council Paper No. 5, *Federal Council Proceedings* (1938), pp. C66, 72.

75. 'Selangor Eurasian Association: A Brief History', *Eurasian Review*, 1, No. 2 (October 1934), 12–14.

76. Selangor Eurasian Association, *Golden Jubilee, 1921–1971* (Kuala Lumpur, 1971). I am indebted to Mr. J. de Souza, General Secretary of the Selangor Eurasian Association, for sending me this booklet.

77. Letter from Talalla, in G. Hawkins and W. S. Thaddaeus, compilers, *Rotary International Golden Jubilee, 1905–1955* (Kuala Lumpur: Kuala Lumpur Rotary Club, 1955), p. 9.

78. *Malay Weekly Mail*, 13 May 1926.

79. Quoted in editorial, 'A "Concord" Club?', *Malay Weekly Mail*, 29 April 1926.

80. Letter from 'Interested', *Malay Weekly Mail*, 29 April 1926.

81. 'A Concord Club', *Malay Weekly Mail*, 29 April 1926.

82. *Times of Malaya*, 21 November 1928.

83. Report by Singapore correspondent, *Times of Malaya*, 19 December 1928.

84. *Straits Echo*, 19 May 1926.

85. Ibid.

86. 'A "Concord" Club?', *Malay Weekly Mail*, 29 April 1926.

87. *Malay Weekly Mail*, 13 May 1926.

88. *Malay Mail*, 23 July 1928.

89. L. D. Gammans, 'Rotary in Malaya', published in *Rotary International* in January 1933 (RH), p. 5.

90. *Malay Mail*, 23 July 1928. Caldecott was speaking at the club's first monthly dinner.

91. Gammans, 'Rotary in Malaya', p. 4. See also Francis F. Cooray, 'The Rotary Movement in Malaya', *British Malaya*, 4 (November 1929), 213–15; E. W. Gilman, Personal Recollections (RH), p. 81.

92. Editorial, *Malaya Tribune*, 9 July 1934.

93. Report on annual general meeting of Singapore Rotary Club, *Times of Malaya*, 11 July 1934.

94. Annual report of the Ipoh Rotary Club, *Times of Malaya*, 4 July 1934.

95. Editorial, 'Is Rotary Failing in Malaya?', *Times of Malaya*, 11 July 1934.

96. *Malay Weekly Mail*, 1 August 1935.

97. Editorial, *Malay Mail*, 17 August 1935.

98. *Malay Mail*, 9 February 1939.

Notes for Chapter 8

1. Purcell, *Memoirs*, p. 250.

2. See Banks, *Feminism and Family Planning*.

3. H. D. Traill, quoted in Peter T. Cominos, 'Late-Victorian Respectability and the Social System', *International Review of Social History*, 8 (1963), 48.

4. G. E. Brooke, 'Medical Work and Institutions', in Makepeace, *One Hundred Years of Singapore*, I, 507–9.

5. 'Annual Report of the Chinese Protectorate in Perak, 1894', *Perak Government Gazette* (24 May 1895), p. 211; *Report of a Committee Appointed to Report on Straits Settlements and Federated Malay States Women and Girls Protection Amendments, 1927*, 1928–9, V (Cmd. 3294), pp. 4–5; and materials used for the preparation of this report in file 52032 (and sub-files) (1928), CO 273/543–544.

6. Letter from Dr. E. A. O. Travers, in 'Report of Venereal Diseases Committee', Council Paper No. 86, *Proceedings of the Straits Settlements Legislative Council* (1923), pp. C316–317; Anderson to Elgin, 11 of 16 January 1908, CO 273/339.

7. Memorandum by Swettenham, 16 September 1891, in *Contagious Diseases Regulations (Perak and Malay States)*, 1894, LVII (H.C. 146), p. 10.

8. 'Marriage in the East', *Malay Mail*, 17 March 1897.

9. W. N. Willis, in Mrs. Archibald Mackirdy and W. N. Willis, *The White Slave Market* (London, 1912), pp. 123–4. Chapters 7 and 8 of this book contain the life story of Madame V., an Austrian woman reputed to have the best brothel in Singapore.

10. Anderson to Lyttelton, 95 of 15 March 1905, CO 273/308.

11. 'White Slaves in Singapore', *Straits Times*, 6 August 1912. See also Lockhart, *Return to Malaya*, p. 108.

12. Lockhart, *Return to Malaya*, p. 109; D. C. S. Sissons, 'Karayuki-San: Japanese Prostitutes in Australia, 1887–1916—I', *Historical Studies*, No. 68 (April 1977), 323–41.

13. 'Report of Venereal Diseases Committee', p. C291.

14. Memorandum by Swettenham, 16 September 1891, *Contagious Diseases Regulations*, p. 9.

15. 'Report of the Secretary for Chinese Affairs for 1911', *F.M.S. Government Gazette*, supplement of 24 May 1912, p. 2. There were 2,164 'known' Chinese prostitutes, 50 Malays, and 10 Indians.

16. F.M.S. 1911 Census, Table 47.

17. Winstedt, *Start from Alif*, p. 52. The interior of a Japanese brothel is described by Robson, *People in a Native State*, pp. 45–7.

18. Mabel Marsh, *Service Suspended* (New York, 1968), pp. 35–6.

19. Memorandum by H. C. Belfield, 11 February 1909, enclosed in Young to Crewe, confidential of 11 March 1909, CO 273/349.

20. E. Cameron to Protector of Chinese, 3 November 1909, and other correspondence, HCO 238/1909.

21. Interview with Mr. Ginder Singh, February 1973.

22. Anderson to Elgin, 11 of 16 January 1908, enclosing letter from Resident General and statement by Ohana, CO 273/339; evidence given by Mr. Bernard Day, file 52032 (sub-file VI) (1928), CO 273/544.

23. *Malay Mail*, 19 March 1897.

24. Robson, *People in a Native State*, p. 49.

25. O'Grady, 'If You Sling Enough Mud', pp. 146–7; interviews.

26. This was William Proudlock, whose case is discussed in Appendix 2.

27. Watson, during discussion on Culpin, 'An Examination of Tropical Neurasthenia', p. 920.

28. Ibid.

29. Lockhart, *Return to Malaya*, p. 141, chapter 7. Other references are on pp. 30, 197.

30. Winstedt, *Start from Alif*, p. 18.

31. Wells, *Six Years in the Malay Jungle*, p. 69.

32. H. R. Cheeseman, in Biographical Notes on Hubert Berkeley, 1959 (BAM). Cheeseman says that he did not accept the second part of the offer.

33. 'Birds of Passage', *Malay Weekly Mail*, 16 November 1922.

34. *Malay Weekly Mail*, 16 November 1922.

35. *Malay Weekly Mail*, 23 November 1922.

36. Ibid.

37. 'Nilai', *Planter*, 3 (May 1923), 563.

38. Letter from Lionel van Geyzel, *Malay Weekly Mail*, 23 November 1922. Van Geyzel was the only writer to give his name during the debate.

39. *Malay Weekly Mail*, 23 November 1922.

40. *Malay Weekly Mail*, 16 November 1922.

41. *Malay Weekly Mail*, 23 November 1922.

42. Ibid.

43. W. Somerset Maugham, *The Complete Short Stories of W. Somerset Maugham*, 4 vols. (New York: Washington Square Press, 1967), III, 957. Similar reactions are described in another work of fiction, which is set in Malaya or British-controlled Borneo: Peter Blundell, *The Sin of Godfrey Neil* (London, 1920), pp. 115–18, 130, 212.

44. Letter from 'Not Born Yesterday', *Malay Weekly Mail*, 23 November 1922.

45. Letter to a British newspaper from a doctor in the F.M.S., *Planter*, 4 (August 1923), 15.

46. Bailey, *We Built and Destroyed*, pp. 129–30.

47. Neither of the writers cited in the two preceding footnotes approved of such relations. Both were arguing in favour of early marriages.

48. Clifford, *Since the Beginning*, quotation from p. 134. The remainder of the novel describes the tragedy which occurs when Maimunah discovers that Frank has returned with a wife.

49. *The Times*, 6 July 1927. The Bishop did not give the name of the book as he did not want more people to read it.

50. Watson, in discussion on Culpin, 'An Examination of Tropical Neurasthenia', p. 921.

51. *British Malaya*, 10 (August 1935), 89.

52. Letter from W. Scoresby Routledge, *The Times*, 3 December 1908.

53. Letter from 'Political Officer', *The Times*, 7 December 1908; letter from Charles F. Harford, 9 December 1908; editorial, 'The East Africa Protectorate', 26 December 1908.

54. 198 H.C. Debs. 4s., 68–73 (7 December 1908), 2125–26 (17 December 1908).

55. Confidential Circular of 11 January 1909, CO 854/168. It is interesting to note that at about the same time the Governor-General of the Netherlands East Indies, van Heutsz, issued a *concubinaats-circulaire* containing similar prohibitions. 'Prostitutie', *Encyclopaedie van Nederlandsch-Indie*, tweede druk, derde deel (1919), 515.

56. Purcell, *Memoirs*, p. 298. At least three of Charleton Maxwell's five children were born before 1909. Maxwell spent his retirement at Lumut in Perak. In November 1940 he and his wife were murdered, apparently by a former servant. George Maxwell, *Annals of One Branch of the Maxwell Family*; *Straits Times*, 8 and 9 November 1940; Blackwell, 'Malay Curry', p. 178.

57. W. T. Chapman, 'Memorandum on Sly Prostitution in Kuala Lumpur and other large Towns in the Federated Malay States', in Selangor Secretariat file 4974/1919 (ANM). I am indebted to Paul Kratoska both for bringing this memorandum to my attention and for sending me a copy.

58. Bucknill Report, p. 165.

59. Letter from 'Looking Ahead', *Planter*, 3 (April 1923), 541.

60. Waugh, *The Coloured Countries* (London, 1930), p. 131.

61. Bailey, *We Built and Destroyed*, p. 130.

62. Interview with Mr. Hugh Allen, July 1972. One work of fiction and another of semi-fiction which are set in planting districts in East Sumatra illustrate similar attitudes on the part of European women: Madelon H. Lulofs, *Rubber*, translated by G. J. Renier and Irene Clephane (London, 1933), p. 91; 'Huwelijk en Concubinaat', *De Indische Gids*, 33 (1911), 418.

63. Letter from 'R. H. P.', *Straits Times*, 5 August 1935.

64. Boulle, *Sacrilege in Malaya*, pp. 138–9.

65. I.S.P., *Statement Upon Questions Relating to Salaries*, pp. 18–19.

66. Guy Hutchings, 'Rubber Planting in Malaya, 1928–32', written in 1963 (BAM), p. 68.

67. This was mentioned by several informants. See also R. C. H. McKie, *This Was Singapore* (Sydney, 1942), p. 65; Francis Thomas, *Memoirs of a Migrant* (Singapore, 1972), pp. 36–7; and a novel by G. W. de Silva, *Only a Taxi Dancer* (Kuala Lumpur, 1939), pp. 64–5.

68. J. S. Potter, 'Malayan Experiences 1934–57', written in 1967 (RH), p. 3.

69. A. van Marle, 'De groep der Europeanen in Nederlands-Indie, iets over onstaan en groei', *Indonesie*, 5 (1951–2), 491.

70. Statement by R. N. Nathan, paraphrased in M. R. Stenson, *Industrial Conflict in Malaya* (London, 1970), p. 29.

71. This was suggested by Hutchings, 'Rubber Planting in Malaya, p. 43.

72. Concerning the periods both before and after the First World War, I have almost no information on the actual day-to-day relationship of European men and their mistresses, how mistresses reacted when the man with whom they lived decided to marry a European woman, and what became of the children created by these unions. The second of these issues is dealt with in the following works of fiction: Clifford, *Since the Beginning*; Maugham, 'The Force of Circumstance'; John Angus, *Apa Suka, Tuan* (London, 1913), chapter 12 ('The Fore-Doomed Bride'); and Knocker, 'And Never the Twain Shall Meet', *Malayan Miscellany*, pp. 131–7. As for the third issue, Mr. G. L. Peet (interview, January 1978) recalls that men often arranged to have their children enrolled in a mission school and would, after that, have nothing to do with them. If a man had married a European woman then the existence of the children by his Asian mistress was completely hushed up.

73. Swettenham, *Malay Sketches*, p. 83.

74. Clifford, *Since the Beginning*, p. 62.

75. W. C. Dawe, 'Amok', *Yellow and White* (London, 1895). See also 'J. A. S. J.', 'Zora—A Malay Tragedy of the Old Days', *Times of Malaya*, 21 December 1922; Clive Dalton, *Child in the Sun*, chapter 6.

76. Lockhart refers to him as the 'deposed Sultan'. I assume, but have been unable to prove, that this was Mohammed Yusuf, Dato Klana of Sungei Ujong from 1880 until he was removed from office by the British in 1887.

77. Lockhart, *Memoirs of a British Agent* (London, 1932), pp. 13–26; *Return to Malaya*, pp. 200–8.

78. Blackwell, 'Malay Curry', p. 207.

79. Interview with Haji Omar bin Mahadi, February 1973.

80. Waugh, *Coloured Countries*, p. 132.

81. Bilainkin, *Hail Penang!*, p. 97.

82. Boulle, *Sacrilege in Malaya*, p. 138.

83. Henri Fauconnier, *The Soul of Malaya*, translated by Eric Sutton (London, 1931), p. 48. Emphasis added.

84. Dr. D. J. Galloway, *Proceedings of the Straits Settlements Legislative Council* (1921), p. B225.

85. 'Report of Venereal Diseases Committee', p. C300. Other information in this paragraph is taken from this report.

86. Memorandum by Secretary for Chinese Affairs, F.M.S., in file 52032A (1928), CO 273/543.

87. Acting Under-Secretary, F.M.S., 30 September 1920, HCO 1654/1920; Chapman, 'Memorandum on Sly Prostitution in Kuala Lumpur'.

88. Hutchings, 'Rubber Planting in Malaya', p. 42.

89. Ibid.

90. Dr. B. Day, Bucknill Report, Appendix V, p. 148. Day was an authority on prostitution and venereal disease in Selangor.

91. Hutchings, 'Rubber Planting in Malaya', p. 44. A very high proportion of Europeans who were treated had gonorrhoea, a less serious form of venereal disease than syphilis but requiring more prolonged treatment. Chinese

tended to seek treatment only if they were suffering from syphilis. *Annual Report of the F.M.S. Medical Department* (1929), p. 114.

92. Editorial, 'The Social Evil', *Malay Mail*, 6 February 1931.

93. 'Report of Venereal Diseases Committee', p. C289.

94. R. S. Morton, *Venereal Diseases*, second edition (Penguin Books, 1972), p. 33.

95. 'Report of Venereal Diseases Committee', pp. C292–300.

96. *First Report of the Advisory Committee on Social Hygiene*, 1924–5, XV (Cmd. 2501), pp. 4–5, 12.

97. *Report on Women and Girls Protection Amendments, 1927*, p. 18.

98. See, for example, Braddell, *Lights of Singapore*, pp. 51–2.

99. *Malaya Tribune*, 5 February 1931. Another long report is in the issue of 14 January 1931. See also McKie, *This Was Singapore*, pp. 101–12.

100. 'The Social Evil', *Malay Mail*, 6 February 1931.

101. O'Grady, 'If You Sling Enough Mud', p. 145.

102. Scott, *Eastern Journey*, pp. 36–7.

103. This is also mentioned by Bailey, *We Built and Destroyed*, p. 33, referring to Eurasian taxi girls in Singapore and Penang. A detailed and very interesting study of cabaret girls in Singapore was conducted by Miss S. E. Nicoll-Jones, 'Report on the Problem of Prostitution in Singapore', 1941 (RH).

Notes for Conclusion

1. 'Rubber Planting in Malaya', *Planter*, 17 (January 1936), 18.

2. Letters of P. Samuel, 3 December 1931.

3. Quoted in Bailey, *We Built and Destroyed*, p. 45.

4. See, for example, E. M. Glover, *In 70 Days* (London, 1949), pp. 24–5. Glover was editor of the *Malaya Tribune* before the Pacific War.

5. See Leslie H. Palmier, 'Changing Outposts: The Western Communities in Southeast Asia', *Yale Review*, 47 (March 1958), 405–15.

Notes for Appendix 1

1. Frost to Commission, 29 August 1922, in *The Final Report of the Retrenchment Commission* (Federal Council Paper No. 16 of 1923), p. 24.

2. *Report of Retrenchment Commission*, p. 8; Emerson, *Malaysia*, pp. 158–9.

3. *Report of the Federated Malay States Retrenchment Commission* (Federal Council Paper No. 31 of 1932), p. 25.

4. Reid, 'H. B.', memories of Hubert Berkeley, written in 1959 (RH), p. 1; personal communication from Mr. E. C. G. Barrett, 4 June 1973. 'Koh Dhulu', meaning 'Go Slowly', was a command used in handling elephants. Personal communication from Mr. J. Innes Miller, 3 September 1974.

5. Blackwell, 'Malay Curry', p. 86.

6. F. S. Physick, in Biographical Notes on Berkeley.

7. Guillemard, *Trivial Fond Records* (London, 1937), p. 123.

8. British Malaya 1921 Census, Table 6 (F.M.S.).

9. Reid, 'H. B.', p. 1.

10. Diaries of Hubert Berkeley (BAM), No. 2.

11. Reid, 'H. B.', p. 2.

12. Letter written by J. M. Laidlaw while in Upper Perak, January 1911, *British Malaya*, 1 (April 1927), 336–7; Reid, 'H. B.', p. 2; Berkeley Diaries. A *wayang kulit* is a shadow-play, directed and recited by a *dalang*. A *mayong* is a dramatic performance, using plots from the Ramayana.

13. Berkeley Diaries, No. 3, p. 162.

14. The will, dated 28 February, is enclosed in Berkeley Diaries, No. 2.

15. Berkeley Diaries, No. 2, pp. 145–6.

16. Reid, 'H. B.', p. 3.

17. Baxendale, *Personalities of Old Malaya*, pp. 24–5. There are several versions of this story, but Baxendale claimed to have checked his with Berkeley (p. 22).

18. Reid, 'H. B.', p. 4; 'An Upper Perak Appeal', *Times of Malaya*, 9 November 1922.

19. Allen, 'Malayan Civil Service', p. 167.

20. *Debrett's Illustrated Peerage* (London, 1935), p. 122.

21. Reid, 'H. B.', p. 5; obituary, *British Malaya*, 16 (May 1942), 10.

Notes for Appendix 2

1. Maugham, *Complete Short Stories*, II, 423–56. The story was first published in 1924. While visiting Kuala Lumpur Maugham was the guest of E. A. S. Wagner, one of Mrs. Proudlock's counsels in the trial. Personal communication from Dr. H. A. L. Wagner, 11 July 1973. Dr. Wagner is E. A. S. Wagner's nephew.

2. Except where otherwise stated this account is based on reports in the *Malay Mail*, 24 April, 1 and 3 May, 7–10 and 12–16 June 1911, and the transcript of the trial enclosed in Brockman to Secretary of State, confidential of 11 July 1911, CO 273/374.

3. In an article based on newspaper accounts of the trial Norman Sherry has made a close comparison between the Proudlock case and Maugham's story: 'How Murder on the Veranda Inspired Somerset Maugham', *Observer Magazine*, 22 February 1976.

4. This was apparently R. Charter, Clerk of Works of the Public Works Department, Kuala Lumpur. During the trial William Proudlock learned that Mrs. Charter was not his wife's mother.

5. In the months after Steward's death Europeans contributed nearly $3,000 to a fund for his mother. *Straits Times*, 19 March 1912.

6. Swettenham to Mitchell, 28 June 1899, and Jackson to Swettenham, 26 May 1899, enclosed in Mitchell to Chamberlain, 169 of 11 July 1899, CO 273/251.

7. Letter from 'Irishman', *Malay Mail*, 17 June 1911. See also letters from 'Two Britishers' in the same issue and 'A Husband, Brother and Father' in issue of 19 June.

8. *Malay Mail*, 19, 21, and 26 June 1911; Brockman to Secretary of State, telegram of 23 June 1911, CO 273/374.

9. Mrs. Proudlock to E. A. S. Wagner, *Malay Mail*, 29 June 1911.

10. *Malay Mail*, 2 November 1911.

11. Letters from the High Commissioner on 14 August and 21 October 1911 were among those which related to the Proudlock case. which were destroyed by the Colonial Office. Register of Correspondence, Straits Settlements, CO 426/18.

12. Report by acting Resident of Selangor (Anthonisz), 9 July 1911, Sercombe Smith to Sir John Anderson, 13 July 1911, Anderson to Sercombe Smith, 7 August 1911, enclosed in Brockman to Secretary of State, confidential of 11 July 1911, CO 273/374.

13. *M.A.P.*, 2 September 1911.

14. Young to Harcourt, confidential (1) and (2) of 4 October 1911, and Wilkinson to Harcourt, confidential of 27 November 1911, CO 273/375; *Malay Mail*, 1, 2, and 11 November 1911.

15. Young to Harcourt, 428 of 27 September 1911, CO 273/375.

16. Letters to the *Daily Mail* from Bleackley, a Selangor resident, and Mrs. M. S. Phillimore, reprinted in *Malay Mail*, 28 July 1911.

17. Editorial, *Malay Mail*, 29 July 1911.

Bibliography

I. Bibliographies

Arkib Negara Malaysia, *Senarai Penerimaan: Accessions List, 1957–1967*, 1969.

Catalogue of the Colonial Office Library [now the Foreign and Commonwealth Office Library], Boston, 1964, volume 8, pp. 159–76 ('Malay Peninsula').

Cheeseman, H. R., *Bibliography of Malaya*, London, 1959.

Frewer, Louis B., *Manuscript Collections (excluding Africana) in Rhodes House Library Oxford*, Oxford, Bodleian Library, 1970.

Lim, Beda, 'Malaya: A Background Bibliography', *JMBRAS*, 35, Parts 2 and 3 (1962).

Robson, J. H. M., *A Bibliography of Malaya*, seventh edition, Kuala Lumpur, 1941.

Simpson, D. H., *Manuscript Catalogue of the Royal Commonwealth Society*, London, 1975.

Wainwright, M. D., and N. Matthews, *A Guide to Western Manuscripts and Documents in the British Isles Relating to South and South East Asia*, London, 1965.

II. Unpublished Official Records

(a) PUBLIC RECORD OFFICE

Confidential Circulars issued by the Secretary of State, CO 854/168.

Federated Malay States, Original Correspondence, CO 717.

Straits Settlements, Original Correspondence, CO 273, and Register of Correspondence, CO 426.

(b) ARKIB NEGARA MALAYSIA

Chapman, W. T., 'Memorandum on Sly Prostitution in Kuala Lumpur and other large Towns in the Federated Malay States', Selangor Secretariat file 4974/1919.

High Commissioner's Office Files (HCO), 1905–1921.

III. Published Official Records

(a) COUNCIL PROCEEDINGS AND REPORTS (aside from those published as Federal Council Papers)

Annual Reports of the Federated Malay States, the separate states, and various government departments.

Civil Service Committee, Federated Malay States, *Reprint of Memorials, Minutes, Correspondence, Despatches, and Schemes, 1900 to 1917*, Kuala Lumpur, 1917. British Library.

Development of the Cameron Highlands up to the End of 1934 and Information Concerning the Highlands, Kuala Lumpur, 1935.

Federal Council Proceedings, 1909–1940.

Government Gazettes.

Proceedings of the Commission Appointed to Enquire into the Disturbances in Kuala Lumpur and District at the Chinese New Year, 1912, Kuala Lumpur, 1912. FCO, Eastern Pamphlet No. 301.

Proceedings of the Straits Settlements Legislative Council, 1912, 1917, 1921, 1924, 1933, 1939.

Report of the Commission on the Temporary Allowances 1931, Singapore, 1931. FCO, Eastern Pamphlet No. 308.

Report of the Malayan Public Service Salaries Commission (Sir John Bucknill, President), Singapore, 1919. FCO.

'Report of Venereal Diseases Committee', Council Paper No. 86, *Proceedings of the Straits Settlements Legislative Council* (1923).

(b) FEDERAL COUNCIL PAPERS (published in *Federal Council Proceedings* unless otherwise stated)

'Report of Mr. R. E. Stubbs on the Salaries and Classification of the Cadet Service in the Malay Peninsula', No. 10 of 1911.

'Further Memorial from the Cadet Service Regarding the Report of Mr. Stubbs', No. 1 of 1912.

'Correspondence Regarding Appointments and Salaries of Officers on the Sterling Scheme', No. 21 of 1918.

The Final Report of the Retrenchment Commission, No. 16 of 1923, printed separately. FCO, Eastern Pamphlet No. 194.

'A Report by the Chief Secretary on a Visit to Cameron's Highlands in March 1925', No. 13 of 1925.

'Chronicle of the Development of the Cameron Highlands . . . 1926–1931'; No. 13 of 1932.

Report of the Federated Malay States Retrenchment Commission, No. 31 of 1932, printed separately. FCO, Eastern Pamphlet No. 324.

'Memorandum on the Report of the Committee Appointed to Enquire into Unemployment in Selangor', No. 5 of 1938.

(c) PARLIAMENTARY PAPERS (page references cited in the footnotes are for the page *within* the particular report)

Contagious Diseases Regulations (Perak and Malay States), 1894, LVII (H.C. 146).

Report of the Royal Commission on the Public Services in India, 1916, VII (Cd. 8382).

First Report of the Advisory Committee on Social Hygiene, 1924–25, XV (Cmd. 2501).

Report by W. G. A. Ormsby-Gore on His Visit to Malaya, Ceylon, and Java in 1928, 1928–29, V (Cmd. 3235).

Report of a Committee Appointed to Report on Straits Settlements and Federated Malay States Women and Girls Protection Amendments, 1927, 1928–29, V (Cmd. 3294).

(d) PARLIAMENTARY DEBATES, HOUSE OF COMMONS
Fourth series, volume 198 of 1908.
Fifth series, volumes 31 to 40, 1911–1912.

IV. Censuses (Listed by date)

Census of the Population of Selangor, *Selangor Government Gazette*, 11 December 1891, pp. 956–7. Includes results of 1884 census.

Census of the State of Perak, 1891, Taiping, 1892. Includes results of 1879 census. ANM.

Hare, G. T., *Federated Malay States: Census of the Population, 1901*, Kuala Lumpur, 1902.

Pountney, A. M., *The Census of the Federated Malay States, 1911*, London, 1911.

Nathan, J. E., *The Census of British Malaya, 1921*, London, 1922.

Vlieland, C. A., *British Malaya: A Report on the 1931 Census*, London, 1932.

Census of England and Wales 1931: General Tables, London, 1935.

V. Sources of Biographical Data, Handbooks, and Directories

Belfield, H. Conway, *Handbook to the Federated Malay States*, London, 1902.

Civil Service Lists, F.M.S., Straits Settlements, and Malaya. FCO reference: JF 1521.

Colonial Office List, London, annual.

Debrett's Illustrated Peerage, London, 1935.

Dictionary of National Biography.

Federated Malay States Railways, *Pamphlet of Information for Travellers*, 1914. ANM.

German, R. L., *Handbook to British Malaya*, London, 1926 and 1937.

Harrison, C. W., *An Illustrated Guide to the Federated Malay States*, London, 1910, 1920, and 1923.

———, *Some Notes on the Government Services in British Malaya*, London, 1929.

Malayan Information Agency, *British Malaya: General Description of the Country and Life Therein*, London, 1929.

The Perak Annual Hand-Book and Civil Service List, 1892, Taiping, 1892.

Singapore and Straits Directory, continued in 1922 as the *Singapore and Malayan Directory*. School of Oriental and African Studies, University of London.

Who Was Who, London.

Wright, Arnold, and H. A. Cartwright, *Twentieth Century Impressions of British Malaya*, London, 1908.

VI. *Manuscript Sources*
(other than unpublished official records)

(a) ARKIB NEGARA MALAYSIA, KUALA LUMPUR
Clifford, Hugh, Diaries for 1888 and 1893. ANM reference: SP2.

(b) BRITISH ASSOCIATION OF MALAYA PAPERS, ROYAL COMMON-WEALTH SOCIETY, LONDON (item number given after each entry)
Berkeley, Hubert, Biographical Notes on, by R. O. Winstedt, H. R. Cheeseman, F. S. Physick, C. C. Brown, and J. Theisberg, 1959. IX/1.
_____, Office Diaries. I/9.
Bryson, H. P., 'Twenty-Nine-and-a-Half Years in the Malayan Civil Service', written in 1963. III/8.
Clayton, R. J. B., 'An Account of a Trip from Taiping to Upper Perak, 1899', copied from an original letter. IV/2.
Hutchings, Guy, 'Rubber Planting in Malaya, 1928–32', written in 1963. III/15.

(c) LAKE CLUB, KUALA LUMPUR
Candidates Book, 1890–1941.

(d) RHODES HOUSE LIBRARY, OXFORD
Blackwell, K. R., 'Malay Curry', autobiography written in 1945.
Corry, W. C. S., Typescript of Tape-recorded Interview Covering Career in the Malayan Civil Service, 1923–1953, conducted in 1969.
Davison, Agnes, 'Some Autobiographical Notes and General Reminiscences', written after World War II.
Evans, Mrs. D. B., Household Accounts Ledger for 1920.
Gammans, L. D., 'The Development of Cameron Highlands: Some Marketing Problems', apparently written in 1933.
_____, 'Rotary in Malaya', published in *Rotary International* in January 1933.
Gilman, E. W., Personal Recollections.
Morkill, A. G., Diary Kept While in Kelantan, 1915–1917.
Nicoll-Jones, Miss S. E., 'Report on the Problem of Prostitution in Singapore', 1941.

O'Grady, G. J., 'If You Sling Enough Mud', autobiography written in 1945.

Peel, Sir William, Colonial Service Notes, 1897–1935, written in early 1940s.

Potter, J. S., 'Malayan Experiences 1934–57', written in 1967.

Reid, J. S. W., 'H. B.', Memories of Hubert Berkeley, written in 1959.

Samuel, P., Letters Home, 1930–34.

Stratton-Brown, Mrs. W. A. H., 'Long Ago in Selangor', life in Selangor 1896–97, written after World War II.

Topham, D. F., 'Autobiography of Douglas Frank Topham, formerly of Harper Gilfillan & Co. Ltd. of Malaya, covering the years in Malaya, 1907–1935', written in 1963.

(e) SELANGOR CLUB, KUALA LUMPUR

Minutes of the Club Committee, Minute Book No. 1, March 1885 to March 1892.

'Selangor Club Rules and Bye-Laws, 1935', with amendments to September 1946.

(f) UNIVERSITY OF HULL, CENTRE FOR SOUTH-EAST ASIAN STUDIES

Bateson, Mrs. Nancy, Letters from Malaya to family in Hull area, 1940–41 (the writer was Mrs. Alfred Wynne at the time).

VII. Memoirs, Travel Books, and Other Published Primary Sources

Abraham, J. Johnston, The Surgeon's Log, London, 1911.

Ahpa, Teed [J. Nield], By Jungle Track and Paddy Field to Rubber Plantation and Palm Grove, Liverpool, 1913.

Bailey, Douglas, We Built and Destroyed, London, 1944.

Baxendale, Cyril, Personalities of Old Malaya, Penang, 1930.

Bilainkin, George, Hail Penang!, London, 1932.

Bird, Isabella L., The Golden Chersonese and the Way Thither, London, 1883 (reprinted Kuala Lumpur, 1967).

Bleackley, Horace, A Tour in Southern Asia, London, 1928.

Bowen, C. D., 'British Malaya As it Was' (excerpts from letters written in 1880s and 1890s), Asiatic Review, 46 (1950), 896–910.

Braddell, R. St. J., The Lights of Singapore, London, 1934.

Cameron, John, Our Tropical Possessions in Malayan India, London, 1865 (reprinted Kuala Lumpur, 1965).

Chelvasingam-MacIntyre, S., Through Memory Lane, Singapore, 1973.

Clifford, Hugh, Malayan Monochromes, London, 1913.

———, Studies in Brown Humanity, London, 1898.

'Colonial Criticism', reprint of articles in Pinang Gazette, September–October 1893, concerning About Perak by Frank Swettenham. FCO, Malay States Pamphlet No. 9.

Curle, Richard, *Into the East: Notes on Burma and Malaya*, London, 1923.

Dalton, Clive, *A Child in the Sun*, London, 1937.

Foster, Harry L., *A Beachcomber in the Orient*, New York, 1923.

Furse, Ralph, *Aucuparius: Recollections of a Recruiting Officer*, London, 1962.

Gibson, Ashley, *The Malay Peninsula and Archipelago*, London, 1928.

Glover, E. M., *In 70 Days*, London, 1949.

Guillemard, Laurence N., *Trivial Fond Records*, London, 1937.

Harrison, C. R., 'Ramblings of the Last of "The Creepers"—1', *Planter*, 37 (1961), 341–50.

Harrison, C. W., *The Magic of Malaya*, London, 1916.

Hawkins, G., and W. S. Thaddaeus, compilers, *Rotary International Jubilee, 1905–1955*, Kuala Lumpur, Kuala Lumpur Rotary Club, 1955.

Henshall, Mary, 'The Good Old Days', *Straits Times Annual 1940*, p. 139.

Hill, Anthony, *Diversion in Malaya*, London, 1948.

'Huwelijk en Concubinaat', *De Indische Gids*, 33 (1911), 410–32.

Incorporated Society of Planters, *A Statement Upon Questions Relating to the Salaries Emoluments and the General Conditions and Terms of Service of Planters on Rubber Estates and other Plantations in British Malaya*, Kuala Lumpur, 1934. FCO, Eastern Pamphlet No. 354.

Innes, Emily, *The Chersonese With the Gilding Off*, 2 vols., London, 1885.

Innes, J. R., 'The Malayan Civil Service as a Career', *National Review*, 77 (March 1921), 102–7.

Kennedy, Raymond, *The Ageless Indies*, New York, 1942.

Keyser, Arthur, *From Jungle to Java*, Westminster, 1897.

———, *People and Places: A Life in Five Continents*, London, 1922.

Knocker, F. W., *A Malayan Miscellany* (edited by 'Palia Dorai'), Kuala Lumpur, 1924.

'A Lady's Experiences in the Singapore Mutiny', *Blackwood's Magazine*, 198 (December 1915), 781–94.

Lim Boon Keng, *The Great War from the Confucian Point of View, and Kindred Topics*, Singapore, 1917.

Lockhart, R. H. Bruce, *Memoirs of a British Agent*, London, 1932.

———, *Return to Malaya*, New York, 1936.

Lovat, Lady Alice, *The Life of Sir Frederick Weld*, London, 1914.

Low, Hugh, *Sarawak*, London, 1848.

McCarthy, E. T., *Further Incidents in the Life of a Mining Engineer*, London, 1922.

[Macfadyen, Eric], *Eric Macfadyen, 1879–1966*, privately published collection of some of his letters and other writings, 1968. Brynmor Jones Library, University of Hull.

McKie, R. C. H., *This Was Singapore*, Sydney, 1942.

Mackirdy, Mrs. Archibald (Olive Christian Malvery), and W. N. Willis, *The White Slave Market*, London, 1912.

McNair, J. F. A., *Perak and the Malays: Sarong and Kris*, London, 1878 (reprinted Kuala Lumpur, 1972).

Marsh, Mabel, *Service Suspended*, New York, 1968.

Maugham, W. Somerset, *A Writer's Notebook*, London, 1949.

Maxwell, Sir William George, *The Annals of One Branch of the Maxwell Family in Ulster*, second edition, Kuala Lumpur, 1959.

_____, 'Has Gunong Tahan Been Jilted?', *Malaya*, August 1952, pp. 27–9.

_____, 'The Early Days of Fraser's Hill', *Malaya*, September 1952, pp. 35–7, and October, pp. 23–7.

Munro, G. I. Gun, 'Malaya Through a Woman's Eye', *Crown Colonist*, 1 (April 1932), 225–7.

Norden, H., *From Golden Gate to Golden Sun*, London, 1923.

Norman, Henry, *The Peoples and Politics of the Far East*, London, 1895.

Onraet, Rene, *Singapore—A Police Background*, London, 1947.

Peet, G. L., *Malayan Exile*, Singapore, 1934.

Pratt, Ambrose, *Magical Malaya*, Melbourne, 1931.

Purcell, Victor, *The Memoirs of a Malayan Official*, London, 1965.

Reid, Arnot, 'More About Perak', four newspaper articles, written about 1894. FCO, Malay States Pamphlet No. 22.

Rennie, J. S. M., *Musings of J.S.M.R.*, Singapore, 1933.

Ridley, H. N., 'The Eurasian Problem', in *Noctes Orientales: Being a Selection of Essays Before the Straits Philosophical Society Between 1893 and 1910*, Singapore, 1913. British Library.

'Rimba', *Bygone Selangor*, Kuala Lumpur, 1922.

Robson, J. H. M., *People in a Native State*, Singapore, 1894. British Library.

_____, *Records and Recollections, 1889–1934*, Kuala Lumpur, 1934.

Scott, J. H. MacCallum, *Eastern Journey*, London, 1939.

Selangor Eurasian Association, *Golden Jubilee, 1921–1971*, Kuala Lumpur, 1971.

Selangor Golf Club, *Twelve Under Fours: An Informal History of the Selangor Golf Club*, Kuala Lumpur, 1953.

Sidney, Richard J. H., *In British Malaya Today*, London, 1926.

_____, *Malay Land*, London, 1926.

Sim, Katherine, *Malayan Landscape*, London, 1946.

Straits Chinese and the Great War (Report on a patriotic meeting, 29 September 1915), Singapore, 1915.

Swettenham, Frank A., *About Perak*, Singapore, 1893.

_____, *British Malaya*, London, 1908.

_____, *Malay Sketches*, London, 1895.

_____, *The Real Malay*, London, 1900.

Talaivasingham, A., *Malayan Notes and Sketches*, Singapore, 1924.

Thomas, Francis, *Memoirs of a Migrant*, Singapore, 1972.

Thomson, J. T., *Some Glimpses into Life in the Far East*, London, 1864.

Treacher, W. H., 'British Malaya, With More Especial Reference to the Federated Malay States', *Journal of the Society of Arts*, 55 (22 March 1907), 493–512.

Walling, R. N., *Singapura Sorrows*, Singapore, 1931.

Waugh, Alec, *The Coloured Countries*, London, 1930.

Wells, Carveth, *Six Years in the Malay Jungle*, Garden City, New York, 1926.

Wheeler, L. Richmond, *The Modern Malay*, London, 1928.

Wilson, Margaret, *Malaya the Land of Enchantment*, Amersham, 1937.

Winstedt, Sir Richard, *Start from Alif: Count from One*, Kuala Lumpur, 1969.

Woolf, Leonard, *Sowing: An Autobiography of the Years 1880–1904*, London, 1960.

Wright, Arnold, and H. A. Cartwright, *Twentieth Century Impressions of British Malaya*, London, 1908.

Wu Lien-Teh, *Plague Fighter*, Cambridge, 1959.

VIII. Fiction

Angus, John [J. A. B. Cook], *Apa Suka, Tuan*, London, 1913.

Blundell, Peter, *The Sin of Godfrey Neil*, London, 1920.

Boulle, Pierre, *Sacrilege in Malaya*, translated by Xan Fielding, London, 1959.

Clifford, Hugh, *Since the Beginning*, London, 1898.

Davidson, Jessie A., *Dawn: A Romance of Malaya*, London, 1926.

Dawe, W. C., *Yellow and White*, London, 1895.

de Silva, G. W., *Only a Taxi Dancer: A Romance of Singapore*, Kuala Lumpur, 1939.

Fauconnier, Henri, *The Soul of Malaya*, translated by Eric Sutton, London, 1931.

Henty, G. A., *In the Hands of the Malays*, Glasgow, 1905.

Keyser, Arthur, *An Adopted Wife*, London, 1893.

Lulofs, Madelon H., *Rubber: A Romance of the Dutch East Indies*, translated by G. J. Renier and Irene Clephane, London, 1933.

Maugham, W. Somerset, *The Complete Short Stories of W. Somerset Maugham*, 4 vols., New York, Washington Square Press, 1967.

IX. Newspapers and Periodicals

(Dates of publication are given only for those used extensively in this study; those which were consulted at the National Newspaper Library, Colindale, are marked 'NNL')

British Malaya, London, Journal of the Association of British Malaya, May 1926 to December 1951 (continued as *Malaya* and then as *Malaysia*).

British Medical Journal, London.

Eurasian Review, Penang. British Library.

Grenier's Rubber News, Kuala Lumpur (issue of 17 February 1912 only). NNL.

Malayan Medical Journal, Singapore.

Malaya Tribune, Singapore. NNL.

Malay Mail, Kuala Lumpur, December 1896 to January 1942 (continued after the Second World War). The National Newspaper Library's collection begins in 1906. Early issues (1896–1905) were consulted at the Arkib Negara Malaysia.

Malay Weekly Mail, weekly edition of the *Malay Mail*. The National Newspaper Library's collection covers the years 1906–1926 and 1931–1939.

M.A.P. ('Mainly About People'), London (issue of 2 September 1911 only).

Planter, Kuala Lumpur, Journal of the Incorporated Society of Planters, 1920–1941 (continued after the Second World War). NNL and Rubber Research Institute, Kuala Lumpur.

Railway Review, London (issue of 5 July 1912 only). NNL.

Selangor Journal, Kuala Lumpur, 1892–1897. Brynmor Jones Library, University of Hull.

Singapore Free Press, Singapore. NNL.

Straits Echo, Penang (all references are to the weekly mail edition). NNL.

Straits Times, Singapore. NNL.

The Times, London.

Times of Malaya, Ipoh (all references are to the weekly mail edition). NNL.

X. Secondary Sources

Allen, J. de Vere, 'The Elephant and the Mousedeer—A New Version: Anglo-Kedah Relations, 1905–1915', *JMBRAS*, 41, Part 1 (1968), 54–94.

———, 'Johore 1901–1914', *JMBRAS*, 45, Part 2 (1972), 1–28.

———, 'The Malayan Civil Service, 1874–1941: Colonial Bureaucracy/Malayan Elite', *Comparative Studies in Society and History,* 12 (April 1970), 149–78.

———, 'Two Imperialists: A Study of Sir Frank Swettenham and Sir Hugh Clifford', *JMBRAS*, 37, Part 1 (1964), 41–73.

Arasaratnam, Sinnappah, *Indians in Malaysia and Singapore*, London, 1970.

Banks, J. A., and Olive, *Feminism and Family Planning in Victorian England*, Liverpool, 1964.

Bauer, P. T., *The Rubber Industry: A Study in Competition and Monopoly*, London, 1948.

Chai Hon-Chan, *The Development of British Malaya*, *1896–1909*, Kuala Lumpur, 1964.

Cominos, Peter T., 'Late-Victorian Respectability and the Social System', *International Review of Social History*, 8 (1963), 18–48 and 216–50.

Cowan, C. D., *Nineteenth-Century Malaya: The Origins of British Political Control*, London, 1961.

Cunyngham-Brown, Sjovald, *The Traders*, London, 1971.

Curtin, Philip D., *The Image of Africa: British Ideas and Action, 1780–1850*, Madison, 1964.

Drabble, J. H., 'The Plantation Rubber Industry up to 1922', *JMBRAS*, 40, Part 1 (1967), 52–77.

_____, *Rubber in Malaya*, *1876–1922*, Kuala Lumpur, 1973.

Emerson, Rupert, *Malaysia: A Study of Direct and Indirect Rule*, New York, 1937 (reprinted Kuala Lumpur, 1964).

Furnivall, J. S., *Colonial Policy and Practice*, New York, 1956.

Gullick, J. M., 'Captain Speedy of Lárut', *JMBRAS*, 26, Part 3 (1953).

_____, *Indigenous Political Systems of Western Malaya*, London, 1965.

_____, 'Kuala Lumpur, 1880–1895', *JMBRAS*, 28, Part 4 (August 1955).

_____, and Gerald Hawkins, *Malayan Pioneers*, Singapore, 1958.

Hodgson, G. A., 'The Incorporated Society of Planters, 1919–1969', *Planter*, 45 (December 1969), 635–60.

Jackson, James C., *Planters and Speculators: Chinese and European Agricultural Enterprise in Malaya*, *1786–1921*, Kuala Lumpur, 1968.

Kennedy, Raymond, 'The Colonial Crisis and the Future', in R. Linton, ed., *The Science of Man in the World Crisis*, New York, 1945.

Khoo Kay Kim, 'The Origin of British Administration in Malaya', *JMBRAS*, 39, Part 1 (1966), 52–92.

Lim Chong-Yah, *Economic Development of Modern Malaya*, Kuala Lumpur, 1967.

Loh Fook-Seng, Philip, 'Malay Precedence and the Federal Formula in the Federated Malay States, 1909 to 1939', *JMBRAS*, 45, Part 2 (1972), 29–50.

Makepeace, W., G. E. Brooke, and R. St. J. Braddell, eds., *One Hundred Years of Singapore*, 2 vols., London, 1921.

Marsh, David C., *The Changing Social Structure of England and Wales*, *1871–1961*, London, 1965.

Marwick, A., *Britain in the Century of Total War*, Harmondsworth, Penguin Books, 1970.

Middlebrook, S. M., 'Pioneers of Chinese Reform in Malaya', *Straits Times Annual 1941*, pp. 83, 85, 87–8.

Mills, C. Wright, *The Power Elite*, New York, 1956 (paperback edition 1959).

Moore, Donald and Joanna, *The First 150 Years of Singapore*, Singapore, 1969.

Mosbergen, Rudolf William, 'The Sepoy Rebellion (A History of the Singapore Mutiny, 1915)', unpublished B.A. (Hons.) Dissertation, University of Singapore, 1954.

Nicolson, Harold, *The Meaning of Prestige*, Cambridge, 1937.

Palmier, Leslie H., 'Changing Outposts: The Western Communities in Southeast Asia', *Yale Review*, 47 (March 1958), 405–15.

Png Poh Seng, 'The Kuomintang in Malaya, 1912–1941', *Journal of Southeast Asian History*, 2, No. 1 (March 1961), 1–41.

'Prostitutie', *Encyclopaedie van Nederlandsch-Indie*, tweede druk, derde deel (1919), 511–15.

Resink, G. J., *Indonesia's History Between the Myths*, The Hague, 1968.

Roff, William R., *The Origins of Malay Nationalism*, New Haven, 1967.

Sadka, Emily, *The Protected Malay States, 1874–1895*, Kuala Lumpur, 1968.

Sharom Ahmat, 'The Political Structure of the State of Kedah, 1879–1905', *Journal of Southeast Asian Studies*, 1 (September 1970), 115–28.

———— , 'Transition and Political Change in a Malay State: A Study of the Economic and Political Development of Kedah, 1879–1923', unpublished Ph.D. thesis, University of London, 1969.

Sissons, D. C. S., '*Karayuki-San*: Japanese Prostitutes in Australia, 1887–1916—I', *Historical Studies*, No. 68 (April 1977), 323–41.

Song Ong Siang, *One Hundred Years' History of the Chinese in Singapore*, London, 1923 (reprinted Singapore, 1967).

Stenson, M. R., *Industrial Conflict in Malaya*, London, 1970.

Stevenson, Rex, 'Cinemas and Censorship in Colonial Malaya', *Journal of Southeast Asian Studies*, 5 (September 1974), 209–24.

———— , 'The Selangor Raja School', *JMBRAS*, 41, Part 1 (1968), 183–92.

Thio, Eunice, *British Policy in the Malay Peninsula, 1880–1910*, Vol. I: *The Southern and Central States*, Singapore, 1969.

Tilman, R. O., *Bureaucratic Transition in Malaya*, Durham, N.C., 1964.

Tregonning, K. G., *The Singapore Cold Storage, 1903–1966*, Singapore, n.d.

Tsou, Pao-chun, *The Urban Landscape of Kuala Lumpur*, Singapore, 1967.

Turnbull, C. M., 'British Planning for Post-war Malaya', *Journal of Southeast Asian Studies*, 5 (September 1974), 239–54.

———— , *The Straits Settlements, 1826–67*, London, 1972.

van Marle, A., 'De groep der Europeanen in Nederlands-Indie, iets over onstaan en groei', *Indonesie*, 5 (1951–52), 97–121, 314–41, 481–507.

Wong Lin Ken, *The Malayan Tin Industry to 1914*, Tucson, 1965.

———— , 'Western Enterprise and the Development of the Malayan Tin Industry to 1914', in C. D. Cowan, ed., *The Economic Development of South-East Asia*, London, 1964.

Yeo Kim Wah, 'The Selangor Succession Dispute, 1933–1938', *Journal of Southeast Asian Studies*, 2 (September 1971), 169–84.

XI. *Writings on Medical Subjects*

Balfour, Andrew, 'Problems of Acclimatization', *The Lancet*, 205 (1923), 84–7, 243–7.

Black, Kenneth, 'Health and Climate With Special Reference to Malaya', *Malayan Medical Journal*, 7 (1932), 99–107.

Carthew, Morden, 'The Aetiology and Prophylaxis of Mental Irritability in the Tropics', *Journal of Tropical Medicine and Hygiene*, 30 (1927), 113–17.

Culpin, Millais, 'An Examination of Tropical Neurasthenia', *Proceedings of Royal Society of Medicine*, 26 (1933), 911–22.

Davidson, Andrew, ed., *Hygiene and Diseases of Warm Climates*, Edinburgh and London, 1893.

Dugdale, J. N., *How to Keep Healthy in the Tropics*, Singapore, 1930.

Duncan, Andrew, *The Prevention of Disease in Tropical and Sub-Tropical Campaigns*, London, 1888.

Fox, S. C. G., *The Principles of Health in Malaya: Some Suggestions to New Comers*, Taiping, 1901. FCO, Malay States Pamphlet No. 18.

Kenney, R. A., *Acclimatization to High Temperatures*, Inaugural Lecture as Professor of Physiology at the University of Malaya in Singapore, September 1961.

Macpherson, R. K., 'Acclimatization Status of Temperate-Zone Man', *Nature*, 182 (1958), 1240–1.

Manson, Sir Patrick, *Tropical Diseases*, fourth edition, London, 1907.

Morton, R. S., *Venereal Diseases*, second edition, Harmondsworth, Penguin Books, 1972.

Neligan, A. R., and others, 'Discussion on the Adaptation of European Women and Children to Tropical Climates', *Proceedings of the Royal Society of Medicine*, 24 (1931), 1315–33.

Renbourn, E. T., 'Life and Death of the Solar Topi', *Journal of Tropical Medicine and Hygiene*, 65 (1962), 203–18.

Singer, Charles, and E. Ashworth Underwood, *A Short History of Medicine*, second edition, Oxford, 1962.

Trewartha, Glenn T., 'Recent Thought on the Problem of White Acclimatization in the Wet Tropics', *Geographical Review*, 16 (1926), 467–78.

Watson, Sir Malcolm, 'Twenty-Five Years of Malaria Control in the Malay Peninsula', *British Malaya*, 1 (January 1927), 245–50.

Selected List of Persons Interviewed

Dato Abdullah bin Mohamed, Johore Bahru, April 1973. Former State Secretary of Johore.

Mr. Hugh Allen, Cattistock, Dorset, July 1972 and July 1974. Planter in Perak, Kedah, and Kelantan.

Miss Nona Baker, Liverpool, March 1972. Sister of V. B. C. Baker, General Manager of the Pahang Consolidated Company, Sungei Lembing, Pahang, from 1929 until the Pacific War.

Mr. E. C. G. Barrett, Cranleigh, Surrey, April 1972. Malayan Civil Service.

Mrs. Nancy Bateson, Hull, December 1971. Lived in Johore before the Pacific War.

Mr. W. L. Blythe, London, June 1972. Malayan Civil Service.

Encik Nasrul Haq Boyce, Klang, April 1973. Planter in East Sumatra before the Pacific War.

Mr. Choo Kok Leong, Kuala Lumpur, March 1973. Son of Choo Kia Peng.

Mr. W. C. S. Corry, London, April 1972. Malayan Civil Service.

Mr. J. S. H. Cunyngham-Brown, Penang, February 1973. Malayan Civil Service.

Mr. J. H. Fenwick, London, April 1972. Chartered Bank, Penang, 1929–34.

Mr. R. H. Fortescue, London, July 1972. Planter in Malacca.

Miss Josephine Foss, London, August 1973. Headmistress of Pudu English School, Kuala Lumpur.

Mr. David Gray, London, June 1972. Malayan Civil Service.

Mr. J. L. Kennedy, London, April 1972. Chartered Bank, Kuala Lumpur.

Tun Sir Henry H. S. Lee, Kuala Lumpur, February 1973. Mine owner, businessman, member of the Kuala Lumpur Sanitary Board.

Mr. Lim Thye Hee, Kuala Lumpur, March 1973. Manager of Majestic Hotel, Kuala Lumpur, at time of interview.

Encik Mohamed Din bin Mohamed Shariff, Kuala Lumpur, April 1973. One of the first Malay police inspectors in the F.M.S.

Tan Sri Dato' Dr. Mohamed Said bin Mohamed, Seremban, March 1973. Doctor in Pahang and Selangor before the Pacific War.

Tun Justice Mohamed Suffian bin Hashim and Toh Puan Suffian, Kuala Lumpur, March 1973. Tun Suffian was the first Malay Queen's Scholar (1938).

Haji Omar bin Mahadi, Kampong Melimbing, Kuala Selangor, February 1973. The *Ketua Kampung* at the time of the interview.

Mr. G. L. Peet, Perth, Western Australia, January 1978. Reporter for the *Straits Times*.

Tan Sri Haji Mubin Sheppard, Petaling Jaya, February 1973. Malayan Civil Service.

Mr. Ginder Singh, Port Dickson, February 1973. Founder of a large transport company.

Mrs. Pauline Stevenson, Spalding, Lincolnshire, October 1972. Lived in Singapore, Seremban, and Ipoh before the Pacific War.

Dato H. F. O'B. Traill, Batang Berjuntai, Kuala Selangor, February

1973. Planter in Johore before the Pacific War.

Dr. D. Reid Tweedie, Sungei Siput, Perak, and Penang, February 1973. Doctor in the Malayan Medical Service in Negri Sembilan and then in private practice in Perak.

Mr. T. M. Walker, London, April 1972. Guthrie and Co., Kuala Lumpur.

Miss Ada E. Weinman, Kuala Lumpur, March 1973. Founder of her own school of music.

Mr. Wong Sin Kit, Kuala Lumpur, March 1973. Entered government service in the 1930s.

Raja Tan Sri Zainal bin Raja Sulaiman, Kuala Lumpur, March 1973. General Manager of the National Electricity Board at time of interview.

Index

Numbers in italics refer to tables and figures

ABDULLAH, SULTAN OF PERAK, 6, 7, 9
About Perak (Swettenham), 58
Abu Bakar, Tunku, *182*
Adams, T. S., Resident of Selangor, 150
Aeria, D. A., 104
Agency houses, 14, 48, 138
Agriculture, Europeans employed in, 29, *29*, 31, 33; *see also* Coffee; Planters; Rubber
Aldworth, J. R. O., 41
Americans, 24, *25*
Anderson, Sir John, Governor, 19, 87, 103, 107–8, 109, 111
Anglo-Dutch Treaty (1824), 4
Anthonisz, J. O., 107, 109
Asian mistresses (of Europeans), 137, 193, 200–1, 206, 213–16; *see also* Concubinage
Australians, 24, 25, 28

BANJERESE, 18
Banks, bankers, 14, 48, 130, 137–8, *155*
Barnes, W. D., 103, 104
Baxendale, Cyril, 45
Bazell, Charles, 179
Belfield, H. C., 37
Berkeley, Hubert, 172, 201; life and work of, 229–32
Bernstorff, Count, 60–1
Birch, E. W., Resident of Perak, 37, 61, 68, 81
Birch, J. W. W., first Resident of Perak, 7, 8, 51
Bird, Isabella, 10, 50–1
Black, Kenneth, 158–9
Blackwell, Kenneth, 174
Bleackley, Horace, 238
Bot, Raja, 102–3, 104
Boulle, Pierre, 138–9, 211, 216

Bowen, C. D., 54, 56
Boyanese, 18, 80
Bozzolo, C. F., 40, 54, 56
Braddell, Roland, 71
British Malaya, 133, 206
Brockman, Sir Edward, 114, 161
Brooke, Rajah, 40
Bruce, Mrs., 144
Bucknill Commission and Report (1919), 39, 42, 43–4, 90–3, 94, 95, 96, 126, 128, 129, 132, 134, 138, 139, 140
Bucknill, Sir John, 90
Bukit Bintang Amusement Park cabaret, Kuala Lumpur, 221–2
Bukit Kutu (Treacher's Hill), 73, 160, *162*
Burlet, J. de, 37
Butler, Mrs. Josephine, 194, 195

CABARETS, 221–2
Cadet Service, *see* Civil servants (Malayan Civil Service)
Caldecott, Andrew, 190–1
Cameron Highlands, 157, 160, *162*; European settlement, 165–6; hill station, 164–5
Cameron, John, 93
Cameron, William, 73, 164
Cantonese Chinese, 18, 80, 114
Casuals (European football team), 118, 119, 233
Censuses, 24–5, 28, 31
Ceylon Civil Service, 42, 43
Chamberlain, Joseph, 78
Chartered Bank, 48, 137–8
Cheah Boon Teat, 101–2
Chellapa Chetty, S. A. S., 104
Chief Secretary, role of, 20, 21
Chiefs, Malay, 5, 6, 8
Chinese, 22, 167; admission into civil service of, 176; British offi-

cials' relations with, 53–4, 67, 97; concubines, 200; cutting off queues by, 114; dance hostesses, 222; dialect groups, 18; élite, 174; European relations during revolutionary period with, 111–17, 121; football team, 118–19; immigration, 17; in Kuala Lumpur, 10–11, 17, 59, 67–8, 83–4, 114–16, 168, 181; medical facilities for, 168; members of European clubs, 181, 182; and Rotary Club, 190; New Year disturbances (1912), 112–13, 114–16, 122; police inspectors, 178; prosperity of, 83–4; prostitutes, 196, 197, 217, 218, 220; Revolution, 97; secret societies, 4, 6, 15; segregation on railways and, 98–106; servants, 79, 80, 113–14; in Singapore, 4, 124; social clubs, 181; spirit farm inspectors, 121; strike by engineering workers, 116–17, 122; tin mining activities, 5, 10, 15–16; trade and commerce, 5–6, 9–10, 53; Weld Hill Club for, 83–4

Chinese Advisory Board, 174

Chinese Chamber of Commerce, 174

Chinese Literary and Debating Society, 101–2, 103

Choo Kia Peng, 170, 181, 182, 190

Choo Kok Leong, 182

Choon Cheok Kee Loo Club (Chinese Millionaire's Club), 181, 190

Cinchona, 13

Civil servants (Malayan Civil Service), 16, 23, 29, 31, 37, 39, 78, 180, 190; Bucknill Report on salaries (1919), 90–3; 126; changing position of, 78–84; colour bar, 96, 97, 107–12; concubinage and, 200–1, 206–8; during First World War, 89–90; educational background, 34–6; examinations, 23, 42–3, 78, 107, 110; marriage and salaries, 84–7, 91, 139; membership of Lake Club, 154–6; monthly family budget of a Perak official, 79, 80; non-European admission to M.C.S., 175–7, 192; occupation of fathers, 36–7; Reconstruction Scheme, 43; recruitment, 40–4, 75; salaries and allowances,

76–7, 79, 78–93, 128–9, 132–4; servants, 79, 80; social origins and recruitment, 33–9; Stubbs Report on salaries (1910), 88–9

Civil Service Clubs, Johore, 183

Clarke, Sir Andrew, Governor, 6–7

Clarke, Dr. Noel, 177

Clementi, Sir Cecil, 21, 22, 164, 169, 188

Clifford, Sir Henry, 41

Clifford, Hugh, 41, 53, 56–7; Since the Beginning by, 57, 201, 205, 213

Clubs, social: Asian, 181; European, 56, 59–66, 147–50, 153–7, 179–83; Rotary Club and race relations, 188–92

Cocoa cultivation, 13

Coffee industry, 13, 28, 45, 66

Colonial Administrative Service, 44

Colour bar in civil service, 96, 97, 107–12, 120, 122, 176; see also Race relations

Commerce and finance, 155; Europeans employed in, 29, 31, 76, 130

Commission on Temporary Allowances (1931), 142

Concubinage: before First World War, 200–1; decline of, 206–13; see also Asian mistresses

Contagious Diseases Acts, 220; repeal of (1886), 194–5, 196

Contagious Diseases Ordinance (1870), 195

Creepers', 45

Crewe, Lord, 206–8

Cricket, 41, 59–60, 63, 76, 115

Curle, Richard, 135, 147–8

DACING RIOTS (1897), 67, 115

Dance hostesses ('taxi girls'), 222

Dato Klana of Sungei Ujong, 214

Davidson, J. G., 61

Debt-bondsmen, 5, 7, 8, 52

Decentralization, 20–2

Dhobis (washermen), 80, 113, 115, 142

Dickson, Sir Frederick, 41

District Magistrates, 8

District Officers, 8, 172; Hubert Berkeley (App. 1), 229–32; role and duties of, 51–2, 55–6, 228–9; and standard of living, 82

Doctors; 178

Douglas, Capt. Bloomfield, 10, 40, 50, 59
Dutch, 4, 24, 25–6, 212
Dykes, F. J. B., 47, 48
Dykes, Major, 48–9

EASTERN CADETSHIPS, 42, 43, 78
Eastern Hotel cabaret, Kuala Lumpur, 222
Eastern Smelting Company, 16
Ebden, L. P., 41
Economy: export (1900–14), 12–18, 226; inter-war years, 126–34, 226
Education, 145; civil service examinations, 42–3, 78, 107, 110; Eurasian, 187; European, 34–6, 46–7, 85; and hill schools, 164–5; King Edward VII Medical School, 178; Malay, 9; professional training for non-Europeans, 178; Queen's Scholarships, 110–11, 125, 176
Education Department, 23, 46, 156
Enger, Robert, 200
English language, 174, 186
Eu Tong Sen, 117, 124
Eurasian Review, 187
Eurasians, 17, 18, 25–6, 28, 31, 40, 61–2, 102, 104, 107, 167, 177; colour bar in civil service, 108, 109, 111; dance hostesses, 222; European relations with, 186–8; occupations, 186–7; prostitutes, 217, 218; Rotary Club members, 190; train drivers, 95; women, 86, 140
European Hospital, Kuala Lumpur, 85, 97, 168, 169, 226
European Unemployment Fund, 127, 132
Evans, Mrs., 143
Exchange rates, 78, 80
Export economy: 1900–14, 12–18, 226; inter-war years, 126

FAMILY BUDGETS, MONTHLY: European and Asian (1930), 130–1; of Perak official (1903, 1906), 79, 80
Fauconnier, Henri, The Soul of Malaya by, 194, 216
Federal Council (F.M.S.), 21, 22, 81, 90; creation of (1909), 19–20
Ferguson-Davie, C. J., Bishop of Singapore, 161

Ferrers, H. N., 238
Fifth Light Infantry regiment, mutiny of (1915), 122–4
Football, 63, 97, 169–70, 174; European teams and the Selangor League, 117–20; multiracial, 170
Foster, Harry, 128
Fraser's Hill, 157, 160, 161, 162, 163–4
Frost, Meadows, 228–9
Furnivall, J. S., 173
Furse, Major, 156

GAMMANS, L. D., 165–6, 191
Gang robberies, 120
General Hospital, Kuala Lumpur, 168–9
Gibson, Ashley, 142
Gold mining, 28
Gordon, Dr. G. A. C., 145
Governesses, 145–6
Green, C. F., 149
Guillemard, Sir Laurence, 21, 129, 139
Gullick, J. M., 10
Gunn Lay Teik, 178
Gunung Angsi (hill station), 161, 162
Gunung Kledang (hill station), 160–1, 162
Gunung Tahan (hill station), 161, 162
Guthrie's, 14, 46, 48, 163, 212

HAILAMS (HAINANESE), 18, 80, 113–14, 124, 148
Hakkas, 18, 114
Hamzah bin Abdullah, 190
Harcourt, Lewis, 109–10, 111–12
Harper, Gilfillan and Company, 48
Harrison, C. R., 44, 45
Harrisons and Crosfield's, 14
Headmasters' Conference, 34, 35, 39, 46, 48
Health, 68–72, 85, 145, 158, 159–60; see also Hospitals
Health resorts, see Hill stations
Heat-stroke, 72
Henty, G. A., In the Hands of the Malays by, 53
High Commissioner, role of, 19–20
Hill stations, 72–4, 157, 160–6, 225
Ho Seng Ong, 191–2
Hokkiens, 18, 114
Holman-Hunt, C. B., 37

Home Civil Service, 42, 78
Homosexual relations (between European men and Asian boys), 194
Horley, Revd. W. E., 86, 101, 113, 198
Horse racing, 66, 67
Hose, E. S., 41
Hose, G. F., Bishop of Singapore, 37, 59
Hospitals in Kuala Lumpur: European, 85, 97, 168, 169, 226; General, 168–9
Hubback, Theodore, 176
Hume, W. P., 108
Hunt Club, Kuala Lumpur, 66
Huttenbach, J., 61, 65

IBRAHIM, SULTAN OF JOHORE, 183
Idris, Sultan of Perak, 20, 108
Illnesses and diseases, 69–72, 158, 159–60; see also Venereal diseases
Immigration, 15, 17–18
Incorporated Society of Planters (I.S.P.), 127, 132, 211
Indian Civil Service, 42, 43, 44, 78, 90
Indians, 22; élite, 174; immigration of, 17, 18; in Kuala Lumpur, 11, 17, 168, 188; medical facilities for, 168; police inspectors, 178; Rotary Club members, 190; in rubber industry, 17; servants, 79, 80
Inspector of Mines, appointment of, 47
International Club, Johore Bahru, 183
Ipoh, 33, 85, 114, 136, 180, 189, 190, 209
Ipoh Club, 180
Ipoh Rotary Club, 191
Island Club, Singapore, 183

JAFFNA TAMILS, 17, 18, 107, 109
Japanese, 18; fall of Singapore (1942), 226–7; mistresses, 200, 216; prostitutes, 196–9, 217–18, 220, 221
Javanese, 18, 217
Jervois, Sir William, Governor, 7
Jockeys, 157
John Little's department store, 85, 94
Johore, 20, 183, 192
Johore Military Forces, 123

Junior Officers, recruitment of, 40–1, 42

KAMPAR, 137
Kang Yu-wei, 101
Kapitan Cina, 6, 10–11, 59, 67, 68
Kedah, 4, 20, 183, 186, 192
Kedah Club, Alor Star, 183
Kelantan, 20, 161
Kenion, A. N., 81
Keyser, Arthur, 41, 54, 62
Khong, Dr., 180
Khoo Keng Hooi, 181, 182, 188
Kimberley, Lord, 6
Kindersley brothers, 44
King Edward VII Medical School, Singapore, 178; see also Hospitals
Kinta, Chinese-European relations in, 114, 116
Klang, 50, 85, 117, 118, 137, 190, 210
Klang Club, 180
Klang football team, 118
Klang Malays, 118
Kuala Kangsar, Perak, 13, 50
Kuala Kubu, 117, 118
Kuala Lumpur, 12, 73, 76, 85; Asian members of European clubs, 181, 182, 183; cabarets and dance hostesses, 221–2; Chinese in, 10–11, 17, 59, 67–8, 83–4, 181; Chinese Literary and Debating Society, 101–2; Chinese New Year disturbances (1912), 114–16, 122; clubs and social structure, 59–67, 147–57, 181, 182, 183, 224; education, 85; European Hospital, 85, 97, 168; European women, 143, 209; football matches, 117; growth of European society, 33, 59–68; 'The Letter' case (1911), 233–8; map of (1930s), 151–2; medical facilities, 85, 97, 168–9; married men, 136; origins and history, 5–6, 10–11; population growth, 17; prostitution and venereal disease, 198, 218–20; residential segregation, 106–7; Rotary Club and race relations, 188–92; shops and hotels, 85, 94; strike of Chinese engineering workers, 116–17, 122; Suleiman Golf Club, 192
Kuala Lumpur Sanitary Board, 11, 181

Kuala Pilah Club, 180–1

LAKE CLUB, KUALA LUMPUR, 64–5, 66, 147, 149, 150, 153–6, 157, 224
Laksamana, Tengku, 180
Larut tin mines, 5, 6
Lawyers, 75
Lee, H. S., 181, *182*
'The Letter' Case (1911), 201, 233–8
Lim Boon Keng, Dr., 110, 111, 125, 176
Limited liability companies, 15, 16
Lister, Martin, 41
Lockhart, Bruce, 171, 200, 213–15
Loke, Alan, 170
Loke Chow Kit, 83, 99–100, 102, 104
Loke Chow Thye, 83, 115, 188, 190
Loke Yew, 67, 68, 83, 98, 99, 100, 102, 103–4, 115, 170, 236
Loo Lew Hoi, *182*
Low, Hugh, Resident of Perak, 7–8, 13, 40, 50, 73

McCLELAND, R. H., 109
Macfadyen, Eric, 44, 81
MacIntyre, Dr. E. T., 109
McNair, Major, 69
Malacca, 4, 25, 190
Malacca Rotary Club, 191
Malaria, 15, 69–70, 71, 135, 158
Malay Administrative Service, 175, 190
Malay College, Kuala Kangsar, 9, 108, 179
Malay Mail, 19, 37, 41, 46, 75, 84, 86, 98, 99, 100, 103, 107, 112, 119, 121, 130, 143, 150, 156, 169, 177, 188, 189, 191–2, 199, 221, 238; letters on sexual relations with Asian women in, 201–3; report of Proudlock murder trial (1911), 234, 236
Malay Rulers, 107, 108, 112, 124, 176, 226; membership of European clubs, 180–1; political roles, 20–2, 74
Malay States, Federated: the British as a percentage of Europeans in, *24*; creation of Federation (1895), 12; definition of European in, *24*; from Intervention to Federation, 7–12; occupational and geographical distribution of Europeans, 23, 28–33; origins of

British control, 4, 6–7; political changes, 18–22; population growth, 16–18; pre-British political and social system, 4–6; role of Europeans in development of rubber and tin industries, 12–16
Malay States Guides, 114, 115
Malay States Volunteer Rifles, 100, 123, 132
Malaya, H.M.S., 16
Malaya Cup (football), 170
Malaya Tribune, 191, 192, 221
Malayan Civil Service (M.C.S.), *see* Civil servants
Malayan Civil Service Committee, 129
Malayan Public Service Salaries Commission, *see* Bucknill Commission
Malays, 11, 20, 22, 68; British officials' relations with, 51–3, 54–8; British rule, 7–9; civil servants, 175–6; and colour bar in civil service, 108; concubines and mistresses, 200–1, 208, 210, 213–16; élite, 8–9, 174; European wives of, 185–6; membership of European clubs, 180–1, *182*, 183; police inspectors, 178; pre-British political and social organization, 4–6; prostitutes, 197, 217, *218*, 220; railway segregation, 102–3; Rotary Club and, 190; Selangor Association Football League, 117–20; servants, 79, 80; Sultan Suleiman Club, 118, 119, 120, 181; western dancing and, 184–5; women, 184–5; *see also* Malay Rulers
Manson, Sir Patrick, 70, 158
Marks, Oliver, 41
Marriage, married life: European, 76, 84–7, 89, 91, 134, 135–47, 208–11; inter-racial, 185–6, 208; separation of husbands and wives, 144, 160; *see also* Women
Marwick, A., 37
Masonic Lodge, Kuala Lumpur, 66
Maugham, Somerset, 39; 'The Force of Circumstance' by, 204; 'The Letter' by, 201, 233, 237
Maxwell Arms, Fraser's Hill, 163
Maxwell family, 37, *38*, 41
Maxwell, Charleton, 208
Maxwell, Sir George, 41, 157, 164, 178, 181, 188, 189
Maxwell, W. E., 40, 41

Maxwell's Hill, 72–3, 160, *162*
'Medical clubs', 195–6
Methodist Mission, 163
Mills, C. Wright, 83
Mining, miners, 29, *29*, 31, 48, 76;
    see also Tin industry
Mitchell, Sir Charles, Governor,
    107
Mohamed Eusoff, Haji (Dato Pang-
    lima Kinta), 180, *182*
Moon Cake Festival, Chinese, 167
Motor-cars, 135
Murray, Capt., 50, 71, 72
Musa-eddin, Tengku, 180

NATIONALITY AND THE CENSUS,
    24–6; *see also* Population
Negri Sembilan, 11, 54, 180, 200;
    European population, *27*; Euro-
    pean women, *209*; joins Federa-
    tion (1895), 12
Neurasthenia, tropical, 159–60
New Club, Taiping, 65, 179, 224
Newspapers, British, 176–7
Ngoh Lean Tuck, Dr. (Wu Lien-
    Teh), 101, 103, 104
Non-cadet services, *see* Professional
    and technical departments
Nutt, W. F., 128–9

OFFICIALS, European (government
    employees), 72, 76–7; Asian
    environment and, 51–8; cadet v.
    non-cadet services, 23; specialist
    departments, growth of, 55–6;
    see also Civil servants; Police
    Department; Professional and
    technical departments
O'Grady, G. J., 175–6, 180, 185
Old Boys' associations, 82
Ormsby-Gore, W. G. A., 158–9,
    163

PAHANG, 11, 161, 164, 181; Euro-
    pean population, *27*, 28; Euro-
    pean women, *209*; joins Federa-
    tion (1895), 12
Pangkor Engagement (1874), 6–7,
    9, 40
Peasantry (*rakyat*), 5, 9, 54
Peel, William, 127
Peet, G. L., *Malayan Exile* by, 159,
    167, 172
Penang island, 4, 190
Penang Peranakan football team,
    120
Pepper, 13

Perak, 5, 6, 9, 11, 21, 50, 60; civil
    servants, 40; and colour bar,
    108; European clubs, 56; Euro-
    pean population, *27*, 28; Euro-
    pean wives of Malays, 185–6;
    and European women, *209*;
    growth of specialist officials, 56;
    hill stations, 72–3; Hubert Ber-
    keley's life and work, 229–32;
    joins Federation (1895), 12;
    monthly family budget of an
    official in, 79, 80; Pangkor
    Engagement (1874), 6–7; police
    inspectors, 177–8
Perak Club, Taiping, 65, 179, 224
Perlis, 20
Pillay, K. Tamboosamy, 61, 67, 68
Planter, 127, 170, 202–3
Planters, 29, 31, 33, 66, 127; Asian
    mistresses and concubines, 200,
    206, 209–12, 215, 216; civil
    servants compared with, 34–9;
    'creepers', 45; during Second
    World War, 134; educational
    background, 34–6; European
    wives of, 144, *209*, 210, 211;
    Highlands settlement by, 165–6;
    inter-war insecurity of, 130–4;
    marriage of, 138–9; membership
    of Lake Club, *155*; occupation of
    fathers, 36–7; prosperity of,
    81–2; recruitment, 44–6;
    salaries, 91, 128, 129–30,
    132–3; social background, 37,
    39; unemployed, 127–8, 132; *see
    also* Rubber industry
Planters' Association of Malaya, 19
Police Department, 23, 31, 46, 47;
    colour bar, 108, 109; married
    employees of, 139; non-
    Europeans, 177–8; salaries of
    inspectors, 86, 90
Political changes, 18–22
'Poor whites', 26, 95, 133, 140, 224
Population growth, 16–18, 26–33
Portuguese, 4, 25, 26
Prestige, British, 77, 93, 95, 121,
    127–8, 132–3, 170–2, 223
Prison warders, 23, 47, 157
Professional and technical depart-
    ments (non-cadet services), 23,
    31, 77, 92; membership of Lake
    Club by officials in, 154–5;
    senior appointments, 46–8
Prostitution, 193, 208; before First
    World War, 194–200; between
    the wars, 217–22; 'sly', 217–18

Proudlock, Mrs. Ethel, murder trial of, 233–8
Proudlock, William, 233–8
Purcell, Victor, 39, 208

QUEEN'S SCHOLARSHIPS, 110–11, 125, 176
Quinine, 69

RACE RELATIONS, 120–2; colour bar in civil service, 107–12; European men and Asian women, 193–222; on football field, 117–20, 169–70; residential separation in Kuala Lumpur, 106–7; Rotary Club and, 188–92; segregation in use of medical facilities, 168–9; segregation on railways, 97–106, 226
Raffles, Sir Stamford, 4
Raffles Hotel, Singapore, 97, 128
Railways, Railway Department, 9, 12–13, 23, 31; European appointments, 47–8; racial segregation on, 97–106, 120, 226; train drivers, 77, 86, 93–6, 157, 223
Raja Musa bin Raja Bot, 182
Raja Uda bin Raja Muhammad, 182
Raub, European Club at, 179
Raub Gold Mine, 28
Reconstruction Scheme (civil service), 43
Recreation Club, Kuala Lumpur, 61–2
Reid, J. S. W., 229
Resident-General, role of, 12, 18, 19, 20, 74–5
Residents, residential system, 6–7, 8, 11, 12, 18, 21, 41, 42, 50–1; cuts in allowances, 74, 78; influence over Europeans, 58, 74–5
Revenue farms, Chinese, 9, 15
Rice cultivation, 52
Ridges, H. C., 101, 116
Ridley, H. N., 13, 186
Rifle Association, Kuala Lumpur, 66
Robinson, Sir William, Governor, 7–8
Robson, J. H. M., 55, 56, 62–3, 66–7, 68, 75, 77, 86, 107, 168, 169, 196, 199
Rodger, J. P., 41, 118
Ross, Ronald, 70
Rotary Clubs, 188–92
Royal Singapore Flying Club, 183

Rubber industry, 12, 13–15, 16, 17, 29, 31, 33, 39, 81, 127–34, 200; boom years, 81–2, 126, 134; plantations and smallholdings, 14–15; post-war slumps, 127–8, 131–4; see also Planters

SAID, DR. MOHAMED, 178
Salaries and allowances, 224; Bucknill Report (1919), 90–3, 96, 126; Civil Service Committee memorial (1909), 87–8; of European civil servants, 76–7, 78–84, 128–9, 133–4; marriage and, 84–7, 91, 134, 137–8, 139; of planters, 91, 128, 129–30, 132–3, 224; of police inspectors, 86, 90; Stubbs Report (1910), 88–9; of train drivers, 93–4, 95
San Ah Wing, 190
Scott, A. MacCallum, 109–10, 111
Scott, W. Ramsay, 37
Secret societies, Chinese, 4, 6, 15
Segregation, see Race relations
Selangor, 5, 7, 10, 11, 50; civil servants, 40; cricket matches, 59–60; Eurasians, 187–8; European population, 27, 28; European women, 209; growth of specialist officials, 56; hill stations, 73; illnesses and diseases, 70, 71; joins Federation (1895), 12; railway segregation, 98–100; rubber industry, 15; see also Kuala Lumpur
Selangor Association Football League, withdrawal of European teams from, 97, 118, 169
Selangor Chinese Chamber of Commerce, 99, 102
Selangor Chinese Recreation Club, 181
Selangor Club, Kuala Lumpur, 59–64, 65, 66–7, 104, 147–8, 149, 150, 153, 156, 157, 163, 224; activities, 59–60, 63, 148; Asian members, 181, 182, 183; fancy dress balls, 63; football team, 118, 120; long bar, 148; nickname ('Spotted Dog'), 62, 148; non-European membership, 61–2; women members, 62–3
Selangor Eurasian Association, 187–8
Selangor Golf Club, Kuala Lumpur, 66, 67, 147, 149–50, 153, 169; Asian members, 181, 182

Selangor Gymkhana (later Turf) Club, Kuala Lumpur, 66
Selangor Journal, 59, 63, 65, 66, 68, 74, 77–8
Selangor Planters' Association, 75
Selangor State Council, 18, 104, 149
Seremban, 33, 50, 136, 190, 198–9, *209*
Seri Mahkota, 118
Servants, 79, 80, 113–14, 142–4, 145, 148
Sexual relations (between European men and Asian women): attitudes toward, 201–6; concubinage, 200–1, 206–13; mistresses, 137, 193, 213–16; prostitution, 193–200, 217–22; *see also* Homosexual relations; Marriage
Siamese, 18; prostitutes, 218, 220
Singapore, 4, 12, 13, 14, 143, 190; European clubs, 183; fall of (1942), 226–7; King Edward VII Medical School, 178; mutiny of Indian Fifth Light Infantry (1915), 122–4; prostitution and venereal disease, 19*3*, 196–7, 217–18, 220, 221; Rotary Club, 191; unemployed Europeans, 128
Singapore Cold Storage Co., Kuala Lumpur, 85, 94
Singapore Free Press, 119
Singapore Volunteer Rifles, 123
Slaves, slavery, 5, 7, 8, 52
Smith, Sir Cecil Clementi, Governor, 11
Socfin, 138–9, 210
Speedy, Captain, 40
Sporting activities, 66, 67, 148, 149, 150; cricket, 41, 59–60, 63, 76, 115; football, 63, 97, 117–20, 169–70, 174
Sproule, P. J., 107, 109
Standard of living: Asian, 83–4, 96, 129–31, 224; European, 77–87, 88–9, 91, 128–30, 128–34, 223–4; of train drivers, 93–6
Status, 77; European–Asian social relations, 183–4; of non-Europeans, 104; of train drivers, 94–5; *see also* Prestige; Race relations
Stevens, Major, 132
Steward, William, murder of, 201, 233–8

Straits dollar, value of, 78, 80
Straits Echo, 111, 189
Straits or Baba Chinese, 18
Straits Settlements, 4, 5, 6, 11, 18; Asian members of European clubs, 183; civil service, 40, 41, 42, 58, 88, 177; and colour bar in civil service, 107, 110–12; Europeans, 27, 29; non-Europeans in government administration, 175–8; prostitution and concubinage, 193–7; social clubs, 62; *see also* Singapore
Straits Times, 112, 124, 169, 176, 177, 197
Straits Trading Company, 16, 163, 198
Strike of Chinese engineering workers, 116–17, 122
Stubbs, R. E., (Stubbs Report), 88–9, 91, 92
Suicide(s), 158, 256
Suleiman, Raja Muda, 61, 180
Suleiman, Sultan of Selangor, 180
Suleiman Golf Club, Kuala Lumpur, 192
Sultan Street Clinic, Kuala Lumpur, 218–19, 220
Sultan Suleiman Club, Kuala Lumpur, 118, 119, 120
Sumatran peoples, 18
Sun helmets, 71–2
Sungei Lembing, European Club at, 181
Sungei Ujong, 5, 7, 11, 50, 52
Sunstroke, 71
Swettenham, Sir Frank, 9, 10, 40, 41, 53, 58, 73, 74, 81, 107, 184, 196, 197, 213, 234
Swimming Club, Singapore, 183
Syers, Capt. H. C., 68

TAIPING, 33, 50, 56, 59–60, 72, 73, 85; European women, *209*; married men, 136; Perak and New Clubs, 65, 179, 224
Talalla, H. Benjamin, 188, 190
Talma, E. T., 107, 109
Tamil Immigration Fund, 15
Tamil Physical Culture Association, 181
Tamil Union football team, 118, 120
Tamils, 17, 18, 61, 67, 102, 118, 172, 181, 197, *218*
Tan Cheng Lock, 176, 177

Tanah Rata, Cameron Highlands, 164
Tanglin Club, Singapore, 183
Taylor, Sir William, 103
Tea, 13
Telok Anson, 54, 85, 137
Thomas, Sir Shenton, 21
Times of Malaya, 177
Tin industry, 5–6, 9, 10, 12, 13, 15–16, 17, 67, 132
Topham, D. F., 48–9, 149, 154
Train drivers, European, 23, 77, 86, 93–6, 157, 223
Travers, Dr. E. A. O., 68, 115, 172
Treacher, W. H., 73, 81
Trengganu, 20
Tropical climate, effects on health of, 68–72, 145, 157–60, 164
Twentieth Century Impressions, 34, 35, 36, 37, 39, 44, 45, 46, 48

UNEMPLOYED EUROPEANS, 127–8, 132, 223
Unfederated Malay States, 20–1, 27, 183, 226
United Chinese (football team), 118–19
Unofficials, European, 18–19, 21, 23, 24, 75, 76, 157, 163; inter-marriage with civil servants, 87; other than planters, 48–9; pros-perity of, 81–2, 126; salaries, 91, 128, 129–30, 132; support for civil servants' salary rises by, 82–3, 90; unemployed, 127–8; *see also* Planters
Utan Melintan, 54

VEERASAMY, S., 190
Venereal diseases, 194–6, 199, 217, 218–21
Venning, A. R., 64

Victoria Institution, Kuala Lumpur, 17
Viswalingam, Dr. A., 178

WALKER, Mrs. Noel, 84
Watson, Sir Malcolm, 200, 206
Waugh, Alec, 210
Waugh-Scott, Dr. G., 159–60
Weld, Sir Frederick, Governor, 8, 40, 41
Weld, F. J., 41
Weld Hill Club, Kuala Lumpur, 84
Wilson, Mrs., 141, 143, 163
Winstedt, Sir Richard, 86, 200–1, 213
Women: Asian/Eurasian, 86, 137, 140, 184–5, 193–222; con-cubinage, 200–1, 206–13; European, 57, 62–3, 76, 98, 134–47, 184, 185, 208–11, 224–5; marriage and salaries, 84–7, 91, 134, 137–8, 139; mis-tresses, Asian, 137, 193, 213–16; prostitution, 193–200, 217–22; railway segregation and, 98–100; ratio in immigrant communities, 17; role in Euro-pean community, 184–6; separa-tion from husbands, 144, 160; wives of Asians, 185–6, 225
Wu Lien-Teh, *see* Ngoh Lean Tuck, Dr.

YANG DI-PERTUAN BESAR OF NEGRI SEMBILAN, 180–1
Yap Ah Loy, 6, 10–11, 59
Yap Ah Shak, 11
Yap Hon Chin, 67–8
Yap Kwan Seng, 11, 67, 68, 188
Yap Tai Chi, 188
Young, Sir Arthur, Governor, 90, 92, 161